POWER AND FOLLY

by the same author

THE LIVING PAST

IVAR LISSNER

POWER AND FOLLY

The story of the Caesars

TRANSLATED FROM
THE GERMAN
BY
J. MAXWELL BROWNJOHN
M.A. (Oxon.)

LONDON
JONATHAN CAPE 30 BEDFORD SQUARE

FIRST PUBLISHED IN GREAT BRITAIN 1958

Originally published in Germany
under the title *Die Cäsaren*

PRINTED AND BOUND IN GREAT BRITAIN BY RICHARD CLAY AND COMPANY, LTD.,
BUNGAY, SUFFOLK
ILLUSTRATIONS PRINTED BY BALDING & MANSELL LIMITED, LONDON & WISBECH

CONTENTS

CONTENTS

ILLUSTRATIONS

MAPS AND DIAGRAMS

ACKNOWLEDGMENTS

I should like to express my sincere thanks to Dr Siegfried Lauffer, Professor of Ancient History at Munich University, for scrutinizing the individual chapters of this book and offering so many valuable suggestions, and to the following sources for having given me permission to reproduce some of the photographs:

ALINARI: Sulla (Villa Albani, Rome), Cicero (Vatican Museum), Claudius (Vatican Museum), Messalina Valeria (Uffizi, Florence), Poppaea Sabina (Capitoline Museum), Nero (Thermae Museum, Rome), Galba (Capitoline Museum, Rome), Otho (Villa Albani, Rome), Aulus Vitellius (Capitoline Museum, Rome), Domitian (Capitoline Museum, Rome), Domitia (Villa Albani, Rome), Trajan (Capitoline Museum, Rome), Antinous (Archaeological Museum, Rome), Lucius Verus (Villa Albani, Rome), Marcus Aurelius (Capitoline Museum), Column of Marcus Aurelius, Publius Helvetius Pertinax (Vatican Museum), Marcus Didius Julianus (Uffizi, Florence), Septimius Severus (Capitoline Museum), Triumphal Arch of Septimius Severus, Caracalla (National Museum, Naples), Plautilla (National Museum, Naples), Opellius Macrinus (Capitoline Museum), Alexander Severus (Vatican Museum), Gordian II (Capitoline Museum), Praetorians.

GERMAN INSTITUTE OF ARCHAEOLOGY: Balbinus, Pupienus, Plotinus, Gordian III, Philippus Arabs, Decius, Gallienus, Diocletian, Constantine the Great.

BILDARCHIV PHOTO MARBURG: Porta Nigra.

LEONARD VON MATT: The Roman she-wolf, Trajan's Column.

JOE NICZKY: Tiberius, Geta, Julia Domna.

POWER AND FOLLY

THE CAESARS

PROUD AND MIGHTY ROMAN WORLD

The history which I have assembled with such accuracy and regard for truth is not unfamiliar or unverified, nor merely borrowed from other sources, but still fresh in the minds of my readers.

Herodian, History of the Caesars, i, 1.

I have therefore decided to deal briefly with Augustus' death and then with the reign of Tiberius and his successors, without either hatred or liking — *sine ira et studio.*

Tacitus, Annales, i, 1.

I HAVE always been fascinated by the knowledge that Julius Caesar's eyes were dark and lively, and that he brushed his hair forward and almost always wore a chaplet of laurel-leaves or gold because he was embarrassed by his baldness.

Cleopatra was a proud young woman. She was no beauty, but her fine bearing and conversational gifts made her an attractive and likable companion.

Emperor Tiberius used to stroll through his gardens on the island of Capri in moody silence, a humourless, obstinate old man with a pathological anxiety neurosis and a marked streak of cruelty in his nature. A modern psychologist would have seen great significance in the way he used his hands. One of this left-handed Emperor's favourite habits was to bore into a crisp apple with his index finger and, on the rare occasions when he joined in a conversation, he would accompany his remarks with a series of affected gestures. It is probable that Tiberius, with his large eyes, nervous mannerisms and penchant for murder, was not actually insane but had been driven to the border-line of insanity by inner loneliness and misery. That is how accurately we can assess his mental condition.

Emperor Claudius was an extraordinary casual and absent-minded person — so vague and forgetful, in fact, that after his wife Messalina had been done away with on his orders he asked his courtiers why the Empress had not come to table.

As for Nero, he not only wrote really good poetry, but wrote it with his own hand. This we have on the authority of an eye-witness who actually saw the original manuscripts covered in the Emperor's corrections.

We owe our knowledge of all these wonderfully vivid details to Roman and Greek historians. But things become blurred by the passage of time, and the facts have been so distorted or suppressed by poets, authors and romanticists of every period that the colourful personalities of imperial Rome have become no more than a row of bloodless caricatures. In this book I have tried to reconstruct a picture of these colourful personalities based on ancient sources. I hope I have brought them to life.

On the other hand, I have not disregarded the results of modern research. Our knowledge has been much enhanced by the individual conclusions and textual criticism of scholars in all the major cultural centres of the world. Yet scholars have been far too quick to challenge the authenticity of old and once-respected sources. Until the middle of the nineteenth century the character-sketches handed down to us by the great classical biographers and historians were taken on trust. It is only now, in a century which has made up for its lack of creative ability by becoming hypercritical, that people have tried to dissociate the magnificent psychological portraits painted for us by Tacitus, Suetonius and Plutarch from historical reality. It is always dangerous to dissect a living thing, and Roman historians have left behind very little that is dead — a fact which ought to guarantee them more respect than they sometimes get.

There is a mysterious link between the past and the present. Only God, who can look across time, knows that there is no such thing as yesterday, today or tomorrow; that our whole notion of time is a delusion because we are mortal and our lives have a beginning and an end; that we are all contemporaries of Tiberius, the Emperor whose reign saw the crucifixion of Christ; and that we are also contemporaries of those who will be alive a thousand years hence and who will, given the opportunity, nail Christ to the Cross once again.

Past and present are firmly interwoven — quite how firmly we are not always aware. We often forget that we are bearing a burden thousands of years old and that future generations will have to bear one which includes all our own thoughts and actions. They will groan beneath the weight of our wars, lost and won, of our nuclear bombs, of our novels and plays, good and bad, of our scientific discoveries, of our ingenuity and stupidity. We have a regrettable tendency to judge everything that is old by the defective and overrated standards of our own day. We are blind to the lessons of past history because we refuse to learn that life will never have anything very new to offer us. There is nothing new under the sun, and no one generation is any more entitled to claim that it has arrived in the world at a 'turning-point' in history than any other.

Most people today are scared of opening a Greek or Roman book. They have a deep-rooted and almost superstitious dread of anything they cannot understand at first glance. Modern so-called literature skirts cautiously round ancient sources like a mountaineer negotiating a crevasse, with the result that the historical novels of our own day all go on repeating the same old errors. Each adds something new to our store of misconceptions until the personalities of the past either become pale shadows of what they really were or are inflated far beyond their true importance. In the end we reach the stage where Claudius, a near-imbecile puppet of his wives and freedmen, is discovered by modern psychologists to have been a complex and, 'in essence', good character.

Our information about Julius Caesar's dark and lively eyes comes from Suetonius, a distinguished scholar who was born in Rome about A.D. 70 and died in A.D. 140. He was an aristocrat who practised law and was later taken by Emperor Trajan on to his personal staff. In his subsequent capacity as Hadrian's private secretary and director of the imperial chancery he had access to the public archives. He must have studied a vast quantity of material during his researches, historical works, records, biographies, imperial speeches, letters, senatorial minutes and collections of anecdotes. Reading his *De Vita Caesarum* is rather like steering a small boat through an immense sea of knowledge. His character-studies are remarkably shrewd, his style is never over-embroidered and his descriptions of the Roman emperors and their strange idiosyncrasies are always invested with an extremely lifelike quality.

Many well-meaning schoolmasters succeed in turning history into something dry and boring, whereas others know how to capture their hearers' imagination. Their secret is quite simple: they follow the example which Tacitus set them so long ago, and intersperse their subject with biographical material. From Tacitus to Ammian, the Roman historian's technique took on an increasingly biographical form. Roman biographers did not so much trace the development of a personality as describe its actual state or being, and by doing so they came — at least in my opinion — very near the mark. The personality of a man is more easily determined from details of his family background and character than from a study of its development, since character is an immutable factor. In this way the biographers of the ancient world supplied us with an extraordinarily objective picture of their imperial masters. Again, classical historians and biographers did not always stick too closely to the chronological order of events, and only introduced political history as far as they considered necessary. This was not a symptom of weakness or partiality, as critical historians of the nineteenth century liked to believe. Suetonius did distort a few facts, it is true, but he never misrepresented the soul or the mental climate of anyone. He acknowledged Nero's poetic talents, for instance, and mentioned that Vespasian could never bring himself to pronounce a sentence of death, however well merited, without sighing and shedding tears. Details like these are of tremendous value, and go a long way towards offsetting the omission of a few dates and figures.

Tacitus grew up under Nero, reached manhood under Domitian, and lived to enjoy the greater happiness and freedom which characterized the reigns of Nerva and Trajan, under whom he held important government posts. He had a sensitive nature and was deeply aware of the evils of his own day. Because of this he matured early and withdrew completely into his private world of ideas, not becoming an historian until quite late in life, at the age of forty. He looked back with nostalgia to the good old days of individual liberty under the Republic, before Augustus came to power. It was true that the imperial regime or Principate, as the Romans called it, was a guarantee of peace. But, however experienced a ruler the emperor might be, the absolute nature of his authority was bound to blur his moral sense and turn his subjects into a crowd of sycophants. In Tacitus' opinion, everyone in Rome who tolerated the imperial regime — whether consul, senator or knight — was sacrificing his personal integrity, and the more distinguished the man in question, the bigger hypocrite he was.

Tacitus lived roughly between A.D.55 and A.D. 120. This true-blue Roman is to my mind the greatest historian who ever lived. He was so great a writer that it almost looks as though no modern scholar is ever going to pin down exactly where the magic of his technique lies. Yet even he has come under attack. People have accused him of taking liberties with factual accuracy and underestimating its importance. But all facts are fragmentary anyway, and the life of individuals, like that of nations, is a tapestry woven out of so many slender and infinitely varied threads that it would be unthinkable to dismiss the services of such a shrewd diagnostician of his times as Tacitus. His lively interpretation and expansion of the facts have nothing whatever to do with invention or fabrication.

Tacitus' style is a model of clarity. He writes concisely, summoning up his characters with a single stroke of the pen, and his taut, vigorous language instantly brings whatever he is describing into sharp focus. His pages are peopled with horrific characters, among them Tiberius, Seianus, young Agrippina and Nero, and his dark forebodings about the Germans, whom he describes more fully and impressively than any other ancient writer, make enthralling reading. Yet the secret of his success was not artistry alone, for artistry was the hall-mark of all the classical historians. There is an almost imperceptible deficiency even in the most precise historical writing of our own day, for wherever it ceases to be art and becomes pure science it fails to arrive at the truth. It is left for Tacitus to show us how to keep the inner truth from being submerged by external truths.

Sallust was yet another extremely impartial historian with a vivid style. Far from being a 'pathological case', as some have tried to make out, he was a plebeian and an ardent admirer of the revolutionary era who felt far too deeply about his subject and took the ills of the Roman people far too much to heart to have written purely as a means of 'suppressing his own vices'.

On reading Plutarch, Goethe declared that he could sense, running through all his brilliant character-studies, the fact that their subjects were human beings. In Plutarch's works, as in those of Horace, can be found the most delicate analysis of Cleopatra's character. We are shown her as she really was, the product of a corrupt world, yet fearless and well-bred, not an Egyptian but a European. I find Horace's description of her, '*non humilis mulier*', or 'a woman without baseness', far more telling than any romantic literary invention of a later age.

I have a strong feeling that people of our own day need something more than historical novels. I think they want some accurate information about the great personalities of the past, but do not know where to look for it.

In writing this book I have enlisted the aid — no less effective, I hope, for being unseen — of masters of classical Latin like Cicero and Horace; Sallust; Suetonius, the diligent and inquisitive biographer of the Caesars; the brilliant historian Tacitus; Dio Cassius of Bithynia; Herodian of Alexandria; Lactantius, whose pages reveal signs of the upheavals to come; and Eusebius, who laid his last book on Emperor Constantine's tomb as a token of his undying loyalty. All these men have been close friends and collaborators of mine, and I have not resorted to translations of their works. The object of this book is to bring Caesars, barbarians and Christians back to life once more and, in an age over-fond of distortion, to paint a picture of them as perhaps they really were, so that they stand before us again, if only for a little while, gay, grave or melancholy just as their fate, character or circumstances made them.

A vanished world?

Far from it.

We must never think of their world as a place which is dead and gone. The story of the ancient world is our own story. We are burdened not only with the evils but also with the blessings of Christian–Roman civilization. Everything we do, everything we are and everything we own comes from the Mediterranean cultural area and was passed on to us by Rome: our religion, our concept of the State, our administrative and legal system, our Church and code of chivalry, our standards of etiquette and fair play, our clothing and art, our astronomy, medicine, mathematical and physical laws, our approach to sport, our ideas about love, marriage and upbringing, our notions of beauty, the names of our months, the choice of Sunday as our national day of rest, and a hundred thousand other things which all have their place in our vast store of customs and go to make up Western civilization — of which we are part whether we like it or not.

Roman history is the history of a city and of what was originally a peasant race whose constructive energy produced the largest empire in the ancient world. The history of that empire represents man's best single lesson in the art of living, since its whole being and development can be traced in the finest detail from its earliest beginnings to its final downfall.

And since, during the imperial era, the destiny of the whole empire lay in the hands of a single man who represented the centre of all activity, attention and, very often, of all religious observance, the story of the individual emperors gives us a clear key to the decline of Rome itself. Not only did the Romans move farther and farther into the world of the Asiatic steppe-races with every eastward step they took, but their emperors, too, became on the whole increasingly oriental and alien in outlook.

Any process of enlargement, aggrandisement and expansion automatically leads towards disintegration. If the blessings of civilization are to remain at their best they can only be enjoyed by a small and cultured minority. Every concession to the taste of the masses, every simplification or blunting of spiritual values, will always result in a watering down of their original substance.

Civilization cannot be bought nor, equally, can it be prohibited. Freedom of thought goes on burning like a small flame during periods of oppression, and burns all the brighter under conditions of enforced secrecy. Like a difficult child, civilization has to be carefully reared, and few know the secret.

Cicero, Rome's finest stylist, politician and lawyer; Pompey, the dry and rather boring man who laid a whole new world at his countrymen's feet; Julius Caesar, the most versatile genius in the ancient world; Augustus, the great and, in his old age, lonely architect of governmental organization; Caligula, the Emperor whose approach was greeted by whispers of 'Here comes the Goat!'; Seneca, the immortal Roman philosopher whom Nero kissed and then murdered; the good emperors Vespasian and Titus; Trajan, Rome's finest army officer; Hadrian and Gallienus, the admirers of Greece; Marcus Aurelius, who spent lonely nights encamped on the frontiers of the barbarian world mentally wrestling for the freedom of his soul; Septimius Severus, the grim Phoenician; Elagabalus, who performed weird dances; Zenobia, the Queen who rode like a boy, and her conqueror Aurelian; Diocletian, the administrative genius; and Constantine, the world's first Christian emperor — in this book we shall be taking a closer look at them all and laying our fingers on the pulse of a great and vanished world.

It is not so hard to imagine that we have all passed through some quarter of the Roman Empire, either in a former life or in our dreams; that we stood in the crowd as Augustus went by, or hailed a dust-stained legionary as he marched courageously, with the simple confidence of every age, to his death; or that we watched prisoners being led off into slavery or thrown into the arena to be torn to pieces by wild animals — cheering with the rest. It is not hard to pretend that we have stood in one of the narrow Roman streets and watched the rich sway past in their litters, hearing the ringing beat of the copper-smith's hammer, the clamouring beggars, the rattling carts and the bargemen's cries echoing from the direction of the Tiber ...

It was a proud and mighty world, the Roman Empire, a glittering and degenerate world wrapped in deceptive glamour. In these pages we shall meet the men who reigned over that world in such godlike splendour, meet them before its power fades altogether and its riches are scattered to the winds, meet them before we become so old and ignorant that we begin to tell ourselves it was all a colourful dream.

MARIUS AND SULLA

RIVALRY AND REVENGE

I have always requited my friends with all that is good, and my enemies with all that is evil.

Inscription on the tomb of Lucius Cornelius Sulla.

These events made it obvious even to the most simple-minded Roman that a change of tyranny, and not deliverance from it, was all that might be hoped for. Marius was harsh and cruel from the very first, and accession to power only stimulated his natural inclinations. Sulla, from his boyhood onwards a friend of gaiety and laughter, only took to murder later in life, when he sated the city with executions beyond number.

Plutarch, Sulla, 29.

IN the year 113 B.C. a remarkable and almost unknown race of men approached the Alpine passes from the north. They were the Cimbri, and their original home lay in the so-called Cimbrian Peninsula, which comprised Holstein, Schleswig and Jutland.

The Greek geographer Strabo records that huge tidal waves tore away whole stretches of the North Sea coasts, forcing the Cimbri to emigrate. They were later joined by the Teutons, a related tribe who probably lived on the Baltic coast of north-east Germany. Together the two tribes pushed on towards the Danube, where they were temporarily held in check by the Celts. It was not long, however, before the Celts' resistance gave way, leaving the restless Cimbri free to wander farther southwards in search of a new home, taking their women, children and all their goods and chattels with them. They, their families and even their pet dogs all lived together beneath the leather roofs of their wagons.

The southerners were astonished at the appearance of these strange newcomers with their tall, slim build, blond hair and pale-blue eyes, their sturdy, junoesque womenfolk, and their children with 'old man's hair' — or so the flaxen heads of the northerners' offspring seemed to Italian eyes.

Having copied their Celtic enemies' up-to-date weapons of war, the Cimbri no longer contented themselves with sword, dagger and shield, but wore richly ornamented copper helmets and used the *materis*, an unusual type of throwing-weapon. They also had cavalry and employed a battle formation in which men in the front rank were lashed together by their belts and thus forced to live or die together.

The German new-comers had some rather rough-and-ready ways. They ate their meat raw, their womenfolk frequently fought alongside them in battle and their commander was not only the bravest man among them but also the tallest. The date and place of a battle were arranged with the enemy in advance, and individual champions challenged each other to single combat before it began. Hostilities were preluded by the hurling of mutual insults, and each side tried to intimidate the other by setting up a terrifying din, the men yelling their battle-cries and the women and children drumming on the taut leather roofs of their wagons. The Cimbri considered that the only worthy way to die was 'on the field of honour'. When they were victorious, their white-robed priestesses used to sacrifice weapons, horses and prisoners to the gods of battle, foretelling the future from their slaughtered captives' blood.

Slowly, like a surging wave, the Germans' wagon-camps rolled southwards, taking rivers and mountains in their stride. When they did move fast, it was only to strike like lightning and then withdraw before their enemies could assemble in strength. The first time a pitched battle was fought between Germans and Romans was in 113 B.C., not far from Noreia, in what is now Carinthia. Only a storm saved the Roman army from total annihilation.

Eight years later the Romans suffered a terrible defeat at Arausio (modern Orange), on the banks of the Rhône. Two Roman armies totalling 80,000 men were wiped out. It was a disaster comparable with the massacre which Hannibal had inflicted on the Romans at Cannae. In 103 B.C. the Cimbri, the Teutons and several Helvetian tribes joined forces and marched on Italy by different routes. By 102 B.C. the Romans had made contact with the Teuton contingent, and a battle was fought at Aquae Sextiae, about fifteen miles north of Marseilles. There, in the warm climate of southern France, the Germans' battle formation failed them for the first time. Their human barricade crumbled and broke. Many of them were killed, while others, the Teuton king Teutobod among them, were taken prisoner. The German women put up a desperate resistance in and around their wagons, spurred on by the knowledge that lifelong slavery awaited them if they were captured.

A year later the Cimbri, too, were defeated by the Romans at Vercellae in northern Italy. The date was July 30th, 101 B.C. (by Roman reckoning, 653 years after the foundation of Rome), and the place the Raudine Fields, an extensive plain in which the Roman cavalry were able to make the most of their superiority. The Cimbri suffered total defeat, and the luckiest among them were those who died in action, since such prisoners as were taken spent the rest of their lives in dread of Roman hatred and the slave-driver's whip.

The vast human avalanche which had terrorized all the races of the south, from the Danube to the Ebro and the Seine to the Po, now lay either under ground or under the yoke of slavery. The homeless Cimbrian race had been exterminated.

Gaius Marius was the son of an agricultural day-labourer, the poorest class of Roman peasant, and was born in the village of Cereatae (now known as Casamare, or 'house of Marius'). After joining the Roman Army and making a name for himself by his bravery in battle, he quickly won a commission and came to Rome, the scars of his war-wounds only outnumbered by his many decorations for gallantry. He tried to secure military promotion by running for political office, but in Rome lack of money and connections made such a thing almost impossible. Then, when he was already forty years old, he met and married a girl of the Julian clan, one of the bluest-blooded families in Rome. She was no less a person than Julius Caesar's aunt.

That marked the real beginning of Marius' career. In 108 B.C. he was elected consul, and two years later he defeated the North African king Jugurtha. He led the Numidian prisoner and his two sons manacled through the streets of Rome to the accompaniment of catcalls and derisive laughter from the inhabitants of the great city, which had never before in all its long history witnessed such a magnificent triumphal procession. (King Jugurtha, it must be added, was later strangled in the prison below the Capitol, the so-called *Carcer Mamertinus*.) After another two years, Marius was given supreme command of the operations against the Cimbri and Teutons, and before long he was marching through the streets of Rome in triumph once more, his defeat of the German tribes having earned him the title 'Saviour of the Fatherland'. Marius, the son of a humble peasant, had now reached the height of his fame. He was elected to the consulship five times and inaugurated a complete reform of the Roman army, eradicating the last lingering traces of class distinction within it. The Roman army, it must be explained, had until then been recruited according to the social and financial status of its members. Marius abolished this rule and laid it down that the sole qualification for acceptance was to be Italian birth and Roman citizenship.

Marius was now the leading figure in Rome. He had saved his country from disaster and his name was universally respected. The aristocracy were forced to recognize him whether they liked it or not, and his humble origins made him popular with the lower classes. He became quite dazzled by the glamour which surrounded him and the acclamation and public enthusiasm which he had aroused. It only remained for the darling of the Roman people to show whether he was equal to the subtler demands of a Roman political career.

Then something terrible happened, something quite unexpected, something which Marius' peasant mind had never reckoned with: peace arrived. It came quite suddenly, as though spirited up out of nowhere. Throughout the length and breadth of the huge empire not a sign of trouble loomed. The three southernmost European peninsulas, Spain, Italy and Greece, together with the northern part of Africa and large tracts of Asia Minor, were all safely under Roman control. The Mediterranean area, the whole of the known world, lay becalmed. Only Marius remained unpacified. His manners were loud and uncouth as ever, and his eyes still blazed as though they could see hordes of Libyans, Cimbri and Teutons swarming to the attack.

Rome was rich and the Romans were a pampered race whose dress was as elegant as their conversation. Roman aristocrats had exquisite manners and lived luxuriously, as befitted the masters of a city which was the centre of the known world. But Marius remained what he was by nature, a plough-boy — hardly the type to feel at home among the refined and perfumed politicians of Rome. He began to pay secret visits to Etruscan fortune-tellers at night, and followed their ludicrous advice as stubbornly as he disregarded the rules of polite society.

One day Marius appeared in the Senate-house dressed in his triumphal robes. He was greeted with hoots of contemptuous laughter, and the news of his ignominious reception travelled through Rome like wildfire. By comparison with other members of the Senate, he was poor. What was worse, he lived modestly. Worse still, he loathed bribery and intrigue. Worst of all, perhaps, he kept a bad chef. But even that did not exhaust the list of blots on his social escutcheon. Being a peasant, he knew no language except Latin, which meant that if anyone spoke Greek in his presence he was reduced to embarrassed silence. In common with most upper-class Romans, he was bored to tears by Greek plays: the only difference was that he frankly admitted it. To immunize himself against the sarcastic gibes of society and the even more distasteful sympathy of his colleagues, he took to the bottle. Consul Marius became a notorious toper.

Marius' sense of insecurity led him to become embroiled in a series of political intrigues which came to a head on December 10th, 100 B.C., when fighting broke out in the great market-place in Rome. The once-victorious general was no longer recognizable in the man who had been consul six times. Marius' role in the first civil war was a deplorable one. He travelled to the

East, and on his return to Rome reopened his impressive mansion with the idea of giving banquets and parties for the capital's upper crust. No one accepted his invitations, however, and he was left to wander through the empty house alone, hoping and praying for an early end to the state of peace which he feared and detested so greatly. But still no war broke out, and peace reigned undisturbed.

In 91 B.C. the Italian provinces rebelled against Rome. The Italici had been demanding Roman citizenship for a long time, but the people of Rome had arrogantly refused to entertain the idea. Finally, the provincial cities took up arms against the capital, and what is known as the Social War broke out. Once again Marius showed himself weak and vacillating. 89 B.C. saw the granting of Roman citizenship to the Italici, and from then on Roman history really became 'Italic' or Italian history.

Meanwhile, a new star was rising at Rome in the person of Lucius Cornelius Sulla. In the year 88 B.C. Sulla became consul and was given command of an expedition against Mithridates, a dangerous oriental potentate who was king of Pontus in northern Asia Minor. His country formed part of what is now Turkey, and took its name from Pontus Euxinus, the Greek name for the Black Sea, which bounded it in the north.

War had come at last, but the ever-ambitious Marius suddenly found himself eclipsed by a new-comer. He resented it that, in spite of all his own past victories, command of the expedition against Mithridates had gone to Sulla. Taking advantage of Sulla's absence on campaign, he seized power in Rome. Sulla returned to the capital and spent some time wandering unrecognized through the streets. Eventually he went to visit Marius in person, but Marius, with his customary sportsmanship, allowed him to leave the city unharmed. Collecting an army in southern Italy, Sulla marched on Rome and took the almost defenceless city without a struggle.

Marius was exiled. He boarded a ship at Ostia bound for Africa, but was forced by unfavourable winds and lack of supplies to land on the Italian coast once more. The exiled general wandered like King Lear, footsore and hungry, through the countryside he had once ruled. He was finally captured by Sulla's police in the coastal marshes at Minturnae, standing up to his waist in mud and hiding his head under a bundle of reeds. From there he was conveyed to prison to await execution. A Cimbrian slave was detailed to carry out the sentence, but the sight of his former conqueror's glowing eyes and the sound of his commanding voice evidently proved too much for him, for the dagger fell from his hand. The officials at Rome were ashamed that a German slave had shown more respect for the old general than his fellow citizens, and they accordingly released him and sent him to the island of Ischia.

All this time, Sulla had been winning repeated victories against Mithridates in Asia. It might be worth our while to take a closer look at this king, who lived between 132 and 63 B.C. and was the Romans' most dangerous adversary in Asia during that period. After conquering the countries of Asia Minor, Mithridates finally ran up against Roman opposition, and when, in 88 B.C. at Ephesus, he ordered a massacre of all the Italians in Asia Minor, between 80,000 and 100,000 people lost their lives. He continued to defeat the Romans at every encounter, and his generals eventually occupied Athens. It was not until 84 B.C. that he at last met an opponent who was a match for him. He was defeated by Sulla and forced to pay an enormous indemnity of 2,000 talents, losing the whole of Asia Minor as well.

By 74 B.C. Mithridates was again master of Asia Minor, and war broke out once more. This time he was opposed by Lucullus, the celebrated Roman gourmet who introduced Europe to the cherry and was a very fine cook — as well as the most brilliant strategist of his day. Mithridates was forced to flee to Armenia, but, tough as always, he rallied his forces yet again and worsted the Romans three times in succession. He was defeated by Pompey in 66 B.C., but as usual he did not stay defeated for long. Once again he reassembled his forces and prepared to undertake a fresh campaign against the Romans. At this point, however, his own son rebelled against him, and the king's heart failed him for the first time. He tried to poison himself, but the poison would not act, and he was obliged to order a slave to kill him. General Lucullus, incidentally, was far from pleased at the news of his enemy's death. He would much rather have dragged him through the streets of Rome in chains, as Marius had once done with King Jugurtha.

The personality of Mithridates is almost like something out of a work of fiction: cruel, autocratic, brutal and indomitable. His own mother was terrified of him even when he was a boy and tried to kill him, but he escaped into the mountains and lived there as a huntsman. On reaching manhood he threw his mother into prison, killed his younger brother and several of his own sons, and eventually murdered his mother for good measure. Mithridates could speak twenty-two languages fluently. He used to award prizes not only to the best poets in the land, but also to the biggest eaters. Like all oriental despots he lived in a perpetual state of fear, seeing everyone around him as a potential assassin. To avoid being poisoned, he deliberately conditioned himself to all the commonest items in the poisoner's repertoire, which was why his first suicide bid failed. He murdered one of his own sisters, whom he had married, and another, whom he had not, and liquidated all the concubines in his harem to prevent their falling into the hands of his enemies.

Mithridates once offered 5,000 gold pieces for the hand of the celebrated Greek beauty Monime. When she insisted that if he did not send her a diadem and make her his queen she would stay at home in Miletus, Mithridates complied with her request, and the lovely girl pined away the rest of her life behind the bars of his harem like a bird in a gilded cage. In the end the king ordered her to take her own life. Monime tried to strangle herself with the diadem, but it broke. 'Wretched bauble!' she is said to have cried in disgust. 'So you were useless even for that.' Then she told an attendant to stab her to death.

To return to Marius and Sulla and the year 87 B.C. Sulla had only just left Italy for his campaign against Mithridates when Marius reappeared in Rome. He was a terrible sight. His hair was matted, his beard unkempt and his mind obsessed with thoughts of revenge. The inhabitants of Rome rose against Cinna, the consul who had been ruling the city with a rod of iron, and drove him out, but Cinna joined forces with Marius and together they marched back into the capital. Completely brutalized now, Marius roamed through the streets with his eyes glazed and his clothes in rags, and anyone whose greeting he did not choose to acknowledge was automatically beheaded on his orders. At the same time he started to drink even more heavily than before, and finally died in a drunken delirium. Only three weeks earlier he had begun a seventh term as consul, this time on his own authority and without the formality of an election. He died on January 13th, 86 B.C., a fine soldier but a deplorable politician.

After three years, Sulla returned from the East. By that time he, too, had been exiled. Like the Athenians before them, the Romans always used to wait until their great statesmen happened to be out of the country, and then overthrow them. In Sulla's case they had executed all his relatives, confiscated his property and declared him a public enemy.

Sulla had scarcely set foot on Italian soil when civil war broke out. Whole legions went over to his side, and he decided to settle accounts with his fellow countrymen. Mithridates was an expert in the art of wreaking revenge, and Sulla had had ample opportunities of studying the king's brutal technique during his campaigns in the East. Thousands of innocent people were slaughtered at his command while he, with a chalk-white face and two hectic spots of red burning in his cheeks, played the role of Lord High Executioner. Public notices or 'proscriptions' were posted daily in the Forum, listing the names of those who had been executed the night before. Rivalling Ivan the

Terrible, Sulla exterminated 12,000 Italians who held out against him in the fortress of Praeneste near Rome. He auctioned off his victims' property and set their slaves free, loaded comedians, singers and whores with extravagant gifts, and invited the whole of Rome to an orgy of eating and drinking, throwing all the left-overs into the Tiber. Curiously enough, he also gave Rome quite a good new constitution and reorganized the legal system. He was, in effect, Rome's first Caesar, for by assuming the office of dictator for an unlimited term he paved the way for those who were to be Caesars in name.

Sulla pandered to the Romans' love of gory spectacles by forcing prisoners of war to fight organized battles in public. During one such entertainment a very elegant lady called Valeria happened to touch the hem of his toga, and he spent the rest of the show flirting with her while prisoners fought to the death in the arena below. Valeria became Sulla's fifth wife. He was fifty-eight at the time.

There came a day when Sulla had had enough excitement for one lifetime. Quite alone and unescorted, he set off for his country estate at Puteoli (modern Pozzuoli,) where he settled down, apparently without considering the possibility of assassination, and spent most of his time in the company of actors and actresses — especially the latter. He also dabbled in poetry and wrote his memoirs. This happy state of affairs only lasted for a year, however. By then a sick man, he fell victim to his easily excitable nature, burst a blood-vessel, and died.

The Romans decreed him a magnificent State funeral, and his body was cremated in the presence of a vast crowd. Before his death he had ordered the following inscription to be carved on his tomb: 'I have always requited my friends with all that is good, and my enemies with all that is evil.'

No one could quarrel with the second part of that statement.

This she-wolf, with her expression of strange disquiet, was already gazing into eternity in the year 500 B.C. At the time of Marius and Sulla she was standing on the Capitol in Rome. Cicero reports that she was struck by lightning and hurled from her pedestal in 65 B.C. (Traces of damage by lightning have actually been found on the bronze.) This work of art, now in the Capitoline Museum at Rome, was probably executed by an Italian craftsman who had been commissioned by the Etruscan rulers of the period. The twins — Romulus and Remus — are a much later Renaissance addition

Lucius Cornelius Sulla (138–78 B.C.). An unbridled libertine and bloodthirsty monster, this dictator was also a statesman of the first rank

Gaius Marius (157–86 B.C.), seven times Roman consul, was a brilliant general but an inept politician. His death is reminiscent of King Lear's

Gnaeus Pompeius (106–48 B.C.), a lifelong soldier who conquered three continents. He married five times. A remarkably shrewd and cautious general, he did not have the luck to die at the height of his fame, like Alexander, but was defeated by Julius Caesar

POMPEY AND CRASSUS

THE SWORD AND THE PURSE

Never before had a Roman, quite apart from defeating so terrible an enemy [Mithridates], subjugated so many large nations and at the same time pushed the frontiers of the Roman Empire as far as the Euphrates.

Appian on Pompey in *Roman History*, xii (War between the Romans and Mithridates), 116.

Pompey settled the pirates, who had hitherto been living in quite a different fashion, in towns. He also made an ally of Tigranes, whom he could have exhibited in his triumphal procession, declaring that he was more concerned with eternity than with a single day.

Plutarch, comparison of Agesilaus with Pompey.

SEVEN HUNDRED THOUSAND people lived in Rome in the year 106 B.C. The city, with its four- or five-storeyed apartment houses, was a maze of alley-ways so narrow that a man could lean out of his window and shake hands with his neighbour opposite. The ill-ventilated houses were a breeding-ground for every kind of disease, and, as in large cities everywhere up to the present day, the people who lived in the busy turmoil of Rome were often lonely. Rents were high, and the inhabitants lived crammed together in a city which was at that time very much smaller than modern Rome. And yet, viewed from the roof of the temple on the Capitol, Rome's citadel, the great metropolis was a beautiful sight. The vista of murky, narrow streets was broken by a succession of splendid marble buildings which soared above them. In the temples and temple courtyards stood the statues which Rome had purloined from the rest of the world, hundreds of works in bronze, magnificent sculptures in marble.

Among these sacred works of art wandered visiting Greeks, shaking their heads sadly as they renewed acquaintance with the gods which had been looted from them. Modern divers are now photographing sunken Roman ships which are veritable museums of classical Greek art.

There were vast warehouses in Rome heaped with salt, wheat, wine and writing-paper from Egypt. If there was a drought in Egypt and the papyrus harvest was poor, the Romans had to write on wax.

During the rainy season people waded through the narrow Roman streets, and the drainage canals beneath the city walls became boiling torrents. Rome did have sewers, however, and no house was without its latrine. In aristocratic households and, later, in the imperial palace, these private thrones — precursors of the modern W.C. — were arranged in a semicircle to facilitate pleasant conversation. The aqueducts, those celebrated masterpieces of Roman engineering, brought over sixty million gallons of drinking and washing water into the interior of Rome each day, and public fountains and bathing-places were located at every cross-roads.

The Gauls introduced trousers into Italy, and the Germans brought furs. But for the most part the Romans dressed in a coloured *tunica*, over which citizens of rank wore the white toga, with sandals or military boots which invariably left the toes bare. They were therefore obliged to wash their feet several times a day — an almost sacred ritual.

'Why do so many Romans become ill?' ask the writers of antiquity. Well, they suffered from lack of sleep, for one thing. Their city was pervaded by an indescribable bustle and din: there were the shouts of the retainers clearing a path for their aristocratic masters, who would only stroll along the narrow lanes if accompanied by a large entourage; there were the throngs of pedestrians, the rumbling carts and hauliers' wagons, the litter-bearers burdened with the swaying wooden frameworks which were a constant cause of traffic congestion, and the tradesmen loudly extolling the merits of their wares. Rome had markets dealing in fish, game, poultry, fruit and delicacies from all over the world.

Outside Rome, some twelve miles away, lay the harbour of Ostia. The island situated at its mouth was later to be crowned by the celebrated Pharos, a lighthouse built on the orders of Emperor Claudius in the year A.D. 48. This gigantic freestone construction with four storeys, of which three were square and the uppermost circular, was modelled on the lighthouse at Pharos, the island off Alexandria, built in about 280 B.C. by the architect Sostratus of Cnidus at a cost of some £350,000. This latter building survived until the fourteenth century, when it was destroyed by an earthquake. It is interesting to note that another lighthouse, built by the emperor Caligula at Boulogne, France, was still to be seen in the seventeenth century. It even appears on old prints of the town. The Roman lighthouse at La Coruña in Spain, erected in A.D. 100, has been in continuous use right up to the present day. Forty-five lighthouse-keepers have served it since it was first built, each of them for an average term of forty years. Looked at in this way, the days of the Roman Empire do not seem so very far off.

The year 106 B.C. saw the birth of two famous men: Cicero, Rome's greatest orator and barrister, and Gnaeus Pompeius, the scion of a plebeian family. Pompey's birthday fell on September 29th, under the sign of Libra, the Scales, whose subjects are reputed to have an equal measure of fortune and misfortune in their lives.

Looking at Pompey's bust, one is compelled to agree with the German historian Theodor Mommsen when he declared him 'a thoroughly ordinary person', rather the 'efficient sergeant-major' type. Yet he was much more than that. He became the most powerful man in the world, if only for a brief time.

A very competent soldier, though not an unduly talented strategist, he applied himself to every task with a remarkable degree of caution, only committing himself when he was quite sure of his ground. He was a fighting-man, rather gauche and awkward, who combined disinterest, honesty and loyalty with a cool and unemotional nature. But his gaucherie was only confined to private life. In the field he was a skilful horseman and fighter. He was less of a peasant and less uncouth than the boorish Marius. Yet he did have one thing in common with him: he was a miserable politician. Marius makes a more sensual and emotional impact. Pompey was rather boring, dry, dignified and formal, a man of higher principles altogether.

Pompey enjoyed greater popularity in the country than in the city. In the outside world he behaved cordially towards all who had dealings with him and tried to grant every request made of him. In Rome, however, he disliked having anything to do with the ordinary citizens, avoided the Forum as much as possible and showed a reluctance to involve himself on other people's behalf, concentrating all his energies on his own plans. He could, when occasion demanded, rise to compelling heights of eloquence, and seems to have been an attractive man, both in appearance and personality. He is said to have been handsome, although our surviving sculptures of him are not exactly flattering. A courtesan called Flora still looked back with pleasure, even in her old age, on her association with him. Plutarch, the Greek historian, tells us that this somewhat promiscuous young lady 'never, when Pompey had enjoyed the delights of love with her, escaped the encounter unbitten'. Her beauty won her so much fame that she was painted and her portrait hung in the temple.

Pompey was the sword. We now come to the purse.

Even from a purely superficial point of view, Marcus Licinius Crassus was the very embodiment of wealth. Crassus meant 'the Fat', and the Fat One had an additional surname: Dives, or 'rich'. He was therefore 'the Rich Fat One', a double cognomen which his father and forefathers had borne before him. The Rich Fat One came from a wealthy family, but he was certainly not a fat man, being no glutton and having little taste for good living. Nine years older than Pompey, Crassus was not particularly cultured or well-read, and was a complete failure from a military point of view. On the other hand, his drive and initiative were scarcely rivalled by any man of his time. He was a great speculator and could, so to speak, 'smell' money. Crassus bought up the goods which Pompey confiscated at dirt-cheap prices. He undertook building projects as magnificent in architectural design as they were shrewdly planned financially. He was an astute banker. Anyone in Rome who needed money, senator and judge alike, called on Crassus. He was only too happy to arrange other people's legal affairs for them, bribing the courts and then taking a cut from his satisfied clients. If his name appeared in a will, it went without saying that it had been forged. Be that as it may, he lived unostentatiously, like any ordinary citizen.

Shortly before his death, Crassus' personal fortune was assessed at 170 million sesterces. He was at that time the richest man in the Roman Empire. A good judge of human nature, he never missed an opportunity to expand his business connections, and took care to greet every Roman citizen of note by name. He was a remarkably likable person, so much so that his constant preoccupation with other people's affairs often seemed almost like philanthropy. Whenever there was a chance of making money his keen commercial sense took him straight to the bottom of even the most protracted and wearisome business deals. He briefed himself thoroughly on every transaction in advance, no doubt partly because he was hard of hearing. Half Rome was in debt to him. He lent money 'interest-free', but with the proviso that the eventual extent of repayment be fixed by himself. In that way the most influential men in the country became dependent on him. Like every wise financier since his time, he took no account of political parties, recognizing that political affiliations exercise a distracting influence upon men of his profession. He lent money to anyone who served his purposes and seemed credit-worthy.

Little by little, however, Crassus did develop political ambitions, not by becoming pledged to an ideal, but merely by taking the line of least resistance as he was borne along on the tide of his wealth, connections and intrigues. Although he took care not to betray it, Crassus had always been jealous of Pompey. In his role as a brilliant business man and a walking bank, he outshone his much greater contemporary only when both of them happened to be in Rome. If Pompey was abroad, his reputation and power far exceeded that of Crassus.

The year 82 B.C. found Pompey, then twenty-four, standing on the rubble of Carthage, watching with amusement as his troops scrabbled among the ruins in a feverish search for the lost treasures of the ancient Phoenician city. When it had at last dawned on them that there was no gold to be found, he led them off to fight Domitius Ahenobarbus, and won the north African campaign in two weeks. Returning to Rome with his army, Pompey decided to enter the city in triumph, drawn by a team of elephants, but the city gate proved too narrow. Sulla, the Roman consul, greeted the twenty-six-year-old general with the title 'the Great'.

When Pompey was thirty the Roman Senate made him proconsul and sent him to Spain against Sertorius, a former supporter of Marius who had set up a Roman exile government in Spain. Sertorius knew every hill and river, every nook and cranny of the Spanish country-side, and his remarkable skill in conducting guerrilla operations against Pompey won him the title, among his followers, of 'the modern Hannibal'. He was assassinated in 72 B.C. while at a banquet, having held out against Rome for eleven years. Pompey defeated his murderer, Perperna, and reconquered the province of Spain.

Meanwhile, rebellion had broken out in Rome. The foreign slaves whom the Romans had captured in battle and trained to be professional fighters or gladiators rose in revolt under the leadership of a certain Spartacus. Spartacus had escaped from slavery in 73 B.C. and, collecting his companions in misfortune from the gladiatorial barracks, had occupied Vesuvius. He forced his way to the foot of the Alps, defeating various Roman armies as he went, and was joined there by Gaulish tribesmen. His new allies soon deserted him, but slaves flocked to join him in ever-increasing numbers. Leaving a trail of burned and looted towns in his wake, he arrived before the gates of Rome with an army of 120,000 men.

Crassus, the Fat One, who had meanwhile become praetor, was now given supreme command of the operations against the slave uprising. His efforts to crush the rebellion which had terrorized Italy for three whole years were totally successful. He erected a grisly avenue of 6,000 crosses, to each of which was nailed a captured slave. Crassus, Rome's greatest slave-trader, knew how to deal with slaves! We are told by Plutarch, incidentally, that he did not treat his own slaves badly.

Pompey was now thirty-five years old. His heart was set on the consulship, but the Senate hesitated to elect him. The outcome was an alliance between the fighter and the Fat One, the sword and the purse. Military force backed by money is an irresistible combination, and the uneasy senators, most of them in debt to Crassus, found their hands forced. In 70 B.C. Pompey and Crassus were elected joint consuls of Rome. Crassus was always the jealous partner in this curious marriage of convenience, the less popular and the much less talented militarily. When Pompey was given the task of clearing the Mediterranean of pirates — a task which he completed brilliantly within the space of forty days — Crassus, anxious to diminish Pompey's influence, joined forces with Julius Caesar.

But in the outside world Pompey gained military successes scarely rivalled by any general before him. He chased Mithridates, the king of Pontus, back behind the Caucasus. He conquered Syria, Palestine and Armenia. The distant Euphrates, the river near which the Tower of Babylon was once built, became the eastern border of the Roman Empire.

Pompey possessed to a marked degree the gift of knowing where to stop. He was an expert at biding his time and using it to best advantage. He founded colonies, continuously strengthened the ties between Rome and her provinces, built cities and organized the whole of the East. He never marched off on wild-goose chases into distant regions which could never mean anything to Rome, never set himself targets which lay in the far off fairy-lands of military ambition like north-west India, the limit of Alexander's advance. But then he never needlessly ran risks, as Macedonia's greatest general did in Gedrosia, or as Napoleon did at Moscow. Pompey was virtually never in danger from strange and hostile nations in distant lands. He only became vulnerable at home, in Rome, at Roman hands, through Roman envy and Roman ambition. The great man carried his destiny within himself, in his own character and the character of his people.

CICERO

ROME'S GREATEST ORATOR

If there had been no Cicero, the Catilinarian conspiracy might well have succeeded, but it would have sunk into the great limbo of the human past. Only the opposition of a Cicero helped Catilina and his confederates to win a place in world history.

The Author.

But should my fate be determined once and for all by my present misfortunes, then, my dear one, I have no other wish than to see you once more and to die in your arms.

Cicero in a letter to his wife Terentia, 59 B.C.

POMPEY was absent from Rome for six long years, from 67 until 62 B.C. Throughout almost the whole of that period Rome was a seething cauldron of conspiracy, haunted by secret unrest and riddled with schemes for revolution and *coups d'état*. The hour of the Roman republic's slow decline had struck. The outlines of the bold plan for a complete political upheaval which Caesar hatched so cautiously, prepared so meticulously and finally carried out with such audacity, now revealed themselves for the first time.

Rome was a republic, as it had been ever since the Romans overthrew their Etruscan rulers in 510 B.C. The Republic survived for about 480 years, until 30 B.C., when the Principate of Octavian marked the technical beginning of the imperial era. Such are the official dates, but Julius Caesar destroyed the Republic several years before its 'official' death.

The period of the Roman Republic's decline is one of the most interesting chapters in human history, not least because it embraces the lifetime of four great contemporaries: Pompey, Caesar, Cato and Cicero.

Rome was now like some ship struggling in the teeth of a storm. Power belonged to any man who could offer the people public festivals and do some judicious bribery during elections. Each tried to outbid the other in the splendour and attractions of his public entertainments. Roman society was morally bankrupt from top to bottom. Money-lenders flourished, great fortunes melted away and property changed hands in a rapid and unmerited fashion. Two large proletariats took shape, one composed of slaves and the other of freemen. 'Only the poor can understand the poor' became a popular catch-phrase. It occurred to people that the penniless masses might be just as capable of constituting an independent political force as the oligarchy of the wealthy. Why shouldn't they play the tyrant for a change, they asked themselves, instead of submitting to tyranny? And, as always in such cases, this movement was aided and abetted by certain sections of the youthful aristocracy. The elegant young bloods with their pomaded locks and modish beards danced gaily to the music of the *cithara* and gossiped over their wine-bowls from morning to night.

Almost everyone was in debt, and all those who had beggared themselves by laziness, extravagance or debauchery joined loudly in the cry for a nation-wide cancellation of liabilities. To many people, the slogan 'divide the land among the poor citizens' seemed their last hope of salvation.

So, while great Pompey held the East in thrall and Rome was winning four Asiatic provinces, the Republic was being internally undermined by a thousand clandestine schemes. Good men now had everything to fear, and bad men everything to hope for. The whole of Roman society, as well as the country-side for miles around, was honeycombed by a vast conspiracy. A cancerous disease, deadly but as yet undeclared, was growing and germinating in secret: the now notorious Catilinarian conspiracy.

Catilina was really nothing more nor less than a cunning criminal with an unstable personality. In spite of this, he managed to gain the office of praetor and even became governor of the province of Africa. He came of a patrician family, and his great-grandfather was a tough soldier who had served with distinction in the campaigns against Hannibal, during which he sustained no less than twenty-seven wounds.

As for his descendant, he was a pale-faced, shy man with a strong liking for the bottle. One moment he seemed the personification of idleness, and the next he was to be seen hurrying, with flying footsteps, about his nefarious business. He had tarnished his name as a young man by joining Sulla's terrorists and indulging in bloodshed and brutality. He later fell in love with Aurelia Orestilla, 'in whom, apart from her personal appearance, no one ever found anything praiseworthy' (Sallust). To clear his house for Rome's most unholy marriage, Catilina murdered his son.

The master-conspirator was impervious to cold, hunger or lack of sleep. He was sly, an expert at hypocrisy and dissimulation, eloquent but not over-intelligent. Every debauched and degenerate young man who had squandered his property or inheritance on loose living, depravity and gambling, was his boon companion by nature. Libertines, adulterers, murderers, internationally-known looters of temples, notorious perjurers, criminals who had already been convicted and other criminals still at large — all of them saw in revolution a chance of regaining their money and reputations.

Catilina himself was motivated partly by an innate lack of moderation, partly by thwarted ambition, partly by the audacity which springs from frequent failure and lack of money, and partly by resentment of the contempt with which society regarded him. He was a victim of his unsavoury past. He also possessed — perhaps as a legacy from his great-grandfather — a certain amount of courage, a degree of military talent, the quick-witted gangster's knowledge of human nature, the fierce energy of a fanatical gambler or criminal and a diabolical faculty for driving the immature or weak-minded to despair and then 'helping' them by making them party to his darkest deeds.

Catilina had twice stood for the consulship, in the years 65 and 64, but had failed on each occasion. An attempt to assassinate the consuls of 65 B.C., intended to be the signal for a *coup d'état*, came to nothing. Then, in the year 63 B.C., he found himself opposed by Marcus Tullius Cicero, the leading orator of his day and the greatest in the whole history of Rome. After this election defeat Catilina secretly laid plans for a grand conspiracy, setting the target date for autumn of the same year. The day of the uprising was to be October 28th, 63 B.C., the anniversary of Sulla's victory.

The object of the revolution was to overthrow the existing government. Behind the revolution stood the leaders of the democratic party, and one of its ostensible aims was a revolt against the divided nobility and the remaining vested interests of the aristocracy. But the democrats had long ago won their battle against the aristocracy, and so there were very few points left at issue on that score. No, there had to be another, concealed aim behind the revolution, something far more important to its instigators, at the back of whom stood the then youthful Caesar. And this far more important factor was the menacing shadow of Pompey. When once Pompey returned from the East they would have to reckon with a military dictatorship, and it was from this danger that the democrats were trying to extricate themselves. Outwardly, they paid homage to the absent general as their leader and the pride of their party. Outwardly, they were rebelling against the nobility. But secretly, at the heart of the plot to seize power, lay a wish to create a counterweight to Pompey, and the conspirators' ultimate objective was Pompey's downfall. That was why they needed a revolution, and that was why, in order to bring it about, they worked away at it in Rome almost solidly from 66 until 62 B.C.

Cicero's bitter struggle against Catilina is one of the most gripping stories in human history. This dramatic contest between the fox and the snake owes much of its fascination to the fact that we can follow its exact course in Cicero's correspondence and speeches. Cicero was Rome's most celebrated barrister. In the year 63 he defeated Catilina for the consulship. By 62 B.C. he had not only frustrated Catilina's hopes of election again, but laid bare the conspiracy, forced Catilina to leave Rome, unmasked the machinations of Catilina's confederates and secured, with the aid of some magnificent oratory, the execution of five of them. Catilina himself was finally run to earth by his enemies and fell, together with 3,000 followers, at the battle of Pistoria, north of Florence.

Rome had been saved from mortal danger. But the man who overthrew Catilina is worth a closer look, for it is upon his intellect and refinement of language that the foundations of European culture largely rest.

Marcus Tullius Cicero's mother brought him into the world at Arpinum, between Rome and Naples, on January 3rd, 106 B.C., 'easily and without pain'. He studied at Athens and on the island of Rhodes, the centres of contemporary learning, and lost his heart to each field of knowledge in turn. Whoever the teacher and whatever the subject, he was always an avid student, and he cherished a secret passion for poetry. The great Demosthenes was his model. Forty-eight of Cicero's speeches are lost, but fifty-eight survive. They hardly represent a code of justice, nor do they ever give the object of his indictments a chance. Piling charge upon charge, accusation upon accusation, Cicero brought mountains of arguments to bear upon his opponents. Employing Attic wit and the subtlest of irony, fair means and foul, he recruited every ounce of available material into the service of his sublime commands of words, an eloquence which left its mark on Latin for all time and made the language of Rome a classical medium of expression.

Apart from this, Cicero was always exceedingly well informed about his opponents. A secret seldom stays a secret for long once a pretty woman hears of it, and in Catilina's case the source of the leak was a woman called Fulvia.

Fulvia was an aristocratic Roman lady of promiscuous habits. Curius, an impudent, immoral and depraved individual who was one of Catilina's fellow conspirators, fell madly in love with her, loading her with so many presents that he completely ruined himself. Since Fulvia's favours were only to be had for gold and tangible gifts, Curius — by this time desperately infatuated — began to tell her about his great prospects and the wealth and prosperity which were shortly to be his. At first he only dropped vague hints, but later, spurred on by desire, he became more explicit. At last, intoxicated by his dreams of the future, he threw caution to the winds. He threatened her with his sword and promised her mountains of gold, generally behaving like a madman. Little by little, Fulvia carefully extracted from the unfortunate Curius the full secret of the conspiracy. And, because she was not altogether discreet, vague rumours of rebellion started to circulate in Rome and continued to do so for several years. Fulvia was always in need of money and her knowledge was valuable and easily converted into cash. It was for money, therefore, that she revealed Catilina's dangerous schemes to Cicero's intermediaries. Curius, too, was easily bought over, and a continuous stream of really reliable information flowed in.

Few men who got caught up in the grindstones of a Ciceronian indictment could hope to escape from their pulverizing jaws unscathed. '*Quousque tandem?*' – 'How much longer?' The famous opening words of Cicero's third speech against Catilina still preserve their ominous ring today. 'How much longer, Catilina, will you abuse our patience? How much longer will your wild behaviour be the object of our scorn? When will you, in your unbridled effrontery, cease glorifying yourself?' Cicero's genius, both as a politician and a lawyer, is clearly recognizable in the unrivalled perfection of the Latin style which graced his speeches.

His letters reveal vanity, ambition and a volatile temperament which made him self-confident in time of success, timidly irresolute and completely unnerved when faced by disaster. Most of these letters are addressed to Atticus, who lived for twenty-three years – from 88 to 65 B.C. – in Athens, where he had taken refuge from Sulla's agents. Atticus was an astute merchant, financier and publisher who owned land in Epirus and was a patron of the arts. He was a practical man, always ready to help people, and he was much wiser in the ways of the world than Cicero, who was a bit of a romantic. Atticus looked after Cicero's finances, published his writings and his correspondence, acted as his lifelong adviser, and provided a sort of placid reservoir into which all his brilliant protégé's miseries, fears, hopes, passions and joys could flow without restraint.

Cicero dictated many of his letters to his secretary and friend Tiro. It was his habit to walk up and down while doing so, and he spoke so fast that Tiro, himself a talented man, invented a shorthand which also enabled him to take down Cicero's speeches verbatim. Latin stenography later took its name from him, and his system, '*notae Tironianae*', was still being used by the monks of medieval times. Tiro, incidentally, was originally a slave whom Cicero freed because of his unusual ability. He was the author of a work on the usage and meaning of the Latin language.

Cicero was well aware that he would go down in human history as a man of very rare genius. He wrote to Atticus: 'As soon as I have completed the history of my consulship I will send it to you, and you can expect yet another one in verse. For since I am to praise myself for once, it shall be done in every possible way. If the world has something great to show, let it applaud it and not criticize. But what I am writing is, in fact, not so much a panegyric as a plain statement of historical truth.' It was a remarkably bold assertion, but it came from his heart, and clearly revealed how far in advance of his time he was in recognizing his own merit, greatness and importance.

Cicero's letters show a lively, attractive mind and a capacity for evolving an inexhaustible wealth of ideas about one and the same subject. They sparkle with intellect, wit, mockery, irony, charm. They bring us face to face with the worries and cares of a hard-working man, of a devoted father, and of a husband who found happiness with his passionate, jealous and energetic wife only when he had plumbed the depths of personal misery. Terentia brought him a dowry of 120,000 denarii on their marriage, and was heir to another 90,000. 'On this fortune he lived in a wise and decent manner, in the company of erudite Greeks and Romans who enjoyed his society,' as Plutarch puts it. In addition, Cicero owned a fine estate at Arpinum, two farms at Naples and Pompeii and a number of beautiful country houses — probably eighteen of them — in various parts of Italy. The houses were all provided with arcades and statues, tastefully decorated ceilings and pillars, hot water, dressing-rooms and steam-baths. There were fowl-houses, too, ornamental shrubberies, little canals and artificial ponds. Cicero asks Atticus to send him the 'Megarian statues and hermae'. 'I await them with great impatience. Rely on my purse and do not hesitate to send me anything of this nature which you think would be worthy of a place in my academy. I am hunting down anything which can help to beautify my gymnasium.' Cicero's favourite property was a villa, formerly owned by the dictator Sulla, at Tusculum, some fourteen miles south-east of Rome, near what is now Frascati.

Cicero wrote a whole library of rhetorical and philosophical works. There were books on orators and the art of rhetoric, on the ideal form of government, on law, on moral obligation, on the nature of the gods, on old age, on fate, on friendship and many other subjects. The sixth of these books, *The Dream of Scipio*, deals with life after death. The earth was popularly held to be a disk in those days, but Cicero describes it — like Plato before him — as a ball: 'For human beings are created on condition that they inhabit this sphere which you see here in the midst of the universe, the sphere which people call the earth. ... The constellations and stars, which are spherical and round, are animated by divine spirit. They complete their circuits and revolutions with marvellous speed. ... But the measurements of the round stars exceeded the size of the earth. The earth itself seemed to me so small that I was overcome by a sense of shame at all our activity, which, when all is said and done, affects but one point upon the tiny earth.'

On December 5th in the year 63 B.C. the Roman Senate was summoned by Cicero to confer on the fate of the captured Catilinarians. Junius Silanus, consul designate for the following year, demanded the death penalty, and all the ex-consuls present supported this proposal. Only Caesar, who had already been elected to the praetorship, rejected capital punishment in favour of life imprisonment, offering plausible and cogent reasons for his attitude of prudent clemency. Of course, he had himself played a secret and unnoticed role in the conspiratorial plan. Silanus and other friends of Cicero were getting ready to vote with Caesar, when Marcus Porcius Cato came down so strongly in favour of executing the Catilinarians that he left everyone in a renewed state of indecision.

Cato, descendant of the Carthage-hater, was an odd individual. Mommsen called him 'the Don Quixote of the aristocracy' and 'a dreamer in the sphere of abstract morality', but this judgment is probably too harsh. Cato was as straight as a die. He was a Stoic, a stickler for the ancient Roman standards and an extreme conservative, a slow-thinking but model citizen who wandered through the vice-ridden capital holding everything up to the mirror of virtue. He always went about on foot and shirtless — like King Romulus, the legendary founder of Rome. Above all else, he yearned for the good old days and made no secret of the fact. He was seldom taken very seriously. Only once did his honesty come in useful, and that was in 58 B.C., when the wealthy island of Cyprus was about to become a Roman province. He was sent there to organize the administration, being the only man who could be trusted not to feather his own nest in the process.

After Cato had delivered his unyielding demand to the Senate to pronounce sentence of death upon the instigators of this liberal, if not anarchical, conspiracy, Cicero rose to speak. He launched into the last of his famous Catilinarian Orations, a veritable masterpiece of psychological persuasion. While managing to give an appearance of complete impartiality, he succeeded, by constantly varying his tactics, in steering his listeners towards their intended destination. The Senate voted for the death penalty. Accompanied by a party of friends and citizens, Cicero personally removed the first conspirator, Lentulus Sura, from his place of detention by the Palatine

Hill and conducted him through the streets of Rome to gaol, where the executioners threw the luckless rebel into a cramped dungeon, the Tullianum, and throttled him with a cord. The dungeon had been reserved for this type of execution ever since the time of King Servius Tullius. The remainder of the condemned men speedily met a similar fate. They were executed the same night, the night of December 5th, 63 B.C.

Cicero felt that the day on which he saved the Republic from the conspiracy was the greatest in his life. He was escorted home in a triumphal procession through the brightly illuminated streets, cheered by vast crowds. People shouted his name from every window and roof-top, hailing him as the preserver and saviour of Rome.

But he was soon to pay a bitter price for his action. When, on the last day of the year, he was about to conclude his term as consul with the customary speech before the assembly, he was brusquely cut short by the tribune Metellus Nepos. A man who had ordered the execution of Roman citizens without a hearing, he said, should not be allowed a hearing himself. Cicero rose to the occasion magnificently, asserting that he had saved Rome and the Republic from the brink of disaster. But, although his speech was publicly acclaimed, he was exiled.

His wife Terentia seems to have had a decisive influence on his life on at least two occasions. Her half-sister, Fabia, was one of the priestesses of Vesta, who were obliged by their vocation to live a life of complete chastity. When the Vestal virgin was suspected of carrying on a secret affair with Catilina, Terentia saw in his removal a chance of nipping this scandal in the bud, and urged her husband to take proceedings against him.

The same thing applied in Clodius' case. Terentia thought that his sister Clodia had her eye on Cicero and was planning to marry him, so she persuaded her husband to bring evidence against Clodius. This man became Cicero's worst enemy and eventually brought about his exile from Rome, putting the great orator's houses up for sale or burning them.

Cicero was deeply hurt by his banishment. He continuously reproached himself, writing touching letters full of love and appreciation to his wife Terentia. 'Unhappy wife, anguished and weakened in body and soul! How can I live without you? If I had you at my side I should not think myself utterly lost.' And later: 'I read, not without bitter tears, how they had taken you from the temple of Vesta by force and led you before the tribunes in the public market-place. My life, my only love!'

Sixteen months later Pompey recalled Cicero from exile. His letters suddenly strike a different note: 'The love of my brother and my daughter compensates me for everything. As for my remaining worry, it is of a strange kind.' His 'remaining worry' was Terentia. At the age of fifty-nine he divorced her, having developed a sudden distrust of her scrupulousness in money matters. Perhaps he had forgotten what a huge fortune she had brought him when they married. At all events, he married Publilia, his young serving-girl. Then something frightful happened. His daughter Tullia died. Beside himself with grief at the loss of the daughter he had worshipped so greatly, Cicero threw Publilia, who had never been fond of the girl, out of his house. But he found life only a pale shadow of what it had been. 'A daughter, and what a daughter? How devoted she was to her father! How clever! How gentle, virtuous and lovable in her whole being! *My* face, *my* way of speaking, *my* intellect!' That was how Cicero wrote to his brother Quintus. Nothing could console him for the death of 'Tulliola', as he used to call her. Shutting himself up in Astura, he spent days and nights by himself in the lonely woods. Was there a life after death? Cicero had pondered the question before. And, if there was such a world hereafter, could one be reunited there with somebody dear to one? Cicero found no answer to that last and most vital problem of existence, death and eternity. He made plans for a temple to his daughter, an abode for her immortal soul. He eventually found solace in work, and the writing of his beautiful essay *On Consolation* brought him peace of mind. Two years later, however, he won the hatred of Mark Antony, whose violent measures he had strongly attacked in his Philippic Orations. He had survived Caesar, Pompey and Cato. But how? It seemed to him that he had done nothing all his life except work, worry and fret. 'You urge me, as you do so often, to be ambitious and to work,' he once wrote to his brother. 'I want to make the most of my abilities. But when am I to *live*?' Well, it was all over now, and he no longer wanted to stroll through his lovely gardens, write poetry or philosophize. Now it was his turn to die. He looked death boldly in the eye, as befitted a great philosopher — nor did his courage fail him at the last moment.

Plutarch does the old man an injustice by suggesting that he should not have hidden from his assassins, who were, after all, only anticipating Nature by a few years. Cicero did not hide. It was true that he got into his litter intending to make for the coast. It was true that he tried to escape from his enemies. But he was a philosopher, not a fool, and knew the value of human life.

When he noticed that his pursuers were gaining on him he ordered his litter to be set down and deliberately leant out. The best head Rome possessed fell beneath the assassin's sword on December 7th, 43 B.C. Cicero may have guessed in those last moments that he was going to see his beloved Tulliola again.

And, that being so, he had nothing more to fear.

Marcus Tullius Cicero (106–43 B.C.), politician, barrister, orator, teacher of philosophy, stylist, and one of the greatest educationalists in history. He is the only genius in the ancient world whose personality is intimately known to us, the majority of his private correspondence having survived

Gaius Julius Caesar (100–44 B.C.). 'All scholars of any ability have pictured Caesar with the same essential traits, yet none has succeeded in reproducing them clearly. The secret lies in Caesar's perfection. Humanly and historically, Caesar stands at the point where the great antitheses of existence merge into one another.' (Theodor Mommsen.) This is a posthumous sculpture

POMPEY

UNDER THE SIGN OF LIBRA

My Cornelia, you have so far known only one aspect of life: good fortune. And, because it has stayed with me for longer than is usual, you have perhaps been deceived. But since we are mortals we must also endure ill fortune.

Pompey to his fifth wife, according to Plutarch.

To return to Pompey. In summer of the year 62 B.C., after an absence of six years, he began his slow return to Italy from the East. The victorious general's homeward progress was one long pageant of splendour, acclaimed by people of many races and marked by presentations to various cities. Pompey did not land at Brundisium until the end of 62 B.C. He had completed the edifice of Roman sovereignty in Asia and temporarily secured it against all threats. It was true that his encroachments on Parthian spheres of interest in the East had sowed the seeds of subsequent retaliation, but he had conquered many lands, destroyed ancient cities, founded new ones — among them Nicopolis, Megalopolis, Zela, Diopolis and Pompeiopolis — and deposed and enthroned kings. There has seldom been a general with so much power who made such sparing and prudent use of it. Pompey's moderation was probably not, as Mommsen believed, due to a lack of self-confidence and initiative. He was remarkably wise and circumspect, if only as a general and strategist. He served Rome tirelessly for nearly thirty years as a cavalryman and a soldier — a cautious and unhurried man who rarely struck quickly, kept a sharp and attentive eye on his enemy's smallest move, and often operated with an almost Asiatic patience.

For all that, aristocratic society in Rome favoured General Lucullus. It was he, they said, who was the real conqueror of the East. Pompey had only supplanted him in order to snatch the laurels of victory from his grasp. This was a malicious distortion, of course, for when Pompey took over supreme command, all Lucullus' earlier successes had been cancelled out and the whole of Pontus had been lost. It was Pompey who chased Mithridates, then Rome's most dangerous enemy, back into the inaccessible depths of Asia, and Pompey who indirectly drove him to suicide, even though Pharnaces, the eighty-year-old king's son, was the immediate cause of his death. In contrast to the aristocracy, the common people of Rome were loud and rapturous in their praises of Pompey. They raised him to the status of a hero, and Pompey let them do it. Life is like a mountain path. It rarely ends at the highest peak. Plutarch says, quite rightly, that it would have been far better if Pompey had ended his life at this point, when his name ranked with that of Alexander the Great.

In 61 B.C. the greatest triumphal procession the world had ever witnessed passed through the streets of Rome. Pompey was hailed as the conqueror of three continents, Europe (Spain), Africa and Asia. His arrival caused a furore. Through the streets came prisoners from distant lands and treasures of unimaginable splendour: five sons and two daughters of the great Mithridates; the Jewish king Aristobulus; Tigranes, son of the Armenian king, together with his wife and daughter; hostages from Albania, Iberia and northern Syria; Olthaces, commander of the Colchians; the rulers of the Cilicians; women from the royal harem of Scythia; Menander, commanding general of Mithridates' cavalry; massive chests containing huge fortunes in coin, and emblems of victory. The procession was preceded by placards listing the countries and peoples conquered by Pompey. There was a picture of Mithridates dying, surrounded by the girls who 'voluntarily' shared his death. Pompey had captured 1,000 fortresses and over 900 large towns, and had defeated twenty-two kings. He handed over to the public exchequer minted money and gold and silver vessels worth 20,000 talents — about £83 million pounds[1]. His own appearance as he passed through Rome in the midst of this gigantic triumphal march was modest and unassuming, but he is said to have been wearing an over-garment, 260 years old even at that time, which formerly belonged to Alexander the Great and had been found among the treasures of Mithridates.

And the people? They did what they always do on such occasions: they cheered.

It was September 28th, 61 B.C., or 692 years after the founding of Rome. It also happened to be the eve of Pompey's forty-fifth birthday. Rome struck coins in his honour.

But who could keep his footing on such a pinnacle of success? Slowly the tragic process of decline and disillusion set in. For thirty years without a break, Pompey had been on active service. For thirty years he had been without a home. Now sleep deserted him and he was startled from his slumbers by troubled dreams of dying oriental kings, charging cavalry, burning cities. The Roman aristocracy laughed at him a little and gave him

[1] At present monetary values one talent is equivalent to a little over £4,000.

ridiculous nicknames. They could not stomach greatness. Their sense of humour and penchant for sarcasm would not allow them to.

As for Pompey, his one passionate desire was for rest. He longed to settle down with his wife and lead a quiet family life. Then he made his great mistake. He disbanded his army, whereupon the Senate refused to confirm his administrative measures in Asia or grant his soldiers their promised small-holdings in the colonies.

It was during this period that Pompey concluded a pact of friendship with Julius Caesar. Caesar, a man of forty-two, was a very influential politician and a brilliant orator, barrister and army officer from the proud patrician family of the Julians, who numbered kings and gods among their ancestors. To set the seal on this pact of friendship, Pompey married Caesar's only daughter Julia, a very beautiful girl of twenty-three.

Pompey was twice as old as Julia. His marriage to this graceful daughter of the Julian clan lasted only six years, for she died at the early age of twenty-nine. Their only child died, too. The scales of fortune were tipping more and more to Libra-born Pompey's disadvantage. But we are still in the year 59 B.C. when Pompey, Caesar and Crassus formed the first Triumvirate or three-man government. Pompey was the general, Caesar the politician and Crassus the capitalist. Pompey's veterans at last got their promised plots of land, his Asian policy was approved and he became master of the greater part of the Roman Empire. Caesar only received the governorships of Illyria and Gaul, which were to form his stepping-stones to subsequent power.

While Caesar was subduing Gaul from 58 to 51 B.C., Crassus endeavoured to conquer Persia, but was captured and put to death. The Persians hit upon a gruesome way of wreaking their revenge on the Fat One, the millionaire, the greatest slave-trader in Rome: they poured molten gold down his throat.

After the death of Julia, Caesar's lovely daughter, the rift between Caesar and Pompey increased. On Pompey's insistence, the Senate ordered Caesar to relinquish his Gallic provinces and disband his army. Caesar, however, crossed the Rubicon, the frontier between Italy and Gaul. 'The die is cast,' he declared, and before long he was master of Rome and all Italy.

Pompey fled to the East, was defeated at Pharsalus in Thessaly, was pursued by Caesar and finally sought refuge in Egypt. The Egyptian court had learned of the disaster at Pharsalus and were preparing to resist Pompey's landing when the Egyptian king's court chamberlain devised a better scheme. A general was dispatched to Pompey's ship with a message inviting him to become king of Egypt. The water being shallow, Pompey went on board the Egyptian barge to be ferried ashore. However, as he was stepping on to the beach, he was stabbed from behind, in full view of his fifth wife and his son, who must have witnessed the murder from the deck of their own ship. Pompey took his toga in both hands and drew it over his face. His code forbade him to utter any word of complaint, and all that escaped him was a deep sigh. If was September 28th, 48 B.C., the very date on which he had, thirteen years earlier, been drawn through the streets of Rome in triumph. Pompey's life had indeed been ruled by Libra, the Scales. The man who had borne the lifelong title 'Great' and had laid the world and treasures without equal at Rome's feet, met his end on a sand-dune on the Egyptian coast.

Not long afterwards, still on Pompey's track, Caesar arrived in Egypt. They brought him the severed head of his son-in-law and former friend.

Deeply moved, Caesar averted his eyes and wept.

JULIUS CAESAR

THE VERSATILE GENIUS

A hurricane was lashing the open sea. Caesar leapt into a fishing-boat. The fisherman wanted to put about before the storm, but Caesar said: 'Take courage! You have Caesar and his destiny aboard!'

Plutarch, Caesar, 38.

Not even in the provinces were married women safe from him.

Suetonius, Vita Caesarum, 50.

'BUT you have no reason for putting such a young man to death,' fellow-Romans told the dictator Sulla. Sulla replied that they were unintelligent if they failed to see any danger in the boy. His name was Julius Caesar.

As a member of the blue-blooded Julian clan, Caesar was one of the most aristocratic youths in Rome and a leading light in fashionable Roman society. He could declaim and recite, he was on good terms with men of letters, he wrote poetry and he enjoyed the favours which the pretty girls of Rome lavished upon him. Scarcely any other young man wore his hair so stylishly or was so versed in the mysteries of the Roman toilette. But life was very, very expensive, and young Caesar spent so much money that he was always having to borrow to pay off his debts. He was frivolous, but he had a good head on his shoulders. The gods only knew how he managed to lead his sort of life and still keep physically fit, but he did, perhaps because he fished, rode and swam.

His father had died early, but he was very fond of his mother Aurelia, a highly respected woman. Theodor Mommsen says that Caesar was a passionate man, since without passion there can be no genius; for all that, his passions never got the better of him.

At the age of seventeen Caesar became engaged to Cossutia, the daughter of an extremely rich man. It was not long, however, before he broke off this betrothal and married Cinna's beautiful daughter Cornelia.

Life was sweet, Rome was a wonderful place and Caesar was young. But he had heard what Sulla was saying about him and was conscious of the dictator's hatred. He therefore moved to the country and roamed about from place to place. When he fell sick he had himself carried about on a litter, spending each night in a different house in turn, until Sulla's soldiers, who were always on his track, eventually discovered his hiding-place and arrested him. Caesar bribed them, fled to the coast and sailed for Bithynia, where he sought refuge with King Nicomedes. He was later accused of having surrendered himself to this king's unnatural desires.

Soon afterwards Caesar set sail once more, only to be captured by pirates. He laughed them to scorn when they demanded a ransom of only twenty talents, scoffing at them for not realizing who their prisoner was. Offering them fifty talents, he sent his companions off to various cities to raise the money and meanwhile lived among the pirates in high style. He harangued them into keeping quiet when he wanted to sleep, joked and gambled with them, read them satirical poems, jeered at them and threatened that he would some day hang them. The bandits found themselves behaving like his bodyguard. It was almost as though he were their leader.

The ransom money arrived and Caesar was set free. He manned several ships, sailed against the pirates, caught most of them and got his ransom back as prize-money. In Pergamos he made good his playful threats by having all the pirates crucified.

After Sulla's death Caesar returned to Rome and demonstrated his brilliant command of language as a defence lawyer. He was polite, affable and civil in his demeanour towards everyone, and very soon won the love and affection of the people. His banquets were the talk of all Rome. His prestige in the State grew until it finally became apparent that his aim was to destroy it.

The great orator Cicero compared Caesar's political ability with the smiling serenity of a calm sea. He found it suspicious and menacing. Looking behind Caesar's mask of friendliness and cordiality he not only saw the man's aristocratic nature but scented his tyrannical aspirations, too. 'When I see,' said Cicero, 'how artistically arranged his hair always is, when I see how he scratches himself with a single finger, it almost seems as though the overthrow of the Roman constitution could never enter his head.'

Before long, Caesar was able to do things in Rome which another man would never have dared to do. He gave Julia, his father's sister and the widow of Marius, a magnificent funeral oration in the Forum. He also set up portraits of her dead and despised husband in public, at which the people cheered and showed their sympathy with loud hand-clapping and applause.

Well, it was not unusual to give an elderly woman a funeral oration in Rome. But what about a young one?

When Cornelia, Caesar's wife, died at the age of twenty-nine, he accorded her the same honour. The people were touched, and the favour of the masses did not desert him even when he married Pompeia very soon afterwards. He continued to court popularity, and it was not long before his debts totalled 1,300 talents.

On the death of Caecilius Metellus Pius, the Pontifex Maximus of Rome, Caesar immediately applied for the office, which gave its incumbent complete charge of the temples and supervision of ritual and religious observance. There were other candidates for the appointment, and it was a hard fight. When Aurelia, Caesar's mother, weepingly accompanied her son to the door on the day of the election, he told her: 'Today, dear mother, you will see your son come back either as Pontifex Maximus or as an exile.' Caesar was elected. He was then thirty-nine.

Next, Caesar aimed for the praetorship, one of the two highest Roman legal appointments. But carving out a career in Rome was not easy. Everyone wooed the populace as best he could. Cato proposed that the Senate should dole out grain to the people, and, since Caesar could not hope to match the Senate's vast distributions, his popularity inevitably suffered. It was a rule in Rome that success went to the highest bidder.

But there was yet another incident which lowered Caesar's prestige. One of Rome's leading gallants was a dissipated and arrogant individual named Publius Clodius, a man who was not only of noble birth but wealthy, too. Clodius was in love with Pompeia, Caesar's wife, and Pompeia was not altogether indifferent to him. However, her quarters were constantly under the eagle eye of Aurelia, Caesar's strait-laced and virtuous mother, who put insurmountable obstacles in the lovers' way.

The Romans had a goddess called Bona Dea, in whose honour they held an annual women's festival from which men were excluded. Clodius, who was beardless and girlishly handsome, dressed himself up as a female harpist and slipped into Caesar's house. He wandered round the rambling building for quite a while, avoiding the more brightly illuminated rooms, until one of Pompeia's slaves recognized him by his masculine voice. Aurelia at once suspended the festivities, covered up the sacred shrines and threw Clodius out of the house. Early next morning the whole of Rome was buzzing with the scandal, and Caesar decided to divorce Pompeia. When the case came before the courts Caesar treated Clodius with remarkable friendliness, declaring that he personally had no knowledge of the man's guilt. Replying to people who asked him why, in that case, he had divorced his wife, he said: 'Because I demand of my wife that she be above suspicion.'

Caesar was appointed governor of the province of Spain. His creditors made such an uproar about his departure that he appealed to Crassus, the richest man in Rome, and the latter paid off his most pressing debts. During his stay in Spain, Caesar read the story of Alexander the Great, and tears came to his eyes. His friends inquired the reason. 'Wouldn't you say,' asked Caesar, 'that I had cause to be sad, seeing that at my age Alexander was ruler of so many nations, while I have never yet done anything great or glorious?'

After a very successful tour of duty in Spain, Caesar returned to Rome and effected a reconciliation between Pompey and Crassus. It was agreed, privately and unofficially, that Caesar, Pompey and Crassus would co-ordinate their policy from then on. The triumvirate had been born. Caesar gave Pompey the hand of his daughter Julia and contracted a third marriage himself, this time to Calpurnia, the daughter of Piso.

In the year 59 B.C. the Roman people's assembly and the Senate granted Caesar the governorship of Gaul, which comprised modern France, Belgium, Holland and upper Italy from the Po northwards. He was given four legions, or about 24,000 men, and his term of office was initially set at five years, although he later got it extended by another five.

It is quite certain that Caesar was deeply influenced by his study of the campaigns of Alexander the Great and other notable generals. Equally certain is the fact that he cherished great plans for conquest, even if he prevented any advance information about them from reaching the ears of an eternally mistrustful Senate. In his work *De Bello Gallico* he justifies his policy of conquest to the Romans, and is always at pains to show how the successful completion of a 'defensive operation' forced him to undertake a fresh one.

Following his defeat of the Helvetii, Caesar came up against Ariovistus, the German king of the Suebi. Ariovistus is really the first tangible figure in German history, and the Suebi were what are now the Swabians. We owe our knowledge of Ariovistus almost exclusively to Caesar's vivid descriptions of him.

After a long series of campaigns, Ariovistus set his cap at Gaul, but was defeated by Caesar between Besançon and Schlettstadt in the year 58 B.C. Although he escaped over the Rhine, he died shortly afterwards of wounds sustained in battle against Caesar.

Caesar's next target was present-day Belgium, and he did, in fact, manage to subdue the whole of northern Gaul.

But he went even farther afield. On two occasions, in 55 and 54 B.C., he crossed the Channel and landed in Britain, but contented himself with exacting tribute from the king of the Celts, 'since among this wretched and poverty-stricken nation there was nothing worth while to be found' (Plutarch). The forefathers of the English, incidentally, never paid the tribute Caesar imposed upon them.

Caesar never tried to conquer the countries east of the Rhine, or modern Germany, although he did make a show of force by crossing the Rhine twice, in 55 and 53 B.C. In those days the Rhine formed the frontier between the Gauls and the Germans, between Roman sovereignty and the 'barbarians' who were still fighting their way obscurely towards a higher level of civilization.

This ability to call a halt when once the limits of his objective had been reached seems to me to be the true secret of Caesar's genius. At the Thames, as at the Rhine, Caesar turned back of his own free will. He never failed, once he realized that his run of luck was at an end, to obey this inner voice.

In this respect Caesar seems a greater man than either Alexander or Napoleon. Alexander was compelled to retreat at the Black Sea river Hypanis. Napoleon turned back from Moscow because he had to. Both Alexander and Napoleon chafed at their luck. Only Caesar knew how to break off every battle on the crest of victory, went just as far as his luck permitted, and was content to leave it at that.

Vercingetorix, a chieftain of the Celtic Arverni from central Gaul, rallied the Gauls in a great national uprising against Caesar and Roman domination. With extraordinary bravery he defended his mountain home, the town of Gergovia, against every attack by Caesar, who was for a time in a highly dangerous position. But Caesar finally blockaded Vercingetorix in Alesia, and the Gaulish hero was forced to surrender. In 46 B.C. he was led through Rome in a triumphal procession, later to be decapitated in the Carcer Mamertinus. The French still regard Vercingetorix as a national hero, as the Germans do Arminius, and, just as the Germans have erected a memorial to their Cheruscan prince in the Teutoburger Wald, so the French have honoured Vercingetorix in Alesia and on the site of Gergovia.

Caesar spent seven long years fighting in Gaul. The Greek historian Plutarch considers that, as a strategist, he surpassed all the Roman generals before him, the Fabii, the Scipiones, the Metelli, Sulla, Marius, Lucullus and even the great Pompey. He points out that Caesar conquered immense areas, fought the most battles and killed the greatest number of enemies. He took 800 towns by storm and subjugated 300 different tribes. He fought 3 million people and killed or captured over a million of them.

Caesar boldly met all his dangers half way, and never shirked any difficulty or hardship. He despised death and astounded everyone by the toughness of his constitution, for he was a lean man whose white skin made him look almost pale. What is seldom known is that he suffered from epilepsy and regarded military service as a kind of therapy, hoping that forced marches, an extremely simple diet and continuous outdoor exercise would cure his attacks. He normally slept in a carriage or a litter. By day he used to inspect fortresses, camps and towns. A secretary was in constant attendance on him, ready to take dictation even while on the march, and behind him usually stood a solitary soldier armed with a sword.

Caesar used to travel so fast that it only took him a week to get from Rome to the Rhône. When he rode it was at a brisk trot, with his hands resting on his charger's neck. During campaigns he would dictate even on horseback, employing two or more scribes for that purpose. In Caesar's view 'written conversations' saved time, and he found short letters far less irksome than long conferences. We can see, therefore, that Caesar between the ages of forty-three and fifty was quite another person from the spoilt, versifying youth of twenty.

It was true that he still had his affairs and successes with women, but he only toyed with them and never allowed them to exert any influence on his decisions. Even so, he probably retained some of his youthful vanity, for he carefully concealed his baldness with the laurel wreath.

Caesar was possibly the most versatile genius ever born. He was a consummate politician, a general who always subordinated his military measures to the overriding considerations of his political aims, an author with an extraordinarily graphic style and great simplicity of expression — rather like Churchill in that respect — and a born ruler who knew how to captivate everyone, from the common citizen and the tough non-commissioned officer to the noble ladies of Rome; from the princesses of Egypt and Mauretania to his two ill-assorted partners, the brave cavalry general and the crafty banker.

All the historians, authors and poets who have tried to capture something of his unique perfection have failed in one respect: they have never managed to catch the strange lustre, the glow, the sheer positive radiance which endued all his deeds and actions and his personality itself.

THE SECRET OF SUCCESS

When, at supper on the day before, they were discussing which death was best, Caesar alone cried in a loud voice: 'An unexpected one!'

Plutarch, Caesar, 63.

THE connection between genius and success is something which the little minds of this world will never understand. Like a radiant sun, Caesar walked the earth — so grey and dismal-seeming to millions of other men — as though pursued by luck. Yet it was not 'luck' as such. Caesar forged his own luck, and knew how to retain it.

We call him Caesar, but the name which became a title of supreme rulership all over the world was actually pronounced 'kaisar' by the Romans.

Crassus had met his death after fighting against the Parthians. Only one man now stood in Caesar's way: Pompey, his great rival and the general whose victories in Asia had almost eclipsed Caesar's own reputation.

Rome was like a ship without a helmsman. Near anarchy reigned, and power belonged to anyone who could set up tables in the public squares and entertain the people. The Senate was corrupt, the constitution on the point of collapse and the speakers' rostra only too often stained with blood. Filibustering orators frequently left the platform as corpses.

At Rome, Pompey tried to prevent Caesar's re-election to the consulship in 48 B.C. On reaching the Rubicon, the river which separated Cisalpine Gaul from Italy, Caesar paused, lost in thought. After lengthy deliberations as to whether he should try a bold *coup* against Rome, the Senate and Pompey, he decided to cross the Rubicon. Within sixty days he had won a bloodless victory and was master of all Italy.

Then came the chase. Caesar pursued his former son-in-law, the man who had once been the stumbling-block to all his aspirations, to Pharsalus. There a battle was fought on August 9th, 48 B.C., which decided the issue once and for all. Pompey suffered a crushing defeat and was later murdered on the Egyptian coast.

Caesar landed at Alexandria and, with godlike self-confidence, began to reorganize the state of utter chaos which prevailed there. Egypt was being governed by the king's prime minister, a eunuch called Potheinus. The king and queen were Ptolemy Dionysus and his sister Cleopatra. Following the normal Egyptian custom, brother and sister were married, but Ptolemy was then only ten years old, while Cleopatra was nineteen. Cleopatra had been driven out of the country by Potheinus and was in Syria at the time, scheming to regain her royal prerogatives by force of arms.

The wily regent Potheinus was far from overjoyed by Caesar's arrival. Having been responsible for Pompey's murder, his next move was to plan an attempt on Caesar's life. Caesar, however, was aware of this and was wise enough never to go to bed, spending his nights at banquets and entertainments. The father of the ten-year-old king owed him seventeen and a half million drachmas, and he now demanded the repayment of ten million for the upkeep of his troops. Potheinus advised him to quit Egypt and carry out his world-wide projects, but Caesar replied that Egyptian advice was the last thing he would take. Instead of leaving the country, he secretly sent for the exiled Cleopatra.

Accompanied only by a Sicilian called Apollodorus, the princess entered a small boat and landed near the royal palace at twilight. In order to reach Caesar's presence undetected she hid herself in a mattress (not a carpet, by the way!) which Apollodorus tied up with cord. The good Sicilian then shouldered the fateful little bundle and brought it to Caesar.

We can well imagine how affected the tough, middle-aged soldier must have been at the sight of the Egyptian girl. She may not have been beautiful, but she was certainly attractive. In Plutarch's own words: 'Her society and charms made a great impression upon Caesar.' Caesar reconciled Cleopatra with her brother, Cleopatra naturally having stipulated that she should take a share in the government from then on. There followed a ceremonial banquet designed to seal the reconciliation.

The attempt on Caesar's life planned by Potheinus and his general, Achillas, was unmasked by Caesar's barber, a slave who, although he was the most timid man in the camp, was an expert spy and eavesdropper. Caesar posted guards all round the conspirators' rendezvous, but, although he got rid of Potheinus, he failed to catch Achillas. The latter immediately took up arms against him. The Egyptians blocked all the canals and sources of water supply, with the result that Caesar's troops nearly died of thirst. Then Achillas tried to make off with Caesar's fleet. Caesar set fire to the naval arsenal and the spreading flames destroyed the famous Alexandrine library.

The burning of this library in the year 47 B.C. was one of the most tragic events in the history of human civilization, for it contained 400,000 papyrus rolls, a literary treasure which would have rescued from the darkness of antiquity an era of pre-Christian history and culture stretching back hundreds and probably thousands of years.

Caesar was himself exposed to great danger during this mêlée. The battle was raging near the island of Pharos and its celebrated lighthouse, when he jumped off the mole into a small boat to go to the aid of his troops. Egyptian vessels came swooping down on him from all sides. He plunged into the sea to elude them and swam to safety through a hail of shots, holding some important documents above the water with one hand. The young king had meanwhile gone over to Achillas, but Caesar turned on him and inflicted a decisive defeat on the Egyptians. The boy-king was probably drowned in the Nile.

Leaving Cleopatra behind as queen of Egypt, Caesar travelled to Syria. Cleopatra, it may be added, shortly afterwards gave birth to a son whom the Alexandrians, logically enough, called 'Caesarion'. Caesar's next step, in 47 B.C., was to defeat Mithridates' son Pharnaces at Zela, south of the Black Sea. His way of transmitting the news to Rome as speedily as possible was to write to his friend Amintius: 'I came, saw and conquered.' Caesar's defeat of Pharnaces, incidentally, was the work of a single hour.

The brilliance with which Caesar parried the blows of fate, his genius for improvisation and his deliberate independence of what is commonly called luck, are all demonstrated by his African campaign during the winter of 47–46 B.C.

What is luck, after all? Isn't it merely the knack of doing the right thing at the right moment?

The campaign in Africa is a perfect illustration of how Caesar managed, despite a succession of mishaps and the most unfavourable prospects, to come home with total victory in his pocket.

Africa was the chief stronghold of Republican opposition, for it was there that all the opponents of Caesar and tyranny in general were concentrated. They included the survivors of the army defeated at Pharsalus, the garrisons of Dyrrhachium (Durazzo), Corcyra and the Peloponnese, and the remnants of the Illyrian fleet. The senior general, Metellus Scipio, Pompey's father-in-law, had also arrived there with his second-in-command Petreius, as had the leader of the Republican anti-Caesarian faction, Marcus Cato, the man who 'would sooner have let the Republic fall in ruins for a proper cause than save it by irregular means' (Mommsen). There, too, were to be found Pompey's two sons, Gnaeus and Sextus, as well as Labienus, an efficient officer who had earlier been Caesar's most able subordinate in Gaul but had now gone over to his enemies' side. In all, the stubborn remnant of Pompey's former supporters had collected ten legions together. The chief backer of this menacing coalition was the ferocious African king Juba, who rewarded those showing pro-Caesarian sympathies with extermination.

While Caesar was assembling forces in southern Italy in preparation for the African expedition, mutiny broke out. The morale of his legionaries, wearied by an endless succession of campaigns, had fallen to zero. They were discontented, and the rewards and privileges they had been granted had not come up to their expectations. They became insubordinate. Still worse, they went marching off to Rome in wild and undisciplined bodies with the declared intention of telling Caesar to his face how they felt. Such officers as tried to halt the gangs of mutinous soldiery were massacred on the spot. Before long the legionaries had reached Rome. They found themselves standing before Caesar, who came out to greet them suddenly and unannounced. His manner was quite calm.

'What do you want?'

Their general asked the question coolly, without any loss of composure or visible sign of emotion. The legionaries informed him that they wanted their discharge. They knew that Caesar needed them, needed them more urgently than ever before, for his African enterprise and they knew that he could not afford to let them go. That was why they were so sure he would comply with their demands. Now was the moment for them to cash in.

Caesar did not discuss the matter. His reply was as succinct as it was unexpected. 'You are right, *Quirites*,' he said. 'Heavy fighting and wounds have tired you out. You may go.'

'*Quirites*' or 'fellow-citizens', he called them, not 'comrades' — as though they had ceased to be soldiers and were already civilians! After his next victory, he told them, after his triumph, they too — together with the victorious soldiers — would receive gifts and grants of land. But they would not be allowed to take part in the triumph itself. 'I do not need you any longer,' he said. 'I discharge you. You will receive your gratuities without any deduction.'

For a moment the soldiers stood there dumbly.

Then they begged to be allowed to remain with him.

Reading this, one cannot quite grasp why the mutinous legionaries let themselves be pacified so easily. But it was not just Caesar's words which did it. It was something quite different, something which, after almost 2,000 years, one finds hard to comprehend. Once again Caesar's extraordinary personality had fascinated and enthralled his soldiers. Once again they stood there before him, captivated, abashed, irresolute, like wax in his hands. Mommsen says: 'History knows no greater psychological stroke of genius.'

The actual expedition in Africa was a long series of mishaps, with one single exception: the battle of Thapsus, the final struggle and the only decisive engagement, which Caesar, true to form, won. No sooner had he sailed for Africa on December 25th, 47 B.C., when an equinoctial storm blew up, and his fleet went astray among the storm-tossed waves. He landed at Hadrumetum (Sousse) with a mere 3,000 men, most of them recruits. Stepping ashore, Caesar stumbled and fell, an occurrence which struck terror into his superstitious soldiers. With great presence of mind he pretended that he had thrown himself to the ground on purpose. 'I seize you, Africa!' he cried.

The remainder of Caesar's ships eventually hove in sight. He managed to extricate his legions from a surprise attack by Labienus, but only with the greatest difficulty and heavy losses. In this kind of situation Caesar revealed an iron nerve and inexhaustible reserves of patience. Stage by stage, he gleaned for his side whatever advantages he could, always avoiding a decisive battle. He mobilized Gaetulian tribes of herdsmen against Juba, drew Mauretanian kings into an alliance, won over various towns and their citizens and incited the native inhabitants of the African coast against the Republicans. He seized the harbours of Ruspina (Monastir) and Leptis Parva, conveniently situated in case of a possible 'Dunkirk', and there dug himself in. Then he settled down to the difficult task of playing for time with inferior forces. He thought of everything. When horse-fodder ran out, he ordered his men to gather sea-weed. When his troops showed that they were incapable of dealing with the enemy's war-elephants, he had circus elephants brought over from Italy. He trained his younger soldiers in African-style guerrilla warfare and conducted daily manœuvres. He showed himself an expert at the waiting game, at keeping cool and holding himself in check. For almost four months he wisely waited until his veteran legions arrived with their complement of tough and battle-seasoned men.

And then, near the enemy-occupied naval fortress of Thapsus, Caesar chose precisely the right moment to lure his adversaries into a fatal trap. On February 7th, 46 B.C., Scipio was stationed with his army only a mile away, on the narrowest point of the isthmus in front of Thapsus, the open sea on one flank and a lagoon on the other. Caesar's veterans could hardly be restrained. At their head he galloped towards the enemy — a man of fifty-four, let it be remembered, with a long history of successful campaigns behind him. His veterans wreaked terrible havoc in the enemy's ranks and also took the opportunity of eliminating several of their own officers with whom they had long-standing scores to settle. Caesar won a total victory.

The enemy commander-in chief, Metellus Scipio, committed suicide when his escaping fleet was trapped. As for King Juba, he had personally devised a dramatic end for himself. He intended to be burnt on an immense pyre in Zama, his capital, accompanied by his family, his treasures and all his citizens. The people of Zama, however, were not over-keen on playing their part in this mad orgy of death and destruction, so they shut the city gates on their king as he approached. After a sumptuous banquet, the savage monomaniac challenged Petreius to mortal combat. Petreius fell, and Juba, who was wounded, had himself stabbed to death by a slave. Labienus and Pompey's sons escaped to Spain.

Cato's death at Utica marked the spiritual end of the civil war and the end of the conflict between the Republican forces and Caesar. This indomitable man chose to die a martyr's death for the Republican cause. Caesar would have been quite happy to pardon him, if only for the sake of gaining a reputation for magnanimity, but Cato, a true friend of freedom, felt that Caesar's mercy would close the gates of immortality to him for ever. When he recommended his son to go to Caesar, his son asked: 'Why do you not do the same?' 'I was born in an era,' answered Cato, 'when one could act and speak freely. At my age I cannot accustom myself to servitude so quickly, but you are a child of the times and must make friends with the spirit of your century.' The greatest Republican of his day, Cato sat down to read Plato's treatise *On the Soul*. At midnight he drove a dagger into his body and, when they bandaged him up, tore out his own entrails. Thus even Caesar's genius foundered on the inflexibility of this reactionary Roman nobleman, Stoic and idealist. 'He did not even grant me the glory of allowing him to live,' snapped Caesar.

Nevertheless, the monarchy had been forged, and Caesar's triumphal march through Rome after all these wars was the triumph of a man who had defended and enlarged the Empire, not that of a victor in a civil war. One day of the festivities was set aside for Gaul, another for Egypt, another for Pontus and yet another for Africa. The triumphal procession included, apart from huge quantities of booty, prisoners such as Princess Arsinoë of Egypt, young Prince Juba of Numidia and the famed Vercingetorix, former hero and leader of the Gauls. Then came Caesar himself and the wagons full of gold for his soldiers. Each legionary received a gratuity of 5,000 denarii, and each centurion 10,000.

Caesar was elected dictator, first for a term of ten years, and then, as *dictator perpetuus*, for life.

The murderous battle against Pompey's sons, which took place near the town of Munda in Spain, led Caesar into such personal danger that when it was over he declared that, although he had often fought for victory, this was the first time he had fought for his life. It was the last battle he ever fought.

The Romans had become used to Caesar's triumphs. The victor was now their absolute master, and Rome stood at the mercy of his whims. It was hoped in the capital that one-man rule would at last bring relief from civil war and its attendant tribulations, and so the Romans willingly elected Caesar dictator for his lifetime. The moment he was granted unlimited power for an unlimited term, Caesar became a tyrant and a dictator in the modern sense.

Then began the grotesque game of flattering a man who was ultimately bound, because of the sheer plethora of the honours heaped upon him, to make himself look ridiculous. An orgy of adulation and exaggerated hero-worship, taking strange and often offensive forms, made Caesar a detested figure even in the eyes of the good-natured citizenry. Most extravagant of all in their panegyrics and eulogies were Caesar's enemies.

Caesar re-erected Pompey's statue. Several of his friends advised him to provide himself with a body-guard, but he replied: 'It is better to die once than always to be expecting death.' Distributions of grain, entertainments, grants of colonial land to veterans — all these things Caesar tossed at the people like so many pieces of bait. At the same time he forged great plans. He wanted to outdo his existing military successes. He wanted to march against the Parthians. He wanted to push down to the Caucasus, skirt the Black Sea and force his way into Scythia. Then he proposed to return to Italy by a long and circuitous route through Germany and Gaul, conquering every country on the way, until he reached the oceans which marked 'the frontiers of the world'.

Caesar planned to cut through the isthmus of Corinth. What was there left, he asked himself, for a man with so much power? What worth-while enterprise still lay open to someone who was master of the world? He decided to dam the Tiber and divert it into the sea near Terracina. A vast project involving thousands of people hovered before his eyes — the draining of the Pontine marshes. He intended to construct moles on the coast, eliminate the dangerous reefs and shoals in the port of Ostia and install harbours and anchorages. He summoned the greatest philosophers and mathematicians of the day and ordered them to devise a new time-system. He introduced the whole Roman Empire to the solar year and the Julian calendar, which was adopted by the world at large and is still, as amended by Pope Gregory XIII in the year 1582, in force today.

Even that was not enough for Caesar. He wanted to become a king, the greatest king in the world. But there the people jibbed. Caesar's boundless ambition was sowing seeds of hatred everywhere, so, when the Senate tried to hail him as king and bestow on him even more exaggerated marks of honour, Caesar refused to rise from the rostrum and declared that the offer should be withdrawn. That, too, went down badly, both with the Senate and the people. Everyone was offended. Caesar went home, laid aside his toga and told his friends that anyone who wanted to kill him was free to do so. Then he apologized. It was his illness, he said. A man with epilepsy easily became confused if he had to address the people in a standing position. Any shock or violent movement made him dizzy. A sycophant named Cornelius Balbus cut short Caesar's apologies by telling him: 'Do not forget that you are Caesar. Let yourself be revered as a superior being.'

Caesar sat on a golden chair in his triumphal robes. He was proffered a laurel wreath and a diadem. A faint, half-hearted round of organized applause broke out. When Caesar pushed the diadem away, the people clapped loudly. He was again offered the diadem. Again he refused it, and again the crowd clapped. Reluctantly, he stood up and ordered the wreath to be carried to the Capitol.

However, Caesar's enemies secretly adorned his statues with diadems. Two tribunes of the people were detailed to remove them, and the men who had hailed Caesar were thrown into prison on the dictator's own orders. The convicted men were accompanied to gaol by a jubilant mob.

Marcus Brutus was an enemy of tyranny. Caesar had pardoned him after Pharsalus, where he had fought for Pompey, and he enjoyed the dictator's particular confidence. He was praetor, and Caesar was backing him as a candidate for the consulship. When Brutus arrived at court in the mornings, he would find notes left on his judgment seat. 'You are asleep, Brutus,' they ran, or 'You are not Brutus'.

Cassius, who instigated the plot against Caesar's life, knew that Brutus could be won over because he was ambitious. It was of Cassius that Caesar once said: 'I do not like Cassius' paleness'. On another occasion, when someone tried to cast suspicion on Antonius Dolabella, the dictator remarked: 'I am not afraid of well-covered gentlemen, only lean and pale ones.' The inference was plain.

The Greek geographer Strabo tells us that sinister portents were observed at this time. Fiery figures were seen, for instance, and when Caesar sacrificed he could find no heart inside the victim. A soothsayer warned Caesar to beware of great danger on the 15th of March. On the morning of that day, Caesar greeted the soothsayer on the way to the assembly with the words: 'Well, the fifteenth of March is here.' Whereupon the soothsayer replied: 'Here, yes, but not yet gone!'

When, at supper the day before, they were discussing which death was best, Caesar called out loudly: 'An unexpected one!' During the night all the doors and windows of his bedroom sprang open and his wife Calpurnia sighed and talked in her sleep. When morning came Calpurnia begged Caesar to postpone the session in the Senate and not to venture out. Caesar was disturbed, for he had never noticed any superstitious tendencies in his wife before.

He had decided not to attend the sitting after all, when one of his favourites took him by the hand and pulled him outside, pouring scorn on all the soothsayers' predictions. An unknown slave came to beg a quick word with Caesar, but failed to get there in time. He told Calpurnia that he had a message of the utmost importance to deliver to her husband. A certain Artemidorus even pushed a note into Caesar's hand which would have unmasked the whole conspiracy, but Caesar just took it and handed it to an attendant. Artemidorus stepped close to Caesar and told him: 'Read it, Caesar, quickly and without delay.' Caesar took the letter back, but was prevented from reading it by the pressure of the crowd.

The Senate was assembled in the magnificent hall which Pompey had built on to the theatre, and which also housed a statue of him. Gazing at Pompey's statue, Cassius mutely called upon the figure for support. Then Caesar entered the chamber and the senators rose respectfully to their feet.

A man called Tullius Cimber handed Caesar a petition on behalf of his exiled brother and followed him to his chair, pleading with him as he went. But Caesar, taking his seat, flatly rejected the petition. Then Tullius took Caesar's toga in both hands and dragged it from his neck. The first to strike was the tribune Casca, who stabbed him in the neck with his dagger. Casca's hand trembled, however, and the blade did not penetrate deeply. Caesar wrenched the weapon away from him, shouting: 'Casca, you madman, what are you doing?'

At that, each of the conspirators drew a weapon, for they had agreed that each of them should participate in the murder. Caesar was hemmed in on every side. He eluded the dagger-blows aimed at his face and eyes, squirming under his murderers' hands like a cornered beast. Then Brutus dealt him a blow in the chest. Caesar had been writhing to and fro, screaming at the top of his voice, but when he saw the sword in Brutus' hand he pulled his toga over his head and offered no further resistance. He fell near the base of Pompey's statue, spattering it with his blood. It was almost as though Pompey were taking his own revenge on his erstwhile friend. Rome's greatest general and politician died with twenty-three wounds in his body.

The powerful guardian angel which had always watched over Caesar during his lifetime followed him into death as the avenger of his murder. It tracked down his assassins wherever they went, on land or sea, and all of them met a violent end or took their own lives. Brutus, defeated at Philippi by Octavian and Antony, fled to the top of a steep hill and there plunged a sword into his breast.

'It is better to die once than always to be expecting death,' Caesar had said.

MARK ANTONY AND CLEOPATRA

THE BEAR AND THE HONEY

> Her appearance and her words had such an effect that she drew into her toils even the most unemotional man, the most inveterate woman-hater.
>
> *Dio Cassius*, xlii, 34.

> There was an irresistible charm in her closer acquaintance, and her appearance, engaging conversation, fine manners and general demeanour never failed to make a deep impression.
>
> *Plutarch, Marcus Antonius*, 27.

SOON after Caesar's death his murderers were forced to acknowledge that, while they killed the man, they had not killed his popularity. Furthermore, the soil which had produced the dictatorship of a Caesar remained as fertile for Caesardom and monarchy as it ever was. The daggers of a Cassius and a Brutus, the fervent speeches of a Cicero, the hatred and opposition of a Cato—all these had done virtually nothing to change the course of history.

It is unwise to assassinate a dictator: far wiser to let him destroy himself.

Fourteen years after Caesar's death began the age of the mighty Caesars, the Roman emperors, the great monarchs, the capricious and often iniquitous rulers of the world. The main candidates for power in the interim were Antony and Octavian.

Marcus Antonius had served under Caesar in Gaul and later became consul in the shadow of Caesar's dictatorship. He was now the most prominent man in Rome, having managed to prejudice Caesar's veterans and the citizens in favour of Caesar's memory and against his assassins.

Octavian was just eighteen years old. Caesar had adopted him, made him heir to his immense fortune and appointed him executor of his political testament. Octavian became 'Gaius Julius Caesar Octavianus'. It took courage to be a Caesar's heir.

Before long Mark Antony and Octavian were in action together against Cassius and Brutus, and at the battle of Philippi (42 B.C.) Caesar's murderers were defeated. Mark Antony became ruler of the eastern part of the Roman Empire, while Octavian took over the West, reigning supreme over Spain,

Italy, Africa and Gaul. Mark Antony was happy and so was Octavian — extremely happy.

But there is always latent danger in any such partition of the world. The feud between Caesar and Pompey was still fresh in the minds of everyone. Pompey had married Caesar's daughter, yet even so the two great Romans became deadly enemies. Mark Antony and Octavian wanted to do better. They wanted to get on together. But ambition and ambition make bad partners, and therein lay the seeds of the momentous conflict to come.

Mark Antony was a fine-looking man with broad shoulders, a strong nose, and manliness and decision in his every movement — altogether a Herculean figure. He was tough, boastful, sarcastic and fond of the bottle, courageous and daring in battle, yet never bereft of a good general's caution.

His soldiers loved him because he was fond of chatting with them, sat down at their tables, drank with them and gave them presents. He was exceedingly generous. He hated to skimp or save and had nothing in common with the parsimonious. He threw out anyone who came to him with complaints, and flatly refused to listen to anyone else's worries.

Women, on the other hand, were his ruling passion. He spent his nights feasting and theatre-going with comedians, jesters, ladies of easy virtue and, above all, with the former slave-girl Cytheris, who enjoyed a most unsavoury reputation. During the day he either slept or stumbled round with a thick head. He had the vice-raddled Cytheris carried behind him in a litter from town to town when he went travelling. On reaching a grove of trees or a beautiful river he would set up marquees and serve banquets on golden plate. Sometimes he used to hitch his chariot to a team of lions, and he made a practice of billeting his favourite whores and musicians of the moment in the houses of respectable men and women. His third wife, Fulvia, had enough energy and exactly the sort of temperament needed to control such a difficult husband. But Antony was not often in Rome. In Asia he spent his time with flute-players, dancers, buffoons and evil riff-raff, and his bouts of debauchery were so open and unabashed that they became the gossip of Rome.

Antony was a frivolous and carefree character, but he was utterly without guile. He liked laughing at others but was just as fond of being laughed at himself, thinking that his ostensible friends' witticisms were not meant in earnest. His court was therefore invaded by an absurd rabble of flatterers who took advantage of his good-natured gullibility. But they took care to season their lies with a little frankness occasionally, so that Antony would think they were men who dared to speak openly and were not afraid to tell him the truth.

With his honey-fuddled bear's nature, Antony might have come through life quite successfully, if fate had not marked him out for a piece of very bad luck. He fell in love with Cleopatra, and Cleopatra knew how to smother the reasonable side of his nature completely.

Antony was at Tarsus in Cilicia, near the Mediterranean coast of modern Turkey, making preparations for a campaign against the Parthians or Persians. He ordered Cleopatra to visit him so that he could interrogate her about the financial and military support which she was alleged to have given to Cassius, Caesar's murderer.

Cleopatra was no longer the young lady who had once been brought to Caesar in a mattress. She remembered her effect upon him; she knew how he had fallen under her spell, and she hoped to have a far easier time with Antony. Now twenty-nine, she had reached her prime and was a woman of much more mature intelligence. She amassed a large number of gifts for Antony, including money and jewellery, but she pinned her main hopes on her own fascination and charm.

Antony became impatient and ordered Cleopatra to speed up her progress, but Cleopatra was quite unmoved by this admonition. She laughed as she lay beneath the purple sails of her royal yacht, propelled by silver oars which moved to the rhythm of harps, flutes and shawms.

Cleopatra had arrayed herself like one of the contemporary pictures of Aphrodite. Pages cooled the air with fans, and slave-girls of unusual beauty, dressed as Nereids and Graces, stood at the steering-oars and ropes. Thousands of incense-candles wafted their perfume to the banks of the river up which the fairy-tale ship had to pass on its journey inland. Throngs of spectators accompanied it all the way from the estuary to its destination.

Antony was sitting in judgment in the market-place when he suddenly found himself deserted. All the inhabitants had run off to see the new 'sensation' from Egypt. As soon as he learned of the ship's arrival he invited Cleopatra to dinner, but Cleopatra replied that it would be better if Antony came to her.

Antony came.

He was dazzled by the splendour of the ship. Cleopatra had ordered the lighting of tens of thousands of torches arranged in circles and ornamental patterns.

On the following day she paid Antony a return visit, but the pomp and splendour which Antony had hastily thrown together were rather modest by comparison. Antony himself ridiculed its lack of taste, and Cleopatra immediately realized, from Antony's jokes, that she was not dealing with a cultivated man like Caesar. Always adaptable, she played the role of a pert and unaffected girl.

It is interesting to set aside the labyrinth of biographies, novels, plays and romantically distorted portrayals of later times, and search for the truth about Cleopatra and her relationship with Antony in ancient sources alone. According to them, Cleopatra was neither abnormally beautiful nor did she seem, at first sight, particularly desirable. But her closer acquaintance — as Plutarch expressly remarks — had an irresistible charm. Her winning conversational ways, her well-bred, elegant demeanour, her figure — all these things added to her attraction. She had a pleasant speaking-voice and had mastered a remarkable number of languages, Ethiopian, Troglodytic, Hebrew, Arabic, Syrian, Median and Parthian among them — not to mention Latin and Egyptian. Plutarch emphasizes that of all the Ptolemaic kings who ruled Egypt before her, not one had even taken the trouble to understand Egyptian.

Cleopatra was Macedonian by birth and her mother-tongue was in all probability Greek. The founder of her ruling house, the Ptolemaic dynasty, had been one of the seven body-guards of Alexander the Great.

Since most of the Egyptian kings were the products of brother-sister marriages, the Ptolemaic dynasty would probably have preserved its Macedonian characteristics intact. We must therefore picture Cleopatra as a white woman, a European who was not dark-skinned like her Egyptian subjects.

Antony had summoned Cleopatra to Tarsus in order to reprimand her. Now he let her bear him off to Alexandria, gave himself up to gambling and pleasure like an indolent youth, and light-heartedly allowed time, that most precious of all commodities, to pass him by. Antony and Cleopatra founded at Alexandria what might be termed the first existentialist club, 'the circle of those who live inimitably'. Day by day they surrendered themselves to their desires and appetites, doing whatever came into their heads. Their chef once roasted eight wild boar one after the other because each dish had to be at its best whenever the lovers suddenly decided to dine, and he could never, he remarked with a smile, guess the time in advance.

Cleopatra never left Antony's side, day or night. She cracked jokes with him, devised one novel form of entertainment after the other and knew when to flatter or scold him. She played dice with him and accompanied him on drinking-bouts, hunting excursions and even military exercises.

At night Antony would stagger tipsily up to commoners' doors and windows and play little practical jokes on them. Cleopatra used to stroll through the streets on his arm dressed as a slave-girl, clapping her hands in high glee whenever her unrecognized hero got himself a sound thrashing. The Alexandrians were delighted with their general and conqueror's entertaining habits, and used to boast that while Antony only showed the Romans his serious side, they were favoured with the mask of comedy.

To impress Cleopatra, Antony made divers swim down and attach fish to his line, triumphantly pulling out two or three at once. The young queen countered by sending down her own divers to put a salted herring on her lover's hook. There were hoots of laughter when Antony thought he had made a good catch. 'Leave fishing to us kings, O Emperor,' Cleopatra mocked him. '*You* must catch cities and countries!'

GOSSIP AT ROME

The Romans who were particularly sorry for Antony were those who had actually seen Cleopatra, for they knew that she was no more beautiful and no younger than Octavia, the wife whom he had betrayed.

Plutarch, Marcus Antonius, 57.

DRUGGED with the ecstasy of his happiness, Antony spent the most wonderful days of his life in Cleopatra's arms at Alexandria.

Meanwhile his third wife Fulvia remained in Rome, ambitious, impatient and extremely worried. There were no newspapers in those days, but gossip travelled fast, and the waiting Fulvia had long known how happy Mark Antony felt at Cleopatra's side.

Like her husband, Fulvia had been married three times. Household affairs interested her little. Her chief love in life was the great game of politics. She was used to acting on her own initiative, giving orders, and even to seeing blood spilt. To dominate an ordinary man was, in her eyes, mere child's play. She wanted to rule kings and order generals about. They used to say laughingly in Rome that Cleopatra owed Fulvia a fee for having taught Antony to accept feminine domination, and Plutarch asserts that when Cleopatra took Antony over from Fulvia he was already tamed and broken in. For all that, Fulvia had always staunchly stood by Antony, even if she was motivated as much by a thirst for power as by love for him. What was more, the Romans considered her a beauty.

Quite on her own initiative and without Antony's knowledge, Fulvia engineered an uprising in Rome, recruited some troops and led them against Octavian, sword in hand. The aim of this savage Amazon was to get rid of Mark Antony's greatest rival and then rule the world through her husband. She may also have been inspired by frustrated ambition or by a hope that disturbances in Italy might prise Antony from Cleopatra's grasp. But Fulvia went to pieces. Jealousy and grief destroyed her health, and she died while on her way to join Antony.

Antony travelled back to Italy. Both he and Octavian behaved as though nothing had happened, and all was as friendly as it had ever been. Fulvia had taken the blame for any dissension between them to the grave with her. Mark Antony and Octavian were genuinely determined to get on with each other. And so Antony married Octavian's thirty-year-old sister Octavia, whose first husband, Gaius Marcellus, had died a short while before. Octavia had brains as well as beauty, and Octavian must have been very fond of her. He had every hope that her relationship with Antony would be a happy one, for the sake of Rome and the world.

But the man to whom Octavian gave his sister's hand was very far from being an ideal marriage partner. He had tasted the opium of Cleopatra's charms and was well on the way to becoming an addict. He made no secret of his affair with her, either, even in Rome, though he did deny that he had married her, his common sense at this stage outweighing his infatuation. His marriage to Octavia did, in fact, last for three very happy years. He took her to Greece with him and on his campaigns against the Parthians, and Octavia saw to it that the friendship between her brother and her husband remained intact.

But then Antony brought his wife back to Italy. Leaving her and his children in the care of his brother-in-law Octavian, he sailed back to Asia on his own. Even while he was still on the voyage to Syria, his old love for Cleopatra revived.

He called her to him, and she came.

Antony celebrated their reunion in Syria by making her some magnificent gifts. He laid whole countries and wonderful islands like Cyprus at her feet.

Rome was shocked. People knew that Antony was capable of conquering countries as well as giving them away, but they were enraged by his motives. The Romans thought it disgraceful to lose bits of their empire merely to satisfy the romantic whims of an ageing and infatuated general. Cleopatra became the talk of Rome once more.

But when Cleopatra gave birth to twins and Antony acknowledged them as his own children (calling the boy Alexander and the girl Cleopatra), when he capped that by giving them the additional names 'Sun' and 'Moon', gossip really ran riot in the city on the Tiber. Everyone pitied the unhappy, beautiful Octavia. Antony, however, tried to justify his behaviour, asserting that the greatness of the Roman Empire lay less in conquering than in giving away. The power of Rome, he declared, would be assured for ever by a large number of royal descendants, and besides, Hercules himself had taken care to perpetuate his kind on the wrong side of the blanket!

Octavia made one last desperate attempt to save her marriage with Antony and prevent a breach between him and her brother. She set off to see her husband in person, but in Athens she received a letter from him telling her to stay where she was.

Cleopatra had seen the red light. She realized that Octavia intended to have a show-down with her. Fearing Octavia's dignity and prestige, fearing her beauty, she now acted as though she were mortally enamoured of Antony. She started dieting. If Antony looked at her, she would go into a sort of ecstasy. If he went out, she gazed after him dejectedly with languishing eyes. She play-acted the whole time. She would make a pretence of crying, and then hastily wipe the tears away when he stole a glance at her, as though she had not wanted him to notice.

Antony was contemplating a campaign against the Parthians, but Cleopatra bound him to her with a thousand chains, with all the artifices of love which 5,000 years of Egyptian experience and her native Macedonian instincts had taught her. Weepingly she complained that Octavia was only clinging to him for political ends, for the sake of her brother and the Romans. She herself, on the other hand, although queen of a great nation, stood there in full view of the world as his lover. She could bear this fate just as long as he remained with her, but she would never survive a parting.

From then on, Antony could never make any plan without wondering if Cleopatra would die of grief as a result. It was under this burden of mental stress that he conducted the whole of his war against the Parthians, a more arduous and dangerous enterprise than any which Roman generals had so far undertaken. He had immense forces at his disposal, and all Asia trembled. But he was governed in everything he did by thoughts of Cleopatra. In order to spend the winter with her, he opened his campaign prematurely and at an unfavourable time of year. He acted rashly and precipitately, never looking where he was going, always dreaming of his love, his mind filled with thoughts of the gorgeous rugs and cushions of the bed-chamber, of the charms of his Egyptian queen, her tears, and her soft, dreamlike voice.

Back in Rome, Octavian ordered his sister to put an end to the scandal and move back into her own house, but Octavia stayed on in Antony's home, not only looking after her own children but those of Fulvia as well. She stood up for Antony's friends and remained loyal and devoted to him, behaviour for which Antony rewarded her ill.

On a silver stage at Alexandria he erected two thrones, one for himself and the other for Cleopatra. He declared Cleopatra queen of Egypt, Cyprus and the eastern part of north Africa, appointing Caesarion, the child of Cleopatra's union with Caesar, as co-regent. Alexander, his own son by Cleopatra, received Armenia, Media and the kingdom of Parthia. His second son by Cleopatra he made king of Phoenicia, Syria and Cilicia. Cleopatra herself was from now on to appear before the people dressed as the goddess Isis, and was christened 'New Isis'. This was all very nice, even if rather undignified. But then came the crucial blow: the Parthian campaign went awry.

Meanwhile, Octavian spent his whole time complaining to the Senate. The Romans were now sorry not only for Octavia but also for Antony. Cleopatra was no stranger to them. She had visited Rome during Caesar's lifetime and was there when he died, so they had seen her with their own eyes and knew that she had no more to recommend her than Octavia, either in age or looks. More and more charges were levelled at her. It was said that Mark Antony had given her the library of Pergamos with its 200,000 works; that he had knelt and fondled his mistress's feet in the presence of a crowd of people. In the end, the Senate voted to declare war on Cleopatra and relieve Antony of his appointments, on the grounds that he had abdicated in favour of a woman. Octavian gave it as his opinion that drugs and love-filtres had robbed Antony of his sanity.

Hardly had war been declared when all the soothsayers, astrologers and augurs came forward to announce that they had seen portents which boded ill for Antony. Pisaurum (modern Pesaro, not far from Rimini), a town on the Adriatic founded by Antony, was destroyed by an earthquake. Sweat oozed from a statue of Antony at Alba, and did not dry up even when wiped away. While Antony was at Patrae, at the entrance to the Gulf of Corinth, lightning struck the temple of Hercules and burned it to the ground. At Athens, the sculpture of Dionysus was caught up by a whirlwind and hurled into the theatre The same gale blew down the colossi of Eumenes and Attalos, on which Antony's name was inscribed.

On September 2nd, 31 B.C., a naval battle was fought between the fleets ot Antony and Octavian at Actium, off the coast of Epirus. During the engagement Antony saw Cleopatra's ships sailing away. Oblivious of all else, he left his forces in the lurch and went chasing off after his mistress. In that moment she cost him an empire.

When Cleopatra saw Antony's standard at the mast-head, she let his ship catch her up. Antony came aboard. Without giving Cleopatra a glance, he went to the forepart of the ship and quietly sat down by himself, resting his head in his hands.

Was he angry with Cleopatra?

Was he ashamed?

For three days he sat there alone in the bows. Only when the ship put in at Taenarum — Cape Matapan, at the southern tip of the Peloponnese — did Cleopatra's ladies-in-waiting manage to effect a meeting between Antony and their mistress.

Antony's fleet put up a prolonged and heroic resistance against Octavian, but it eventually abandoned the hopeless struggle. Sending Cleopatra on to

Egypt in advance, Antony gave himself up to solitude. Nervous, miserable and quite unlike his old heroic self, he roamed about in the company of two friends. He even tried to take his life, but his friends foiled the attempt and brought him back to Alexandria.

Once there, he had to acknowledge that Cleopatra was made of sterner stuff than he. She was still full of daring and initiative. There was no Suez Canal in those days, so Cleopatra now proposed to haul her fleet across the desert sand of the peninsula and down to the Red Sea. From there she intended to sail off into the blue and find a new home in some distant land where Octavian and Rome could not follow, where she could feel safe from enslavement.

But since the Arabs immediately burnt the first ships to be hauled laboriously ashore, and since Antony proved to be mistaken in his belief that his land forces were still intact at Actium, Cleopatra abandoned her project and started reinforcing her frontier garrisons.

Antony built himself a house, surrounded by water, on one of the moles leading out to sea at Pharos. There, weary of disloyalty and jealousy, he meant to lead a lonely life like Timon, the Athenian misanthrope. However, Cleopatra fetched him back into her castle at Alexandria.

The two of them disbanded 'the circle of those who live inimitably' and formed a new club, 'the companions in death', which was joined by many friends who wanted to die with them. Meanwhile they spent their time making merry, drinking and enjoying themselves.

Cleopatra saw clearly what had to come. She began to conduct secret experiments to discover which sort of poison brought death in the most painless way. Using condemned criminals as her subjects, she tried out every conceivable kind of poison. She found that fast-acting poisons were very painful, while slow-acting ones were more pleasant. From criminals she turned to animals. Every day she let snakes loose among mammals.

Finally she found that the bite of the asp, and only the asp, brought drowsiness, an irresistible urge to sleep, a little sweat on the face and then oblivion. She was so thorough in her experiments that she tried to rouse her 'guinea-pigs' from their coma, and was gratified to discover that, once in this first stage of death, they refused to wake up.

What species of asp afforded such a pleasant death?

Asps kill by poisoning the nervous system, vipers and adders by poisoning the blood. Nerve-poisons bring on paralytic symptoms, shortness of breath and death by respiratory paralysis. Blood-poisons result in a much more painful death. We therefore presume that Cleopatra's choice fell upon the Levantine asp, an exceedingly vicious and poisonous creature whose venom affects the nervous system.

Was this snake Cleopatra's great secret? Even today, the Levantine asp raises its head in a sinister question-mark from the baskets of the Cairo snake-charmer.

Cleopatra was ready.

The stage was set for as shrewd a duel with death as the world had ever witnessed.

THE FINAL SACRIFICE

I do not weep because I have lost you. I shall be joining you soon enough. No, what hurts me is that such a great general as I should be surpassed in courage by a woman.

Plutarch, Marcus Antonius, 76.

THE summer of 30 B.C. was a time of uneasiness and fear, both for Cleopatra and Antony. Danger shimmered in the sun-baked streets of Alexandria. There was a sense of impending doom.

Octavian, the victor of Actium, was advancing on Egypt from Syria, and Cleopatra and Antony could scarcely muster any forces against him.

It appears that Cleopatra may secretly have been corresponding with Octavian during the weeks preceding the final disaster. It is also probable that she received a guarantee from him that her life would be spared if she managed to get rid of Antony. Octavian's envoy to Cleopatra was an able young general named Thyrsus. He conducted some extremely skilful negotiations with the queen, who was as convinced as ever of her beauty and charm.

In his despair and loneliness, Antony became jealous. He had Thyrsus watched. He had him arrested and flogged. Then he sent him back to Octavian with a letter telling him that, in spite of his predicament, he, Antony, was still very quick-tempered, and Thyrsus' conduct had offended him. 'And if you are annoyed that I have flogged your ambassador, there is always my freedman Hipparchus. You can have *him* hung up by the arms and flogged, and then we shall be quits.' It must be explained that Hipparchus was one of the first men in Antony's entourage to go over to Octavian.

Weary, irritable and overwrought, Antony saw himself surrounded by enemies. He mistrusted everyone and started — probably with good reason — to regard Cleopatra with suspicion. For her part, she behaved with every tenderness, plying him with sweet words and flattery. She made no mention of her own birthday, but celebrated her lover's with extravagant splendour. Guests who came to this 'last supper' poor, left the festivities as rich men.

Hour by hour Octavian's generals ate up the miles of desert which lay between them and Alexandria. Hour by hour Octavian's shadow loomed larger and more menacing.

Cleopatra had taken care to provide herself with a splendid mausoleum well in advance. Whether it was a pyramid or a monument of some other kind, we do not know. We only know that it was a building of extraordinary beauty and that it stood next to the temple of Isis.

Into it Cleopatra transported the most priceless of her royal treasures — gold, silver, emeralds, pearls, ebony, ivory, cinnamon and, last but not least, numerous torches and large quantities of pitch. On hearing this, the ever-wary Octavian began to fear that Cleopatra would burn her vast store of treasures before he could lay hands on it. Wishing to prevent her from committing this final act of desperation, he sent couriers to her with messages designed to raise her hopes. At last he arrived outside the city with his army.

Antony led a desperate sortie and fought so bravely that he put Octavian's cavalry to flight. But no sooner had he won this victory than he thought proudly of Cleopatra, went back to the royal palace, kissed his beloved and paraded before her in full armour. Then he sent an emissary to Octavian challenging him to single combat. Octavian replied: 'There are many ways of dying open to you.'

Antony realized that his great opponent was right. He was caught like a rat in a trap. He was going to die one way or another, and his only remaining choice was the manner of his death.

At supper he drank liberally and ate with gusto, remarking to his servants that no one could tell whether they would be waiting on him tomorrow, or on a new master. They were alarmed by the thought that they themselves might be dead by the following day.

Antony's friends wept, but he told them that he would not lead them into a battle in which he would be seeking not victory but a glorious death.

At dawn the next day Antony deployed his army on the hills in front of the city. From his vantage-point on the high ground he watched his ships as they left the harbour to engage Octavian's fleet. He stood there quite calmly, watching. But as soon as his ships were near enough to the enemy the crews raised their oars in salute. His whole fleet went over to Octavian, and the combined force moved in on Alexandria. At the same time, Antony's cavalry deserted as well. He rushed back into the city, raving and shouting that he had been betrayed.

Cleopatra had already taken refuge in her tomb. The trap-door fell with a crash behind her, bolts rattled and locks clicked. Before entering her eerie vault, accompanied by two of her most loyal slave-women, Iras and Charmian, she sent a message to Antony telling him that she had taken her life.

Antony was at the end of his tether. He talked confusedly to himself. 'You are waiting. ... What are you waiting for? Until now, fate gave you an excuse for living ... but that excuse no longer exists. It has been torn from you.' He went to his room and put his armour on. 'Ah, Cleopatra!' he said, 'I do not weep because I have lost you. I shall be joining you soon enough. No, what hurts me is that such a great general as I should be surpassed in courage by a woman.'

Antony ordered his faithful slave Eros to kill him. Eros drew his sword, raised his arm ... and stabbed himself. He sank to the ground at Antony's feet.

'Worthy Eros!' cried Antony, 'you were right. You could not do it. But you have shown me what I must do.'

Stabbing himself in the stomach, he fell back on to a bed. Before long, however, the blood stopped flowing from his wound and he regained consciousness. He ordered the onlookers to give him the *coup de grâce*, screaming and tossing about in terror, but his friends ran from the room. Then Diomedes, Cleopatra's private secretary, rushed in with orders from his mistress to bring Antony to her tomb.

In his death-throes, Antony told his attendants to carry him to the mausoleum. Cleopatra would not open the door but appeared at an upper window and let down some ropes. Antony was tied to them, and Iras and Charmian pulled him up. As they did so, Antony's wound started to bleed again. He struggled in agony and stretched out his hands to Cleopatra. The two serving-women began to weaken, but Cleopatra, her features racked with the effort, refused to abandon her hold on the ropes.

She laid Antony on her bed. She tore her clothes with grief. She lacerated her breasts with her nails and wiped the blood from her lover's body with her face, calling him her lord, her husband and emperor. Her own misfortunes were quite forgotten.

Antony asked for wine. He may have been thirsty or he may, perhaps, have wanted to put a speedy end to his sufferings. He told Cleopatra to save herself, always providing it could be done without dishonour. 'Do not mourn me because of my unhappy end,' he said. 'Think rather of the many good things I enjoyed, of my great reputation and power: and remember that it is no disgrace for a Roman to be vanquished by a Roman.' With that, the great man died, still dazzled with love and infatuation.

Meanwhile, they had brought the bloodstained sword with which Antony had mortally wounded himself to Octavian, who went straight into his tent and wept. He wept for the man who had been his brother-in-law, his co-regent and his companion in so many battles and enterprises. He read Antony's letters to his friends to prove that whereas he, Octavian, had always sought friendship, Antony had answered in truculent and aggressive vein.

Then he sent Proculeius off to see that Cleopatra was kept alive at all costs. He was still thinking of her treasures, and probably, too, of his future triumphal march through Rome.

Cleopatra declined to return with Proculeius. Opening a small shutter in her trap-door, she demanded that the government of Egypt be handed over to her sons. Proculeius did his best to cheer her.

Next, Octavian sent a general called Gallus to speak to Cleopatra. There was another conversation through the trap-door. While Gallus spun the interview out, Proculeius climbed up a ladder and in through the upper window. One of the serving-women cried out: 'Poor Cleopatra! They have trapped you!'

Catching sight of Proculeius, Cleopatra tried to stab herself with a dagger, but he twisted the weapon out of her hand. He also searched her clothing, for fear that she had some poison on her. A sentry was posted in the tomb and ordered to treat Cleopatra with every courtesy.

A few days later, Octavian came to speak with the captive queen in person. He found her in a terrible condition. She was a mass of cuts, her breasts were bruised and inflamed, she was in a high fever and she had deliberately starved herself almost to death. On his entrance she jumped up from her couch, wearing a loose-fitting *chiton*. Her hair tangled, her eyes swollen with weeping, her voice trembling and her face twisted with grief, she threw herself at his feet. Even now her old trust in her looks was not quite gone, and something of her old self-confidence lurked in her ravaged face. Octavian told her to lie down again. She at once began to justify herself, blaming her everlasting fear of Antony for all that had happened. But Octavian demolished her arguments one by one, so she resorted to pleading and tried to arouse his sympathy. She behaved as though she wanted to cling to life with every fibre of her being. At last, in desperation, she gave Octavian an inventory of her treasures.

One of Cleopatra's stewards, who was present, accused her of having neglected to mention several items of value. Jumping up in a rage, she took the man by the hair and rained blows on his face. Octavian laughed and tried to soothe her. 'Do you deny,' she shouted, 'that it is insufferable for me to be reproached by my own slaves while you treat me honourably, even in my present circumstances?'

Octavian was now convinced that Cleopatra wanted to live. He assured her that he would treat her magnanimously and that she would be allowed to go and live in Italy, surrounded by all that was dear to her. He left feeling sure that he had taken her in completely, his real intention being to lead the

Egyptian queen in triumph through the streets of Rome. Cleopatra, however, knew or guessed this, and the very fear of such an indignity steeled her determination to give Octavian a big disappointment.

She begged permission to take Antony a funeral offering. Going to his tomb, she threw herself on his coffin. 'Antony,' she cried, 'I bring you this offering as a closely guarded prisoner. I must not injure this body of mine, enslaved and guarded as a symbol of triumph over you, with tears or blows. These are the last funeral offerings which Cleopatra will ever bring you. In life nothing could part us. In death we shall not, in all likelihood, lie beside each other.'

She then decorated the coffin with garlands and ordered a bath to be prepared for her. After her bath she sat down to a sumptuous meal.

A little later a man arrived from the country carrying a small basket. When the sentries asked what it contained the fellow opened it and, removing some leaves on top, showed them that it was full of figs. The sentries marvelled at the size and beauty of the fruit, and the man smilingly offered them a few. They allowed him to take the basket inside.

After her meal Cleopatra wrote on a tablet, sealed it and sent it to Octavian. Then, ordering everyone to leave the room, she locked herself in with her two serving-women.

Octavian unsealed the writing-tablet. In it he read Cleopatra's fervent request to be buried at Antony's side. Realizing what had happened, he hurriedly sent messengers to Cleopatra. But it was too late. They found her dead on a golden couch, dressed in her royal finery. One of her attendants, Iras, was dying at her feet. The other, Charmian, swayed and stumbled, still trying to adjust the diadem encircling Cleopatra's brow.

'That looks nice,' mocked a soldier.

'It is only befitting,' answered Charmian, 'for a descendant of so many kings.' Then she collapsed.

Hidden beneath the leaves and figs had been the asp whose venom Cleopatra had tested so carefully. She had removed a few leaves, seen the snake and, crying: 'There it is!' presented her bare arm to its fangs.

Some say that Cleopatra teased the asp with a golden needle until it struck at her arm and hung there. They also say that her arm bore the marks of two minute punctures. At all events, Octavian later had a picture carried in his triumphal procession which showed Cleopatra with an asp hanging from her arm.

On Octavian's orders, Cleopatra was buried in regal state at Antony's side.

AUGUSTUS

'HAVE I ACTED OUT THE COMEDY WELL?'

After the main meal he would withdraw to the couch in his study. There he stayed until far into the night, until he had completed the rest of the day's affairs. Then he went to bed, but seldom slept longer than seven hours, and then not uninterruptedly. He used to wake up three or four times. If he could not get to sleep again he would summon a reader or story-teller to his bedside and thus induce himself to fall asleep once more ... He never lay awake without someone sitting by his bed.

Suetonius, Augustus, 78.

WITHIN fourteen years Octavian had rid himself of every other contender, actual or potential, for supreme power: first Caesar's murderers, Brutus and Cassius, then Pompey's son, then Lepidus, and finally, after the naval battle at Actium, Mark Antony and his mistress, the Egyptian queen Cleopatra.

He continued to reign, a cool-headed and competent ruler, for another forty-five years. He ushered in a new era of world history which not only outlasted his lifetime but survived for century after century and has extended, despite tumbling thrones and abandoned sceptres, into our own day. He became master of the world, the first real Roman emperor. His Greek motto ran *speude bradeōs* or 'make haste slowly', the watchword of any statesman with lasting achievements to his credit. What is done well, Augustus used to say, always happens soon enough.

He always held several government appointments at the same time. He commanded the army in his capacity as Imperator. Later, he got himself appointed Pontifex Maximus, the supreme religious authority, and so became a sort of heathen Pope. The Senate also voted him the honorific title Augustus, which meant roughly 'the exalted and piously to be revered'. Sextilis, the month in which Octavian conquered Egypt in 30 B.C., was rechristened Augustus in his honour and has become our August. Many towns still bear his name today, among them Augsburg, Aosta, Autun and Saragossa. Yet, despite all the authority he himself possessed, Augustus was wise enough to surround himself with the ablest men of his day. Agrippa fought his battles and Maecenas was his diplomat.

Augustus' whole career is an object lesson to us that a State should be headed not by a general but a statesman; that a statesman can always achieve more than a soldier, and that a brilliant politician — with or without a cigar in his mouth — is worth more than all the generals put together. No victory delighted Augustus more than his treaty with the Parthian king, which guaranteed peace on the eastern frontier of the Roman Empire and effected the return to Rome of all the legions' standards ever captured by the Parthians. The *Ara Pacis Augustae* or Altar of Peace at Rome is the most important work of art produced during the classical Augustan age.

Octavian returned to civilian life at the early age of thirty-three, and after the conquest of Egypt he never personally touched a sword again. His method of keeping fit was to play hand-ball and take short walks.

It is said that he once fell asleep just before a battle. When Publius Quinctilius Varus, defeated by the Cheruscan prince Arminius in the famous battle of the Teutoburger Wald, threw himself on his sword, the only measure which occurred to the seventy-two-year-old emperor was to let his beard and hair grow long in mourning. He even developed an aversion for his German body-guards and dismissed them, sturdy, loyal men though they were. They had suddenly become sinister in his eyes.

Modern historians are becoming increasingly convinced that Augustus is harder to understand than any other historical figure. Although he spent fifty-seven of his seventy-seven years in a fierce blaze of publicity, he kept his motives and secrets concealed behind a veil of silence.

For all that, Augustus is not really such a mysterious figure. In the year 40 B.C. he was still the cold, inexorable avenger and tyrant. One has only to think of Perugia and the massacre which he instigated there in front of the altar of Julius Caesar on the anniversary of his death, the Ides of March. '*Moriendum est*' — 'Let there be death,' he said. Yet from 30 B.C. to A.D. 14, a period of forty-four years, the same Augustus was the most fortunate, just and intelligent ruler that Rome, so used to bloodshed, had ever known. Never did the Romans enjoy a time of greater peace and prosperity than when Augustus was their absolute ruler.

Considering the high aesthetic standards of the day, we can form some idea of Augustus' appearance from the fact that the Romans considered him a strikingly handsome man. He was 'approaching blond' and not very tall, hence his fondness for wearing shoes with built-up heels. It was a joy merely to watch him when he moved. He had a very pleasant voice and peculiarly radiant eyes, of whose effect he was well aware. His eyes were unusually large, too, which was held by the people to be a sign of divinity. He was hurt if anyone looked him straight in the eye, much preferring ordinary mortals to avoid his gaze. He had no difficulty in conquering womanly hearts.

Almost as notorious an adulterer as Caesar, he seduced the wives of friends and political opponents alike, countering any reproaches with the plea that he was sacrificing everything for Roman policy. Fortunately, his wife Livia was wise enough to put up with his philandering habits, even going to the lengths of providing him with young girls whenever the warm summer nights made him restive.

Livia was one of the shrewdest women in Rome, and became, as the years went by, a co-regent and sort of unofficial Secretary of State. Her marriage to Octavian at the age of twenty caused great indignation in Rome at the time. Her first husband, Tiberius Claudius Nero, 'passed her on' to Octavian when she already had one child (the future Emperor Tiberius) and was shortly expecting another. Even Rome found such a marriage slightly disreputable.

It is understandable that historians find Augustus hard to analyse, for his dual personality was apparent in everything he did. The man who was so fond of philandering behaved in other respects just like an ordinary citizen. Indeed, his only wish was to be first citizen, which was why he liked to be known as *Princeps*, 'the First'. He wept on receiving the title 'Father of the Fatherland', and refused to be addressed as *Domine* or 'Lord', even in the family circle or in fun. When offered the title *Dictator*, which Caesar had held, he declined with horror. He gave the State a constitution which was not supposed to be a monarchy but a form of improved republic. His house on the Palatine was deliberately unostentatious, even though all subsequent 'palaces' in history take their name from that building. He insisted on a frugally run household, allowing himself only the plainest fare and hardly ever drinking. When he did drink, his favourite was a Tyrolean wine from Rhaetia. He also had something in common with Frederick the Great, being a collector and a patron of the arts. He built himself a villa on Capri where he collected interesting fossils, mammoth-bones among them. He was almost Spartan in his habits, detesting military parades, parties and firework displays. He believed in shaving himself daily, which was by no means the rule among the Roman males of his day.

When it came to civil engineering, Augustus built on a bolder and a grander scale than any Roman ruler before him. Nile canals in Egypt, aqueducts and bridges in southern France, the controlling of the river Tiber, the Temple of Apollo on the Palatine in Rome — all these projects were born in his mind and then transformed into marble and stone. Rome ceased to be a city of brick and became a city of marble. Augustus re-erected eighty-two temples and built a pantheon large enough to contain not only the ancient gods of Rome but also the new gods she had inherited from her subject peoples, on the principle that one could never tell with gods and it was better to be sure! His other works included the Baths of Agrippa, the Temple of Neptune, the Theatre of Marcellus, promenades and a kind of triumphal avenue — all of it borrowed splendour, of course, because it was all a reflection of Greek art.

Augustus was lucky enough — or deserving enough — to be a contemporary of great poets like Virgil, Horace, Propertius and Ovid. He spent happy hours discussing ancient Roman history with Livy of Padua, the great historian. It was these men who really set Octavian–Augustus on the pedestal of divinity and endowed him with his halo of immortality. Some of it stuck to him, as something always does, and no other Roman emperor was worshipped as a god after his death with such pious sincerity.

During his lifetime, however, Augustus was really neither hero, saint nor philanthropist. He loved nobody. It was probably the thought of Caesar's end which made him attend the Senate wearing a suit of mail beneath his toga, and during the most important sessions ten strong men sat in his immediate vicinity.

His health was not good, either, even though he did reach the age of seventy-seven. He had himself frequently rubbed with ointment, sweated over a fire and took sulphur-baths in the Albula springs between Rome and Tibur. He fished, threw dice and played marbles with little slave-boys. He took great pleasure in the laughter of these unaffected, unspoiled and garrulous youngsters, and had them fetched from all parts of the world, especially Syria and Mauretania. His personal physician Antonius Musa prescribed a cold-water treatment which cured him of a serious illness when everyone else had given him up for lost. When Marcellus, his heir-presumptive, tried the same treatment he dropped dead. Augustus believed in giving the people *panem et circenses*, 'bread and circuses', and his public entertainments included animal-baiting, gladiatorial shows and a sham sea-battle fought on an artificial lake by 3,000 combatants.

In the course of centuries the Romans had become increasingly dissolute and self-indulgent, and childless marriages were common. Augustus disqualified all unmarried men from inheriting. Atlas-like, he pitted his strength against the decline of the West, which was being vociferously foretold by a dozen Spenglers even in those days. In his books and tracts he waged a bitter fight for morality, at a time when the Jewish people were witnessing the birth of the Messiah in Palestine.

With the growth of his power and responsibilities, the young and unscrupulous despot in Augustus gave way to the mature statesman. Then, with shocking suddenness, his youthful misdemeanours sprang to life again in his daughter Julia. Her impudent and shameless behaviour became such a public scandal in Rome that Augustus was eventually forced to punish her like a common criminal and send her out of the country. He brought her up very strictly as a young girl, never allowing her to do anything which might cause public offence. She had been compelled to sit there — entirely cut off from the outer world — and spin wool. And once, when a well-mannered young nobleman had called on her in Baiae to pay his respects, Augustus sent him a letter reproving him for his lack of tact.

Now that his daughter had been exiled, he saw to it that she was denied all the creature comforts. No wine was allowed to pass her lips, and no man, not even a male slave, could visit her without first obtaining Augustus' permission. Even then, a careful note was taken of the visitor's age, height, colour of eyes and possible scars or blemishes. Nobody was to be allowed to insinuate himself into Julia's presence, and she was never to escape surveillance again.

Augustus spent a lonely old age, most of his friends having died before him. His greatest misfortune was to have had no sons of his own, for he outlived all the men whom he designated as his successors, including Marcellus, Agrippa and his two grandsons Lucius and Baius, who were the comfort of his declining years.

The whole of Italy and the Roman Empire had reached a golden age. Augustus was tired now, very tired. At Nola, near Pompeii, he sent for Tiberius, Livia's son by her first marriage, to name him heir-apparent. He was aware that Tiberius was an unknown quantity and probably guessed that he would not make an ideal successor, but time was running out.

'Are the people outside already mourning?' he asked, shortly before his death. 'Have I acted out the comedy well? If the spectacle of my life has pleased you, applaud!'

Augustus died in Livia's arms. During his lifetime he had built himself and his family a mausoleum on the Field of Mars, a magnificent circular building of great size which has survived the millennia until our own day. In it were placed his ashes and a record, compiled by himself, of all his achievements, engraved on two bronze plaques. The plaques have disappeared, but a copy of this *index rerum gestarum*, the celebrated Monumentum Ancyranum, was discovered on a temple wall in Ankara, 1,500 years after Augustus' death.

There were some of Augustus' friends who swore that, as the flames blaze up beneath the great man's pyre and the sparks flew hissing into the sky, they saw the Emperor rise heavenwards.

TIBERIUS

THE SINISTER RECLUSE OF CAPRI

'Into the Tiber with Tiberius!' shouted the people of Rome. It was A.D. 37, and the seventy-eight-year-old emperor looked as though he was never going to die. No other emperor ever occupied the throne at such an advanced age.

The Author.

I am very well aware that much of what I have related and shall further relate may be found trivial and unimportant. Yet it is probably not valueless to subject events which are at first sight unimportant to closer scrutiny. For they are often the causes of great upheavals.

Tacitus, Annales, iv, 32.

A JOYLESS, gloomy and extremely mistrustful man who was at odds with himself and the world, Emperor Tiberius cuts a tragic and sinister figure.

He is one of those great historical personalities whose characters have almost eluded the grasp of historical research, the main reason being that he was nearly always doomed to be the pawn of other people whose machinations obscured his own character and destiny.

When the Roman historian Tacitus produced his main work, the sixteen-volume *Annales*, in about A.D. 115, he was writing only seventy-eight years after Tiberius' death. In the *Annales* Tacitus gives us a picture, remarkable for its keen observation, of the dangerous world of intrigue which surrounded the dramatic figure of Tiberius. He was by no means unfair to the Emperor. Tiberius' cold and rigid nature really was as he described it: a curious blend of mistrust, tenacity, hatred and fear of humanity, moderation, intelligence and, sometimes even, the occasional spark of genius.

The imperial era, which lasted for 500 years, had got off to a flying start with the first emperor, Augustus, and his forty years of one-man rule. No successor, however strong, could hope to maintain such greatness and impetus.

Who, then, was Augustus' successor, of whom the crumbling ruins of villas and palaces on the island of Capri still stand as a mute reminder?

There is a passage in the Gospels (St Matthew xxii, 17–22) which describes Jesus holding a coin in his hand. 'Whose is this image and superscription?' He asks. 'Caesar's.' 'Render therefore unto Caesar the things which are Caesar's,' He replies, 'and unto God the things that are God's.' The coin in

Jesus' hand was a *denarius*, a silver coin worth about 1*s*. 8*d*., and the head on the denarius was that of Emperor Tiberius. When Christ was born — perhaps in the seventh year before the beginning of our chronology — the throne was occupied by Emperor Augustus, and Tiberius was thirty-five years old. When Christ, having been condemned to death by the Roman procurator Pontius Pilatus, was nailed to the Cross — in about A.D. 30 — Emperor Tiberius was seventy-two years old. 'Crucify Him!' shouted the Jews in Jerusalem. A little later the mobs in Rome were shouting: 'Into the Tiber with Tiberius!' — '*Tiberium in Tiberim!*' Pun or not, it was made in grim earnest.

Tiberius' father was a certain Tiberius Claudius Nero, one of Julius Caesar's officers. His mother was Livia Drusilla, the woman who really made him what he was. She was remarkably beautiful. The great Octavian, later to be Emperor Augustus, saw her and fell madly in love with her. Livia, as we have heard, was already married and the mother of a four-year-old child, but Octavian took her away from her husband in spite of that, whether against her will or not is uncertain. Octavian was in such a hurry that he did not wait for her second confinement but took her into his house when she was far gone with child. Three months later Livia gave birth to her second son, Drusus.

Livia was an exceedingly ambitious woman and kept a sharp eye on every aspect of her growing sons' careers. Tiberius spent half his life on active service in Spain, Armenia, Gaul and Germany, where he fought at his brother Drusus' side. The soldiers soon got used to his strict ways and, even though their private name for him was not Tiberius but *Biberius*, 'the drinker', they obeyed him. At the age of twenty-nine, his brother fell from his horse and later died of his injuries. Livia only had Tiberius left now, and it was her secret wish that he should become emperor. She was the wife of all-powerful Augustus. In her eagerness to manœuvre herself and her son on to the highest rung of the political ladder, she had wasted no time in buttressing Tiberius' position. He and the Emperor were not blood-relations, it was true, but Livia shrewdly devised a means of strengthening the ties between them. Augustus' daughter Julia, whom we met in the preceding chapter, had been married to Agrippa, Augustus' best friend and one of the victors of Actium, but was now a widow with five children. On his mother's insistence, Tiberius married her.

This would not have been so bad, perhaps, if Tiberius had not already been married to a woman called Vipsania, with whom he was very much in love. What was more, Vipsania was Agrippa's daughter by an earlier marriage.

Tiberius was thus being forced to marry his wife's step-mother. This was the first bitter cup which Tiberius had to accept for political reasons. He was compelled to part with the only woman he had ever loved and marry the uncongenial Julia — Julia, whose depravity was the talk of the capital, Julia, whose loyalties — as the whole of Rome knew — lay with no one but herself.

Once, later on, when Tiberius accidentally met Vipsania, he gazed at her steadily with tears in his eyes. From that day forth they made sure that he never again set eyes on the woman he had really loved.

Emperor Augustus adopted his step-son and son-in-law, appointed him co-regent and co-partner in the tribunician power, and presented him to all his armies as the successor to his throne. After Agrippa's death he also entrusted him with all the most difficult military assignments. When the subject peoples between the Danube and the Adriatic staged a concerted uprising, it was Tiberius who quelled it after three years of heavy fighting. When the Roman province of Germania collapsed after the battle of the Teutoburger Wald, it was he who secured the Rhine frontier.

Yet Augustus was not happy about his successor. Tiberius was not a blood-relation, after all, and he did not altogether trust him. Perhaps he did not want the splendour, fame and magnificence of his own reign to be overshadowed. He passed the title of Caesar on to Tiberius in his political testament, but in the same document he also appointed his own wife Livia as co-regent.

Julius Caesar was fifty-six when he died. Tiberius was fifty-six when he came to the throne in A.D. 14. Until then he had stood, almost insignificantly, in the shadow of a more than life-size Augustus. Now he was to rule under the influence and guidance of a woman, his mother Livia. This was logical enough, since it was to her that he owed his throne, but it was unpleasant, equally, to submit to continuous restraint. He wavered uneasily between fear, suspicion and hatred.

Tiberius was evasive when the Senate asked him to assume power. He made all sorts of allusions to the magnitude of the Empire and his own inadequacies. Only a mind like that of the dead Augustus, he said, was equal to such an immense task. Augustus had allowed him to share in the problems of government, so he already knew from personal experience what a Herculean task the over-all administration of the Empire was. The State had such a wealth of brilliant men that there was really no need to burden any one individual with everything. ...

There was a fine, estimable ring about all Tiberius' arguments, even if they were insincere. Everyone applauded the new man; no one believed him.

But that was always Tiberius' way: he had an innate or habitual fondness for indulging in obscure and ambiguous turns of phrase, quite regardless of whether there was any necessity for them. At this point, on the threshold of his reign, he intended to exercise the utmost caution. He therefore expressed himself even more vaguely and obscurely than usual. His fear and his conviction that he was menaced on every side made him unwilling even to accept the title Imperator, and he rose from his seat when the consuls entered the chamber.

The senators, on the other hand, had but one fear. They wondered whether it was obvious to their future master that they could see through him. Redoubling their pleas, they implored Tiberius to accept, embracing his knees with tears in their eyes and raising their arms to heaven and to the effigy of Augustus. Their adulatory and obsequious attitude also extended to his co-regent, Livia, who now bore the title 'Augusta'. They proposed that she should receive the additional honorific 'Mother of the Fatherland'.

Tiberius did not take kindly to this. The marks of respect paid to a woman, he declared, must be kept within bounds. He also tried to limit to reasonable proportions the honours bestowed upon himself.

He was afraid of his uncommonly astute, clever and calculating mother, afraid of her measureless ambition, afraid of the woman who had managed her marriage to Augustus with such subtle intuition and remarkable adaptability.

Tiberius at first showed himself a determined and experienced ruler. He abandoned the Germans to their everlasting feuds and contented himself with holding the Rhine frontier. He maintained peace and order in the provinces, and his conduct of governmental affairs at Rome was characterized by intelligence and lack of coercion. As long as his mother was alive to share the sovereignty, she could provide a last resort in cases of injustice or faulty decision, for Tiberius still accorded her the same old deference, fear and obedience.

Livia Augusta did not die until A.D. 29, having reached the ripe old age of eighty-four. Thereafter conditions deteriorated considerably. Without more ado, Tiberius turned the mild imperial regime of Augustus into a dictatorship. The Senate lost its power, and the people were no longer permitted to elect their own officials, who were now chosen for them by the Senate acting on the Emperor's recommendation. Indicting senators for *lèse-majesté* became the order of the day.

The introduction into world history of trials for *lèse-majesté* is, sadly enough, one of Tiberius' main claims to fame. Anyone who opposed him was hauled before a tribunal. Informers flourished, judicial murder became rife, and not a day passed without executions taking place, even on feast-days, religious festivals and at the New Year. There was a very steep flight of steps, known as the Gemoniae, leading down from the Aventine Hill to the Tiber. In earlier times the custom of dragging people down them on the end of a hook and throwing them into the Tiber had been reserved for common criminals. Now, no one who had been convicted was spared, not even women and children, and twenty executions in a single day became quite commonplace. The public prosecutors found their hands full because fees were now paid not only to themselves but also to the witnesses in a successful prosecution. Accusations, depositions and impeachments began to pile up. A large force of secret police came into being, its ramifications even extending into private households, where, as always, domestic slaves provided the most lucrative source of information. They could think up treasonable remarks of every description and put them into their masters' mouths, or at least make their life a hell with blackmail. Children, too, informed on their own parents.

Tiberius silently directed this spate of persecution, punishment and execution from behind the façade of a penal code, often trying, with a solemn face and head held high, to give the impression that his dearest wish was to reduce the many well-merited sentences he had to pronounce. The fact that he was probably a practised hypocrite seems to have escaped many of our modern historians. Tacitus, whose *Annales* gives us a pregnant description of the conditions prevailing at the time, has been regarded with unwavering scepticism by historians from the nineteenth century onwards. He has been accused of distorting and misrepresenting the figure of Tiberius. Ever since Mommsen, modern research into Roman history has been pervaded by a feeling of 'we know better', and it is now thought fair to dismiss the accounts of Suetonius, Dio Cassius and Tacitus as exaggerated. Fervent attempts are made to be 'fair' to emperors like Tiberius, Caligula and Claudius. Only in very recent times and after thorough-going research has the reliability of the ancient Roman and Greek historians been acknowledged and an attempt been made (as with Erich Köstermann and H. Drexler in the case of Tiberius) to put the classical sources back into their true perspective.

Tiberius grew more and more suspicious as time went by. He sought solitude and avoided people. He discovered hidden allusions to himself in the most harmless remarks and dinner-table jokes, so that whenever he entered a room conversation dried up. Tiberius had simply forgotten how to get on with people. There was only one man in all his dreary life whom he trusted completely, and unfortunately he was a criminal, though not a conventional one. He was one of those artful, cunning, self-effacing, mealy-mouthed, ever-smiling, almost Shakespearian villains whom we find exaggerated on the stage and hardly ever recognize in real life.

Lucius Aelius Seianus was born at Vulsinii. Like Iago in Shakespeare's *Othello*, he was an officer, and his resemblance to that Shakespearian figure also extended to his character. Seianus became prefect, or commander, of Tiberius' body-guard. His power in Rome was virtually unlimited. Nothing could happen without his permission, and it was literally fatal for anyone to approach Tiberius without his knowledge. He was always devising new ways to secure the Emperor's favour, having long ago won that of his soldiers. The cohorts of the Praetorian Guard had formerly been housed in various parts of the city. They were now concentrated in one vast barracks where they were more easily controlled, more conscious of their numerical strength, more self-confident and more impressive. Seianus visited this barracks frequently, often stopping to have a chat with individual officers and men. He exercised the right of promotion on the Emperor's behalf. Far from causing him any trouble, Tiberius commended him before Senate and people as his partner and collaborator, and gave permission for statues of him to be erected in theatres, public squares and military establishments. He trusted Seianus.

And Seianus?

He had but one aim: to become Emperor of Rome himself. The only way to achieve this aim was to get rid of all the potential heirs to the throne, a task rendered formidable by the number of children in the royal family. 'It was,' as Tacitus puts it, 'an uncertain business, taking violent action against so many people at the same time. Their removal by stealth demanded time, and could only be accomplished at certain intervals.' It was this secret course of action which Seianus chose. He decided to start with Drusus, Tiberius' son by his beloved wife Vipsania. Seianus cherished a particular loathing for Drusus, who was a forceful person violently opposed to anyone with open or secret designs on his father's throne, and who had once hit him in the face during a quarrel.

It is intensely interesting to watch how Seianus went about the removal of Drusus. Anyone who reads what follows should bear in mind that it is history, not the imaginary plot of some stage play.

Seianus did not launch a frontal attack on Drusus. That was not his way. Still like Shakespeare's Iago, he went to work with subterfuge and slander, studiously keeping himself in the background. His first move was to

Emperor Augustus was born in 63 B.C. and died in A.D. 14 at the age of seventy-seven. 'His outward appearance was distinguished by remarkable beauty and always by extreme grace, though he scorned all aids to beauty', writes Suetonius. The month of August is named after him

Tiberius, the grim and sinister figure who died in Capri at the age of seventy-eight. This emperor's character was marked by hatred and contempt for humanity, and his behaviour in his island retreat was extremely brutal

A silver denarius bearing the head of Tiberius. This was the sort of coin which Christ held in his hand when the Pharisees asked him whether it was right to pay tribute to Caesar. The reverse depicts Livia Augusta, the Emperor's mother and co-regent

approach Drusus' wife. This woman, also called Livia, had been plain as a child but had later developed into a raving beauty. Seianus wooed her so ardently that he finally succeeded in inducing her to commit adultery. Having attained his first objective, he went on to arouse her hopes of marriage, painting a glowing picture of himself upon the imperial throne with her, revered by the whole Roman Empire, at his side. Once he had kindled her imagination to this extent, he stopped beating about the bush and urged her to murder her husband. And Livia, grand-niece of Augustus, daughter-in-law of Tiberius and wife of Drusus, actually agreed to jeopardize her name for the sake of this risky and criminal undertaking.

Livia's friend and physician Eudemus, who often visited her on the pretext of giving her medical treatment, was initiated into the secret. To reassure his female accomplice, Seianus drove his wife Apicata, who had borne him three children, out of his house. All was now agreed between the conspirators and everything had been carefully planned. But the enormity of their intended crime perturbed Seianus, Livia and Eudemus the physician, and they postponed it.

Drusus often complained about Seianus, both to the Senate and his father. He pointed out that while he, the Emperor's own son, was there, the Emperor's chief adviser and right-hand man was a stranger. Before they knew it, Seianus would be co-regent. Admittedly, the first steps to the throne were steep but, once they were past, friends and helpers would always be to hand. They could only ask the gods to take this fellow Seianus down a peg. Such was the gist of Drusus' remarks.

Seianus was afraid now. There was no time to be lost. He had received accounts of what Drusus was saying about him in private from the unfaithful Livia, and he could hardly wait to get the murder over. He ordered a poison to be prepared, something very slow-acting which would bring on the symptoms of a normal illness.

The poison was administered to Drusus by the eunuch Lygdus. Little by little it took effect, and Drusus became seriously ill.

Emperor Tiberius continued to attend the Senate daily. Perhaps he was indifferent to his son's illness, or perhaps he merely wanted to exhibit his transcendence over family worries. Drusus died, and Tiberius still continued to attend the Senate. When the senators tried to offer their condolences he reminded them of their dignity. 'I may be reproached for appearing before the Senate so recently bereaved,' he declared, 'but my devotion to the State has lent me strength and consolation.' Was his grief genuine? We do not know.

As long as Drusus was alive, things were not too bad. Seianus did not dare to do all he had in mind. He took care to justify his measures to the Emperor because he was afraid of Drusus and knew how sharply he criticized him in his father's presence.

But when he saw that Drusus' murder had passed off unnoticed and relatively unmourned, Seianus began to think out ways of eliminating the remaining heirs to the throne. These were the sons of Germanicus, Tiberius' nephew, and their right of succession was indisputable. Since it was impracticable to kill off three people 'just like that', Seianus began to spread slanderous stories about them and simultaneously organized an insidious whispering-campaign against their mother Agrippina. His intrigues were highly successful.

Meanwhile, Livia had become impatient and was demanding that Seianus should marry her as he had promised. Seianus obediently went to the Emperor and asked for Livia's hand in marriage. The Emperor refused his request in a letter as polite as it was devious.

Seianus then hit upon the idea of persuading the Emperor to leave Rome. He believed that Tiberius would find the privacy of new surroundings so congenial that he would leave him, Seianus, free to conduct affairs of State in his own sweet way. He therefore outlined to the Emperor the advantages of peace and privacy.

Tiberius fell for the suggestion. He went to Capri and lived on that beautiful, peaceful island for eleven years, until his death. Only twice during this period did he travel to the mainland, and even then he dared not enter Rome, but skulked in its vicinity. People scared him enough individually, let alone in the mass.

One of Tiberius' twelve houses on Capri stood on a cliff-top high above the sea. This was probably the Villa Io, which took its name from Zeus' mistress. Somewhere near there, too, was the place of execution from which condemned men used to be hurled into the sea on the Emperor's orders, while fishermen stood by below to finish off any survivors with poles and oars.

The Emperor apparently had no time either for the gods and their worship or for the dictates of conscience. He was completely wrapped up in astrology. Only one man, a freedman, was initiated by Tiberius into the secrets of his horoscope. It was the duty of this man, an uneducated but well-muscled individual, to escort all visiting astrologers who met with the Emperor's disapproval out of the house in a friendly manner, and then hurl them off a high cliff into the sea. When Tiberius asked the astrologer Thrasullus what his own horoscope portended and what else would happen to him, Thrasullus, that very day, the star-gazer blanched and started to shake with fright. He was threatened, he said fearfully, by terrible and almost mortal danger. Tiberius at once embraced the alarmed man and warmly congratulated him. From that day forth he treated him royally, regarding him as the *ne plus ultra* of clairvoyants, a walking Delphi and an oracle on two legs.

What else the Emperor did on the island is not quite clear, but the most incredible rumours circulated. Tacitus tells us that 'he was able to indulge his cruelty and lust with less distraction there than at Rome'. But, although he wanted to withdraw himself and his 'peculiar talents' from the Roman gaze, he never neglected affairs of State and maintained written communication with the capital.

Eight years after Drusus' murder, Seianus received his just deserts. The Emperor conducted such a thorough investigation into his crimes that, in his zeal, he mistakenly had a friend of his from Rhodes stretched on the rack. He looked out across the sea from the highest peak on the island, waiting for the signals which would inform him the moment Seianus' conspiracy had been suppressed. The old fox was so cautious that he refused to leave the Villa Io for nine months after Seianus' arrest. Seianus was led to his execution with a cloth over his head and a rope about his neck. Panic-stricken, he cried out for his friends, but the streets and squares were empty. His children were also handed over to the executioner. The sight of these innocent victims drove their mother, Seianus' divorced wife Apicata, to such despair that she committed suicide. Eudemus the physician and Lygdus the eunuch became quite talkative on the rack. ...

Six years later Emperor Tiberius died, still in Capri. He was seventy-eight years old. Mentally deranged and afflicted with hallucinations, he tried, to the very last, to conceal his deterioration behind a mask of artificial gaiety. On March 16th, A.D. 37, his breathing appeared to have stopped. 'Tiberius is dead,' the imperial couriers announced. His successor, Gaius Caesar Caligula, started to accept congratulations on his accession to power.

Then it was suddenly announced that Tiberius had regained consciousness, that he had recovered from his coma and was asking for food. Everyone went pale. Some pretended sorrow, others indifference. Caligula was rigid with fury. Having just seen his dearest wish fulfilled, he would now have to go on waiting for the death of a man who simply refused to die.

He ordered heavy rugs to be thrown over Tiberius, and the old man died of suffocation.

CALIGULA

'HERE COMES THE GOAT!'

On one occasion he summoned three consuls to his palace at midnight, and told the men, who were half dead with terror and feared the worst, to take their places on a stage. Appearing suddenly, amid a tremendous din of flutes and foot-tapping, dressed in a long cloak and a tunic which reached his ankles, he performed a dance, and then disappeared again.

Suetonius, Caligula, 54.

As long as Emperor Tiberius was alive, people in the Roman Empire went about their business grumbling and grousing secretly. One incautious word spelt arrest. 'Death itself is afraid of him,' they whispered in the streets. But when the old man of Capri who refused to die had finally given up the ghost, all gave vent to their feelings. Curses rent the Roman air, and many people loudly demanded that the dead man should be refused an honourable burial. At last, they thought, at last they were free from the constant danger of arrest, sham trial and execution.

But the senators trembled. They trembled even now that all life had left Tiberius' body. They had trembled for years, and now — from sheer habit — they went on trembling. They dared not throw open the prisons. It happened that the date fixed for several executions coincided with the news of Tiberius' death. The executioners were conscientious officials who lived by the book. Heedless of their unfortunate prisoners' pleas for mercy, they garrotted them as ordered. After all, who could tell what the coming days and weeks held in store? Who could tell whether Tiberius was really dead? The effects of the Emperor's inhumanity persisted long after his death.

Soon couriers were speeding through the country-side. Travelling in relays, they could cover 125 miles, or the distance from Misenum to Rome, in a mere forty-eight hours. Straight from the death-bed of the old Emperor came the name of the new, and the Senate convened an immediate session to hail the new master of Rome.

Gaius Caesar, also known as Caligula, was only twenty-four years old. His mother was the Agrippina who had been exiled by Tiberius, and his father was the long-dead and once very popular general Germanicus. Caligula belonged to the family which had suffered so much from the murderous treatment of Seianus and Tiberius, and only owed his survival to the fact that he had seemed too young and insignificant to merit killing. Apart from him, three of his sisters were still alive.

After his mother's arrest, Caligula had at first been cared for by his grandmother Antonia, and had later, at the age of nineteen, gone to the old Emperor's court at Capri. He was forced, whether he liked it or not, to learn the art of dissimulation. Tiberius tried to draw him out by telling him things which might give him cause for complaint. But Caligula never gave himself away. He appeared to remember nothing of his family's dreadful fate and acted as though Tiberius had never harmed a hair of their heads. He was amazingly self-controlled. His manner towards Tiberius was one of willing obedience and steadfast loyalty. So obsequious was his behaviour that someone later said of him, very neatly, that there had never been a better slave or a worse master.

The young man's easy-going façade probably concealed, even at this stage, a leaning towards sadism, extravagance and self-indulgence. He used to watch the torturing and execution of condemned men with avid interest. Dressed in wigs and flowing robes he visited disreputable taverns and brothels. Emperor Tiberius was not unaware of this. Indeed, he once said: 'Gaius has survived to the detriment of myself and everyone else.' Fools and knaves were all that remained of the great line of Emperor Augustus. However, there flowed in Caligula's veins not only the blood of his great-grandfather Augustus but also that of Antony, so that in this young and easily corrupted fruit of an old and venerable tree both the victor and vanquished of Actium lived on. We shall see how Antony's blood declared itself in him, with his weakness for Egypt, for mawkish oriental romanticism and incest.

The rumour went round that Caligula had poisoned Tiberius, that he had removed the Emperor's ring while the old man was still breathing and that, when Tiberius refused to die straight away, he had throttled him with his bare hands.

It was a slow procession which moved along the ancient Via Appia from Misenum to Rome. Tiberius' body was carried by common soldiers. At the head of the cortège as it journeyed from village to village and town to town came Caligula, cheered by crowds of hurriedly assembled onlookers. From altars erected on each side of the road clouds of incense and the smoke of thank-offerings rose to the sky. In order to reach Rome before the main body arrived, Caligula hastened on in advance. The royal proclamation was greeted with senatorial enthusiasm and roars of approval from the crowds outside. As usual, the Romans let themselves be carried away far too easily. Without any inkling of what they were in for, they solemnly swore by all the gods to die for Gaius Caesar. He was still called Gaius Caesar, by the way, Caligula being only a nickname which he would not tolerate, even in private. As a boy his mother Agrippina had put him into military uniform and heavy top-boots or *caligae*, and the soldiers had adopted the diminutive of this word, *caligula*, as their pet name for him.

Caligula decreed Tiberius a modest funeral and gave him a funeral oration in which he said little about the dead man and a great deal about his own father Germanicus and his great-grandfather Augustus. That done, he set off for the islands in the Gulf of Campania where his mother Agrippina and his brothers had met a ghastly end. Bringing his relatives' remains back to Rome, he ceremoniously interred them in the Mausoleum of Augustus. He then requested the Senate to bestow every conceivable honour on his three sisters, the only surviving members of his family. That still left a young cousin and co-heir of his called Tiberius to be 'taken care of'. Caligula, then twenty-five, adopted seventeen-year-old Tiberius as his son, gave him the title 'Prince of the Youth', and then ordered him to carry out his own death sentence.

Caligula's next victims were Macro, the prefect of the Praetorian Guard, and his wife. As successor to the notorious Seianus, Macro had helped Caligula to secure the throne, but the Emperor now found him a nuisance, so he appointed him viceroy of Egypt and then, before the unfortunate couple had a chance to set sail, sent him and his wife an order to commit suicide. Caligula's chief aim was to win over the masses. He distributed largesse and arranged spectacular entertainments, including chariot-races and lion-, bear- and panther-hunts on a huge scale. He ordered 800 wild beasts to be brought to Rome. He organized poetic contests and competitions in Greek and Roman rhetoric. The poet who did worst had to lick his composition off the writing-tablet and was birched or ducked in the river. Caligula did promise, however, to abolish prosecutions for *lèse-majesté*, to recall those who had been exiled, and to publish a regular statement of public finances. In that respect he made a promising start.

People had been sickened by Tiberius and his dismal reign. Caligula dangled before them the prospect of halcyon days to come. In an attempt to emulate Augustus, he imported obelisks from Egypt. He did not notice that, while the pillars once brought over by Augustus were adorned with interesting hieroglyphics, his own obelisks had been forged.

Shortly after his accession, Caligula became ill. People waited for nights on end in the streets near his palace. All were deeply concerned for his recovery, and some made a vow that they would sacrifice their lives if he were cured. No sooner had the Emperor recovered from his illness than he started to show his true colours. On January 1st, A.D. 38, he had induced the Senate to swear, one by one, that they would lay down their lives not only for himself but also for his sisters. By January 1st, A.D. 40, two of those sisters were already imprisoned on lonely islands. The third, Drusilla, had died previously, and the Emperor was inconsolable over her loss. Having betrothed her to a man called Lucius Cassius Longinus, he had then abducted her and publicly treated her as though she were his own legal wife. He had also named her his heir. When she died Caligula stormed from one end of Italy to the other, demanding that anyone he met should share his grief. He decreed days, weeks and even months of public mourning. He prohibited laughing, bathing and taking meals in the company of parents, wife and children, on pain of death. He even arranged Drusilla's admittance to the Pantheon, the national temple of Rome. Hitherto, only Julius Caesar and Augustus, the twin founders of the imperial regime, had been represented there as gods. Caligula now erected altars for the new deity and sponsored a nation-wide 'Drusilla craze'. One young senator who solemnly asserted that he had seen Drusilla ascending into the sky when she was cremated received a handsome reward.

Caligula twice abducted the brides of Roman noblemen in the middle of their weddings, only to repudiate them later. His real passion in life was a woman called Caesonia, who was as extravagant and dissolute as she was lacking in looks and youth. He often made her ride at his side, arrayed in military cloak, helmet and shield, for the benefit of his troops, and occasionally exhibited her naked to his friends. When Caesonia presented him with a daughter he officially declared her his consort and the mother of his child — whom he recognized as his own flesh and blood by its ungovernable behaviour. Then he began to 'rule'.

He made the most highly respected senators trot along beside his chariot in their togas or wait behind his couch at table, dressed in linen aprons like slaves. Other senators were secretly killed on his orders. He had his quaestor flogged, commanding that his clothes be ripped off him and laid beneath the soldiers' feet beforehand to give them a better foothold when plying their whips. During gladiatorial games he ordered the huge awning over the arena to be drawn back. The audience sweltered, but no one was allowed to leave the theatre. From time to time he had half-starved wild beasts brought into the arena to be fought not by gladiators but by decrepit old grey-beards or respectable family men who had some physical defect or other.

But Caligula did not stop there. He wanted to play at being a god. Closing the granaries, he declared a state of famine. He combed the gaols for prisoners to throw to the beasts. When he could not make up his mind which to choose, he simply ordered all the prisoners 'between the first bald head and the last' to be marched off. Some convicts he branded or personally condemned to fight wild animals. Others he locked up like beasts of prey in cages where they could only move on all fours. He underlined the inhumanity of his behaviour with gruesome jokes. For instance, he sent his exiled sisters a message saying that he not only had islands for them 'but swords, too'. And when he signed death-warrants he would murmur to himself: 'I am settling my accounts.' His favourite instruction to the executioner was: 'Strike him so he feels he is dying.'

'Let them hate me, as long as they fear me!' — *oderint dum metuant*, was Caligula's motto. When the popular favourite in a race was not his own, he called out: 'Oh that the Roman people had but a single neck!' He grumbled about the general state of prosperity in the country. Believing that people would soon forget his reign if it was not distinguished by some great disaster or defeat, he prayed for famines, plagues, fires and earthquakes. During one sumptuous feast he suddenly became convulsed with lunatic laughter, and when the two consuls reclining near him asked why, replied: 'I am laughing at the thought that I could have both your throats slit on the spot.' He never kissed his wife or mistress on the neck without gently remarking: 'This lovely head will fall, too, as soon as I give the order.' He played an unpleasant practical joke on the officials responsible for organizing the customary festival of remembrance for the battle of Actium. As great-grandson of Augustus and Mark Antony, he made the following announcement: if the celebrations took place it would be an insult to the vanquished Antony, and the officials' heads would roll. But if the celebrations did not take place it would be an affront to Augustus' memory, and the officials would still forfeit their heads.

But all this was not enough for Caligula. He wanted to be a god here on earth, not a god of marble — a golden statue of him already stood in the temple — but a living god. He accordingly had himself decked out in the sort of robes in which Greek sculptors usually portrayed their gods. His courtiers declared themselves thrilled at his appearance, so he paraded before the people dressed as Hercules, Bacchus or Apollo, and presided over the courts in the garb of Jupiter. The Roman people set about enrolling their

Emperor among the gods during his lifetime, and the Senate voted him a temple out of public funds.

Caligula's only failure was with the Jews, who protested loudly when the Roman administration tried to erect a statue of him in the Temple at Jerusalem. If the Emperor had not died in the nick of time, war would have broken out. There were also disturbances in Egypt when attempts were made to introduce emperor-worship into the Jewish synagogues there. Led by Philo, the greatest Jewish philosopher in the ancient world, a delegation arrived in Rome to lodge a protest, but was curtly dismissed by the Emperor.

Caligula designed a new sort of bath, thought up absurd dishes and exotic drinks. His pleasure-boats on Lake Nemi, near Rome, boasted unheard-of luxuries. When the lake was drained twenty years ago, remains of them were found lying ransacked on the bottom. Caligula built moles where the sea was deepest, bored tunnels where the rock was hardest, turned plains into mountains and mountains into plains. Everything had to be done at top speed, and anyone who dawdled forfeited his head. After a year of this, Caligula had run through 2,700 million sesterces, the sum total of the fortune left him by Tiberius. He started levying ridiculous taxes and wherever possible got himself named as 'heir' to the richest men in the land. Anyone who lived too long after making such a will received a gift of poisoned delicacies from his imperial beneficiary. The public exchequer was also replenished by reckless confiscation.

Anxious to gain a military reputation, Caligula crossed the Rhine. There was obviously nothing much to do there, and the Emperor's commanders were hard put to it to collect any prisoners of war. Eventually Caligula's German body-guards were sent across the Rhine and told to hide in the undergrowth until they were 'captured'. The Emperor's next objective was 'the conquest of Britain'. Leading his troops to the Channel coast, he deployed them in battle order. Then, having forgotten to provide the necessary transport for the crossing, he ordered them to collect sea-shells. Only a few ships were available, so Caligula took a short pleasure-cruise and then ordered a general withdrawal, at the same time dispatching couriers to the Senate to describe his heroic part in this victory. The only tangible result of the expedition was a lighthouse, 200 feet high, which Caligula built at Boulogne. It was not demolished until 1544.

Caligula arrived back in Rome on his birthday, August 31st, A.D. 40. He now proposed to become a sort of super-god and settle in Egypt, making Alexandria the capital of the Roman Empire. But first he wanted to give the Roman aristocracy a final taste of his mettle.

Caligula was a tall man with a pale face, an abnormally plump body, a scrawny neck and skinny legs. His eyes were deep-set and his brows receding, while his forehead was broad and threatening. He tried to enhance the naturally ferocious expression on his ugly features by making frightful grimaces and contorting his face in front of the mirror. Although he was bald, his body was very hirsute. 'Here comes the Goat!' his subjects whispered; but whispers like that could prove fatal.

The Emperor found it impossible to rest. Three hours' sleep a night was all he could manage. He crawled under his bed and cowered there. He donned women's clothes and a golden beard. In his right hand he brandished a lightning fork, a trident or a snake-entwined rod, all emblems of the gods. He also gave ballet performances in the palace at night, with himself as soloist.

The half-mad Emperor reigned for no less than three years, ten months and eight days. His crazy regime would have lasted even longer if one of his army officers had not decided to assassinate him.

Caligula's orgy of inquisition, murder and oppressive taxation had been an anathema to the officer corps. The man who put a stop to it was Cassius Chaerea, tribune of one of the Praetorian cohorts. He was an elderly soldier with a great military career behind him, and had never in his life shrunk from danger. The Emperor had always singled him out for the most unpleasant assignments and was fond of baiting him in front of his brother officers — unwisely, as it turned out.

Chaerea organized a small conspiracy. On January 24th, A.D. 41, he lay in wait for the Emperor in the underground gallery of the theatre. Caligula was just leaving when Chaerea dealt him a heavy blow on the neck with his sword. Another sword pierced his chest. 'So let your destiny be fulfilled!' Chaerea is said to have cried. Caligula writhed on the ground in agony. 'I am still alive!' he screamed. There were thirty wounds in his body by the time they had finished with him. His wife Caesonia was killed by a centurion and his little daughter's brains were dashed out against a wall.

The news of Caligula's assassination was received with incredulity. 'The Goat has thought up the rumour himself,' people whispered. 'He's spreading it to test our reactions!'

Yet another madman was living on for a little while after his death. ...

CLAUDIUS

THE POOR BOOBY

Sickly from childhood onwards and living in a state of perpetual fear which made him pretend to be more stupid than he really was, reared for a long time beneath the eye of his grandmother Livia, then of his mother Antonia, and of women generally, he lacked that masculine disposition which distinguishes the free man. The master of Rome and the provinces was himself a slave.

Dio Cassius, lx, 2.

At the confluence of the Rhône and the Saône stands Lyons, the French city famous for its silk. Once called Lugdunum, it was the capital of Gaul, the Roman province conquered by Caesar. It was also used by the great Roman general Drusus as an operational base during his campaign against the Germans. Drusus was the younger brother of Tiberius and would probably have made a better emperor, but he lost his life after falling from his horse in Germany.

It was in Lugdunum, on August 1st, 10 B.C., that a son was born to Drusus and his wife Antonia. The child was given the names Tiberius Claudius Drusus.

Half a century later, in the year A.D. 41, Claudius was destined, as a man of fifty, to become Emperor of Rome. He was the uncle of Emperor Caligula and the nephew of Emperor Tiberius, but he lost his father in early childhood and had, as a youth, to contend with persistent ill-health.

He was considered, probably with justification, to be a physical weakling. He was also considered, perhaps with less justification, to be stupid — almost insane. His own mother, Antonia, called him 'a monster', and declared that Nature had 'only begun, not completed' him. 'More stupid than my son Claudius', she used to say when she regarded anyone as particularly idiotic. His grandmother Livia Augusta also treated him with contempt. She seldom spoke to him. If she had to reprove him for anything, she either wrote him a few curt lines or acted through a third party. When Claudius' sister Livilla heard that her brother would some day inherit the throne, she bemoaned the unhappy fate of the Roman people.

Emperor Augustus was also worried about his young relative. In a letter recommending that an adviser be appointed to guide him, he wrote: 'We shall always be sweating with fear in case he does something which might, perhaps, seem offensive or ridiculous.' He also took care that young Claudius never sat in the imperial box at the Circus, so that he was not seen by the public. In his will he treated him like a stranger by putting him among beneficiaries of the third class.

When young Claudius went to Tiberius and asked to be given consular duties, his uncle sent him a modest forty gold pieces and told him to have a good time at the Saturnalia. That was all he thought him capable of.

Claudius' house burned down, and the Senate proposed to build him a new one at public expense, but Emperor Tiberius annulled the decision. He would make good the damage out of his own pocket, he said, Claudius being weak in the head. When Claudius was deputed to congratulate Emperor Caligula, his nephew, on the unmasking of a conspiracy, Caligula flew into such a rage because they had picked on his uncle, of all people, for the job, that he had Claudius thrown into the river to cool off.

If Claudius was late for a meal, the other diners let him wander round the royal table for a long while before he found a seat. When he fell asleep during meals, as he often did, they would amuse themselves by throwing olive-stones and date-kernels at his head. And if he snored at table they used to put slippers on his hands, so that when he woke and rubbed his eyes, he got a shock, to the huge enjoyment of everyone present.

Not having anything worth-while to do, Claudius spent his time either strolling in the garden of his suburban property or living quietly by himself in his villa in Campania. But he also drank, gambled and, according to the historian Suetonius, associated with some very unsavoury characters.

Was Claudius really nothing more than an oaf? Well, he was tutored by the great historian Livy and associated with Greek scientists and scholars. He took an interest in philology and phonetics. He made an exhaustive study of history and was himself the author of some extremely interesting historical works, none of which, unfortunately, has survived. On his accession he introduced three new letters into the Roman alphabet, creating a distinction between *u* and *v* which had not until then been customary. (The new letters never really caught on.) It is not difficult to understand why an oddity like Claudius, whom no one had entrusted with any duties or offices, who had been subjected to continuous repression and contempt, and who had been left in the tender charge of a tough and brutal riding-master, was hardly destined to be the ideal emperor for Rome.

Claudius was already fifty years old when the strange workings of chance set him upon the throne. Before assassinating Emperor Caligula the conspirators decided to remove anyone who might disturb the proceedings, and Claudius was left in a summer-house. When he heard that the Emperor had been murdered he ran to a near-by balcony and hid himself behind some curtains. A passing soldier, noticing a pair of feet peeping from under the curtains, pulled Claudius out, threw himself at his feet and hailed him as Imperator. Then he took him along to his unit, where the troops deposited him in a litter and carried him into their camp. Claudius was dejected, terrified and quite ignorant of what was happening. Passers-by who recognized him in his litter thought he was being taken off for execution. Mobs thronged the streets of Rome and loudly demanded a new emperor. The Senate met to discuss whether it would not be better to abolish the Principate altogether. But it was too late. The troops were clamouring to swear allegiance to Claudius, who at last acquiesced. He promised each soldier 15,000 sesterces, or about £250 per head. By doing so he set a precedent. In future, no Roman Emperor could take up office without giving the Guard a gratuity in cash, and the size of that gratuity often determined the length of his reign.

Claudius celebrated his accession by declaring a general amnesty. He had his grandmother Livia Augusta enrolled among the gods and insisted on according his family the honours due to them. 'By Augustus!' was his favourite oath.

The people soon realized to their surprise that Claudius had a peculiar hobby. His idea of real bliss was to play the judge. He conducted interrogations, passed sentences and presided over court sessions even during the height of the Roman summer. He was extraordinarily inconsistent, however. Sometimes he acted with prudence and deliberation. Once, when a woman refused to recognize a young man as her son, the Emperor extracted an admission from her by ordering her to marry him. On other occasions he became childish and behaved like a buffoon. If one of two parties failed to appear in court, he always decided in favour of the party present.

Perhaps the most remarkable feature of the Emperor's judicial career was the amount of insolence he tolerated in court. When a witness who had been subpoenaed failed to turn up, his legal representative merely went on repeating that it would have been quite impossible for him to appear. Only after exhaustive questioning by Claudius did he add: 'The man has died. I suppose he was allowed to.' Another lawyer thanked the Emperor extravagantly for having permitted him to defend a client, and then remarked: 'Though defence is an established practice, of course.'

Barristers took gross advantage of the Emperor's extraordinarily patient attitude. When he got down from the seat of judgment they would loudly call him back, holding him fast by the toga or even by the leg. One Greek lawyer shouted at him: 'As for you, you're a poor booby!' A Roman who had been charged with criminal offences against women on the evidence of prostitutes bribed by his enemies called Claudius 'simple-minded' and 'inhuman' and hurled a stylus and some wax tablets in his face, cutting him quite badly.

The Emperor's public prosecutors were lazy and negligent, and red tape flourished. People whom Claudius charged with celibacy and childlessness demonstrated that they were respectable married men with large families. Someone who was accused of trying to commit suicide with a dagger calmly undressed and exhibited his unmarked body. The Emperor imposed penalties out of the blue because this man or that had left Italy 'without the Emperor's knowledge', or 'without leave'. This was something quite new to the Romans, who had hitherto been able to travel anywhere they pleased.

But Claudius was not merely a stupid and inconsistent judge with sudden flashes of inspiration. He made genuine efforts to deal with public affairs and achieved some positive results. In particular, he considerably improved the administration of justice in the provinces. He granted Roman citizenship to a large number of Gauls. (His address to the Senate on that occasion has been found inscribed on a bronze plaque at Lyons, the city of his birth.) Theodor Birt thinks that Claudius' lasting achievements in the spheres of policy and administration set him on a far higher plane than Tiberius or Caligula. To a large extent, however, Claudius owed these achievements to his freedman Narcissus, whom he appointed chief of the imperial secretariat. Narcissus was a man of sound judgment who carried out his administrative duties without worrying too much about the vagaries of his royal master.

Claudius always applied himself conscientiously to the problem of Rome's food supplies. When one district of the city caught fire, he summoned every citizen to help. Ordering baskets of gold to be set before him, he personally rewarded each man according to the amount of fire-fighting he had done. He guaranteed supplies of grain during the winter months. He granted large concessions to the shipbuilding industry. He dredged the harbour at Ostia, which had become completely silted up, an unusual technical achievement which Julius Caesar had attempted without success. Diverting spring-water from the mountains nearly forty miles away, he brought it across the Campagna and into Rome, to the Palatine, which had only been provided with storage-tanks until then. The 'Aqua Claudia' survives today as one of the most impressive feats of Roman engineering. Claudius diverted the waters of the Fucine Lake into a canal which 30,000 people took eleven

Agrippina, mother of Caligula and wife of Germanicus. She starved herself to death in A.D. 33, after she had been exiled and imprisoned by Tiberius

Emperor Caligula. If not actually insane, he was certainly prone to crazy ideas and probably constituted a 'border-line case'. The historian Suetonius reports that 'Once, when the sacrificial beast stood ready at the altar, he appeared in the rôle of sacrificial slaughterer, swung the axe high in the air – and struck the assistant priest dead'

1, 2

3, 4

1. *Emperor Claudius* was born at Lyons in 10 B.C. and died in A.D. 54 – probably poisoned by Agrippina. Some modern scholars and novelists have tried to explain away and excuse, on inadeq grounds, the grotesque actions which Tacitus, Dio Cassius and Suetonius attribute to the influen the Emperor's womenfolk and freedmen

2. *Antonia* (36 B.C.–A.D. 37) used to call her son Claudius 'a monster of a man' whom Nature begun but never completed. She was the daughter of Mark Antony and Octavia, Augustus' s

3. *Messalina Valeria*, wife of Claudius. Notorious at Rome for her dissipated way of life, she event contracted a bigamous marriage with her lover Silius. She was put to death in A.D. 48 at the comm of Claudius

4. *Julia Agrippina* (A.D. 15–59). She married Claudius, who was her uncle, in the year A.D. 49, a said to have participated in his murder in order to put her son Nero on the throne

years to build. Before the last soil was removed and the lake allowed to drain away, he held a mock sea-battle. Those who had been forced to take part in it raised the customary cry: '*Ave, Imperator, morituri te salutant!*' or 'Hail, Emperor, they salute you, those who are about to die!' 'Or aren't, as the case may be,' answered the Emperor. The men took this flippant remark for a pardon and flatly refused to fight, whereupon Claudius jumped up and hobbled all round the lake, ranting and raving at them to proceed, which they eventually did. The battle was fought between a Sicilian squadron and a squadron from Rhodes, each consisting of twelve three-deckers. The signal for the attack was blown on a conch by a silver Triton which rose from the lake by mechanical means.

Emperor Claudius presented spectacular entertainments and barbaric animal-baiting displays. There was always 'something on' in the Circus Maximus for the spoilt and sensation-loving people of Rome. It might be chariot-racing, or hunting wild animals from Africa, or the famous Thessalian horsemen who drove wild bulls around the arena until they were completely worn out, then leapt on to their necks and brought them down by the horns. The Emperor announced a fairly minor gladiatorial show in the following terms: 'I invite the people to take pot luck, as it were.' He played the jovial host, personally rewarding the victors with gold pieces and encouraging the spectators to enjoy themselves.

Claudius only conducted one war. Setting sail from Ostia he landed at Marseilles, marched to the Channel coast, and, without bloodshed, subdued part of Britain within the space of a few days. Six months later he returned to Rome and staged a splendid triumphal march. The campaign had been carefully prepared by Narcissus. Claudius had sent him on in advance to persuade the legions to leave their comfortable quarters on the Rhine frontier and take part in the expedition, for which they showed not the least enthusiasm.

The Emperor's reign was a motley succession of good things and bad. He forbade certain persons to go farther from Rome than the third milestone. He conferred honours on elderly people and dished out sets of triumphal regalia by the thousand. In the same edict he could publish important government decrees and recommend the population to take a certain cough-cure. Many owners of ailing and decrepit slaves used to put them off on the Island of Aesculapius, a small island in the Tiber inside the city limits of Rome. Claudius decreed that, in the event of their recovery, such slaves should receive their freedom.

Claudius banished the Jews from Rome 'because, egged on by Chrestus, they constantly stir up unrest'. (Even at this date, the elders of the Church frequently used the form Chrestus for *Christus.*) The expulsion of the Jews from Rome occurred in the year A.D. 49, the crucifixion of Christ having already taken place during Tiberius' reign.

Envoys from Germany were allowed by Claudius to sit in the *orchestra*, the best seats in the theatre. On one occasion, when they had been allotted seats in the amphitheatre normally reserved for the people, they saw that the Parthian and Armenian ambassadors were sitting in the Senate's seats. Proudly declaring that they were in no way inferior, either in bravery or rank, they seated themselves in the orchestra. The Emperor sanctioned their autocratic behaviour.

Claudius pronounced and carried out sentences of death with a complete lack of compunction. Thirty-five senators and more than 300 Roman knights were executed on a single occasion. But, being absent-minded, the Emperor sometimes forgot that he had ordered such executions shortly after they had taken place. He invited the dead men to his house and then wondered why they did not turn up.

Claudius was a prodigious eater. Slaves had to tickle his throat with a feather as he lay on his back after a meal, snoring, to help him void his stomach. Since he slept little at night, he used to get most of his sleep at court in the day-time. And however loudly the barristers bellowed their speeches, however much they shouted, nothing roused the royal 'Lord Chief Justice' from his oblivion.

Behind all the Emperor's activities, two sinister influences were at work: emancipated slaves, and women. And dominant among the women was the notorious Messalina.

CLAUDIUS AND MESSALINA

'WHY DOESN'T THE EMPRESS COME TO TABLE?'

She was bored by her love-affairs because she never encountered any opposition.

Tacitus, *Annales*, xi, 26.

EMPEROR CLAUDIUS was a tall man, and could hardly have been called thin. He looked his best when reclining on a couch, but there is even said to have been a certain dignity about his appearance when standing or seated. His gait was rather unsteady, he foamed at the mouth when angry, his nose ran, he stuttered, and his head had an habitual tremor which grew perceptibly worse in moments of agitation. He was all right in other respects — except for a stomach ailment which often gave him pain!

There is little doubt that he had pronounced sadistic impulses. He was always reluctant to forgo any opportunity of conducting a gruelling interrogation in person, and insisted on attending executions. On one occasion he was so taken with the idea of witnessing an 'old-fashioned' execution that, when the executioner did not turn up, he left the criminal tied to his stake all day and waited there until a substitute executioner could be fetched from the capital. At mass-executions he used to lull his conscience by turning the statue of Augustus round so that his milder forebear could not see the bloodshed.

He took a special delight in fights between wild beasts and also in *meridiani*, or 'midday' gladiators, who had to fight to the death in the midday heat without any defensive armour. Augustus' humane rule that gladiators should no longer fight to the death had long ago been abolished. Claudius used to hurry to the arena early in the morning and remain glued to his seat even in the long intermissions during which the spectators went off to eat. When he could not find enough professional fighters he used to condemn stage-carpenters, mechanics and other members of the Circus staff to mortal combat in the arena. The slightest pretext was sufficient: it only needed some scenery or scaffolding to collapse or some machinery not to function properly.

As is often the case with such natures, Claudius' marked streak of cruelty was allied with extreme timidity and perpetual distrust. He refused to visit an invalid unless sick-room, bed and bed-clothes had been carefully searched in advance. He never felt happy at table unless he was surrounded by bodyguards armed with spears. Everyone who visited the Emperor had to submit to a thorough search. Only after lengthy remonstrances about the indignity of such a measure did he waive it in the case of women, boys, and young girls. He often complained bitterly that there was nowhere where he could feel safe.

The whole of this peculiar man's reign was subject to the influence, principally, of emancipated slaves and women. The Emperor was at times merely the pawn of these two groups, their interests and whims. The eunuch Posides, the freedmen Felix and Harpocras, his financial administrator Pallas, and, in particular, his private secretary Narcissus, were all responsible for the wildest intrigues at court. They also became, in a short space of time, the richest men in Rome.

Claudius was twice engaged. He broke off his engagement to Aemilia Lepida before their wedding, and Livia Medullina died of a severe illness on the wedding-day itself. He then married twice, and got divorced shortly afterwards on each occasion, in the first instance because of petty irritations, and in the second because his wife was promiscuous and he suspected her of murder.

Then he married again, this time to Valeria Messalina, the daughter of his cousin Barbatus Messala. Who was this notorious woman whose very name has such an infamous ring even today?

When Claudius became Emperor, she was just seventeen. She was therefore thirty-three years younger than her imperial husband with the waddling gait. She was slim, and probably golden-haired, although Juvenal casts doubt on this by alleging that she wore a wig. One thing is certain: she had a passionate and volatile temperament.

Messalina presented Claudius with an heir — probably the only positive contribution she ever made to history. Its true significance can only be measured when we reflect that neither Caligula, Tiberius nor Augustus had any direct heir. Claudius was delighted. He named the boy Britannicus in memory of the partial conquest of Britain which was his only military achievement.

As the person who had brought this child into the world, Messalina could do no wrong. She certainly made the most of her opportunities. She had affairs with every conceivable — and inconceivable — sort of man: with gladiators, with dancers, with the handsomest and, sometimes, if she had a fancy, with the ugliest men in Rome. In all these activities she took the fullest advantage of her position and revenged herself pitilessly on anyone who was foolhardy enough to rebuff her. One murder more or less meant nothing to her. She made enough pin-money for her amusements by doing a brisk traffic in patents of citizenship, official appointments and other concessions.

But in the end it all became rather boring. The longer Messalina's list of amours grew, the less opposition she encountered. She abandoned herself to a career of debauchery such as even Rome had never known before.

All this left Claudius quite cold, so Messalina set to work on a certain Gaius Silius, the handsomest beau in Rome. She broke up his marriage and made him her lover. Silius realized what a dangerous game he was playing, but he knew that it would be equally dangerous to throw in his hand. Messalina showered him with gifts, and he, privately hoping that everything would turn out for the best, decided to enjoy the situation while it lasted. Clandestine love-affairs seemed to have lost all their savour for Messalina, and the only way she could titillate her jaded palate was to shock the whole of Rome. She never left Silius' side, showed herself in public with him, and visited his home accompanied by a large retinue. Tacitus tells us: 'There came a stage when the Emperor's slaves, freedmen and whole court were located at her lover's house, as though the throne had already passed to him.' If Claudius knew of his wife's adulterous goings-on with Silius, he at least acted as though he was blind to them, with the result that Messalina and Silius grew even bolder and more presumptuous. It occurred to Silius that actual danger might prove a remedy for potential danger. Not wishing to wait for the ageing Emperor to die, he decided to marry Messalina, now twenty-four, and adopt Britannicus.

They were married with due ceremony.

Messalina waited for Claudius to divorce her. She was now bigamously married, after all, and everyone in Rome knew it. But the Emperor did not act. Perhaps the enormity of the situation made people afraid to tell him. Perhaps Tacitus' assertion that Emperor Claudius knew nothing about it is really true.

Narcissus, the Emperor's private secretary, was more than a mere intriguer; he was a very competent civil servant, and Messalina's meddling in public affairs had always irritated him. While Claudius was staying at Ostia, he persuaded two of the Emperor's mistresses to inform him of the affair. One of them, Calpurnia, fell at the Emperor's feet, crying: 'Messalina has married Silius!' and the other woman confirmed the news. At Calpurnia's suggestion, Claudius consulted Narcissus. 'Don't you know that you are a divorcé?'

Narcissus asked him. 'The people, the Senate and the army all witnessed Messalina's wedding to Silius. If you do not act quickly, Silius will be master of all Rome.'

It was autumn, and Messalina was throwing a wild party to celebrate the vintage festival. Women were dancing about in animal-skins like frenzied Bacchanals, while Messalina, more brazen than ever, disported herself with Silius, she with her hair unbound and dishevelled and he crowned with ivy. At the height of the orgy a man called Valens, another of Messalina's lovers, climbed a tree. 'There's a heavy storm blowing up from Ostia!' he shouted. He was right. Claudius was approaching from Ostia, and with him was a detachment of Praetorians under the command of Narcissus. He was not coming in the role of a vengeful husband, however, but trembling for his own safety and repeatedly asking his friends if he was still Emperor. Messalina quickly made up her mind to go and meet her husband. Everyone had suddenly deserted her, including Silius, who excused himself by saying that he had business to attend to in the Forum. She rode along the high road to Ostia in a humble dung-cart. No one sympathized with her. All that people could remember were her vices.

The Emperor sat in his carriage, brooding apathetically. His head was trembling as usual. When Messalina drew near he simply looked the other way.

Messalina fled with her mother to the gardens of Lucullus. For the first time in her life she was at a loss. She thought of pleading for mercy, but her mother advised her to forestall the executioner by taking her own life. Her dissipations had ruined her, however, and the last vestiges of honour had died within her. Before she had time for further deliberation the assassins had arrived with orders from Narcissus to settle matters quickly. Taking a sword, Messalina pressed it fearfully against her breast, then her throat. But her nerve failed her and one of the executioner's assistants stabbed her to death.

Claudius received the news just as he was sitting down to dinner. They did not tell him whether Messalina had died by her own hand or another's. He did not ask. He merely called for a goblet and indulged in his usual bout of drinking. Then, suddenly, he seemed to remember something. 'Why doesn't the Empress come to table?' he asked.

The fifty-eight-year-old Emperor later announced to his troops: 'Since I have been unlucky in my marriages, I shall remain a bachelor from now on. If I fail to remain one, you may kill me.'

Hardly had he made this declaration when he started courting again. He developed a fresh interest in Paetina, whom he had once divorced. Then he wooed Lollia Paulina, formerly the wife of Emperor Caligula. But it was Julia Agrippina who finally won the day.

Agrippina was the daughter of Germanicus, Claudius' brother. Thirty-three years old, ambitious, ruthless and calculating, she took advantage of her close relationship by kindling her elderly uncle's passions with blandishments and caresses. A union with Agrippina would normally have counted as incest, so Claudius saw to it that the Senate 'compelled' him to marry her 'for the good of the State'. What was more, marriage between niece and uncle now became legally permissible by general decree.

'Rome was as if transformed. From now on, everything went according to Agrippina's wishes. She did not merely toy with the State like the frivolous Messalina. Hers was a rigid and utterly masculine regime.' That is how Tacitus describes the atmosphere in the capital in his famous *Annales*. As the *éminence grise* behind the throne, Agrippina was the real ruler of Rome. Whereas Messalina had not taken the least interest in politics, they were Agrippina's meat and drink. Tacitus informs us that she was born in 'the capital of the Ubii' and that she arranged for a veterans' colony to be founded there. It was after her, not Claudius, that the place was named in A.D. 50, becoming Colonia Agrippinensis, or what is now Cologne, Germany.

Claudius, thoughtless or absent-minded as ever, added to the scandal that his latest marriage had already caused by publicly referring to Agrippina as his 'little daughter' or his 'foster-child', and by remarking, in his speeches, that he had carried her in his arms from birth. For all its vices, Rome found it hard to swallow this form of legitimized incest.

Agrippina's aim was to secure the right of succession for Nero, her son by her first marriage, and she was prepared to achieve that aim by fair means or foul. She succeeded in arranging the betrothal of her twelve-year-old son to Octavia, Claudius' daughter. By becoming step-son and son-in-law of the Emperor, little Nero was now on an equal footing with the heir apparent, Claudius' own son Britannicus. At the same time, Britannicus was edged farther and farther out of the lime-light, while Nero was schooled for a great career and given the famous philosopher Seneca as his tutor. Claudius eventually adopted Nero and gave him the title of prince. Agrippina had attained her objective. She now had to hold her ground and dig in. But she had to act quickly, knowing that many people at court saw through her plans, and that her numerous crimes might one day bring about a change of heart in Claudius. Accordingly, she served him a dish of his favourite mushrooms — poisoned, of course. Enlisting the aid of the notorious poisoner Locusta, whose deadly wares found a ready market in the unscrupulous Roman society of her day, she had obtained a marvellous poison which induced first mental derangement and then death.

It is said that Claudius lost the power of speech after enjoying his mushrooms. He tossed and turned all night in frightful pain. By next morning he was dead. According to another story, he brought up the poisoned food but was immediately given another dose, either in gruel or an enema.

Agrippina put all the entrances to the palace under guard. To prevent the innocent Britannicus from finding out, like Hamlet, that his father had been murdered, she clasped the youngster tightly to her as though she were beside herself with grief and needed comfort.

On October 13th, A.D. 54, the gates of the imperial palace were flung open and out stepped seventeen-year-old Nero, to be greeted by rousing cheers from the soldiery. In the side-streets, old women whispered that Claudius had been distinctly heard to mutter over and over again, during his last session in court, that he had reached the end of his earthly life. What was more, a comet had appeared and his father's tomb had been struck by lightning; and everyone knew that they were omens of death.

NERO

HE REALLY WAS A POET

Writing tablets and books have come into my possession bearing very familiar verses written in his own hand. One can see at first glance that they are neither borrowed from another nor written at another's dictation, but by someone taking trouble and using his own ability.

Suetonius, Nero, 52.

AGRIPPINA was now thirty-nine years old. Her life had so far been dedicated to a single end: the securing of imperial status for her son Nero. She had been co-regent with Claudius and now, having murdered him, she was the true ruler of Rome. '*Optima mater*' or 'best of mothers' was how Nero, on the evening of October 13th, A.D. 54, addressed the woman who had murdered her husband the day before.

'Our Emperor is no orator,' the citizens told each other. 'He is the first master of Rome to have his speeches made up by others.' There were smirks all round, and some people laughed out loud.

But seventeen-year-old Nero was not discouraged. This was Claudius' funeral, and he, Claudius' adoptive son and the new Emperor, he, Nero Claudius Augustus Germanicus, was giving the funeral address. He had originally been surnamed 'Ahenobarbus', like his father. The latter had been a red-bearded man, as the name implied, and the first traces of red down were just beginning to appear on Nero's own cheeks.

In his oration Nero spoke of the long history of the imperial family. He enumerated its ancestors, the consulships and triumphs they had won. He pointed out that during the reign of his adoptive father Rome had sustained no losses anywhere in the Empire.

Greatly moved, the senators at once offered Nero the title 'Father of the Fatherland'. The new Emperor made a very favourable impression by thanking them courteously and declining the honour, remarking that he was too young for it.

He went on to speak of the prudence and sagacity of his predecessor. But that was the moment for smiles to break through. It was too much. Nobody could keep a straight face. Tittle-tattle, gossip and scandalous stories went the rounds of Roman society faster than they do in London, Paris or Washington today. Domestic slaves passed on whatever they picked up. The whole of Rome had enjoyed a generous sample of Claudius' 'sagacity' and 'prudence'. And to hear these words from the mouth of Nero, the son of Agrippina, whose poisoning of Claudius was even then being discussed in whispers behind closed doors. ...

The speech had, of course, been composed by the philosopher Seneca, Nero's friend and adviser. Seneca had his wits about him. He knew what Rome expected of Nero. Everyone knew that it was not Nero's speech. Nero was not capable of composing one — or delivering one, either, the people now noticed. They were to learn later that he preferred to sing.

The Romans were spoilt. They had heard the best orators that ever mounted a platform. They had known Cicero. The dictator Caesar had been an expert rhetorician. Augustus had been more ready-tongued than anyone in the Empire and had spoken magnificently, like a real emperor. Tiberius, although he deliberately indulged in ambiguity and *double entendre*, was a reliable speaker who weighed his words with care. Even the stuttering Caligula had been an effective orator, and Claudius' elegant style of public speaking had always been impressive.

But Nero! He was a truly peculiar youth to be entrusted with the destiny of an empire. He sculpted, painted, took singing-lessons, had a secret penchant for racing and even wrote poetry. With such a versatile and talented man as Emperor — even if he couldn't make speeches — the Romans saw golden times ahead. But then the Romans always saw golden times ahead when, after all the disillusionment he had aroused, an emperor was buried on the Field of Mars and his successor treated them to the customary farce of a funeral oration.

Nero was too good to be true. He declared that he was nobody's enemy, that he harboured no ill-will against anyone and that he was mounting the throne free from any desire for revenge. He intended to do away with favouritism, lobbying for appointments and corruption. He was going to wage no wars, to clean up the courts and give the Senate every freedom. Like his predecessor, he naturally invoked the name of Augustus, still the only bright star in Rome's murky imperial past.

But, before he could devote himself to carrying out these good resolutions, he had some family business to attend to. Britannicus, Emperor Claudius' own son and the potential Hamlet who might avenge his father's murder, was still alive. This fact in itself spelt danger for Nero.

At the festival of Saturnalia, Nero, surrounded by a circle of friends, ordered Britannicus to stand up and sing a song, convinced that the boy would make a fool of himself. But Britannicus was quite unembarrassed and sang a ballad which told how he had been deprived of his inheritance and his father's throne.

That was probably the moment when Nero decided to do away with his step-brother. He went to Julius Pollio, tribune of one of the Praetorian cohorts, who was holding the celebrated Locusta in gaol. He brought pressure to bear on the tribune and threatened Locusta with execution if she did not speedily prepare him an efficient poison: something which would, as he put it, bring him some peace of mind! Locusta brewed him a particularly deadly concoction which she guaranteed would act like a sword-thrust.

History has handed the scene down to us in all its details. Nero shared his dining-room with the royal children, among them Britannicus. The children took their meals seated while the older people reclined on couches.

Since the servant who had to taste all the food and drink intended for Britannicus might have given the game away by dropping dead, a subterfuge was employed. Britannicus was handed a very hot drink which the servant had already tasted. When, as he was meant to, he refused the drink because it was too hot, some cold water was hastily poured into it. This water contained the poison. It permeated his body so quickly that his voice and breathing failed at once.

The children who were sitting near Britannicus fled. The adults in the secret stared at Nero without moving. As for him, he lolled comfortably on his couch, looking as if nothing out of the way had occurred. Quite calmly, he said that it was probably just another of those epileptic seizures which had afflicted Britannicus since his early childhood. It would soon pass.

Agrippina was numb with shock and bewilderment. Perhaps she guessed that her son would one day murder her with the same cool deliberation. Octavia, who had been compelled to marry Nero, just three years older than herself, when she was only twelve, had long ago learnt to suppress grief, love or any other emotion. And so, after a short pause, the meal resumed its merry course. Britannicus, the last male descendant of the Claudian line, had mutely met his death under the very eyes of his sister, step-brother and step-mother, four months after his father's murder and Nero's accession.

Nero rewarded Locusta for her help by granting her immunity in respect of all her previous crimes, giving her some real estate and sending her some pupils to be instructed in the deadly art of poison-brewing.

The Emperor celebrated his murderous act by giving handsome presents to his closest friends. Then he took care of the people. He distributed a vast sum of money, 400 sesterces per head, to the population of Rome, and presented noblemen and senators who owned no property with a year's income.

Rome did not have a bad time during the first year of Nero's reign. Through the influence of Seneca and Burrus, the efficient prefect of the Guard, many improvements were made in the judicature and the administration. Agrippina, too, supervised her son as best she could and gave him appropriate advice. While out walking, Nero always greeted Roman noblemen by name, and made a hobby of remembering them all. When the Senate wanted to offer their thanks to him, he modestly replied: 'If I have deserved them.'

Nero began to recite poetry, at first only at home, but later in the theatre. His audiences went wild with delight. When a death-warrant was put in front of him for signature, he cried: 'I wish I could not write.' Emperor Trajan later described the first five years of Nero's reign as the happiest period in the imperial age of Rome. If he was right, it was due to Seneca's influence.

Humane, affable, courteous, talented: that was the new Emperor. He showed interest in the theatre and organized a large variety of entertainments, including youth sports or *Juvenalia*, Circus games, theatre performances and gladiatorial contests. There were races between chariots drawn by four camels, and a leading member of the Roman aristocracy is said to have ridden an elephant down a tight-rope into the arena. A comedy called 'The Fire', during the course of which an actual building was burned down, had a great success. Among the presents distributed to the people were birds of every variety, delicacies, and coupons for grain, gold, silver, precious stones, pearls, articles of clothing, slaves and breeding-cattle. But Nero's exuberant desire to be 'kind' did not stop there. He gave away ships, real estate and whole blocks of houses.

Nero saw to it that contestants in gladiatorial games did not fight to the death. Then he suddenly ordered 400 senators and 600 knights into the arena to fight a sword-battle, and insisted that it should be a gory one. 'Just an odd whim,' people said in the Emperor's defence.

Naval engagements were staged on artificial salt-water lakes with sea-monsters swimming about in them, and there were pantomime ballets with very risqué passages. To the great excitement of all present, an unknown Icarus made his first attempt at flight, but plunged to the ground close to Nero's box and spattered the Emperor with blood.

Nero awarded prizes for Latin rhetoric, poetic composition and lute-playing. He took the prizes for poetic composition and rhetoric himself, but modestly declined the victor's wreath for lute-playing. During court sessions he would have the case for each side put to him verbally and then announce his verdict the next day, in writing. He introduced Rome to a completely new style of architecture. Porches had to be built in front of every house so that their flat tops could serve as fire-fighting platforms, fires being a constant source of annoyance and danger in the capital. Nero built these arcades at his own expense.

He also tried to limit the growing extravagance of wealthy Roman society. Public feasts were to consist of a fixed number of courses. Inns were only allowed to sell cold snacks, not cooked meals.

From A.D. 54 until A.D. 59, Nero reigned with wisdom and moderation. They were the first five of his fourteen years on the throne.

While describing the young Emperor and this portion of his reign, the Roman historian Suetonius makes an abrupt but interesting remark. Among Nero's 'praiseworthy' measures he includes the death-penalty which the Emperor imposed upon the Christians. Suetonius calls them 'the Christiani, a sect which had given itself up to a new superstition harmful to the public interest'. This is the first explicit reference to the Christians made by the non-Christian Suetonius.

Some of Nero's laws not only demonstrate a genuine desire to remedy abuses but also show how thoroughly he went into matters. He issued some very sensible decrees against forgery, 'gold-digging' and the falsification of wills.

Nero had no taste for campaigns of conquest. This was partly due to Seneca's wise influence and partly because it was in keeping with his own character. For he was not a mere buffoon or charlatan, but possessed genuinely great artistic ability. At all events, the beginning of his reign was not marred by any of the acts of inconceivable folly which characterized its latter years.

Despite his ridiculous love of ostentation, despite his quite grotesque vanity and despite his pathological yearning for recognition as an artist and a genius, the Emperor was almost always meticulous in observing the rules of a competition. Should he ever modify the rules in his favour, he at least tried to delude himself that he had not.

One more thing: later historians and, in particular, historical novelists have denied Nero, whose morbid propensities make him seem an outcast of Hell itself, even a nominal claim to poetic ability. In reality, Nero appears to have been a fluent poet. Writing between thirty and fifty years after Nero's death, Suetonius mentioned that he had seen tablets and papyrus scrolls bearing familiar verses written in Nero's own hand. He had immediately recognized, by the corrections and deletions, that these verses could not have been copied or dictated but must have been written by a man with a mind of his own who was carefully thinking things out for himself. Nero is also said to have tried his hand at painting and sculpture with no little success.

Here may lie one of the root causes of his pathological striving for approbation. If he had been utterly without talent, his lust for recognition might not have reached such insane proportions. But since he was obviously activated by strong artistic impulses (a fact which historians frequently disguise from us); since he gradually lost the ability to distinguish between flattery and genuine appreciation; since, as time went by, his impulses were no longer curbed by his intelligence; and since he was eventually deserted by all the prerequisites of artistic creation — a sense of proportion, self-discipline, modesty, reverence, self-criticism, and faith — all that was left of Nero was a caricature of an artist and a dictator, tottering in the throes of near insanity.

STAGE-FRIGHT

Nero wanted to call the capital of the Roman Empire 'Neropolis'. He rechristened the month of April 'Neroneus'. In his morbid craving for fame, he wanted to be immortal.

The Author

IMMEDIATELY after his accession, Nero engaged as his court musician a man called Terpnus, one of those singers who accompanied themselves on the *cithara*. The cithara was a lyre-like instrument which the performer held in his hand and played in a standing position. Our words 'zither' and 'guitar' are derived from the Latin *cithara*, which was, in turn, borrowed from the Persian *sithtar*, an instrument with three strings.

Terpnus was the greatest cithara virtuoso of his time. Every night until dawn Nero listened while Terpnus sang. The dangerous, capricious Emperor and the lyre-player with the splendid voice, late at night in the hushed palace: it was a scene reminiscent of the court of Saul, the first king of Israel, who made young David sing for him.

Before long, Nero began to study singing and lyre-playing himself. He conscientiously followed all his teacher's instructions. To strengthen his voice he lay on his back for hours with slabs of lead on his chest. He rid himself of any 'waste-matter' which might obstruct his singing by taking laxatives and emetics. Singers were at that time advised to avoid eating fruit, and Nero extended this ban to include any food which might prove detrimental to his voice. To spare his throat he instituted monthly fast-days during which he would not even touch bread.

We have already learned that Nero was no orator. His voice did not carry and lacked resonance. But, like so many people who suffer from some physical disability, he made his weakest point the focus of his greatest aspirations. Nero wanted to sing, and sing in public. He practised diligently, lured on by the attractions of the stage. 'Unheard melodies are never sweet,' he said.

With its blasé fondness for ridicule and criticism, Rome was hardly the right venue for his first appearance. Nero's first public performance took place at Naples. All the town's most important citizens were invited to the theatre, and the news of the Emperor's appearance also attracted the curious inhabitants of neighbouring towns. Even then, the Neapolitan theatre was not full, so numerous Campanians received compulsory invitations to attend.

After the performance was over and everyone had left the theatre, the town was shaken by an earthquake and the theatre collapsed. Seeing this as a mark of divine Providence, Nero continued his series of recitals.

Anxious to preserve his health in general and his voice in particular, Nero took a Turkish bath. He did not stay there long. The theatre beckoned him once more. He went and dined with the actors, promising them that when he had downed a few drinks to oil his vocal chords he would give them something to make the rafters ring. Some visitors from Alexandria were so loud in their applause that he sent for more ship-loads of them.

As time went by, no kind of applause was loud enough for the Emperor. He had young Roman aristocrats trained in the art of applauding and selected five thousand hefty young commoners, whom he divided into groups. Each group was coached in a certain type of applause. There was *imbrex*, or clapping with the hands cupped, which got its name from the hollow roof-tile; *testa*, or clapping with the hands flat, named after the flat building-brick; and *bombus*, a bee-like hum of applause. Nero's claqueurs were distinguished by their fine clothes and elegant hair-styles. They were obliged to remove their knight's rings in case these hindered their applause. Their leaders received a salary of 400,000 sesterces, or about £6,800.

Nero decided to sing in Rome and arranged a concert there. (The word concert originally meant 'competition'.) It was a grand contest on the Greek pattern, with events which included music, singing, poetic composition, rhetoric, field sports, chariot-racing and riding. Nero christened these games the *Neronia*, and built special baths and a gymnasium for the competitors. The Neronia were to take place every five years. Nero sat impatiently in the orchestra, the rows of seats reserved for senators, while the vast circle of spectators clamoured to hear his heavenly voice. Drawing his lot from the urn like all the other lyre-players, he joined the queue and, when his turn came, mounted the rostrum. Officers of his body-guard carried his lyre for him. Having made the usual introductory speech, he bade the ex-consul Rufus announce that he would sing the opera *Niobe*. He sang for a very long time, roughly from midday until four o'clock in the afternoon. Then, to give himself ample opportunity for more singing in the future, he postponed the award of victor's wreaths and the rest of the events until the following year.

Nero now began to take part in tragedies, complete with costume and mask. He saw to it that the masks of gods, heroes and heroines resembled his own features or those of his current mistresses. Among the shows in which he played the lead were *Orestes the Matricide*, *Oedipus Blinded* and *Frenzied*

Poppaea Sabina became Nero's mistress and persuaded him to murder his mother Agrippina and his wife Octavia. Nero married her in A.D. 62 but kicked her to death three years later because she nagged him for coming home late

He was a red-head. Emperor Nero ruled Rome for fourteen years, from A.D. 54 to 68. At the age of fifteen he married Octavia, who was three years younger than himself, and at seventeen came to the throne. Nero had genuine poetic ability

Nero's Golden House was not redis
covered until the Renaissance. Th
rubble-filled rooms were christene
'grottoes' and the murals on the
walls inspired the Renaissance artis
to paint their 'grotesques'. This is th
origin of our modern expressio
'grotesque'

Sinister, endless passages. The vast ha
and corridors in the Golden Hou
which Nero built himself in Ron
covered ten times the area of the hu
Colosseum for 87,000 people whi
later arose on the site of his palace an
gardens. Emperor Trajan erect
public baths above some of Ner
buildings

The octagonal domed chamber in Ner
Golden House. Nero spent imme
sums on building suites of roo
banqueting and reception ha
magnificent baths, colonnades a
artificial lakes – all 'so that he co
at last live like a human bei

Hercules. Then he turned to equestrian sports. At first he was content to play with model horses on a table, but he soon began to visit the Rome races in secret. In the end, he announced quite openly that he was very keen to take part in races and augment the number of his prizes. He started by practising in his garden in front of slaves, and eventually appeared in the Circus Maximus as a charioteer.

The whole world was now familiar with Nero's weakness for prizes. All the Greek cities which held musical contests sent him victor's laurels for lyre-playing. 'Only the Greeks have a fine ear for music. They alone are worthy of my art,' declared Nero, and set off for Greece. He visited all the festivals. If they had already taken place, they were held all over again. Nobody was allowed to leave a theatre once Nero had started to sing, not even women in labour. Their children's first impression of the world was the Emperor's voice. Men who simply could not stand his singing any longer climbed out furtively over the walls. Others pretended to be dead and were carried from the theatre feet first. During the Neronia of A.D. 65 many people were crushed to death or succumbed to the heat and lack of air.

The imperial artiste was always very nervous and jumpy before a performance. He spoke to the judges and warned them to exclude the factor of chance. That done, he observed the rules with a punctiliousness which amounted almost to anxiety, but was only too happy to declare himself the winner when he was offered the laurel wreath. His way of obliterating the memory of earlier victors in the competitions was to have their busts and statues thrown into the latrines.

During a race at Olympia in Greece, Nero was thrown out of his chariot. He was picked up and installed in it again, but failed to complete the course. Needless to say, he was still awarded a prize. The Olympic Games, which had been held regularly for 800 years at four-yearly intervals, were postponed for two years until Nero could come to Greece. On his departure he rewarded the whole province of Achaia by exempting it from taxation. He marked the occasion by giving an address at Corinth, the verbatim text of which has fortunately survived in an inscription: 'My magnanimity, noble Greeks, always leaves room for the highest hopes, it is true, but I am granting you a boon which you would never have dreamed of. You are to receive freedom such as you never knew even in your happiest times, since you were for ever defeating one another. Other rulers have given cities their freedom. Only a Nero can give a whole country its freedom.'

Admittedly, this speech reflected Nero's inordinate self-conceit, and to any

Greek with a sensitive ear it must have sounded offensive. Moreover, it was all play-acting. But it was a first-class and even sincere piece of play-acting, for the truth was that Nero admired and revered everything Greek. He loved the Greeks and was convinced that their good taste, their festivals, their theatre, their arts and their artistic appreciation had never been rivalled by any other people in the world. The Emperor set the seal on this doubtless quite genuine conviction by granting the Greeks their freedom, which secured him their lasting affection. Indeed, after his death the Greeks saw Nero in a transfigured light as their saviour and benefactor, and considered him worthy of divine worship. During the trials and tribulations of their later history they looked for his return, unwilling to believe that their Grecophile emperor could really be dead. Nero, who strove for immortality and eternal renown throughout his life, at least found posthumous fulfilment of his dream in Greece.

The Emperor firmly believed in his mission as an artist, actor, poet and singer, and the most modern researchers (M. P. Charlesworth, for instance) are beginning to regard Suetonius' evidence of his great ability in these fields as entirely credible. Suetonius and Tacitus both showed in their writings that they were far from being admirers of this unique emperor in other respects, so a few favourable remarks on their part surely deserve to be taken at face value.

Nero re-entered Rome in Augustus' triumphal chariot, dressed in a purple robe and a Greek cloak embroidered with golden stars, the Olympic victor's wreath on his head and a second, the Pythian, in his hand. He now slept with his precious wreaths of victory arranged about his bed. To avoid 'wasting' his voice, he ceased to communicate with his troops except in writing. He was constantly accompanied by a voice-trainer whose job it was to remind him to spare his lungs or carry a handkerchief before his mouth.

Nero took to slinking out of his palace in disguise after dusk had fallen. He frequented disreputable taverns, beat people up as they walked home through the streets, and threw them into privies, or broke into shops and robbed them, later auctioning off the loot at his house. Once, when he made an indecent assault on a senator's wife, he was nearly beaten to death. From that day onwards he never sallied forth unless followed at a distance by an escort of soldiers.

He spun out his meals from midday to midnight, now and then refreshing himself with warm baths or cold, according to the weather. Prostitutes and dancing-girls from all over the city served him at table. When he travelled down the Tiber to Ostia, brothels were set up for him at intervals along the banks.

Agrippina, Nero's mother, kept a sharp watch on her son's activities and frequently reprimanded him. Octavia was still his wife, of course, but he scarcely noticed her. His current mistress was an emancipated slave called Claudia Acte. When he spoke of ultimately marrying her, his mother made a scene. A person of noble birth could not contract a legal marriage with a former slave, so Nero put it about that Acte was of royal descent. Slave or not, she remained true to him until his death and was buried at his side.

While still on intimate terms with Acte, Nero began to court Poppaea Sabina, a woman of great beauty and intelligence. He sent her husband, who had abetted the affair from the outset, off to Lusitania (modern Portugal) as governor. But as Nero's attachment to his lovely and ambitious mistress grew deeper, and as Poppaea herself made greater efforts to take Octavia's place and force Nero to divorce her, so the relationship between mother and son became more and more strained, until, finally, there was a breach. Agrippina and Poppaea loathed each other. Only one of them could dominate Nero, and one of them had to go.

Nero decided to murder his mother. Poisoning her would have been too risky, since she kept her household under strict supervision and only ate at home. He therefore lured her aboard a ship and sank it. Agrippina succeeded in swimming ashore and at once informed her son that she was still alive, even though everyone knew that he would kill her. The Emperor summoned his two councillors of State, Burrus and Seneca. Burrus declined to give his Praetorians the fatal order. Seneca had always been an opponent of Agrippina. Together, Burrus and Seneca advised that the murder be entrusted to Anicetus, a former slave who had at one time been Nero's tutor. Agrippina's house was surrounded, her servants cut down and she herself killed. She died on March 20th, A.D. 59, at the age of fifty-four. As she saw the sword poised above her, she cried: 'Smite the body that brought Nero into the world!'

Nero had tried to strangle his young wife Octavia several times. He eventually divorced her on Poppaea's insistence, declaring that she was barren. Then he ordered her to be executed for conjugal infidelity. Every witness called during the judicial inquiry protested Octavia's innocence, save one: Nero arranged for his former tutor Anicetus to give evidence for the prosecution and declare that he had secretly deflowered her. Just twenty years old, Octavia had her veins opened. When the blood would not flow, they asphyxiated her in a steam-bath.

'THE IGNOMINY AND DISGRACE OF IT!'

Nothing was to be seen but fire after fire, and nothing to be heard but: 'Fire! Look, fire! Where? How? Who started it? Help!' There was frightful chaos everywhere. Everyone ran wildly to and fro. Children, women, young men and old, all sent up such a monstrous babble of shouts and screams that, what with the smoke and the clamour, it was impossible to hear or see a thing.

Dio Cassius, xxii, 16.

THERE was no point in having money, thought Nero, unless one spent it lavishly. Hence his admiration for Caligula, his uncle, who had squandered the immense fortune left him by Tiberius in such a short space of time.

Nero spent enormous sums on building-projects. The vestibule of the Golden House, his new imperial palace, was so vast that it easily accommodated a colossal statue of himself, some 115 feet high, The hall, which consisted of three pillared arcades, was over 1,600 yards long. It contained a lake surrounded by buildings intended to represent cities, grain-fields, vineyards, pastures, woods inhabited by animals tame and wild — and all this inside a single hall. The dining-rooms had fretted ceilings with sliding panels of ivory concealing pipes which sprinkled the guests with sweet-smelling water. There were also baths with salt and fresh water, a luxury hitherto unknown even in Rome. Nero's verdict on the completed building was: 'Now at last I can begin to live like a human being.' The *Domus Aurea* or Golden House was only discovered about 400 years ago, in 1500. Sixteenth-century Romans christened the huge rooms 'grottoes', and the murals in them, so different from the usual ecclesiastical paintings of those days, became 'grottesco' or 'as in the grottoes'. It is to Nero therefore that we originally owe our expression 'grotesque'.

Since Rome could not provide enough labourers to carry out all the Emperor's building schemes, he imported prisoners from all over the Empire and ordered that, in future, criminals should be sentenced to penal servitude wherever possible.

It was not long before the funds in the public exchequer were exhausted. Provision still had to be made for the army's pay and veterans' pensions, so Nero resorted to petty larceny. The estates of all persons who had neglected to mention the Emperor in their wills automatically went to the public treasury. Most government appointments had to be bought for hard cash. 'You know what I need,' Nero used to say. 'We must take care to leave no one with anything.' In the end he even laid hands on the dedicatory offerings in the temples and melted down silver images of the gods.

There came a day when Poppaea, whom he had now married, was forced to suffer the fate which she had so heartily wished on Octavia. Nero killed her by kicking her in the stomach when she was pregnant.

There was scarcely one of his relations, close or distant, whom Nero did not try to do away with. He compelled his tutor Seneca to take his own life. Seneca had long guessed that he would one day fall prey to the Emperor's blood-lust. He applied for leave of absence and offered the Emperor his whole estate, but Nero assured him that his worries were groundless and that he, Nero, would rather die than do him any harm. The Emperor sent his second councillor of State, Burrus, some medicine for a sore throat. Burrus dropped dead. As for Corbulo, Nero's ablest general, who had defended the whole eastern frontier of the Roman Empire from the Caucasus to the Euphrates, we can readily understand why he incurred the Emperor's jealousy and was obliged to commit suicide.

When a conspiracy against him was discovered, Nero's blood-thirsty tendencies reached insane proportions. The plotters appeared in court triply chained. Some of them confessed without more ado, but others proudly declared that the best service anyone could render Nero was to kill him. Both the condemned men and their children died by poisoning or starvation. The Emperor's homicidal mania knew no bounds, and Romans were now condemned to death on the slightest provocation. A man called Thrasea was ordered to commit suicide 'because he had an expression like a cross schoolmaster'. People who failed to carry out their own death-sentences were 'taken care of' by Nero's doctors, which meant, in the Emperor's vocabulary, that their veins were opened. It is even said that he took delight in giving people to a notorious Egyptian glutton who was used to eating anything, including raw meat, and letting him devour them alive. As Nero himself declared in proud and happy tones: 'No prince before me ever realized the extent of his power.'

Displeased by the ancient buildings and narrow, winding streets of Rome, Nero set fire to the city. Everybody knew that he was responsible, but even when householders caught his servants red-handed, setting fire to their homes with burning torches, they dared not lay a finger on them. The fire raged for seven days and six nights, and two-thirds of Rome were burnt to the ground. The inhabitants sought refuge in vaults, tombs and temples. Most of the city's places of interest were gutted, including numerous temples and large palaces. Nero watched the fire from the tower of the Palace of Maecenas on the Esquiline Hill. Overwhelmed by the beauty of the scene, he sang a ballad called *The Fall of Ilium* and remarked that at last he could really picture the burning of Troy. He made as much money as possible out of the catastrophe by taking on the job of clearing away rubble and corpses and forbidding anyone to touch the ruins of his own property. He then proceeded to impoverish the citizens by demanding 'voluntary' contributions to a relief fund.

Broad new streets were laid out and buildings were not allowed to exceed a certain height. Nero undertook to build arcades in front of apartment houses. The installation of water-mains was supervised to prevent anyone drawing off more than he really needed, and it became compulsory to keep fire-fighting apparatus in the forecourt of every house. But, although the city's appearance was somewhat improved, the Romans were discontented. They grumbled that the narrow alley-ways and tall houses had been cooler than the broad, unshaded streets, whose heat they found intolerable. They also suspected that Nero's sympathetic offers of reconstruction were only designed to camouflage the enormity of his act of pyromania. The dreadful rumour that he himself had set fire to the city spread from house to house like a virulent disease. To silence this dangerous gossip, Nero put the blame on the Christians. In this connection, Tacitus, who was born in northern Italy in A.D. 55, has given us some of the earliest non-Christian evidence about Jesus. The authenticity of the passage in question (*Annales* xv, 44) is acknowledged by philologists all over the world with the exception of Hochart and Drews. Its great value lies not only in its explicitness but in the fact that it comes from a Roman who regarded the Christians as a criminal sect. 'This name (Christians) comes from Christus, whom the procurator Pontius Pilatus condemned to death during the reign of Tiberius. But the abominable superstition, which had been suppressed for a while, soon became wide-spread once more, not only in Judaea, its place of origin, but also in Rome, where all the shocking and odious religious cults in the world forgather and find adherents.'

We so often hear the cry that there is no real historical evidence of Christ's existence. Well, that is exactly what this passage in Tacitus *is*. The historian goes on to relate that people who openly acknowledged themselves to be Christians were arrested. They were not explicitly accused of arson, it is true, but were charged with 'hatred for the human race'. Nero turned the persecution of the Christians into a festival. The faithful were sewn up in animal-skins and torn to pieces by dogs; nailed to the cross; or set on fire and turned into human torches. Tacitus gives us a subtle indication that, even at this stage, the Romans began to be stirred by sympathy for the Christians 'although they were guilty and had merited the harshest penalties'. But they were victims of one man's ferocity, victims of Nero, and no one really took any pleasure in their death except the Emperor, who opened his own gardens to the public for the Christian-burning display.

It is interesting to picture this man who ruled so autocratically on the brink of madness. Nero was of medium height. His skin was covered with blemishes and Suetonius expressly states that he suffered from body-odour. His auburn hair was dressed in ringlets like a woman's, which greatly scandalized everybody. His features were not unhandsome. He gazed out rather timidly, through very short-sighted grey-blue eyes, at a strange world which tolerated his every whim. He had a bull-neck and a protuberant belly, and his heavy torso was supported by a pair of extremely spindly legs. He was probably blessed with a very robust constitution, for in spite of his dissipations he was ill only three times during his fourteen years on the throne.

For fourteen years the world tolerated him. Then, on the eighth anniversary of his mother's murder, he received news of a rebellion in Gaul under the leadership of Julius Vindex. Nero greeted the information with peculiar impassivity, almost as though he had a premonition of his downfall and death and felt he could not avert it. However, when he learned that the whole of Spain had joined the revolt, he fainted dead away. On regaining consciousness he rent his clothes and beat his brow, crying: 'It's all up with me!' His old nurse pointed out that other rulers had been in similar straits, but Nero replied: 'Never! Never has there been a misfortune like mine. I am losing my throne during my lifetime!' And taking his two most precious crystal goblets he dashed them to the floor.

The Emperor now planned to poison the whole Senate, murder all his military commanders and put Rome to the torch once more, turning wild animals loose on the population to hinder any attempt at fire-fighting.

Then he relapsed into moody apathy. He declared that if he lost his throne he would live by his art. He would betake himself to Alexandria, where people had some artistic appreciation, and become a humble singer and lyre-player. ... But soon that plan, too, was discarded. Nero announced his intention of going out to meet the rebel army alone and regaining their loyalty with his heart-rending tears. Next day, he said, he would be chanting paeans of victory. He at once started to compose lyrics for these songs.

But his remaining armies deserted him. Nero tore the gloomy dispatches into little pieces. He ordered Locusta to brew him a poison, but could not summon up the courage to take it. He now proposed to appear before the people dressed in mourning and beg their forgiveness for all he had done. The completed draft of a speech on these lines was discovered after his death.

One night, towards midnight, he suddenly started out of his sleep. His body-guards had abandoned him. He called for his court officials, but no one answered. There was no one there. All the doors were closed. The servants had even stolen his bed-linen and his box of poison. The Emperor looked around for Spiculus, a famous gladiator, to give him the *coup de grâce*. But there was no one, absolutely no one there. 'Have I neither a friend nor a foe, then?' he shouted, and rushed out of the palace intending to throw himself into the Tiber.

Then he changed his mind. His freedman Phaon offered him refuge at his country house. Nero jumped on to his horse and galloped through the night, his face covered with a handkerchief. There was a peal of thunder, an earth-tremor and the sound of soldiers shouting. His horse shied at a putrefying corpse by the roadside and the handkerchief fell from his face. A Praetorian guardsman recognized him but let him pass. Arriving at Phaon's house, Nero threw himself on to a bed, whimpering.

His friends advised him to avoid dishonourable treatment by taking his life. Nero ordered them to dig a grave to his measurements, so that his body might be accorded a decent burial without delay. While they did so, he wept and cried out repeatedly: 'See, what a great artist is dying!' On hearing that the Senate had decreed that he should be flogged to death with rods, he picked up two daggers, intending to kill himself—and put them down again. 'The ignominy and disgrace of it all!' he exclaimed. 'This won't do for Nero. No, it won't do at all.' Then, seeing horsemen galloping up to take him prisoner, he stabbed himself in the throat with the help of one Epaphroditus. The cavalryman who had been detailed to kill Nero now pretended that he had come to rescue him. 'What loyalty!' gasped the dying Emperor. It was the last mistake he ever made.

Nero died at the age of thirty-two, on the sixth anniversary of his wife Octavia's murder. There was jubilation in Rome and throughout the Empire. And yet there were some who decked his grave with spring and summer flowers for a long time afterwards. Suetonius writes: 'Twenty years later an unknown man appeared among the Parthians claiming that he was Nero. I was only a young man at the time. But Nero's name was still held in such esteem, even at that date, that the Parthians revered the mysterious individual for a long time and only handed him over to the Romans with the utmost reluctance.'

That was how long he took to die, this man who kindled and rekindled the imagination of far-off races; who offered people of many lands not serious policies but entertainment, sport, art and theatricals; who conquered the world's inhabitants not with logic but with startling and sensational pleasures – and all without their recognizing the perilous madness which lay beneath his actor's mask.

PETRONIUS

THE FEAST OF TRIMALCHIO

'Here lies Gaius Pompeius Trimalchio Maecenatianus. He was upright, staunch, true. He started with nothing and left a fortune worth thirty million sesterces. He never followed any particular philosopher. Farewell, you that read this.' That was how the self-made freedman Trimalchio pictured the inscription on his tomb while in his cups.

Petronius, Satyricon.

AMONG Nero's many victims was Petronius, of whom Tacitus tells us in the *Annales* (xvi, 18). He was a strange person who slept during the day and pursued his pleasures by night, achieving an unparalleled mastery in the arts of hedonism and idleness. A man who insisted on calling a spade a spade, he was regarded by his contemporaries as agreeably frank and unaffected. He had a mordant wit and a strong sense of humour, but he also showed, as proconsul of Bithynia and subsequently as consul, that under certain circumstances he could become an energetic and skilful political administrator.

Nero appointed Petronius his *arbiter elegantiae*, the celebrated Latin expression meaning, roughly, Minister of Pleasure or master of ceremonies. His job as a sort of judge in matters of taste won Petronius the surname 'Arbiter'. Whatever Petronius Arbiter recommended, Nero was certain to find pleasing and acceptable. Petronius probably succeeded in lending the thoroughly debased standards of entertainment at court some fresh refinement and splendour. But, since his manners, his connoisseur's knowledge of genuinely worth-while things and his self-assured good taste put him head and shoulders above all the other men in Nero's entourage, it was only natural that he soon made enemies. Tigellinus, one of Nero's favourites, became jealous of him. He bribed a slave to make perjurious allegations against him which led to the arrest of the century's most elegant man at Cumae in A.D. 66.

To escape execution, Petronius opened his veins. True to his lifelong pursuit of pleasure, he arranged for someone to read cheerful poems and light verse to him while he was dying, applied tourniquets from time to time to prevent his life ebbing away too quickly, chatted with his friends, and rewarded his slaves or had them flogged, whichever they merited. He completed a list of Nero's vices, sent it off to his lord and master as a final dig, and died at the dining-table as though death had come naturally and not as a violent form of punishment.

If this Petronius and the author of the *Satirae* are identical — which is now a fairly unanimous assumption — the dead man was one of the most impudent rascals in the history of literature. His treatise on etiquette probably comprised twenty volumes. Although only fragments of the fifteenth and sixteenth books have survived, they are a veritable thesaurus of contemporary slang and shed light on the lowest stratum of Roman society, its manners, good and bad, its amusements and dissipations. The *Cena Trimalchionis* or *Feast of Trimalchio* gives us a taste of how a self-made man used to amuse and entertain his guests in those early days. There is almost nothing in the whole of classical literature, apart from the mural inscriptions at Pompeii, which gives us a more direct and vivid impression of the Roman *nouveau riche* and the Roman in reduced circumstances. 'Do you know who's got something on at his place today? Trimalchio, a very elegant gentleman. He's got a clock in his dining-room and a trumpeter who blows the hours, so that he always knows how much of his life is behind him.'

A bald-headed old man in slippers and a red tunica, Trimalchio is discovered playing hand-ball with some curly-haired boys. The evening begins with a steam-bath followed by a cold plunge. Trimalchio is anointed with perfumed waters and then dried — not with linen towels but with the softest wool — wrapped up in scarlet rugs, and carried home in a litter. A musician playing a small flute accompanies him all the way. On the door of his mansion is a sign-board bearing the legend: 'Any slave who leaves the house without his master's permission will get a hundred lashes.'

Before the start of the meal Alexandrian slaves pour snow-cooled water over the guests' hands, while other slaves give them a pedicure. They sing as they work, for, like all the servants, they are trained in choral or solo singing.

A Roman feast consisted of at least seven courses, including hors d'œuvres, two entrées, two meat courses and a sweet. At Trimalchio's a third meat course is added.

The first of the hors d'œuvres is a donkey of Corinthian bronze carrying panniers, one filled with green and the other with black olives. The donkey also carries silver bowls with small plates brazed on to them containing roast dormice steeped in honey and sprinkled with poppy-seeds. There are damsons and pomegranates, too, and sausages smoking on a silver grill. Trimalchio, ensconced on a pile of small cushions, is carried in to the strains of music. Then comes the first entrée, a wooden hen with outspread wings and under it some peahen's eggs bedded in straw. But in the eggs — a little surprise for the guests — are plump beccaficos in peppered egg-yolk. The dishes are borne away by a chanting choir. Jugs of vintage Falernian wine 100 years old are served. Trimalchio claps his hands and intelligently observes that wine lives longer than men. A second entrée is placed on an enormous centre-piece, a circular disk ornamented with the signs of the zodiac, and on it twelve bowls of food appropriate to the various signs. Then comes the first of the three meat courses: a gigantic wild boar. As it is carved, live thrushes fly out and flutter round the room, to be caught by bird-catchers equipped with poles smeared in lime. One privileged boy hands round grapes, singing poems composed by his master. When a guest begins to tell a story about a rich man and a poor man who were enemies, Trimalchio interrupts him with the question: 'What does "poor" mean?'

At the bidding of a jester, a boy dances in time to music on the rungs of a ladder, jumps through burning hoops and balances a jug in his teeth. The host declares that he gets more fun out of jugglers and trumpeters than anything in the world, and that nothing else matters. He says that he has also provided some actors, but he would sooner let them play the fool. Meanwhile, the boy — a slave, like all entertainers — falls from the ladder, and Trimalchio groans as though injured. He at once grants the youth his freedom in case anyone should say that a great man like Trimalchio was hurt by a mere slave.

'Everyone can have a cock, a dish of white chicken-meat and other trifles,' the millionaire announces condescendingly. 'My chefs are used to cooking whole calves in cauldrons.' When, shortly afterwards, a roast pig is brought in, the host finds that it has not been gutted. The chef is summoned. He confesses that he has forgotten to gut the animal. 'Clothes off!' orders Trimalchio. 'He shall be thrashed on the spot.' Then he countermands the order. 'Gut the pig in front of us,' he bids the chef. Donning his clothes again, the man takes his knife and makes some incisions in the pig's belly — and out pours a cascade of roast sausages and black puddings. This jape is loudly applauded by the other servants. A toast is drunk to the chef and he is crowned with a silver wreath. The third meat course consists of a stewed calf.

To emphasize Trimalchio's wealth, his secretary reads out a list of facts. In a single day, thirty boys and forty girls were born on his master's country estate at Cumae, ten million sesterces were paid into his account, a slave was crucified for having made fun of him and fire broke out in Trimalchio's gardens at Pompeii. 'Let's see, when was the park at Pompeii bought for me?' inquires our Roman profiteer.

Panels in the ceiling slide apart and a huge ring descends. On it hang golden wreaths and flasks of scented ointment, presents for the guests. They begin to crack smutty jokes. Fortunata, Trimalchio's wife, behaves rather badly, and the womenfolk get tipsy. A slave, pouring out wine and water, gives an imitation of a nightingale. 'Something else!' bellows our bald-headed Croesus. 'Something else, go on, something else!' Before long, the slaves of Trimalchio, a former slave himself, are allowed to join in the drinking. Their master announces that anyone who doesn't want a drink will have it poured over his head. Two boys enter carrying large jars. They pretend to quarrel and start scuffling. As they do so, oysters and mussels fall out of the jars and are collected in a bowl by another boy, who hands them round. Novelties like this go down well with the guests.

Trimalchio becomes maudlin. He asks for his will to be brought in and reads it aloud to the sound of his servants' lamentations. Then he describes what his tombstone will look like. Guests weep and slaves sob. 'We know we must die one day,' says Trimalchio. 'Why shouldn't we enjoy life? As true as I have your welfare at heart, let's take a bath. It's like an oven in here.'

Later in the feast — and by this time tipsy as a fiddler — Trimalchio shows the guests his funeral toga trimmed with purple. 'I hope it will become me as a corpse as well as it became me in my lifetime,' he says. 'Try and imagine you have been invited to my funeral.' To trumpeters who enter the room, he adds: 'Pretend I'm dead, and play something nice.' One of the slave musicians blows his instrument so lustily that he rouses the neighbourhood. Thinking that Trimalchio's house is on fire, night-watchmen come rushing up with water-buckets and axes and break the door down. 'We seized this favourable opportunity,' the narrator tells us, 'and took to our heels as though we really were escaping from a fire.'

Just as the narrator of the 'ludicrous feast' poked fun at himself and his surroundings, just as he unleashed his amazing powers of observation on all that he despised and brilliantly described it, just as the newly emancipated slave-boy, a nervous guest at Trimalchio's table and in his bath, was forced to celebrate with his fat and stupid host whether he liked it or not, so it was, probably, with Petronius at Nero's court. Setting the fashion with a smile, this brilliant Cervantes of the ancient world played the part of an elegant fool and accepted the crumbs from his stage-struck master's table for as long as fate permitted. But no one, either before or after him, ever captured the vices of a decadent metropolis and held them up as a mirror before the face of posterity with such covert amusement or resigned candour.

SENECA

WHAT IS MAN?

A weak and fragile body, naked, defenceless by nature, dependent on the help of others, susceptible to all the iniquities of fate, apprehensive about his food, over-abundance or lack of which both spell his destruction.

Seneca.

BEFORE dismissing the dark days of Nero, let us take a rather closer look at Nero's contemporary, Seneca. It is a quirk of history that Seneca, of all people, who was one of the greatest educationalists in the field of Western culture, should have been Nero's tutor. The Nero–Seneca combination proves that character is always stronger than upbringing and that a teacher can only mould and develop his pupil's natural inclinations, never fundamentally change them. Parents take note!

Seneca was without doubt the most brilliant thinker of his century and, where humanity, virtue and wisdom were concerned, one of the greatest pioneers of all time. Strangely enough, Seneca's arrival in the world at Cordoba in southern Spain almost coincided with the Christian Saviour's birth at Bethlehem. It was in the shadow of Christ's presence that Seneca wrote the following lines: 'Divinity is near you. It is at your side. It is within you. There dwells in us a holy spirit, the observer and guardian of all that is good and evil in us. He treats us as we have treated him. No one is a good man without God.' (Seneca, *Letters to Lucilius.*)

Was he ever granted the grace to know of Christ, or did his pagan mind evolve all these ideas spontaneously?

While Gallio, Seneca's brother, was governor of Greece, St Paul arrived in Corinth to preach the Gospel. He was so remarkably successful that the Jewish community there tried to get his teachings banned. In the year A.D. 52 Gallio decided the issue between the Jews and St Paul in the latter's favour. It is quite possible that Seneca read of these events in Gallio's letters, for he was on good terms with his brother and dedicated several of his works to him. But, apart from that, Seneca must have been aware that there were Christians in Rome. The whole world knew how Nero had blamed them for the great fire. Since Seneca's views were so closely related to the concepts of Christianity, an idea subsequently grew up that Seneca was a Christian and had corresponded with St Paul. St Jerome believed in the authenticity of the letters which have survived, but today they are regarded as forgeries. Seneca spent a long time in Egypt, where his uncle was governor. There, too, he must have heard something of the Christian point of view, since a fierce controversy was raging between the Jewish and Christian communities in Egypt at the time.

Seneca's father was a Roman knight. He was also an orator and the author of several works on history and rhetoric. It was not long before he brought his young son Lucius Annaeus to Rome and sent him to study under Sotion and Attalus the Stoic. Seneca himself said of his tutors: 'Whenever I listened to Attalus inveighing against the vices, fallacies and errors of this life, I pitied humanity and saw Attalus reigning high above all other mortals. I am not ashamed to confess the deep love for Pythagoras which Sotion inspired in me.' Seneca was, incidentally, a dramatic poet of considerable repute. His tragedies, among them the *Medea*, *Phaedra* and *Oedipus*, all left their mark on world literature.

Under Emperor Caligula, Seneca became quaestor. He gave such impressive judicial addresses that the young Emperor grew jealous of him. He even made plans to have him killed, but was murdered before he could carry them out. In the year A.D. 41 Emperor Claudius banished Seneca to Corsica. Seneca owed his eight years on that rugged island to Messalina's hatred. There is something both touching and sublime about the way in which Seneca, far from home, comforted his mother Helvia. His words could serve as consolation to any mother waiting for her son to return from far away. 'Let us traverse every land. There is no place in the whole world which does not belong to man. Eyes turn towards heaven everywhere in the same way; the same space divides all that is divine from all that is human. Well, then. What does it matter where I am, as long as my eyes are not deprived of the scene at which they can never gaze their fill; as long as I am permitted to look at the sun and moon, to capture the other stars with my glance, to study their rising and setting, their intervals, and the reasons for their faster or slower progress; as long as I am with them and in communication, as far as man is allowed to be, with the heavens; as long as my soul, which strives for a glimpse of congenial things, can always spend its time in higher spheres — what does it matter?'

Seneca was not recalled to Rome until after Messalina's death. Agrippina, Claudius' second wife, secured him a senior government post at Rome and appointed him her son Nero's tutor.

Seneca did his utmost to keep his pupil on the straight and narrow path.

Lucius Annaeus Seneca was born at Cordoba in the year 4 B.C. He was tutor to Nero who ordered him to commit suicide in A.D. 65. This remarkably lifelike bronze bust was found in the Villa dei Papyri at Herculaneum, but it is highly doubtful whether it actually portrays Seneca himself

Servius Sulpicius Galba was proclaimed emperor by the Spanish legions in A.D. 68. A bent old miser of seventy-three, he did all he could to make himself unpopular. Being a sufferer himself (he was afflicted with gout) he did not mind if other people suffered too

Otho (A.D. 32–69) was as vain as a peacock and always wore a wig. He was so extravagant as a young man that he said, with justification: 'My last hope lies in becoming Emperor.' His end: suicide

Aulus Vitellius (A.D. 15–69) was a clumsy giant of a man with a limp. His face was puce with wine-drinking and his body bloated by debauchery. Even taking Galba and Otho into account, Vitellius was the prize failure of the year A.D. 69. (Ancient sculpture in the Capitoline Museum)

Young Nero often saw him as a mere kill-joy who wanted to clip the wings of his imagination. But when he came to the throne he found he needed advisers. In Seneca and Burrus we are confronted by the unusual picture of two men who shared a single position of authority yet remained friends. Together they held the reins of world power, Burrus the Praetorian prefect and Seneca the shrewd but kindly orator. 'The blood-letting would have continued ...' writes Tacitus, but Burrus and Seneca opposed it. When Burrus died (obviously one of Nero's victims), Seneca's position also began to deteriorate. '*Mors Burri infregit Senecae potentiam*,' we read in Tacitus (*Annales* xiv, 52).

In the end, Nero's murderous and all-embracing grasp fastened itself upon his old tutor. As Seneca himself admitted: 'Who was ever unaware of Nero's cruelty? Having murdered his mother and his brothers and sisters, what was there left for him to do but murder his teacher and tutor?'

The man who received his orders to die was probably better prepared for death than any mortal before or since. In the whole course of human history, rich as it is in murder and injustice, only one other philosopher went to his death with such utter serenity, with the aura of immortality shining so brightly about him: Socrates the wise. It is no mere accident that Socrates the Greek was the spiritual father of Seneca the Roman. One cannot describe Seneca. To appreciate what a really full life means and how it is possible to lay down that life with complete peace of mind, one must hear him.

Long before Seneca guessed that the Emperor would one day force him to commit suicide, he had recognized the brevity of human existence, the value of each passing day and the danger of letting time slip by unheeded and unfulfilled. 'I have looked on each day as my last,' he wrote to Lucilius. There is quite an alarming note in some of Seneca's admonitions, and his essay *On the Brevity of Life* should be compulsory reading for everyone every ten years. 'You live as though you will live for ever. It never occurs to you how poorly provided you are. You squander time as though you had it in plenty, although the very day you devote to someone or something may be your last. You fear everything like creatures that must die, yet hanker after everything as though you could live for ever. ... Just as travellers are beguiled by a conversation or a book until they suddenly notice to their astonishment that they have arrived, so busy men never notice their uninterrupted and remarkably swift journey through life until they have reached their destination. ... Time runs out inaudibly, intangibly, noiselessly, unrecognized and unfamiliar. Yet it is the most precious commodity and the only real treasure we possess. Your lifetime,' Seneca says, 'will make no sound. It will not remind you of its haste. Silently it will flow away. ... There is no more difficult art than that of living. But you must learn how to live while you live.'

How should we use our time? How should we make sure that it is not wasted? Seneca gives us a clear answer. 'Man is a being endowed with reason. This advantage attains perfection when he fulfils what he was born for. What does reason demand of him? The simplest thing in the world: to live in accordance with his nature. ... Be safe: constantly remind yourself what a fine thing it is, having perfected your life before you die, to live out the rest of your time quietly, the possessor of a happy life. ... We tear life into little pieces and dismember it. ... I wish you possession of yourself, so that your soul, driven this way and that by restless thoughts, finds a firm foothold at last and stands secure, so that it finds favour with itself and, because it has recognized the true blessings in our possession, heeds no increase of years.' Seneca advises us to ask ourselves every evening what we have done better during the day than ever before, and in what respects we must make more progress.

Seneca had clearly recognized that there is only one worth-while thing in a man's life, namely what he *is*: his own faculties, his own ability to think, his own character. These are immediate values, values which accompany him everywhere and at all times. What he *has*, on the other hand, is much less important. 'Never consider him unfortunate who is dependent upon externals. The man who takes pleasure in things that come from outside has built upon fragile foundations. Each joy that comes from there will return there. But that which springs from within oneself is steadfast and true, grows, and stays with us to the end. The other things which arouse such great admiration are only fruitful and pleasant when the possessor of them is also in possession of himself. ... Mightier than the whole of destiny is the soul. ... It is a mistake to model our lives on those of others and to do something only because many others show us how. To belong to oneself is a blessing beyond price.'

Seneca knew that the only happy person is one who can follow his natural bents. He also knew that that is just what one should and must do, and that only these inner predispositions have any value. He had, in general, an amazingly deep insight into the secret of 'the happy life'. 'I deny that wealth is a good thing. For, if it were, it would make men good.'

On the other hand, Seneca was not so simple as to be unaware that money or prosperity is a useful attribute, provided its importance is not over-estimated. 'For the rest, I acknowledge that it is allowable to possess wealth, that it is useful and brings life many advantages. ... Can there be any doubt that a wise man has a greater opportunity to develop what is within him in wealth than in poverty? ... Stop forbidding philosophers to possess money, therefore. No one has yet condemned wisdom to poverty.'

But man must not be the servant of what he owns: what he owns must serve him. 'Among the wise, wealth remains subservient; among fools it gains the upper hand. The wise man makes no concession to wealth; but *you* become used to it and depend on it as though someone had promised you everlasting possession of it.'

It is amazing what a modern, up-to-date ring there is about every word this spiritual giant wrote, nineteen hundred years ago. He grasped at every aspect of life, laying its meaning bare and tearing away the veils obscuring it until he reached the ultimate mysteries of the world to come. In this, he was always indifferent to popular opinion. 'Things are not so well with mankind that the majority always prefers what is best. A large proportion always supports what is worst. In voting, one and the same thing is approved or condemned: that is the outcome of every decision made on a majority basis.' Anyone suffering from 'managerial disease', lack of leisure or pressure of work, should take time off to read Seneca's essays *On Peace of Mind* and *On the Brevity of Life*. 'Busy men have no time to review the past, and, even when they do, the memory of regrettable things pains them. Thus they are averse to thinking back on time misspent, and dare not hold their mistakes up before the light. ... Anyone who ambitiously craves for much, arrogantly despises much, obtains much by force, extorts much by trickery, avariciously acquires much and wastefully squanders much, must necessarily fear his memory. The reward of a man with a carefree and tranquil mind is an ability to review every part of his lifetime. The soul of the busy man cannot look back. His life has vanished into the abyss.'

From *On Peace of Mind:* 'Thus each man eternally flees from himself. But what good is it, if he cannot escape himself? He is his own escort and most burdensome of companions. ... Hence restless journeys are made and sea-coasts traversed. Vacillation, ever hostile to the present, tries first the sea, then the land. ... Many an old man well advanced in years can produce no evidence of his having lived long other than his tale of years. ... But do not believe that someone has lived a long time because of his grey hairs and wrinkles. He has not lived a long time, only existed a long time. ... Living happily and living naturally are two ways of saying the same thing.

'We live naturally when we watch our physical proclivities and the requirements of our nature carefully but not fearfully, as if they were something fleeting and only bestowed on us temporarily. ... Virtue is to be found everywhere, in the temple, in the forum, in the assembly, standing before the walls, covered in dust, fresh-faced, with calloused hands; but sensual pleasure is to be found hiding in corners and seeking darkness, in bath-houses, sweat-rooms, and places feared by the police, feeble, enervated, sodden with wine and scented oils, pale, rouged, painted with cosmetics. But the true mind never changes, nor is it ever repugnant to itself, and, since it is the best, it never changes anything within itself. The greatest blessing is harmony with oneself ... insight and discernment, health, freedom and beauty of the soul. Why speak you of pleasure? I see the happiness of man, not of the belly — which is more capacious in cattle and animals. ... Therefore learn how to enjoy yourself, but know that true joy is a serious matter.

'What a splendid thing a good conscience is!' Seneca exclaims. 'Men spend the greater part of their life doing evil, a large part of their life doing nothing, and the whole of their life doing anything other than that which they really should. ... All that part of our lifetime which lies behind us holds death in its hands. Place all your hours side by side: you will be less dependent on the morrow if you make the most of today. The more you postpone life, the faster it hurries by. ... The man who is everywhere gets nowhere. You must spend time with certain individual minds and draw sustenance from them if you wish to derive anything from them.'

Not even Nero could alarm a man who had attained such heights of knowledge. Of course, Seneca did not heedlessly throw his life away. When he realized that people who bore him a grudge were blackening him in the Emperor's eyes, he requested an audience. He thanked the Emperor with the utmost courtesy for all the favours he had received, declaring that he had been blessed with too much good fortune and that humility and moderation would be the losers. He begged Nero for aid 'because I can no longer sustain my wealth. Allow my resources to be merged with your own'. He wanted to lay everything at his former pupil's feet and end his days in peace.

Nero declined: 'It is you who hold me back when, in my youthful inexperience, I stray from the path and stumble. It is you who direct my energies for the best and take such good care of me. If you give me back your property, talk of my covetousness and your fear of my cruelty will be on every tongue.' So saying, Nero embraced Seneca and kissed him. Seneca expressed his thanks — 'which', as Tacitus remarks, 'is how conversations with a ruler usually end.'

After this interview, Seneca lived a very retiring life and was rarely seen in Rome. In A.D. 65 destiny caught up with him. The Emperor charged him with complicity in the Pisonian conspiracy, and eventually sent the tribune Silvanus to order him to commit suicide. With absolute composure, Seneca asked for permission to make his will, but was prevented from setting down his last wishes. Noticing that his friends were weeping, he asked: 'Where is that self-command in the face of adversity for which we have been girding ourselves all these years?' He embraced his wife Paulina, who announced her intention of dying with him. (She slashed her veins, but was later saved.)

Seneca died slowly. He severed his arteries with a single stroke, but the blood oozed reluctantly from his old and meagre frame. He tore open the veins in his legs and at the back of his knees, trying to disguise his frightful agony. Even at that late stage, he dictated a longish speech to his amanuensis. When death still refused to come, he asked his doctor Annaeus to give him some poison. The poison, too, failed to act. Finally, Seneca climbed into a hot bath. He sprinkled his favourite slave with water, declaring that he was offering a libation to Jupiter the Deliverer. Then he had himself carried into the steam-room, where he eventually died of asphyxiation.

'No one takes care to live wisely. Everyone worries about living long. But anyone can live a wise life, while no one can rely on a long one. He has comprehended wisdom who dies as free from care as he was born.'

GALBA

THE OLD MISER

It is universally acknowledged that Sulpicius Galba was the wealthiest man ever to enter the house of the Caesars.

Plutarch, Galba, 3.

NERO's death marked the end of Julius Caesar's line. Nero had no heirs. His successor, Galba, was unrelated either by birth or adoption to the man who set fire to Rome. Not a drop of the first six emperors' blood flowed in the veins of the seventh.

Galba was born on December 24th, 5 B.C. He came of a very aristocratic family, and called himself 'descendant of Quintus Capitulus Capitolinus', tracing his ancestry back to the god Jupiter and to Pasiphaë, the wife of Minos. More important to his status than these legendary forebears, however, was his distant relationship with Livia, the wife of Augustus. It was uncertain, even during the lifetime of this Emperor, what the name 'Galba' meant. *Galbanum* is the resinous gum from a Syrian plant. *Galbeum* was a woollen sling containing medicaments which Galba wore because of some ailment or other. *Galba* was the Gallic expression for fat, and *galbae* were silkworm grubs. Galba's grandfather was a historian who wrote a history of Rome from its foundation to his own day. Galba's father, a small misshapen man, was a very hard-working but not unduly talented lawyer. When Livia Ocellina, a rich and outstandingly beautiful woman, declared her intention of marrying him for his noble birth, he showed her his physical deformities. She was quite undeterred.

The man who later became Emperor Servius Galba was not, however, a son of Livia Ocellina, who was his father's second wife, but of his first wife, Mummia Achaica. When astrologers prophesied to Tiberius that young Galba would come to the throne late in life, the gloomy old misanthrope said: 'He can stay alive, then: he won't ever bother me.'

As a young man, Galba lived like any other rich and pampered nobleman. He spent his summers on a fine estate at Tusculum, a sort of Roman suburb where well-to-do families had their villas. (Ruins of this place were found near Frascati, fifteen miles from Rome.) Young Galba insisted on feudal deference from his inferiors. His freedmen and slaves were obliged to parade before him twice a day, in accordance with ancient Roman custom. Men and women alike had to wish him good morning and good night at the beginning and end of each day. He received instruction in the principal branches of contemporary education, and also studied jurisprudence. He married once, but after the death of his wife Lepida steadfastly remained single — not, it may be said, because he had been particularly devoted to Lepida, but because his personal preference was for himself and stalwart young men. Agrippina, Nero's widowed mother, had at one time taken an interest in him, but he was astute enough to avoid her.

Galba became praetor at an early age. The Floralia, or games in honour of the plant-goddess Flora, were held each year in May. Praetor Galba made Circus history at one of these festivals by exhibiting rope-dancing elephants, to the delight of Rome. Consul, governor of the province of Aquitania in south-west France, legate of Upper Germania and successful commander in action against the Germans — those were the high-lights of a career which culminated in Galba's accession to the throne as an elderly man of seventy-three.

Caligula murdered! The news travelled through the Empire like wildfire. People tried to talk Galba into letting himself be proclaimed Emperor, but he prudently refrained, thereby winning himself the undying affection of Claudius, Caligula's successor.

Galba's next appointment was the governorship of Africa. The troops had been afraid of him during his time in France, and in Africa he fully maintained his reputation as a martinet. Acting on the principle that the only way to toughen soldiers, whether veterans or recruits, was to keep them permanently on active service, he rejected all applications for leave. When one of his soldiers sold a bushel of his grain ration for about £8, Galba ordered that if food ran short he should receive no rations at all. The man starved to death.

Galba finished his term in Africa loaded with honours and triumphal regalia.

Nero was now Emperor. Galba became increasingly cautious. He lived in complete retirement. Whenever he went on a trip he was followed by a second carriage. This mysterious vehicle contained a million sesterces in gold, roughly £17,000, designed to cover any contingency from greasing palms to financing a quick get-away.

Galba was eventually given the governorship of Hispania Tarraconensis, a province which included territory in the north and east of the Iberian Peninsula. It was there, while he was sacrificing to the gods in a temple, that a miracle occurred. The hair of the boy holding the censer suddenly turned snow-white. This was interpreted as a sign that an old man would succeed a young man as Emperor — *i.e.* that Galba would succeed Nero. But it took some time to happen. Galba administered his Spanish province for eight years. Once again he was an object of fear. Discipline became tighter wherever he went. The local inhabitants were delighted, because former procurators had plundered the country to their hearts' content. Galba was energetic, strict — even cruel. He chopped off a fraudulent money-lender's hands and had them nailed to his counter. A guardian who had poisoned his ward was sentenced to crucifixion. He claimed his right of appeal to the Emperor. Being a Roman citizen, he could apply to Nero in person. Galba at once 'commuted' his sentence by erecting a considerably higher cross and having it nicely whitewashed. Otherwise the penalty remained the same.

In the end, however, Galba became perturbed by his own severity. Rather than do anything to offend Emperor Nero, he became indifferent and adopted a policy of laissez-faire. 'No one can be prosecuted for doing nothing,' he told himself. But two things occurred to change the mind of the man whose one desire was to be left in peace. First, Galba intercepted a letter in which he read that Nero had issued a general order to the procurators to kill him; and, second, someone reminded him of an ancient prophecy which stated that 'the master of the world' would come from Spain. Like Charles V and Philip II after him, Galba took this prediction to apply to himself. He declared a state of war, recruited fresh legions and posted reliable sentries outside his sleeping-quarters.

Galba was very nearly killed before he reached the highest rung of the ladder which he had climbed so painstakingly. While walking down a narrow lane to the baths, he heard someone exclaim: 'Are we going to miss this fine opportunity?' 'What fine opportunity?' thought Galba. He arrested two slaves, who confessed on the rack that Nero had hired them to assassinate him.

Then the incredible news arrived from Rome. Nero was dead. Galba learned that he had been accorded the oath of allegiance. The name *Caesar* had now become a title reserved for the possessor of supreme power. Galba assumed that title in the warm June of A.D. 68.

The new Emperor was preceded by a bad reputation. Seventy-three years old, completely hunch-backed and bald, Galba did just about all he could to make himself unpopular. He was afflicted with gout, and being a sufferer himself he did not worry if others suffered, too. Whenever his crooked nose showed itself at the dining-table his head steward knew what to expect. Galba would carp at the amount of food being served and quietly tot up what it was going to cost him. He was a miser. While his watery blue eyes stared vacantly at the first theatrical performance he attended as Emperor, the actors sang: 'Here comes the skinflint from his farm', and the audience joined in. The Emperor's shoes pinched him in the truest sense, for his limbs were so racked with gout that even the lightest sandals made him wince. He could not hold a scroll, either, since it was agony for him to open and close his fingers. Three men followed him everywhere like shadows: Titus Vinius, Cornelius Laco and the freedman Icelus. Vinius, who was known to have filched a silver bowl from Emperor Claudius' table when invited to dinner, was rapacity personified; Laco was the walking embodiment of idleness; and Icelus was vice incarnate. Bereft of all will-power, the gouty old man 'reigned' in the shadow of these three ne'er-do-wells. On occasions when his gout was particularly painful he became indescribably harsh and avaricious, and the merest breath of suspicion would suffice to send someone to the executioner without a hearing.

Enlisting the help of a committee of fifty prominent Romans, the old miser annulled all the bequests made by Nero. He protected notorious criminals like the eunuch Halotus and the former Praetorian prefect Tigellinus, who had both been henchmen of Nero, even though the people repeatedly demanded the death of Tigellinus on the grounds that he had been one of the chief offenders during the Neronian regime.

Finally, there was Galba's behaviour towards his troops, which was fraught with danger. He treated them all, soldiers and officers alike, with a complete lack of consideration, never hid his distrust of them and constantly insulted them. The first unit which swore allegiance to him was the army in Upper Germany. The unpleasant old man, by this time afflicted with a painful fleshy protuberance on his right side, imagined that the officers despised him for his childlessness. Calling a parade, therefore, he publicly adopted a young nobleman called Piso Frugi Licinianus. The young man did not have long to enjoy his stroke of luck. Five days later, on January 15th A.D. 69, he was to die with Galba.

Galba's last five days passed quickly. The bandage which was meant to support the peculiar excrescence on the right side of his body had to be loosened repeatedly. The Emperor had developed a mysterious appetite. He no longer groaned at the sight of twenty or thirty dishes on his table, but got up before daybreak, consumed with hunger. He selected as his companions some even taller and more stalwart young men, the sight of whom was his sole remaining joy in life.

Galba started to do odd things. Sorting through his magpie's hoard of treasures, he picked out a necklace of pearls and precious stones, intending to adorn his Fortuna, a little bronze statuette which he kept on his estate at Tusculum. He had found the bronze goddess lying forlornly on his doorstep. Now he wanted to give her the finest piece of jewellery he possessed.

But his avarice got the better of him. He only wanted to sacrifice *one* piece of jewellery, so he dedicated the necklace which had been earmarked for his Fortuna to Capitoline Venus instead. The very next night, Fortuna appeared to him in his sleep. She was screaming with rage. Half dreaming, half delirious, he saw her bundling together all she had ever given him. The old man awoke with an effort, groaning. He decided to make an expiatory sacrifice. Preparations were to begin at once. Frenziedly, with the icy fingers of dementia already clawing at the fluttering hem of his toga, Galba raced off to Tusculum. But there, instead of a burning flame on the sacrificial altar, he found only hot ashes, and instead of a youth in a white robe, a trembling old man in deep mourning. 'Your murderers are not far away,' the augurs warned him. Standing close by was Marcus Salvius Otho, whom Galba had just greeted with an embrace.

The same day, Otho seized power, and Galba was advised to take refuge in the Praetorian camp. But he was weary, and searing pains shot through his limbs. He decided to stay in his palace, and mustered some troops for his personal protection. Then he donned a linen corselet made of eighteen thicknesses of cloth stiffened with vinegar and salt. 'Ah!' he groaned, 'even that will not avail me against many swords.'

Loud voices were heard. Apparently the revolt had been crushed. Messages of congratulation were pouring in, and everyone was re-affirming his loyalty to the Emperor. Deciding that good news ought to be met half way, Galba left the palace. A soldier shouted to him that he had killed Otho. 'On whose orders?' snapped the Emperor, characteristically reluctant to give a reward.

While Galba was passing the Lacus Curtius on his way to the Forum, some horsemen galloped up. The crowds scattered. In a moment the gouty old monster was deserted by his whole escort. Galba bowed to the inevitable. Baring his neck to the assassins, he uttered the formula used by Romans when slaughtering an animal for sacrifice: 'Forward, strike home, since so it must be!'

Nobody made any move to save him. Everyone stared at the gory spectacle in silent horror. The old man lay where he had been felled. A passing soldier cut off his head, intending to take it with him. Finding it difficult to grip because of Galba's lack of hair, he put his thumb into the imperial mouth and, like that, carried it to Otho. Otho threw the head to some camp-boys, who stuck it on a spear and sang a refrain which went: 'Enjoy your old age, Galba!'

Argius, Galba's major-domo, later buried his master's head and trunk in the imperial gardens by the Aurelian high-road. Galba was seventy-three when he became Emperor: he was still seventy-three when he died, having reigned for only eight months. Had he never become Emperor, remarks Tacitus, everyone would have gone on believing that he might have made a good one.

OTHO

BETTER AT DYING THAN RULING

That was Emperor Otho's verdict on himself. 'Scarcely had the freedman departed when Otho stood the sword upright between his hands and threw himself upon it. He experienced only enough pain to make him utter a single groan, thus betraying what had happened to those standing outside.'

Plutarch, Otho, 17.

ROME was now a sink of iniquity, a den of vice, a festering sore on the face of the world. Gluttony and perversion, adultery and pederasty, sadism, treachery and injustice all made their repulsive presence felt among the seven hills which ruled the world. Caligula, Claudius, Nero and Galba had prepared the morass into which the new Emperor, Otho, was to wade still deeper. Between the years A.D. 30 and A.D. 69 Rome's moral barometer showed its lowest reading.

Doomed to the fate of all tyrants, the Emperors everlastingly shivered in their shoes. Their nights were made hideous by the memory of bloodshed, poison and judicial murder. They could scent conspiracy everywhere. More and more spies had to be employed. Every wall had ears. Terror reigned supreme. A down-trodden and humiliated band of toadies and sycophants danced a witches' dance about the infallible person of the Emperor, who could trust no one.

In the time of Augustus it was still customary to obtain senior political appointments on merit, by showing courage and competence. In Claudius' day the best method of making headway was to unmask a plot against the Emperor's life. That was precisely the course adopted by Lucius Otho, Emperor Otho's father. It did not take much doing. The conspiracy, which had been organized by a Roman knight, was revealed to Otho by a slave. The fawning Senate at once erected a statue of Otho in the Palatium, and Emperor Claudius elevated him to patrician rank. 'I could not wish for a better man than Otho,' declared Claudius, 'even among my own children.'

Lucius Otho was a man who adapted himself skilfully to the poison- and intrigue-ridden age in which he was born. Tiberius had been fond of him, and it may have been his good fortune to bear a remarkable resemblance to that Emperor. On April 28th, A.D. 32, his wife Albia Terentia, a woman of aristocratic birth, bore him a son. The child was bow-legged, and this imperfection — common enough among babies — stayed with him throughout the thirty-six years of his life.

However, young Marcus Salvius Otho developed other physical imperfections which did not suit his pronounced and precocious vanity half as well. The unscrupulous, degenerate and lascivious youth roamed nightly through the narrow Roman streets, waylaying drunks and beating them up. There were large gangs of these aristocratic teddy-boys in Rome during this period, although one might add that the comic dramatist Plautus had described an equally vicious type of young Roman more than 200 years earlier.

Otho senior soon awoke to his son's peculiar inclinations and thrashed him soundly and often. Marcus Salvius lurked in his corner like some small and vicious animal, ever poised to run off and hatch fresh mischief or spend more money than he possessed. He accepted his beatings and waited for the old man to die.

Lucius Otho had scarcely breathed his last when his son started to pay court to a dissipated wreck of a freedwoman whose only redeeming feature was the fact that she was on good terms with Emperor Nero. By affecting a passion for her, Marcus Salvius Otho insinuated himself not only into the Emperor's clique but also his affections. His success was not really so surprising, of course, because young Otho and the singing Emperor were fairly similar in character. Like the mistress of some vain and stupid tyrant, Otho could twist Nero round his little finger.

It goes without saying that Otho was party to Nero's most intimate secrets. It was he who inveigled Poppaea Sabina, Nero's mistress, into committing adultery and then contracted a mock marriage with her. Having done so, he was unwilling to surrender her to his impatient lord, master and employer. Nero had to send Otho off to Lusitania (modern Portugal) as governor, before he could have Poppaea Sabina to himself. His indignation at his friend for having committed 'adultery' with his own wife caused great amusement in Rome.

Otho administered his province for ten years, and we learn with some surprise that he made a thoroughly good quaestor. He was in on Galba's coup against Nero from the start, though even at that stage he cherished secret ambitions of becoming Emperor himself, encouraged in this hope by the astrologer Seleucus. Seleucus (called 'Ptolemaeus' by Tacitus and Plutarch) had long ago told him that he would survive Nero. Now the astrologer suddenly turned up with another prediction: 'In a short time you will be Emperor.'

Otho made systematic preparations for his accession to the throne. Whenever Galba came to dine with him, he distributed largesse to the Emperor's body-guard. Indeed, he made such a lavish bid for popularity with the Praetorian cohorts that he soon had every guardsman favourably comparing his own open-handedness with Galba's skinflint habits and wishing that he were Emperor instead. For a while Otho hoped that Galba would adopt him, but, as soon as he saw that it was not to be, he started to plan a *coup d'état*. Working on the snowball system, he confided his schemes to five bodyguards and instructed each of them to enlist two more. A large sum was paid for each new man recruited. Friendly as ever, Otho went to call on the Emperor, taking his leave when word came that 'the architects had arrived'. That was the signal for the *putsch*. The soldiers who murdered Galba acted on Otho's personal instructions.

Otho was now Emperor. He did not know that his triumph was to last for only ninety-five days. One of his first measures was to honour Nero by re-erecting his statues — a remarkable thing to do such a short time after Nero's death. He even made the people address him as 'Nero' and granted fifty million sesterces towards the completion of Nero's Golden House.

One morning screams were heard issuing from Otho's bed-chamber, and he was discovered lying on the floor by his bed. It seems that his murdered predecessor's ghost had appeared and hurled him to the ground. Then Otho stumbled during a storm and was distinctly heard to mutter, over and over again, in Greek: 'Why did I have to choose the longest and most difficult flute?' (Suetonius, *Otho*, 7). His throne was tottering even before he had settled himself properly upon it.

News arrived that the army in Germany had sworn allegiance to Vitellius. Otho ordered the Senate to inform Vitellius by messenger that he, Otho, had already been elected Emperor. Undeterred, Vitellius marched on Italy. Otho fought two successful battles at the foot of the Alps, but was defeated at Betriacum, between Mantua and Cremona.

Otho had never been a hero. He hated civil war. When a soldier announced that his army had been defeated at Betriacum, nobody believed him, and the imperial camp merely laughed. Then, before Otho's very eyes, the man threw himself on his sword. Among those present was the father of Suetonius the Roman historian. He later told how Otho had called out in despair: 'I shall no longer subject brave and devoted men to danger.'

Otho said goodbye to his brother and several friends, burned his correspondence, distributed gifts and held an audience for anyone who wished to speak to him. Then, having drunk some cold water, he put a sword beneath his pillow and fell sound asleep.

Although the cold-blooded determination with which Otho committed suicide early next morning may seem surprising, it was quite in keeping with his character. One sword-thrust in the left side was enough. He groaned aloud. Servants rushed into his bed-chamber. Otho put his hand over the wound. He showed it to them, covered it again and died.

There he lay, bow-legged as ever. Only then was it discovered that Otho did not have a single hair on his head. He had deceived his entourage for years by wearing a well-fitting wig. His dearest wish was to have a soft, smooth skin, and he had depilated himself by rubbing his face daily with moist bread.

Otho's death was in such striking contrast to his life that several of his soldiers wept, kissed his hands and feet, called him a brave man and, running on their swords, followed their Emperor into death. Roman citizens who had cursed him during his lifetime started to praise him now that he was dead. 'Duels of imperial loyalty' were fought at Rome, the losers joining the Emperor in the next world as though by divine decree. It was a strange age of aberration and debased values, an age when humanity had nothing to cling to. The Gospel of Christ was on its way — it already had its martyrs — but it had not yet conquered Rome in the year A.D. 69.

Emperor Flavius Vespasianus was a commoner. He occupied the throne for ten years. The destruction of Jerusalem (A.D. 70) falls within his reign, as does the building of the Roman Colosseum

Emperor Titus ruled well under the most ad-
erse conditions. His short reign (A.D. 79–81)
vas beset by a series of disasters which in-
luded the destruction of Pompeii and Her-
ulaneum, the Plague, and a great fire at Rome

Bloodthirsty gladiatorial contests and animal-baiting displays took place here. The huge amphitheatre at Rome was started by Emperor Vespasian and opened by his son Titus in A.D. 80 with Games lasting a hundred days. The Romans called this building the Flavian Theatre, after the two Emperors' family name. In the Middle Ages it became known as the Colosseum, from the colossus or huge statue of Nero which had been set up nearby. It could seat 87,000 spectators and had gallery-space for 20,000 more. The seats could be sheltered from the sun by means of huge awnings, and spectators reached their places via sixteen stairways and eighty arcades

VITELLIUS

THE IMPERIAL GLUTTON

Roman historians could only explain this emperor's huge and unnatural capacity for food by assuming that he emptied his stomach after every meal by tickling his throat with a feather.

The Author.

THE pen balks at describing Lucius Vitellius, father of Vitellius the Emperor. To put it bluntly, he was a toady and a boot-licker of the first order. Having held the governorship of Syria, he later became the highest official in the Roman Empire, deputizing for Emperor Claudius during his campaign against Britain. Despite this, he aroused a great deal of scorn and ridicule by his infatuation for a former slave-woman. He waited on her hand and foot and followed her around like a pet dog. Declaring that he was hoarse and that it would soothe his sore throat, he publicly drained a goblet of her saliva mixed with honey.

'Caligula is a god,' he announced. With these words he ushered in a vogue of Caligula-worship. The Romans were no novices at this sort of thing. They had seen it all — insanity, perversion and men who were a blend of emperor, god and animal — yet even some of them were taken aback. Lucius Vitellius carried toadyism, flattery and sycophancy to grotesque and idiotic lengths. There was little enough left to offer Caligula in the way of honours, but Lucius Vitellius could always be relied on for new ideas. He made Caligula his god and danced attendance on him, spinning like a top in the fervour of his devotion.

Caligula's successor, Claudius, that tool without a mind of its own, that slave of women and freedmen, laughed at him delightedly. He liked Lucius. Lucius lay on his belly before Messalina and begged for one of her shoes. Messalina put out her right foot and Lucius pulled the shoe off. From then on he always carried it between his toga and his tunica. He liked people to be watching when he suddenly produced the shoe and kissed it passionately.

Then he had a stroke and died the next day. The father was gone. What was the son going to be like?

We are still in A.D. 69, the undistinguished 'year of the three Caesars'. None of them, Galba, Otho or Vitellius, reigned for more than a matter of months. All of them were failures. But one of them at least won the booby prize, and that was Vitellius junior.

His real name was Aulus, but he was always known by the obscene nickname 'Spintria'. Aulus spent his early years in Capri as one of the band of degenerate adolescents whom Tiberius collected about him in the seclusion of that island and christened 'Spintriae'. Having won Tiberius' affections with such success, Aulus Vitellius ingratiated himself in turn with Caligula, as his chariot-driver, with Claudius, as his gambling companion, and with Nero, as his *vox populi* or 'spokesman of the people'. (Once, when Nero was leaving the Circus — reluctantly, because he was itching to take part in a lyre-playing contest — Aulus Vitellius coaxed him back with an assurance that the public were clamouring to hear him.)

With the backing of so many emperors, Vitellius could hardly fail to get on in life. The stages of his political career covered a senior priesthood, the proconsulship of Africa and, finally, the Roman equivalent of the Ministry of Public Works. He murdered his son by his first wife, Petronia. His second wife, Galeria Fundana, bore him another son whose tongue was so badly malformed that he could hardly speak — a living proof of the Roman ruling classes' physical and mental degeneration at this period.

In the year A.D. 68 something quite unexpected happened. Galba sent Vitellius to Lower Germany. It was a strange thing to do, because Vitellius could well prove dangerous in his new job. But Galba said, and he was probably right, that the least dangerous people are those whose main interests lie in the direction of eating and drinking. And Vitellius was a glutton such as even Rome, the home of gluttony, could seldom boast.

Vitellius was also bankrupt. He rented an attic for his wife, son and daughter, so that he could let his house, but he lived at such a rate that all he amassed was debts. Now that he had been posted to Germany he needed money. He attacked his mother and tore a pearl ear-ring out of her ear. He was dogged by duns and creditors wherever he went, plagued by people whom he had cheated, whose taxes he had embezzled. Vitellius turned, at bay. His omnipresent tormentors, who worried him by day and even knocked him up at night, had to be stopped or silenced, either by counter-accusations or blackmail.

Vitellius was not without a certain native cunning. He made a practice of warmly embracing and kissing his private soldiers. Whenever he met liverymen and travellers on the road he would greet them cordially, asking them how they were and whether they had breakfasted — belching, because he personally had already taken his first great batch of food on board. In camp he played the paternal, generous, benevolent general. He cancelled punishments, dismissed charges, extended leave and distributed presents. It was late one evening when his soldiers finally gave vent to their affection for him. They hauled him out of his quarters in his night-shirt and proclaimed him Emperor.

They had not chosen a very auspicious time. It was January 2nd, A.D. 69, and the second day of each month was regarded as unlucky. Bleary-eyed with sleep, Vitellius was carried through the streets of Colonia Agrippinensis, now Cologne, holding a sword which had once belonged to the deified Julius Caesar.

As dawn broke, flames leapt into the sky. It was the second unlucky omen. ... The General's dining-room had caught fire. He quickly dispelled any superstitious presentiments by exclaiming: 'The sky is shining for us!'

Vitellius adopted the surname Germanicus, defeated Emperor Otho, ordered some executions and sat back to enjoy his triumph. When told that his cohorts were burning and looting, he merely laughed. Slaves were set free and free men were enslaved. There were floggings galore. Vitellius used brute force on anyone he disliked.

Mountains of dead lay on the battle-field at Betriacum, where Otho's forces had been defeated. Vitellius' staff recoiled from the mounds of decomposing flesh. Not so Vitellius. 'Ah!' he cried, 'slaughtered enemies smell good, don't they? But dead Romans smell even better!' He handed round some flagons of wine and took a drink with his officers and men.

Then came the entry into Rome. Trumpet-calls heralded a new era of madness on the throne as, followed by his legions with their banners and standards, the Emperor marched in, arrayed in his general's cloak. Vitellius seems to have modelled himself on Nero, for he held a memorial service in his honour and led the applause when some of Nero's songs were performed afterwards. He even tried to out-Nero Nero. Referring to Nero's Golden House, he said that it was beyond his comprehension how Nero could have lived in such poor style. Such of Nero's courtiers as were still alive rubbed their hands gleefully and looked forward to a return to the good old days.

Vitellius did not have much time to spare for his official duties. He left the administration of public and private affairs to his favourite, Asiaticus, an emancipated slave with whom he was on only too intimate terms. Once, growing tired of his master's whims, Asiaticus ran away to Puteoli and became a lemonade-seller. Vitellius caught up with him, clapped him in irons, then freed him again. But his favourite became fractious once more, so he sold him to an itinerant trainer of gladiators. However, when the time came for young Asiaticus to enter the arena, Vitellius impulsively withdrew him from the contest and set him free.

Breakfast, lunch, dinner and, after it, a drinking-session: those were the most important events in the Emperor's daily life. Roman historians could only explain his huge and unnatural capacity for food by assuming that he emptied his stomach after each meal by tickling his throat with a feather. Constant practice had made him an expert at vomiting. Unfortunately, he seldom had any money, so he made a habit of paying calls on several Romans every day. Anyone who was honoured in this way and spent less than 4,000 gold pieces on entertaining his imperial guest was likely to forfeit his head.

To celebrate the Emperor's arrival in Rome, his brother gave a banquet at which 2,000 rare fish and 7,000 fowl were served. But perhaps the high-spot in the history of the royal cuisine was when Vitellius dedicated to the goddess Minerva an immense silver dish containing pike-livers, pheasant-brains, peacock-brains, flamingo-tongues and lamprey-milt, all blended with the rarest oils and sauces. Every galley in the Mediterranean — and beyond the Bosphorus, even — had to go fishing to collect the ingredients. But Vitellius' appetite grew with eating. There were times, between meals, when there was nothing to eat at all. The Emperor found this unendurable, especially at night when the chefs were asleep. He would blunder about the palace, ransacking the cellars and leaving a trail of broken jars and pots in his wake. But there was something else in the Emperor's life which brought him anguish: the smell of baked meat and cakes which rose to his nostrils when he was sacrificing. He was supposed to offer sacrifices, not devour the sacrificial offerings himself, but that did not deter him from occasionally snatching titbits from the altar or the sacred fire and wolfing them on the spot. While travelling he would sometimes come upon eating-houses beside the road. Even if they were closed, there would be a little burnt fat, or a few vegetables, or some left-overs from the day before. It all went down.

Vitellius' inordinate appetite was matched only by his infinite cruelty. He ordained all sorts of subtle punishments and was always inventing new ways of getting rid of people. A man in the throes of fever was given a cooling drink of water with poison added. Vitellius was at his most implacable when revenging himself on his creditors. He only had to catch sight of someone who had lent him money in the past to order his arrest. Sometimes, to make revenge even sweeter, he would reprieve men who had just been condemned and then have them killed before his very eyes. It became dangerous to be remembered in a will, since the Emperor frequently ordered the garrotting of heirs as well as testators.

Then there were the astrologers. Known as 'Chaldeans' because Babylon was the home of astrology, they had accurately forecast the date of the Emperor's death. Vitellius banished them from Rome and persecuted them, killing many of their number. He is said to have starved his mother to death when she fell sick because a Chattian woman had prophesied that he would reign in safety if he outlived her.

Vitellius reigned for eight months 'in a constant stupor', as the Roman historian Dio Cassius puts it. Then his armies began to defect. They swore allegiance to Vespasian. Vitellius became scared. He bribed anyone whom he could still hope to win over with vast sums of money and made promises which he could never have kept, even if he had won, to those who volunteered to fight for him. He dispatched a fleet against the enemy under the command of his brother, but his army was defeated at Cremona in northern Italy by Vespasian's legions. Vitellius abdicated and announced his intention of retiring into private life, but was immediately dissuaded by his flatterers. Falling upon Sabinus and other supporters of Vespasian who had just laid down their arms, he drove them into the Temple of Jupiter on the Capitol and burnt them alive. He watched the scene from the palace — still munching.

But his position deteriorated once more, so he suggested that the Senate should send envoys to discuss peace terms. By this time, however, Vespasian was close at hand. Vitellius fled, accompanied only by a baker and a cook. He had scarcely set off when the news reached him that Vespasian was suing for peace. Back he went to the imperial palace in Rome, only to find it forlorn and deserted. Buckling a belt full of gold pieces about his massive body, the Emperor shut himself up in the porter's lodge, leaving a dog tied up outside and barricading the door with beds and other articles of furniture. Before long Vespasian's advance-guard arrived. The soldiers searched every room until, finally, they came upon the strange porter.

'Where is Vitellius?' they asked him. The trembling Emperor tried to keep up the charade, but he was recognized. He begged and implored them for mercy. He told them that they could lock him up as long as they did not kill him. He reminded them that he had been Emperor and knew things which could save Vespasian's life. All to no avail. The soldiers tied his hands behind his back and put a halter round his neck. Half naked, his clothes in ribbons, he stumbled through the streets. His captors manhandled and reviled him. They pulled his head back by the hair and strapped a sword to his chest, point uppermost, so that he could not bow his head and hide his face.

'Murderer! Guzzler!' shouted the people, as the Emperor blundered through the streets to his doom like a clumsy giant. His face was puce with drink, his body bloated, and he limped from an injury which he had once received while driving Caligula's chariot in a race.

A man with so many victims to his credit was not allowed to die quickly. He was tortured to death with countless small wounds, then dragged into the Tiber on a hook. His brother and son followed him. The war was over but, as Tacitus remarks, peace had not yet broken out. Vitellius' soldiers and supporters were tracked down, both in Rome and the provinces. and annihilated by the revolutionaries. Vitellius died at the age of fifty-five. The Babylonian soothsayers had been right.

VESPASIAN

HIS WITTY MAJESTY

Caenis, his astute wife, earned money for Rome. 'She received large donations from all quarters. For money, people could secure appointments, governorships, military commands, priesthoods—even favourable verdicts from the Emperor. Once, when Vespasian's son Titus referred distastefully to the urine tax, his father took a gold piece which had come from that source and showed it to him with the words: "You see, my boy, it doesn't smell—*non olet!*" '

Dio Cassius, lxiv, 14.

THE Roman aristocracy had mismanaged things badly.

Galba, Otho and Vitellius had dealt their spirit of leadership a final blow. The aristocratic families could not produce another emperor. The new emperor had to come from the people. The Flavian clan had no distinguished ancestors, it was true, but their country had no need to be ashamed of them. It was as though the dawn of a new age had arrived.

Titus Flavius Vespasianus was born in a small hamlet called Falacrina, above Reate (modern Rieti), in Sabine territory. He was the son of a Customs supervisor. His mother, Vespasia Polla, was an energetic woman from Nursia. She was the sort of ambitious Roman mother who wanted her son to do big things in life and make a great political career. It is interesting to note, incidentally, that the Flavian family was of Etruscan stock.

Titus Flavius was brought up by his grandmother Tertulla on her country estate. Later, as Emperor Vespasian, he was often drawn back to this scene of his youth, and never forgot his grandmother's ministrations. He always drank from Tertulla's little silver wine-goblet on feast-days, and took care to see that her villa was maintained in its original condition, like a museum.

Vespasian married twice. His first wife, Domitilla, who was the former mistress of a Roman knight, bore him three children: Titus, Domitian and a daughter. After her death he married a freedwoman, evidently a most efficient person, who had once been secretary to Antonia, the mother of Claudius.

This second wife was called Caenis. She possessed the two finest attributes a secretary can have: a good memory and a sense of discretion. Not surprisingly, the Emperor remained faithful to her until she died. It was not until after her death that he acquired the numerous concubines who — we are told on good authority — used to lie beside him in a row during his siesta.

Under Claudius, Vespasian had won a great reputation in Germany and, more particularly, in Britain, where he had fought thirty engagements on Rome's behalf, captured twenty towns and conquered Vectis, now the Isle of Wight. In the year A.D. 63 he became governor of Africa, where he ruled extremely badly — according to Tacitus — and extremely well — according to Suetonius. Vespasian was as unsuccessful at ingratiating himself with Nero as he had been successful with Caligula. He obviously could not stand Nero's interminable arias, because he was forbidden further access to the imperial court for falling asleep during performances.

It was at about this time that sudden, repeated and mysterious appearances on the stage of Roman history were made by the little country where Jesus Christ had been born. The Jewish Messianic belief and a sense of guilt at Christ's crucifixion had combined to produce a new and, from Rome's point of view, dangerous ideology. The Roman historian Suetonius records that there was prevalent in the East at this time a firm belief that out of Judaea would come 'mastery over the world'.

Since A.D. 66 the idea that they and their national god were destined to rule over every other nation on earth had added fuel to the Jews' outbursts of hatred and physical violence against nonconformists in Caesarea and elsewhere. Palestine had long been under Roman control. It had been prophesied to the Jews that their god would hold sway over all other nations, but they were thinking of worldly, not spiritual domination. They rebelled — against Rome, every Roman and every friend of Rome.

It was to combat this threat that fifty-eight-year-old Vespasian was given command of the legions in Judaea in the year 67. Taking his son Titus with him as second-in-command, Vespasian occupied Galilee and Samaria. After a series of engagements, he reached the Sea of Galilee. Mount Tabor fell, as did the fortress of Jotapata. Titus was the first Roman to set foot on the walls during the final assault.

The defender of Jotapata was a priest called Joseph ben Mattathias. When the town fell, he saved his life by calmly walking over to the Roman camp. Standing before General Vespasian in chains, he made a momentous prophecy: 'You have put me in fetters now, but in a year's time, as Emperor, you will set me free.'

The priest and prophet Joseph ben Mattathias became known to posterity as Josephus. He is responsible for much of our detailed information about this period. He settled in Rome, became a Roman citizen and wrote, among other important works, a twenty-volume history of the Jews from the Creation to A.D. 66.

The year A.D. 69 saw the fulfilment of the great Jewish historian's prophecy. On July 1st Vespasian was proclaimed Emperor by the legions at Alexandria, and on July 3rd by the army in Judaea. Once again we meet a reminder of Christ. Vespasian's authority lacked divine confirmation. People expected a miracle from him — yet another after-effect of Christ's presence on earth. In Egypt a blind man and a cripple implored the Emperor to cure them. Vespasian would not have anything to do with such superstition and advised them to go to a doctor, but friends talked him into trying to heal the two men, and history relates that he did, in fact, succeed. 'And many false prophets shall rise, and shall deceive many,' said Christ (Matthew, xxiv, 11). The Romans heard rumours of this miracle, and the Emperor's stock rose rapidly.

Many good things are reported of Vespasian. He subjected the Roman army to strict discipline and made sure that his authority was legally ratified by the Senate and the people. The verbatim text of this statute survives on a metal plaque discovered in Rome. Vespasian was a second Augustus, but made of even sterner stuff. He detested effeminacy and abhorred the womanish tendencies of the young men of his day. To one youth who reeked of perfume he said: 'I'd sooner you stank of garlic.'

Rome, large parts of which still lay in ruins as a result of Nero's fire-raising activities, was rebuilt under Vespasian. He personally shovelled away the first pile of rubble. Owners of real estate who left their land vacant could now be dispossessed by anyone who cared to build on it. Near the Forum, Vespasian erected the Temple of Peace, and in the middle of the city, on the site of Nero's Golden House, there arose the great Flavian Amphitheatre which later became known as the Colosseum. It does not owe its name to its size, by the way, but to the immense statue or colossus of Emperor Nero which stood close by.

To bring a morally degenerate Rome to its senses, the Emperor prompted the Senate to enact the following decree: any woman who had an affair with someone else's slave became the slave of her lover's owner. People were not used to having such a virtuous emperor at the helm of the Roman Empire. This commoner who had won the throne apparently wanted to make a clean sweep of everything. It was something quite new, something unheard of — almost scandalous. Amazing rumours went the rounds. Vespasian had no scores to settle. He was not fond of bloodshed. He felt so safe that he did not even post sentries outside his palace. It was true that he presented animal-baiting displays in the amphitheatres, but he took no pleasure in contests between human beings. He sighed and shed tears if ever he had to sign a death warrant. He set no store by outward marks of respect, and was straightforward, unostentatious and kind. His Imperial Majesty even took his own boots off, which was something the court found almost incredible.

One could make jokes about the Emperor and abuse him to his face without risking punishment. Demetrius the Cynic, who was most disrespectful to the Emperor on one occasion, went unpunished. Vespasian merely called him 'dog', that was all. The Cynic philosophers took their name from the Cynosarges College in Athens, where they taught. Since they recommended a return to Nature and despised civilization, they represented a 'dog's philosophy', so to speak, *kuon* being the Greek for 'dog'. What Vespasian meant was: 'You are and will remain a Cynic, which is to say, a dog that barks. And dogs that only bark do not bite. That is why there is no need to punish you.'

Vespasian was always in particularly good form at table. He loved to crack jokes and tell stories. Some of his jokes were indecent, but many were extremely witty, too. On one occasion Mestrius Florus pointed out to him that the Latin word for 'carts' should be pronounced *plaustra*, not *plostra*. From then on the Emperor made a point of addressing Florus as 'Flaurus'.

Vespasian often poked fun at himself, which brings us to the thrifty or perhaps miserly side of the great man's nature. It would be understandable if he really was avaricious, for he found, at the very beginning of his reign, that he needed forty milliard sesterces, or nearly £700 million, to save the nation from the bankruptcy to which his predecessors had reduced it. Vespasian accordingly raised the level of taxation, increased the provincial tributes and did business deals which the most hardened swindler would have been ashamed of. Always keeping in the background and acting almost entirely through Caenis, his well-beloved wife, he bought up scarce commodities and, when his operations made them even scarcer, unloaded them at a large profit. He also sold official appointments and pardons. The Alexandrians called him 'a vendor of tunny-fish steaks'. Once, at the Saturnalia or Roman carnival, when a burlesque of the Emperor's funeral was being presented, with a comedian called Favor giving the customary imitations of his mannerisms and tricks of speech, Vespasian asked how much his funeral would cost. 'Ten million sesterces', came the reply. 'Then give me a hundred thousand down and throw me into the Tiber!' he shouted.

He had undoubtedly inherited some of his business acumen from his father the Customs supervisor.

Vespasian introduced a tax on urine, which was a valuable commodity at this time, being used as a tanning agent. When his son Titus protested about it, Vespasian held a coin under his nose and asked him: Does it smell?' Titus agreed that it did not. Hence the celebrated expression *non olet*, 'It doesn't smell', meaning money is money no matter where it comes from. Vespasian could be very witty. Even on his death-bed, when he realized that his illness was fatal, he cracked: 'Dear me! I think I'm becoming a god.'

Vespasian was of medium height and sturdily built, but not exactly handsome. His face always wore the expression of one who was a martyr to indigestion. He used to get up very early each morning to read the incoming mail and official reports, receiving his friends even while dressing. Then he worked on, allowing himself a break for a short walk, until it was time for his afternoon rest. After that he took a bath. He was particularly fond of taking cold baths, a habit which is said to have brought on intestinal trouble. Even when he was sixty-nine and extremely ill he still transacted affairs of State from his bed, received deputations and supervised the courts and their decisions.

He did not want to die — not lying down, at least. And so, in his last moments, he exerted every ounce of his remaining strength in an effort to stand up. With the words: 'An emperor ought to die on his feet,' the tough and virile old man breathed his last in the arms of the courtiers who were supporting him. Honest bourgeois, Etruscan and son of the Sabine soil, he had lived for sixty-nine years, seven months and seven days.

TITUS

THE ERUPTION OF VESUVIUS

Ashes were already falling on us. ... I looked back. A dense vapour was coming up behind us, like a stream poured out on the ground. ... The darkness returned and, with it, such an intense and heavy rain of ashes that we often had to stand up and shake them off to avoid being covered over and stifled by their weight.

Pliny the Younger to Cornelius, *Tacitus*, Book vi, Letter 20.

TITUS became Emperor at the age of forty. He died two years later, in his prime.

But, although he reigned for only two years, people continued to sing his praises for centuries. He was like a beacon shining in the darkness of the imperial era of Rome. He was, as Suetonius aptly remarks, 'the love and delight of the human race'. Titus Flavius Vespasianus was brought up at Nero's court with Britannicus, whom Nero poisoned. It is said that he was reclining next to Britannicus at the time of his death, and that he drank some of the poison, making himself extremely ill. That was in the year 55, when he was sixteen.

We have already heard how Vespasian took his son to Judaea, how Titus subjugated the whole country and how he was the first to climb the walls of Jotapata. In the year 70 he besieged Jerusalem. Three fortified strongholds had to be taken individually: the Lower City, the Upper City and the Temple. The Jews fought with a fire and determination born of their absolute faith in God, but bastion after bastion fell and the Temple went up in flames. The priests hurled themselves on to their enemies' swords, killed one another or sprang into the flames. As Dio Cassius remarks (lxvi, 6): 'In perishing thus, beneath the ruins of their temple, they all saw not death, but victory, salvation and happiness.'

As Titus was leaving the province of Judaea, the soldiers hailed him as Imperator and implored him to stay or take them with him. A suspicion somehow arose that Titus intended to sever connections with his father and set himself up as Emperor of the East. However, he hurried to Rome as fast as he could and greeted Vespasian with the words: 'Here I am, Father, here I am!' Examples of such mutual trust and understanding between father and son are rarely to be found in the history of the Caesars. Titus played an active part in public affairs. He issued edicts and even dictated letters in his father's name, and was regarded by him as joint regent. As commander of the Praetorian Guard he became known for his forceful methods, and soon earned a reputation for cruelty by killing off anyone whom he suspected of being a threat to his father or himself.

The Romans were not too sanguine about the heir-apparent and his pleasure-loving disposition. He spent night after night drinking with friends; he consorted with a bunch of disreputable young men; and, worst of all, there was his scandalous affair with Queen Berenice.

Berenice was a sister of the Jewish king Herod Agrippa II, with whom she maintained an incestuous relationship, having previously been married to two men in quick succession. We learn (*Acts* xxvi) that she heard St Paul speak in Caesarea. Having helped to put Vespasian, Titus' father, on the throne, she now became the son's mistress, married him in secret and bound him to her with the remarkable beauty for which she was renowned the world over. But the Romans knew too much about this woman. They were worried about Titus and his way of life, apprehensive of him even before he became Emperor.

Their fears were unfounded. The moment he became Emperor of Rome, Titus broke with the worthless cronies of his youth, chose distinguished men as his advisers and banished Berenice from Rome — much to their mutual sorrow.

Few other rulers in human history were better intentioned, yet few had so little time allowed them or were subjected to such severe ordeals. In A.D. 79, just two months after Titus became Emperor, Italy was rent by one of the greatest natural catastrophes in recorded history: the terrible eruption of Vesuvius, which engulfed the towns of Herculaneum, Pompeii and Stabiae, and had been heralded, from A.D. 63 onwards, by a series of devastating earthquakes.

The Roman historian Dio Cassius, who was born in A.D. 155, gives a description, based upon hearsay, of how the eruption began: how flames burst from Vesuvius and 'beings of superhuman size appeared on the mountains and floated through the air', how the air became oppressive and sultry and the ground trembled, how the whole of Campania 'undulated' and the mountain-tops 'skipped'. 'Day turned to night, and light to darkness'. A first-hand and thus more valuable account of the eruption of Vesuvius on August 23rd and 24th, A.D. 79, can be found in the famous letters of Pliny the Younger. Pliny, who was born at Como in A.D. 62, was a wealthy orator, author and patron of the sciences. He was seventeen when

Vesuvius erupted. In the course of the eruption his mother's brother, Pliny 'the Elder', lost his life. Pliny the Elder, besides being an admiral, was a well-known scientist and an extremely erudite man. He fell prey to his scientific curiosity, for, whereas most people fled from the danger-zone, the Admiral sailed off to Stabiae (near the modern Castellammare) in the Bay of Naples. He wanted to get as close to the natural phenomenon as he could, and was undeterred even when the showers of stones and clouds of vapour became intolerable.

Present-day scholars have racked their brains as to how the inhabitants of Pompeii and Herculaneum actually met their end. The lava-ashes which buried them hardened and took on the shape of their bodies in the very moment of death. The bodies then decayed away to nothing, leaving only skeletons in hollow cavities. In 1865 the Italian archaeologist Giuseppe Fionelli hit upon the idea of filling these cavities with liquid plaster of Paris. As a result, human figures were recovered, still wearing on their faces the expressions which they had worn when they died on that dreadful day in A.D. 79. The castastrophe seemed to have taken its victims completely unawares. Their posture still denoted quite clearly that, even at the moment of their death, death itself was very far from their thoughts. Hence the plaster 'reincarnations' of people sitting, sleeping or making love. In one shop a customer was found with coins still lying on the counter before him.

What actually killed all these unsuspecting people? Was it the volcano's poisonous gases? Was it lava? Could the tide of lava have penetrated everything so quickly and thoroughly? Were the inhabitants suffocated by a rain of ashes? Was it the heat?

The historian Tacitus tried to elicit from seventeen-year-old Pliny an exact account of his uncle's death. In Pliny's letter of reply we possess a precise description, by a contemporary, of the way in which the inhabitants of the flat land below Vesuvius met their end. Pliny, who was close at hand with his mother in Misenum, wrote: 'Then the flames and the sulphurous smell which preceded them put the others to flight. But he [his uncle the scientist-admiral] was only heartened by them. He rose to his feet, supported by two slaves, but suddenly sank down again. In my opinion, the dense smoke had obstructed his breathing and blocked his stomach. When day came once more his body was found quite untouched, without injury, and still dressed in the same clothes. His expression was that of a man asleep, not dead.'

The overwhelming of Pompeii and Herculaneum was followed by 'a frightful plague, the like of which had never been seen before.' It was assumed that this epidemic had been spread by the rain of ashes from the eruption. Dio Cassius reports that their volume was so enormous that they even reached Africa and Syria.

Emperor Titus at once set off for Campania. He set up a relief organization, gave financial assistance to the victims of the disaster and used the resources of those who had died intestate as a result of the eruption to help rebuild the damaged towns.

But in the following year, while he was still absent from the capital, Rome was devastated by a fire which raged for three days and nights, gutting the Capitol, the Temple of Jupiter, the Pantheon of Agrippa, the Theatre of Balbus and the Octavian buildings together with their libraries. Although Titus' first reaction was one of despair, he soon pulled himself together and began to lend a hand. He ordered his own houses to be stripped of their ornamentation and used it for the reconstruction of buildings and temples.

Since Nero's time and during the reigns of Galba, Otho and Vitellius, a flourishing community of informers had grown up in Rome. Titus made a regular practice of flogging all informers and slanderers in the Forum. Then he had them paraded in the arena of the amphitheatre and either auctioned them off as slaves or deported them to the most unhealthy islands in the Empire.

No one was ever executed on Titus' orders or with his consent. 'I would rather die than kill others,' he used to say. When two patricians were brought before him on a charge of conspiring to usurp the throne, Titus told them quietly: 'The throne is a gift of Destiny.' He sent a message to the mother of one of the men, who was already having visions of her son being nailed to the cross, reassuring her about his safety. On the following day he assigned them two seats close to his own in the amphitheatre. When the gladiators' weapons were presented for his inspection he handed them over to the throne-struck patricians, regardless of the fact that they had probably been plotting his death — a gesture which excited the boundless admiration of all present.

But then Titus had all the attributes calculated to arouse admiration and affection in others. He must have been a grand-looking man, although he was not built on heroic lines and had a slight tendency towards corpulence. He was a first-class swordsman and horseman, a good speaker and quite a talented poet. He could sing and play the lyre, and was such an expert at shorthand that he used to compete with his secretaries for fun. He was also very adept at imitating handwriting, and claimed that he would have made a successful forger.

Titus' first wife was Arrecina Tertulla. On her death, he married Marcia

Pompeii. The Forum and the Temple of Jupiter

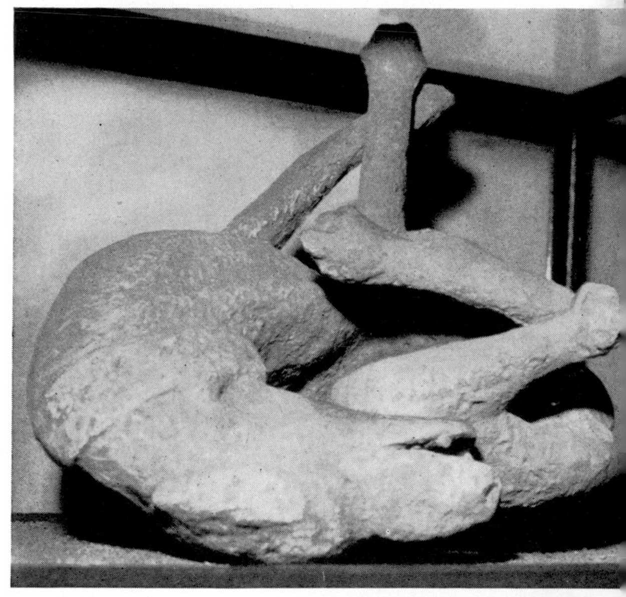

The death-throes of a dog belonging to Vesonius Primus the Fuller. He was chained up during the eruption of Vesuvius and was suffocated by volcanic ash. This 'sculpture' was produced by filling the cavity occupied by his skeleton with plaster of Paris

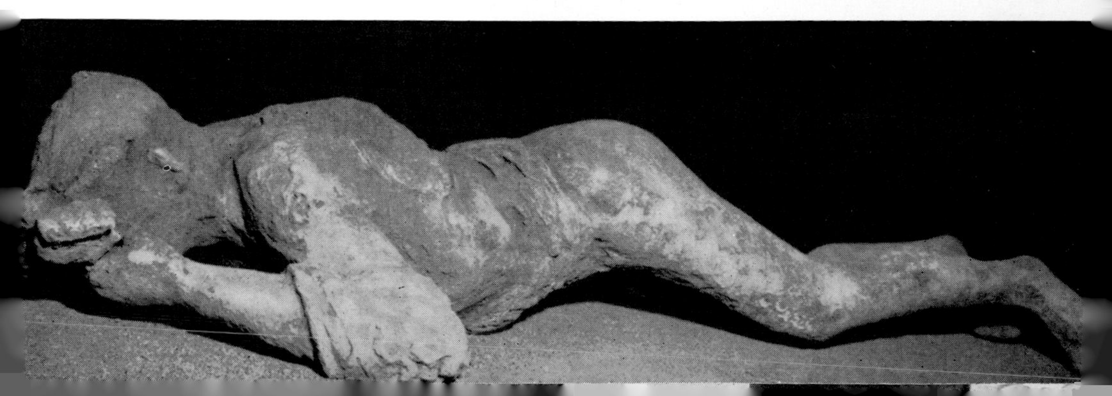

Overwhelmed by damp ashes. During the Pompeii disaster this man fell to the ground, still trying to protect his face with his hands. (Plaster cast of cavity and skeleton)

This head of *Cleopatra* in the British Museum probably gives a good idea of the famous queen's appearance, for it bears a very strong resemblance to reliable portraits of her on the bronze coin from Alexandria and the silver coin from Ascalon. The only factors which cast doubt on the theory that this is the same Cleopatra are the lack of a diadem and a slight variation in hair-style

Furnilla, who bore him a daughter, Julia, and whom he later divorced. Julia became Domitian's lover and was ultimately deified.

The Emperor was completely incorruptible and never accepted gifts or favours from anyone, whether private citizen, city corporation or foreign king, even though the whole of the contemporary world would gladly have laid its treasures at his feet. At the same time, he was extremely generous. He turned the dedication of the amphitheatre or Colosseum, which is still an object of world admiration, into a national festival without equal. Emperor Vespasian had begun the building of this amphitheatre, and now, in the year 80, it was completed. Titus held celebrations lasting a hundred days. He made cranes do battle first with dwarfs, as in the ancient legend, and then with four elephants. Nine thousand beasts were baited to death, some of them by women animal-tamers. Gladiators fought land- and sea-battles (during which the arena of the Colosseum was filled with water), and there were performances by trained horses, bulls and other animals. The Colosseum had 87,000 seats and an additional 20,000 places in the gallery. Since there were eighty numbered entrances and tickets corresponding to them, the vast crowds could always find their seats with ease and file out smoothly after each performance. Emperor Titus may have been the inventor of the lottery. He had the spectators showered with little wooden balls, each containing a small coupon. These coupons could be exchanged for the various articles marked on them, which included items of clothing, silver and gold vessels, horses, cattle, goats, sheep and even slaves.

The baths hurriedly constructed by Titus above Nero's Golden House (the famous Baths of Titus, where the Laocoön group was found) were also completed at this time, and their opening celebrated in a befitting manner. The people accepted all these blessings with a mixture of amazement, bewilderment and delight.

No one who approached the Emperor with a request or petition was ever prevented from stating his case or sent away without hope. When people warned Titus that he would never be able to fulfil all the promises he made, he answered: 'No one who has spoken to Titus shall go away disappointed.' On another occasion, when it occurred to him at supper that he had done nobody a favour all day long, he said: 'My friends, I have wasted a day.' He never lost an opportunity of endearing himself to his subjects. It was almost as though he guessed that he was only to be granted two years on the throne. He never omitted to give the poor free access to the public baths and — a shrewd stroke of psychology — always chose to let them in when he was bathing there himself.

As we have already seen, Fate was unkind to this worthy emperor during his reign, with its volcanic eruptions, earthquakes, plagues and conflagrations. But Titus had another and perhaps even greater worry. His brother Domitian spent his whole time conspiring against him, stirring up disaffection in the army and creating bad blood generally. Titus never let himself be provoked into punishing him. He did not even exile him, but treated him as his partner and successor from the outset, often imploring him in confidence to return the brotherly affection which he felt for him.

When the great festivals of dedication were over, the Emperor wept bitterly in the presence of the people, suddenly aware that his end was near. In the summer of A.D. 81 he set off for Sabine territory, but was struck down by fever the very first night. He continued his journey by litter, pulling the curtains apart time and again and gazing up into the sky with the plaintive words: 'I do not deserve to have my life taken from me. I have done naught to repent of — save one thing.'

The historians Suetonius and Dio Cassius assert that nobody knew what he was referring to. Some people presumed that Titus was thinking of the illicit relationship which he was supposed to have had with Domitia, his brother's wife. Against this, there is Domitia's solemn oath that no such relationship existed. Suetonius argues very plausibly that Domitia would never have denied such a thing if it had been true, since she was only too happy to brag about her other vices. Dio Cassius offers another and equally plausible explanation. He thinks that the Emperor may have considered it a crime not to have executed his brother Domitian, who was quite openly plotting against his life. This would fit in with the belief, prevalent at the time, that Domitian either caused or accelerated his brother's death. There were rumours of poison. Dio Cassius asserts that Domitian put his brother, still breathing and possibly not beyond hope of recovery, into a receptacle filled with snow. He said it was to reduce his temperature, but in reality he probably wanted to hasten his death.

Titus died at the age of forty-two in the same country house, the old family seat in Sabine country, where his father had died before him. The whole nation mourned the dead Emperor, and the Senate heaped him with panegyrics and honours. The Jews, on the other hand, asserted that Titus' untimely end was a punishment for having destroyed the Temple at Jerusalem.

As for Domitian, he galloped off to Rome without even waiting for his brother to die, burst into the Praetorian camp and had himself proclaimed Emperor.

DOMITIAN

THE EMPEROR IS CATCHING FLIES

Domitian was impetuous and quick-tempered, but he was also spiteful and cunning.... He never genuinely liked any human being, a few women excepted, and if he did act as though he liked someone it was sure to be because he had earmarked him as his next victim.

Dio Cassius, lxvii, 1.

'Is anyone with the Emperor?'

The question was directed at Vibius Crispus by a visitor who wanted to speak to Emperor Domitian urgently.

'Not even a fly,' came the answer.

Bewildered, the stranger repeated his question.

'Not even a fly,' Crispus reiterated. The words were not as silly as they seemed. Although it was supposed to be a close secret, the whole court knew that the Emperor returned to his private quarters for an hour each day to catch flies. Having caught them, he would impale them on a sharpened stylus.

His wife Domitia bore him a son, thereby earning the title Augusta, or Empress, but Domitian divorced her at short notice when she fell in love with the actor Paris. This handsome Casanova, who was idolized by ladies of the highest rank, incurred Domitian's jealousy and was murdered in the street. However, the Emperor soon invited his divorced wife to re-join him. 'I don't know how I feel about it,' he said, 'but it is the will of the people.' This was a brazen lie, of course. Domitia was the daughter of a famous general and had previously been married to Aelius Lamia. Lamia was an unfortunate individual. First the Emperor seduced his wife, and then, when someone admired his singing-voice and he was unwise enough to remark: 'Yes, I've given up sex,' the Emperor heard of it and had him executed. Domitia, it may be added, went in constant fear of her imperial husband's displeasure.

Domitian wanted to outdo all the emperors before him. He organized spectacles of quite fantastic splendour. Apart from presenting sea-battles, animal-baiting and gladiatorial contests in the Amphitheatrum Flavium or Colosseum at Rome, Domitian arranged large-scale battles and two- or four-horse chariot-races in the Circus Maximus. Other novelties included gladiatorial contests by torch-light. And, as in Nero's time, women combatants also took part.

Emperor Domitian presented a strange appearance. His face was always red — probably with rouge — not because he wanted to look ashamed but perhaps, as Tacitus suggests, because he wanted to hide his blushes. He may also have wanted to give an impression of vigour and energy. The eyes which stared into the arena were large, but weak. In later years Domitian grew paunchy and bald, and was deeply offended if anyone joked about his baldness. He wrote a small treatise on the care of the hair and presented it to a fellow-sufferer, a friend with a bald head, with the following dedication: 'You see what a tall, handsome figure I have: yet my hair will go the same way as yours. I bear it bravely, though it makes me an old man before my time. Always reflect that there is nothing finer and nothing more fleeting than beauty.'

Whenever the Emperor sat in his imperial box he was accompanied by a scarlet-clad dwarf with an extraordinarily small and malformed head. He was often heard chatting to this dwarf, and it was whispered that the big man discussed things of the utmost importance with his minute companion. (Red was Domitian's favourite colour, and he wore it himself. His purple toga was tailored after the Greek fashion.)

Domitian issued several strange decrees. He forbade actors and dancers to appear in public and only allowed them to perform at private functions. He prohibited castration and reduced the price of such eunuchs as the slave-dealers still had 'in stock'. Women of doubtful reputation were forbidden to ride in litters or benefit under wills. Inchastity among Vestal Virgins was at first punishable by a simple death penalty, but Domitian later treated them 'after the custom of our forefathers'. This meant that (as in the case of the Vestal Cornelia) they were buried alive and their lovers flogged to death with sticks. Domitian instigated many such trials, though Pliny tells us that the priestesses' guilt was probably not established in any instance.

Apparently, Domitian's cruel streak only declared itself gradually. At first he seemed to shun all bloodshed, and even proposed to forbid the slaughter of oxen. Later on he became spiteful and an expert at shock-tactics. Issuing cordial invitations to the people whom he had marked out for brutal punishment, he put on his brightest manner, commended them heartily and then pronounced their death sentence. Whenever Domitian's opening words were kind and affable, people knew that a trial or interview would end in savagery and sudden death.

Domitian slowly bled his subjects white. Property was confiscated on the slightest pretext and trials for *lèse-majesté* took place as they had done under Tiberius, who served as Domitian's model in this respect. The Emperor's palaces swallowed up enormous sums. Each roof-tile had to be overlaid with gold-leaf. We are told that a harsh tax was imposed on Jews. The Jews had formerly paid their taxes to Jerusalem, but since the time of Titus they had gone to the Emperor. It was a sort of protection-money which secured them religious toleration. The Christians probably had to pay it, too, since they came under the category of those 'who disguised their origins'. Ecclesiastical history relates that Domitian actively oppressed the Christians. Flavius Clemens, a cousin of the Emperor and the third Bishop of Rome, was a victim of this persecution, as was his wife Flavia Domitilla. Suetonius recalls that in his youth he was present when a ninety-year-old man was forced to show the procurator and a large tribunal whether he was circumcised or not.

Domitian was quite as arrogant as Nero ever was. On recalling his wife he declared that she was being allowed to take her place in the 'abode of the gods' once more. 'Hail to our Lord and Lady!' shouted the audience in the amphitheatre, and Domitian's edicts were prefaced by the words: 'Our Lord and God commands ... ' He was the first Emperor to demand that the Romans recognize him as a god during his lifetime. Indeed, it became his official mode of address. Domitian took great care to see that the statues erected in his honour on the Capitol were of solid gold or silver. Their poundage was carefully calculated, and woe betide everyone if they proved to be under-weight. The Emperor put up so many triumphal arches decorated with four-horse chariots and triumphal insignia that the people went out at night and scribbled 'Enough!' on them.

The campaigns and wars of conquest which Domitian waged — solely to enhance his reputation — in the Taunus region on the German frontier, in Britain and on the lower Danube, owed their measure of success only to the fact that he had a number of competent military commanders. But, like Nero, he was jealous of his generals' achievements and recalled them whenever they were on the verge of an expedition of any scope, as he did in the case of Agricola, the doughty general who reached Scotland and first brought the Romans definite news that Britain was an island. When Agricola died, everyone was convinced that he had been poisoned by Domitian, who was, incidentally, his son-in-law.

Domitian's kind of regime could never have lasted for very long. The great historian Rostovtzeff compares it with a return to the worst times under Tiberius, Caligula and Nero. Wherever the Emperor went, he aroused fear, alarm and hatred. Conspirators went about their silent and sinister work, aided and abetted by his wife Domitia. As usual, the 'Chaldeans' or soothsayers foretold everything in advance. Domitian sat in his chamber quaking with terror. Pliny tells us that he imported some white, marble-like stones from Cappadocia which shone like a mirror when they were polished, and used them to line the walls of the rooms and passages where he spent most of his time. Trembling, nervous, ever apprehensive of the assassin's dagger, he never took his weary eyes from the mirror-stones. He was happy only if he could see what was going on behind him. When he was interrogating prisoners he now shut himself in alone with them, holding their chains tightly in his hand.

The astrologer Ascletarion had predicted that Domitian would be murdered. Domitian asked him how he, the astrologer, would meet his end. Ascletarion replied that he would shortly be torn to pieces by dogs. The Emperor had him executed and ordered him to be carefully cremated so that no dog could come near him. A storm blew the pyre over, and Ascletarion's half-burned body was, in fact, torn to pieces by dogs. This convinced Domitian that his own end was near. When offered some fruit, he said: 'Keep it until tomorrow — if I am here to eat it.' Sleep deserted him, and at night he would jump out of bed, order torches to be brought in and stare about him wildly.

On September 16th, A.D. 96, the moon entered Aquarius. It was not due to emerge until September 18th. What was more, Mars and Saturn were also under that sign simultaneously, a conjunction which was a sure portent of disaster. The Emperor had been told that he would die at the fifth hour. Somewhere about that time, he asked how late it was. To reassure him, his attendant said that it was six o'clock. Greatly relieved and delighted, Domitian took a bath. Then his steward Parthenius announced that a messenger had arrived and was seeking an immediate audience. Apparently, he had discovered a plot against the Emperor's life. Ordering everyone to withdraw, Domitian closeted himself alone in his bedroom with the messenger, a man called Stephanus, who was steward to his Christian niece Domitilla. Stephanus looked harmless enough. He was wearing a woollen bandage on his left arm because of an injury which he said he had received, but between the bandage and his arm he had concealed a dagger. He handed the Emperor a written denunciation of the alleged conspiracy, and the Emperor started to read it. At that moment, Stephanus stabbed him in the groin.

We are told that after the first thrust Domitian called for his servants and bade them pass him the dagger which lay beneath his pillow, but all they found was a bladeless hilt. Mad with rage and terror, the Emperor hurled himself on Stephanus. Throwing him to the ground, he wrestled with him and tried with bleeding fingers and his last reserves of strength to gouge his eyes out, but Stephanus was too strong for him.

Domitian had reigned for fifteen years. Dio Cassius writes that he was never genuinely fond of any fellow-creature. He is said to have been a fine bowman, and used to shoot poisoned arrows between the outstretched fingers of young slaves without harming them. He could be witty, too. 'I wish,' he once said, 'I were as handsome as Maetius thinks he is.' And, another time: 'The sad thing about emperors is that, if they discover a conspiracy, no one believes them unless they are murdered.'

Domitian led a lonely existence just before his death. He only went out walking in areas which had been carefully sealed off. But he remained dissolute to the last. After his assassination, people smashed his busts with joyous abandon and dragged his statues off their pedestals to be melted down.

TRAJAN

LEAVE THE CHRISTIANS ALONE

Trajan was Julius Caesar resurrected.

Ernst Kornemann.

'I always try, as Emperor, to behave toward private citizens as I would formerly, as a private citizen, have wished Emperors to do.'

Trajan, taken from *Eutropius*, viii, 5.

SOMETHING new happened in Rome in the year A.D. 96. For the first time in history, an emperor was elected from among the members of the Senate. Senator Nerva was sixty-four years old. He had inherited a weak constitution and was in failing health, but he was a good lawyer, and restored some much-needed equilibrium to the State.

All the many people whom Domitian had thrown into gaol for *lèse-majesté* were immediately released, and exiles were allowed to return to Italy. On the other hand, slaves who had denounced their masters during Domitian's reign of terror were now sentenced to death. Emperor Nerva also forbade the prosecution of people 'because of their Jewish way of life' — which probably meant the Christians. Those who had been dispossessed of their property by Domitian had it returned to them, and a welfare fund was set up for the benefit of destitute Romans. Nerva raised money to purchase small-holdings for these paupers. When his court got into financial straits he sold clothing, gold, silver plate and valuable household furniture from the imperial palace, as well as several royal mansions.

The new Emperor enforced his economies on the rest of Rome, too. He abolished extravagant sacrifices and limited expenditure on luxuries such as race-meetings and public entertainments. Castration was prohibited, as was marriage between uncle and niece.

It is not surprising that Nerva was soon able to say of himself: 'I have done nothing which would stand in the way of my abdicating and returning to private life unscathed.'

But the worthy man was wrong. His life, too, was threatened. Minor conspiracies were brewing here and there. The Emperor disconcerted the plotters by calmly appearing in their midst unarmed. Nevertheless, when he got the feeling that people were abusing his kindness, that they even

The shaded area indicates the extent of the Roman Empire between A.D. 117 (death of Trajan) and A.D. 211 (death of Septimius Severus). The size of the Empire remained

despised him, perhaps because he was too old, too good or too decent for a decadent city like Rome, he adopted the Roman governor of Germany as his son and proclaimed him Emperor. It was the best and most important

virtually static until the death of Theodosius in 395, the only territories lost being Dacia (following the Gothic invasions of 250–70), Mesopotamia and south-west Germany

decision Nerva made during his reign. The Roman historian Eutropius called it an act of 'godlike prevision'.

The new Emperor's name was Marcus Ulpius Traianus. He was a

Spaniard and a provincial (which was yet another novelty for Rome), and came of a Roman colonial family from Italica near Seville on the Guadalquivir. Nerva had relatives of his own whom he could have put on the throne, but Rome and the Roman Empire were more important to him than his family, and Trajan seemed to be the man for the job.

Trajan was forty-eight years old. He became Emperor by adoption and on his own merits. That, too, was a new departure, but it became recognized procedure for the next hundred years, thereby guaranteeing Rome a series of efficient rulers which began with Nerva and ended with Marcus Aurelius, and turning the second century A.D. into the happiest and best period in the history of imperial Rome.

Nerva died, having reigned briefly but well for one year, four months and nine days. And Trajan, the great man who wanted to be another Alexander but never attained his ideal, set out on his autocratic and ambitious, but prosperous career.

He made the most of his time. He rebuilt the dilapidated Circus on a larger and more magnificent scale, planned public buildings, high-roads and harbours, built a causeway across the Pontine marshes lined with houses and interspersed by numerous bridges, installed forts and crossing-places on the German Rhine. He carried out further projects in the Neckar region. One of his achievements was a road leading from Mainz, via Heidelberg, to Baden-Baden. His creative energy left its mark deep in the heart of the Danube area. In Africa he reached the borders of the desert and founded the colony of Timgad, the African Pompeii which was discovered under its shroud of sand by archaeologists of our own day.

Trajan loved hunting. He also loved banqueting, but only in moderation, and could drink a great deal of wine without getting drunk. For informers, who were his special bugbear, he reserved a special punishment, which was to flog them, put them on board ship and send them out into a storm. In other respects he was always sparing in his punishments. He treated the Senate with courtesy and walked through the streets of Rome alone and unescorted.

When Pliny the Younger, who was governor of Bithynia under Trajan, wrote to the Emperor asking what he should do with the Christians in his province, Trajan wrote back: 'They must not be persecuted. It is unworthy of our century to give credence to anonymous denunciations.' Trajan's accession ushered in an age of humanity and tolerance.

On the north bank of the lower Danube, in the Seven Mountains region of Wallachia in eastern Hungary, lived the Dacians. From sparse accounts we can glean a vague picture of their king, Decebalus, a highly intelligent, proud and wily barbarian who would never accept defeat at any price.

Trajan advanced on the Dacians and worsted them, whereupon Decebalus behaved as though he intended to negotiate for peace and was prepared to make any concession. Then he fought on. His sister fell into Roman hands. Once more the barbarian king seemed willing to submit. He even paid homage to Trajan, fell on his knees before him and threw his weapons away. Trajan made peace and returned to Italy.

It was not long before news came that King Decebalus and his Dacians had thrown all their agreements overboard. North of the Danube, it seemed, peace treaties were made to be broken. Once again Trajan took personal command of the Roman army. Dacian troops began to desert, and soon King Decebalus was suing for peace again. Simultaneously, he recruited a fresh army, bullied a number of tribes into joining forces with him against the Romans and sent assassins into Trajan's camp. The assassins were captured and tortured into admitting their guilt. Decebalus then tried another ruse. He invited Longinus, a brilliant Roman general who had caused him a great deal of trouble, to pay him a visit. Longinus had scarcely set foot in the barbarian king's camp when he was made prisoner. Decebalus offered to release him in return for all the Roman-occupied territory along the Danube. Trajan's reply was couched in such ambiguous terms that he left Decebalus in the dark, but Longinus was loyal to his Emperor and, before the barbarian king could do any more blackmailing, he poisoned himself.

Trajan then built a stone bridge across the Danube to help keep the Dacians on the run. Dio Cassius of Bithynia, who wrote an eighty-volume history of Rome in about A.D. 229, gives a glowing description of Trajan's bridge at the Iron Gate. Trajan's other feats of engineering were impressive enough, he writes, but this surpassed them all. The man who actually constructed it was a Greek called Apollodorus of Damascus, one of the greatest engineers and architects in the ancient world.

Using the bridge, Trajan began a systematic conquest of the Dacians. The Romans fought with extreme bravery. Decabalus first lost his headquarters and then his whole country. Eventually, when he was threatened with capture, he took his own life. His head was brought back to Rome in triumph, and Dacia became a Roman province. An enormous monument commemorating the victory was built in the Dobrudja, the *Tropaeum Traiani*, whose ruins were discovered by Moltke in 1837. The spot beneath the bed of the Ister where Decebalus had buried his royal treasures was betrayed to the Romans, who dug them up. It was there by the Ister that the stubborn king had built his residence, a strong fortress, so Dio Cassius tells us. This is surprising when we consider that the Dacians were largely a nomadic people. They were subsequently joined by Roman colonists, with the result that the region which they once occupied, now Romania or Roumania, has a half-Latin, half-Slav language.

But Trajan did not stop there. He let his sense of mission, his vigorous character and his spirit of initiative carry him on to further achievements. He decreed victory celebrations lasting 130 days, during which thousands of wild animals tore each other to pieces and thousands of Dacian prisoners of war went through their paces in the arena. These gory spectacles gave the Roman public their first opportunity of seeing the bravery of the men whom Trajan had defeated. The Emperor put up libraries, commissioned the architect Apollodorus to build the *Forum Traiani* — a new square between the Capitol and the Quirinal — and erected the most splendid example of Roman sculpture anywhere: world-famous Trajan's Column, an amazing history-book in stone which depicts the exploits of Roman legions on the Drave, the Save and the Danube in a series of 155 pictures encircling a pillar.

We are shown the bridge under construction; ships sailing along the river heavily laden with supplies; legionaries on the march, on sentry duty and in action; the Emperor himself, on foot as usual, among his troops; Dacian women and children in flight; and repeated portrayals of Quintus Lusius, Trajan's senior general, once a Moroccan sheikh but now the Emperor's right-hand man, an Othello of the imperial era.

Of all the honorific titles which the Senate bestowed on Trajan, only one meant anything to him: *Optimus*, 'The Best'. It was a title which matched his character. He owed all the rest to his military successes.

Trajan's marriage to Plotina was childless. The Empress must have been extremely beautiful, if her coin-portraits are anything to go by. She lived a very quiet life and was a great friend of Marciana, Trajan's sister. On taking up her abode at the imperial palace, she said: 'May I leave this house as free from any guilt as I now enter it.' It was a vow she never broke.

Trajan could not bear inactivity. He was the last great soldier to occupy the Roman throne, a man who was not only a brilliant statesman but a simple, straightforward and uncommonly powerful personality with the military genius of a Caesar burning within him. He made up his mind to march against Parthia, inspired by the fact that there were Greek cities there culturally related to Rome, magnificent cities like Ctesiphon and Seleucia, which were in the hands of the barbarian Parthians.

Trajan victoriously retraced Alexander the Great's footsteps into the East. He reached Babylon and the Euphrates. Ambassadors from India began to arrive in his camp. He pushed on into Media. Satraps and kings laid gifts at his feet. A trained horse fell on its knees before him. His troops marched, without striking a blow, along the endless roads of Mesopotamia, Assyria, Armenia. Never before had the Roman Empire undergone such expansion as it did under Trajan. At Antioch the Emperor was unexpectedly involved in a terrible earthquake which claimed thousands of victims. (We are in the period between A.D. 114 and A.D. 116.) He escaped through the window of a house just before it collapsed, and spent several days in an alfresco bivouac on the local race-course. Then he resumed his campaign. At last he reached the Persian Gulf, and the Indian Ocean lay before him. He built a fleet with the intention of conquering India, the land of Alexander's dreams and the land which Alexander did, in fact, reach.

But behind Trajan, behind the Roman conqueror, rebellion reared its head and conquered nations defected. That was one respect in which Trajan was unlike Alexander: he could not hold cities, kings or rulers under the spell of his personality or turn them into his permanent vassals. He was not a man to make political marriages, a device which Alexander used so successfully. He did not exercise the same effect on orientals as his glamorous and fortunate Macedonian predecessor. 'I should have liked to go to India, too, if I had been younger,' he mused resignedly as he watched a ship sailing off to India.

While the Senate back in Rome was announcing Trajan's victories to the public — with difficulty, because people found it hard to remember all the battles and thread their way through the names of so many distant and unfamiliar countries — Trajan was marching into Arabia against the Atreni, one of the many nations which had rebelled against him. Their capital was neither large nor prosperous, and was surrounded by arid and desolate country. The water was bad, and there was no wood or grazing. It was dangerous to besiege the place, since it stood 'under the protection of the sun-god'. Trajan's cavalry was routed and Trajan himself, the 'worthy greyhead', as he was affectionately known, narrowly escaped being wounded. A sand-storm and a plague of flies compelled the Emperor to abandon the siege. That is all we know. We have no idea where the town of Atra or Hatra stood, or what desert dune now covers it.

Emperor Trajan still had a thousand plans. But he was old and sick, having long been afflicted with dropsy. He wanted to get back to Italy quickly rather than die on foreign soil. Leaving one of his generals, Publius

Aelius Hadrianus, behind in Syria with the army, he travelled to Cilicia in Asia Minor. There his condition deteriorated.

Trajan was smitten by a dreadful suspicion that someone was trying to poison him. He suffered a stroke which left him partially paralysed, and suddenly found difficulty in breathing.

Although the Emperor did not die unexpectedly, he had neglected to provide himself with a successor. His wife Plotina wanted him to adopt General Hadrianus, but Trajan would not agree. He thought him too weak, and had quite different ideas about who should be Emperor. Soon the sands had run out and it was too late. Trajan had reigned for nineteen years, six months and fifteen days.

Emperor Trajan (reigned A.D. 98–117) richly merited the name Optimus, 'the best', which was later bestowed on him. He was one of the most important and powerful Roman rulers, and under him the Roman Empire reached its point of greatest expansion

Plotina, wife of Trajan, was renowned for her modesty, dignity, loyalty and virtue. She helped Hadrian to become Trajan's successor

Trajan's Column, 125 feet high, a picture-book in marble comprising 155 individual scenes. The burial urns of Trajan and his wife Plotina were interred in its base. The column contains a circular staircase and was surmounted, until the Middle Ages, by a statue of Trajan

An interesting scene from the 155 reliefs on Trajan's Column shows Dacian princes reaching for a bowl of poison in their eagerness to commit suicide rather than be brought to Rome in Trajan's triumphal procession

HADRIAN

A STATESMAN ON THE THRONE

There was something almost miraculous in the way he emerged from the darkness of human history. Emperor Hadrian was a wise man such as humanity only sees at intervals of several hundred years, a man of many parts, a prince of peace, order and integrity.

The Author.

EMPEROR TRAJAN was dead. How the legions all over the Roman Empire, from Britain to the Nile, from the Guadalquivir in Spain to the Euphrates and Tigris, would mourn when they heard the news. How the Dacians north of the Danube would sigh with relief. Would it mean their freedom? And the Parthians? Would it raise their hopes of peace?

Emperor Trajan was dead, but there was much whispering around his death-bed.

His wife Plotina was a clever and accomplished woman. She was always one jump ahead of events, both in her ideas and her policies. She and Hadrian had always got on extremely well, and their Platonic friendship had lasted for twenty years. Hadrian was now forty-one. Plotina wanted to make him Emperor, but there was the question of adoption. Although Trajan had entrusted him with the highest political appointments, he had never adopted him.

Still the whispering went on round Trajan's death-bed. Attianus and Plotina were very worried. What were they to do? The news of the Emperor's death had not escaped the room yet, but beyond the heavy curtains stood sentries, senators talking in low tones and tribunes awaiting orders for the legions and their generals in Germany, Britain, Egypt and Parthia.

Plotina had an idea. The Emperor was dead, but nobody outside knew it yet. He could be made to whisper. Perhaps it was Attianus who impersonated him so effectively. Whoever it was, there issued from the bed-chamber of the dead Imperator a weak voice announcing the adoption of Hadrian.

At last the curtains were drawn back. At last the Emperor was dead. At last the dispatch-riders could gallop off, carrying the news to the four corners of the far-flung Empire. They reached the capital of Syria, where Hadrian was governor.

Publius Aelius Hadrianus enjoyed an unrivalled reputation in the Roman Empire. He was also related to Trajan, and his father came from the same interesting part of the world as Trajan's, the banks of the Guadalquivir, where, 1,000 years before Christ, the world's greatest seafaring nations, the Etruscans and Phoenicians, had fought for commercial supremacy.

Hadrian was a Spaniard, and Spanish was his mother-tongue. His mother, Domitia Paulina, was a true child of Cadiz.

Having lost his father at a very early age, Hadrian became Emperor Trajan's ward. He studied the Greek language at Rome with burning enthusiasm. Greece attracted and enthralled him. He was fascinated by Greek art and greatly admired Greek sculptors, statesmen and philosophers, especially Plato. The Romans nicknamed him 'the little Greek'.

Hadrian joined the army in Spain at the age of fifteen. His great passion was hunting, and he pursued it in such a rash, wild and foolhardy way that Trajan was forced to recall him to Rome. The normal stages in a public career followed, including a tour of duty with the legions on the Danube. More hunting, wine-drinking and debts. Then, like a sudden flash of lightning in the European sky, the news of Trajan's accession.

Now twenty-two, Hadrian set off on a break-neck journey from the Danube to Cologne. His carriage broke down, but he pressed on regardless, and arrived in advance of his brother-in-law Servianus, who disliked him and was always trying to bring him into Trajan's bad books. Hadrian congratulated the new Emperor.

Actually, Trajan and Hadrian could never have become intimate friends. They were too dissimilar in character. Nevertheless, with Plotina's support, Hadrian found a way of getting close to the Emperor. He married Sabina, the grand-daughter of Trajan's sister. Trajan was not too pleased with this union, but Plotina managed to reconcile him to it. The Platonic friendship between Plotina and young Hadrian grew increasingly close. And, when the messengers galloped up to Hadrian with the news of Trajan's death, he may well have guessed at once that his friend Plotina was behind the adoption. He informed the Senate of his wish to be confirmed as Emperor. At the same time, he declined to accept, either then or in the future, any of the customary marks of honour.

Peace the world over: that was the new Emperor's prime consideration from the earliest days of his reign onwards. He remained true to that ideal until his death.

There is no doubt that Hadrian's reign was one of the most prosperous and fortunate in ancient history. He was a quite remarkable personality. For sheer versatility, he towered above every Roman emperor since Augustus. He embodied, for perhaps the last time, all the finest qualities which the ancient world produced: humanity and chivalry, insusceptibility to physical hardship, courtesy, an excellent mind and an amazing diversity of natural gifts.

The new Emperor at once abandoned all territory east of the Euphrates and Tigris, recognizing that these areas were untenable with the forces at his disposal. Trajan's conquests in Parthia, Assyria and Mesopotamia were therefore lost to Rome.

Hadrian was a political genius of the first order. So much was obvious from the outset. He acted from personal conviction and relied on his own judgment. Knowing that unrest on such far distant frontiers would overtax the resources of the Roman Empire, he set himself a target: the Roman Empire must become strong in defence. It must remain entrenched in that position of strength and keep the peace.

It was an unpopular policy. There were murmurs from Rome's generals. Ambitious officers are not fond of seeing their careers frustrated by everlasting peace.

But Hadrian won the people's backing. He wrote off all the sums of money owed by private citizens to the Roman exchequer. There was a tremendous outburst of rejoicing as thousands upon thousands of promissory notes went up in flames in the Forum.

Hadrian at once began to put the public finances in order, probing every last detail with remarkable business acumen. He instituted welfare services and granted economic aid to the towns in Campania. He built up a bond of intimacy between himself and the members of the Senate which rendered fruitful co-operation possible from the very start. He attended senatorial sessions punctually and in person. He safeguarded the Senate's reputation by ensuring that unsuitable candidates were not elected. He visited his friends when they were ill. He entertained a good deal, but his banquets were largely devoted to the discussion of affairs of State. He secured the services of numerous shrewd and efficient men.

Hadrian achieved all this without a large outlay. He disliked pomp, luxury and extravagance, but insisted on etiquette and formality, and was himself a model of good breeding, culture and courtesy.

THE MODERN MONARCH

> Who among men had such wide interests, who was so many-sided and mobile, who thought so quickly, knew so much, surprised even those who stood nearest to him by his knowledge of their most secret thoughts? Who was in everything so supple and yet hard as steel, who so cold in calculation and determined in action? He felt the longing of men and gave it fulfilment in philosophical formulae, ideologies, and illusions, but also in deeds, so that they greeted him with exultation where he appeared.
>
> *Wilhelm Weber, Cambridge Ancient History*, Volume XI, Chapter viii, 3.

HADRIAN radiated his own private atmosphere. There was a modernity in his preoccupation with things of moment and his lack of interest in mere emperorship. His education had made him Greek to the core, and under him the Hellenic world experienced a spiritual and material rebirth unequalled at any other stage in the imperial era, either before or since.

Late and indirect as it was, defeated Greece had at last won her victory over Rome.

In the fourth year of his reign, A.D. 121, Hadrian set off on his first journey as Emperor. He was perhaps the most travelled monarch in world history, and this wanderlust was one of his most noteworthy characteristics.

Always accompanied by his large secretariat, he travelled from one end of the Empire to the other, inspecting the administration of justice wherever he went. Travelling along the roads of Europe, North Africa and Asia by coach, horse or foot, he and his staff of officials constituted a mobile 'directorate' with sweeping political powers.

Gaul, Germany, Greece, Asia Minor and Egypt all saw the arrival of the Emperor and his large and silent entourage. Hadrian liked people to be quiet in his presence, and made it the principal task of a senior official to see that they were.

In proof that if anything held up these long journeys it would not be symptoms of royal fatigue, Hadrian sometimes marched twenty miles or so in full armour. He always wore ordinary clothes and shunned gold, jewellery and weapons. He visited soldiers in hospital. He regrouped his armies almost always with an eye to their defensive, not their offensive, potentialities. He recruited bodies of militia in all the frontier provinces of the Empire to defend the civilized world against the barbarians. In his administration of the Roman army he outrivalled all the emperors before him. He forbade officers to accept gifts from their men and prohibited all luxury in the armed forces. Above all, he was endowed with the remarkable talent, as beneficial as it was practical, for sensing with razor-sharp certainty whether an appointment or a contract for military supplies or building materials was useful and expedient, or whether it had been dreamed up merely to provide some organization with jobs, work or perhaps money. Hadrian ruthlessly swept away everything which was at all unnecessary or unprofitable. He kept a tight rein on the money- and time-wasting paper warfare and costly red-tape which are the bane of any large empire. Hadrian built up an ideal type of civil servant.

The Emperor's mental flexibility and lack of prejudice were amazing. His beard was an outward and visible sign of this. It must be borne in mind that ever since the time of Alexander the Great, or 500 years earlier, the whole of the Graeco-Roman world had gone about clean-shaven, the only exceptions being outsiders like Christians and philosophers. Socrates wore a beard, as did Plato and Epicurus. Hadrian's beard was a token of his archaistic leanings. It was precisely this devotion to an ancient past which put him so far in advance of his time. For all her influence over him, Plotina had nothing to do with this. Hadrian defended his beard. In fact, he decreed that only men with beards or potential beards could become officers, a regulation which weeded out the immature. The wearing of beards became universally fashionable under Hadrian and his successors. The wall-statues of this period are all bearded, a fact which enables art historians to date them.

The soldiers adored their Emperor. He drank with them, ate with them and marched with them, never using a carriage.

The Roman Empire grew tremendously strong. It grew strong, yet had no need to wage war. The Dacian war was speedily brought to an end. Hadrian refused the offer of a triumphal procession, ordering instead that the statue of Trajan, his late predecessor and the real conqueror of Dacia, should be carried into Rome through the Porta Triumphalis.

The Parthians looked upon Hadrian as their friend and redeemer. The Armenians now had their own king and not a Roman governor, as in Trajan's time. The Mesopotamians were absolved from paying tribute. Hadrian made large gifts to the kings of the Albanians and Hiberians in the Caucasus, thereby gaining their friendship for the first time. The Bactrian kings of the Hindu Kush sent ambassadors to Hadrian and courted his favour. Rome's international relations had been put on the best possible footing.

But inside the Roman Empire, too, nothing escaped the eyes and ears of the Emperor. He was everywhere at once, since his agents (*frumentarii*) travelled the world over, reporting whether senior government officials were really doing their job. It was a system of internal espionage which the Emperor maintained purely for his own information and never abused in the interests of suppressing personal freedom.

Hadrian wanted to be his people's servant, no more — but no less. He always rose to his feet when receiving senators, but insisted that they should wear the regulation toga on duty or in public. He reorganized the whole judiciary and commissioned the celebrated jurist Salvius Julianus to make a collection of all previous legal decisions, thus paving the way for Emperor Justinian's *corpus juris*. He prohibited denunciations for *lèse-majesté*. Slaves could not be killed by their owners. Sentences of death (this applied to slaves, too) could only be passed by public courts. Hadrian even issued a decree forbidding the sale of male or female slaves to the brutal gladiatorial schools. Henceforth this could only take place under State supervision and after detailed examination of each individual case. The penalty for culpable extravagance was strict, but short and sweet: anyone who had squandered property which he was legally obliged to conserve was flogged in the amphitheatre and then allowed to go home. Hadrian abolished penal servitude for slaves and freemen alike. It was the custom, when a Roman had been murdered in his own home, to use torture when interrogating his slaves. The Emperor did away with this inhuman practice and laid it down that only slaves who had been near enough to have any knowledge of the murder could be interrogated. He extended the concept of *humanitas* to include slaves because, in his eyes, they too were human beings.

Then there was bathing. Hadrian decreed that the sexes should be segregated when taking public baths, and installed new baths for this purpose. We know, incidentally, that he applied this rule to his own villa, where he had two separate baths.

But Hadrian was not a prudish person. He was modern, both in the world of his day and in retrospect. He was a democrat. Anyone could approach him. He spoke to everyone, including the poor, chatted far more often with other ranks than with officers. Once, as he was walking down a street, a woman called to him and asked him something. 'I've no time now!' said the Emperor. 'Then don't be Emperor!' she shouted after him. Hadrian turned back and listened to her patiently.

The Romans, being southerners, regarded Germany as a land of hard winters and intense cold. Hence the admiration of the historian Dio Cassius when he wrote that the Emperor never covered his head either in heat or cold. 'Even in the German snows and the scorching sun of Egypt, Hadrian went about without a hat.'

Aelius Spartianus, the Emperor's Roman biographer, says in his *Historia Augusta:* 'Scarcely ever had an Emperor traversed such vast regions at such speed.' We learn that Hadrian climbed Mount Etna in Sicily to watch the sunrise. His contemporaries found this rather bizarre, but there are many references to his penchant for sun-worship. He may have caught the idea from his study of Pharaoh Ikhnaton and the Amarna period which, even at that time, lay 1,500 years back in Egyptian history.

The Emperor's second great world tour covered the period A.D. 128–134. Gaul, Spain, Britain and Germany were all inspected. In Britain, Hadrian erected the famous rampart or entrenchment which extended for over sixty miles from the Tyne Estuary to the Firth of Solway. He also strengthened the Germano-Rhaetian *limes* or frontier rampart between Andernach and the Danube at Regensburg. Something else of note happened during this period: Hadrian dismissed Suetonius Tranquillus, his private secretary and a well-known historian, together with his assistants. Apparently they had taken liberties with his wife Sabina which infringed court etiquette. He was also very displeased with Sabina because she had grown irritable and perpetually ill-tempered. If he had been a private citizen and not Emperor, he would undoubtedly have divorced her.

Hadrian was an amazingly accomplished and talented person. He was a good prose-writer and an excellent poet, and greatly enjoyed swapping verses with the major poets of his day. He was an authority on Cato, Cicero, Virgil and Sallust, and knew the works of Homer and Plato like the back of his hand. He considered himself such a good astrologer that he set down in writing, every January, what was going to happen to him in the course of the year. Even in the year he died he recorded, with a fair degree of accuracy, all that fate still held in store for him, down to the actual hour and minute of his death.

The philosophers Epictetus and Heliodorus, orators, musicians, mathematicians, painters, astrologers — Hadrian gave them every possible help and encouragement. But he was fond of teasing them and involving them in caustic debate, poking fun at them much as did Frederick of Prussia at Voltaire. His quite phenomenal memory enabled him to dictate brilliantly formulated speeches at high speed, retain whole books by heart and write, listen and chat to his friends all at the same time — 'incredible as it may seem', as his biographer remarks.

Hadrian also had a very good memory for faces, a characteristic which he shared with other great statesmen in world history such as Napoleon, Bismarck and Churchill. He would even recognize private soldiers again after a lapse of years and address them by name without a moment's hesitation. Indeed, he made it a sort of hobby not only to remember the names of thousands of people but also to be able to spell them correctly. This aptitude aroused the greatest admiration in the Senate and among the inhabitants of the many countries he visited.

He could be witty, too. A grey-headed old man made a request which Hadrian refused. Soon afterwards the same man appeared again, this time with his hair dyed. Hadrian recognized him immediately. 'I have already refused your father once,' he quipped.

DIVINE ANTINOUS

Hadrian was not only the first true philhellene to occupy the throne of the Caesars but also the greatest, in whose footsteps Gallienus followed in the third century and Julian in the fourth. Under Hadrian, Hellenism ... became the formative power in the *Imperium Romanum.*

Hermann Bengtson, Greek History, Section 5.

THE Emperor often bathed in the public baths. On one such visit he saw an old man flexing his knees and rubbing his back against the wall. 'Why are you massaging yourself against the marble?' asked Hadrian. 'Because I do not own a slave,' the old man answered. The very same day, Hadrian made him a present of several slaves and enough money to maintain them for years. Next time he visited a public bath the walls were lined with old men bending their knees and rubbing their backs on the marble. Calling them over, the Emperor told them to massage each other for a while.

Here is something else which may be attributed to the great man's whimsical or pungent sense of humour. With the aid of his architect Decrianus, he arranged for the removal of the colossus which Nero had erected in the vestibule of his Golden House. Keeping it in an upright position, he had the statue transported to a spot north-west of what later became known as the Colosseum. The gigantic sculpture must have been some 130 feet high (part of its pedestal still survives), and was so heavy that the Emperor's architect had to use a team of twenty-four elephants in order to shift it. Hadrian erased Nero's features and dedicated the figure to the sun.

The Emperor was so fond of animals that he built tombs for his pets. His hunter, Borysthenes, even got a pillar complete with inscription.

Hadrian visited Athens three times, in the years 124–5, 128–9 and 131–2. Here he built the so-called City of Hadrian, thus becoming, in effect, the second founder of Athens. He completed the Olympeium and built the Temple of Hera, a pantheon, the Stoa and its library, a gymnasium, the Panhellenion (a temple for Zeus) and an aqueduct. He got himself initiated into the mystery-cult of Eleusis. For Athens, Emperor Hadrian was the symbol and author of a fresh lease of life. Hadrian's Gate, which divides the ancient city from the new, still bears the legend: 'Here is Athens, formerly the city of Theseus' on one side, and on the other: 'Here is the city of Hadrian, not of Theseus.' Hadrian was so devoted to the Greeks that he founded a 'panhellenic confederation', which every Greek city in the Roman Empire was to join.

There is no doubt that Hadrian's intentions for Jerusalem, too, were of the best. Ever since its destruction by Emperor Titus the city had lain beneath the Judaean sun like a great open sore. Hadrian began to rebuild it. On the spot where Jehovah's temple lay in ruins he planned to build a shrine for Jupiter. Enraged by this, the Jews rose in rebellion under their leader and champion Bar Kokba. Hadrian retorted by instructing his general, Julius Severus, to destroy all their towns. As a devotee of peace, he found it a hard decision to make. It distressed him and made him morose.

In the year 130, while he was visiting Egypt with his wife and the usual

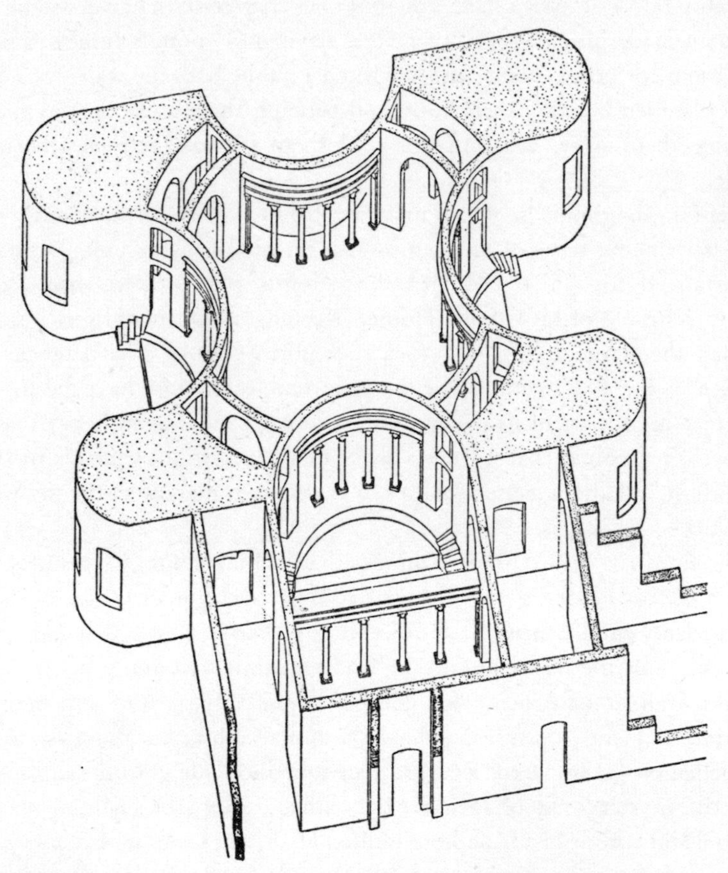

The 'Little Palace' of Hadrian at Tivoli. (ex *Hadrian und seine Villa bei Tivoli*, by H. Köhler)

large entourage, Hadrian suffered a stroke of misfortune which was to cast a shadow over the rest of his life. A lady-in-waiting, Julia Balbilla by name, left a few Greek poems engraved on the Colossus of Memnon as a memento of the imperial visit.

On the Emperor's staff at the time was a very handsome young man called Antinous, of whom he was extremely fond. It appears, though the facts are obscure, that this youth was drowned during a trip up the Nile. That, at any rate, is what Emperor Hadrian is supposed to have said. Dio Cassius, the Bithynian historian, is sceptical, and suggests that Antinous died for love of Hadrian 'because what the Emperor had in mind demanded the voluntary sacrifice of another'.

This death, accident or not, seems to have overwhelmed the Emperor so

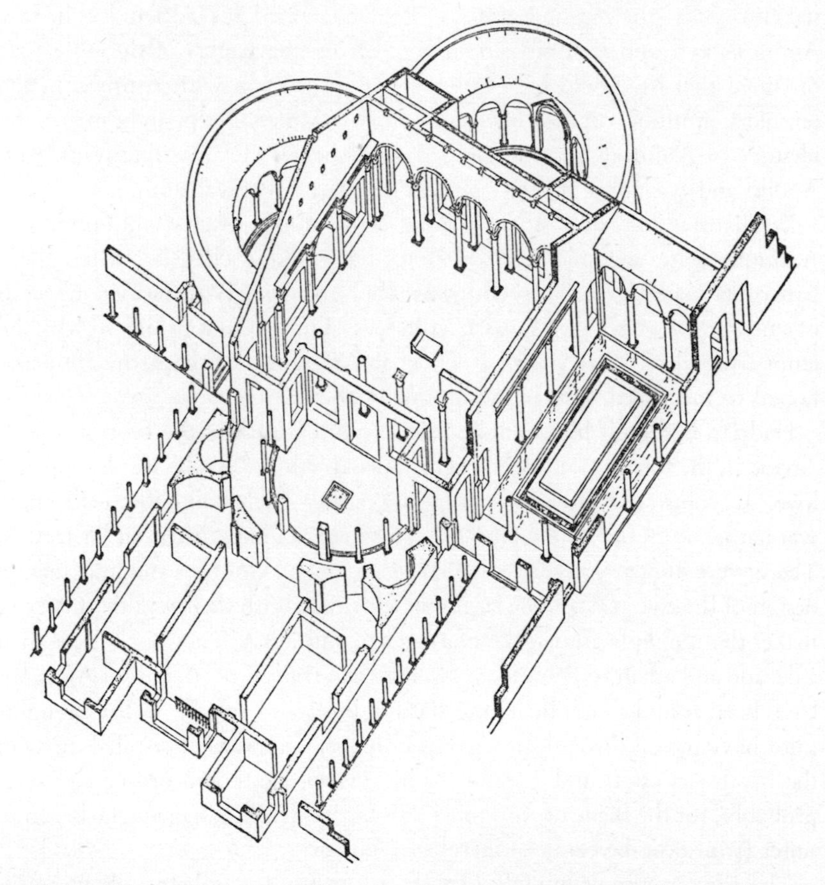

Hadrian's Villa at Tivoli was built to the Emperor's own specifications. This is the spacious dining-room. (By courtesy of the Verlag Gebr. Mann, Berlin)

utterly that he never recovered from his grief. We are told that he mourned for the dead boy 'like a wife'.

At the place where Antinous died, Hadrian founded a town called Antinoe (now Antinoopolis) on October 30th, A.D. 130. The town stands on the east bank of the Nile, not far from Hermopolis on the other side of the river. Whereas the streets of Pompeii were thirty feet across at their widest point, Antinoe had an avenue sixty-five feet wide. Lining this main thoroughfare were baths, temples, a theatre and a building assumed to be Antinous' tomb. All the streets ran at right angles, like those in New York, and were numbered in the same way.

Still unsatisfied, the Emperor set up statues and busts of Antinous all over the Roman Empire. He even came to believe that he had observed a new star in the sky, the star of Antinous. People laughed at Hadrian, but he saw Antinous as a god, as Osiris, resurrected from the waters of the Nile, and ordained that he should be worshipped in association with Ammon in the temple at Antinoe. In the Greek cities of Asia Minor, Egypt and Europe, the identity of Antinous became merged with that of Hermes, Dionysus, Pan, Apollo and Asclepius. In Italy he was associated with Silvanus.

To Hadrian life had lost all meaning if the unique beauty and nobility of Antinous were beyond recall. He built temples and chapels but left them bare of sacred images. For whom were they erected? Was Hadrian in search of a new god? After all, he was an adherent of the gods of Rome, so why the empty temples? One thinks at once of Antinous. Perhaps the Emperor hoped to meet him, resurrected, in one of them.

Hadrian had built himself a beautiful country place at the foot of Monte Arcese in the lonely Campagna. This villa at Tibur (Tivoli) was his especial love. Its ruins cover an area of some 160 acres. Each building on the estate was named after one of the famous places Hadrian had visited on his travels. There were libraries, a theatre, baths, arcades. The vigorous and imaginative design of the two palaces, the large and the small, with their wealth of curves, makes them unique among the buildings of antiquity. They took more than a decade and a half to complete. No less than sixteen portrayals of Antinous have been found there, including statues, busts and reliefs. What thoughts must have passed through the ageing Emperor's mind as he strolled through the rooms, cloisters and grounds of his Tivoli, alone and unescorted save, probably, for the shade of Antinous? His health deteriorated, and he began to suffer from nose-bleeding of increasing violence.

The Emperor built himself a tomb, a gigantic mausoleum which he intended all his successors to use in turn. Although he had seen the pyramids in

Egypt, he wanted his own symbol of eternity to be round, round as eternity itself. A site opposite the Campus Martius became a scene of great activity. Ant-like, slaves hauled stones and mortar into position, and the grandest tribute to Roman emperorship gradually took shape. The tomb is now the Castle of St Angelo. Hadrian wanted the urn containing his ashes to repose there in solitary state until the next emperor joined him, and so on into all eternity.

Hadrian had hoped to live for a very long time, but he now saw that Fate was hovering close at hand, ready to recall him. He had nominated Lucius Ceionius as his successor in the event of his death, but Ceionius appears to have been tubercular.

Hadrian ordered the execution of a ninety-year-old man called Servianus and his grandson Fuscus, aged eighteen. No one had ever seen Hadrian act in anger before. 'Bear witness to my innocence, ye gods!' cried Servianus. 'I see Hadrian. He wants to die and will not be able to!' It was true. Hadrian's condition grew worse and worse. 'It is sad indeed,' he wrote, 'to want to die and not to be able to.'

Lucius Ceionius unexpectedly died of a violent haemorrhage. Hadrian, who was now suffering from dropsy, summoned the most distinguished members of the Senate to the palace and addressed them from his sick-bed. He presented Antoninus Pius to them and announced that he would be taking over the government. Antoninus, for his part, was required to adopt young Marcus Aurelius as his son and successor.

Meanwhile, Hadrian felt his death grow more imminent with each day that passed. Still as restless as ever, he made a last trip to Baiae on the coast. He wanted to look at the sea, the broad and splendid sea which had carried him from country to country, the water which made him feel closer to the soul of his beloved Antinous. But he was in agony. So passionately did he yearn to die that he begged for some poison. Then he called for a sword, but no one would hand him one. He promised money and legal immunity to anyone who would kill him, but no one volunteered. In the end he sent for Mastor, a former prisoner of war. With a mixture of threats and promises, he talked him into killing him. He daubed a cross on his chest to mark the spot where Mastor was to drive his dagger home.

The barbarian took to his heels.

Hadrian wept.

He wept because he could kill others, but not himself. The idea suddenly struck him that he might have regained his health and lived longer if only he had received proper treatment. 'Many doctors are a prince's death,' he is alleged to have said just before he died.

ANTONINUS PIUS

THE GENTLEMANLY EMPEROR

He was a strikingly handsome man of eminent talents and a pleasant disposition. An aristocrat to his finger-tips, he was dignified in manner, an accomplished orator, a fine scholar, extremely moderate and abstemious, an industrious landowner, affable, magnanimous, ever respectful of other men's rights. He possessed all these attributes in the right proportion and never made an exaggerated parade of them. That was why he won the esteem of all people of integrity and truly merited comparison with Numa Pompilius.

Julius Capitolinus, Antoninus Pius, xi.

HADRIAN, the man of peace, had reigned with such success that the machinery of government was functioning with marvellous regularity and precision.

Hadrian's foresight and wisdom are beyond praise. Ill though he was, he made careful provision for his death by designating not only his adoptive heir but his successor's successor. Both Antoninus and Marcus Aurelius fulfilled all Rome's hopes. Neither of them proved a disappointment. Indeed, under these two rulers the world empire maintained its foothold on the highest pinnacle of success ever attained in the whole course of Roman history. Twenty years of peace: forty years of order and justice.

Marcus Aurelius was really the last great figure in this fortunate period. Once he had gone, the ship of State drifted into troubled waters and steered a perilous course among the reefs of disputed succession, assassination and German invasion.

Antoninus Pius was a good-looking man with a likable and even gifted personality. None but the best characteristics were ever attributed to him. He was fifty-two years old when Hadrian died. The Romans compared him with Numa Pompilius, the wise and upright prince of peace who was the second king of Rome. They had to go a long way back in history to find a comparison with the aristocratic and elegant landowner who was now Emperor of Rome. In A.D. 147 the latter-day Numa presided over the celebrations held to mark the nine-hundredth anniversary of Rome's foundation.

Antoninus was born at Lanuvium in Latium, but his family came from Nemausus, now Nîmes in Provence. Since nobody from the provinces could become a senator without owning land in Italy, the Antonini had bought property in Campania. Antoninus lived on his estate, Lorium, fed his chickens and devoted himself to the breeding of cattle and horses. It was there that he brought up young Marcus Aurelius. He took a really paternal interest in his adoptive son, initiating him into the lore of country life and teaching him how to run an estate properly.

Antoninus occupied the Roman throne for twenty-three years, and throughout that time — in complete contrast to Hadrian — he never left Italy. They were the Empire's happiest years. Edward Gibbon, the famous English historian, went so far as to regard the Antonine period (which includes the reigns of Antoninus and Marcus Aurelius) as mankind's happiest era. The German historian Ernst Kornemann, on the other hand, looks upon the reign of Antoninus as 'a succession of grossly wasted opportunities' which caused the Roman Empire to retrogress. There is something in both points of view. The nation was still blessed with prosperity and peace, but the Germans were growing stronger in the north and the Parthians in the east. Antoninus should, perhaps, have waged preventive wars in each case, but he lived 'with his head in the clouds where external affairs were concerned', as Kornemann puts it. However, I think it is unfair to criticize him for that. Every monarch or statesman who genuinely believes in the possibility of lasting peace and wishes to spare his people bloodshed does, fundamentally, live with his head in the clouds. Antoninus was a man of integrity and a good and paternal ruler. Every government decree he issued was painstakingly discussed with his best friends and advisers in advance, for the last thing he wanted was to appear autocratic.

For all that, his name makes less impact on the memory than that of such members of the imperial rogues' gallery as Nero and Domitian, or strongmen like Sulla and Antony.

It seems to be an unfortunate fact that the world's thrifty, gentle and kindly monarchs, who save their subjects from great catastrophes, are doomed to a shadowy historical existence.

Immediately after Antoninus' accession, the Senate refused to confer on his late predecessor any of the customary marks of respect. They could not forgive him for having executed certain distinguished men. Antoninus tearfully implored the Senate not to slam the gates of Olympus in Hadrian's face. 'If Hadrian was really so wicked and ill-disposed towards you, I am not your emperor. You would have to invalidate everything he did — including my adoption.' Antoninus made such an impression on the senators that they eventually awarded Hadrian all the funeral honours due to him.

To Antoninus the Senate gave the surname *Pius*, or 'dutiful', a title which

Sabina was never happy. Emperor Hadrian's wife was a grandchild of Trajan's sister. Hadrian married her in A.D. 100 to help him secure his predecessor's throne ▶

Handsome Antinous was drowned during a trip up the Nile with Hadrian. Hadrian marked the spot by founding the now ruined city of Antinoopolis. The Emperor's passion for this young man from Bithynion-Claudiopolis is one of Roman history's greatest enigmas. It has never been established how Antinous was drowned, but the Emperor never recovered from his grief and built the dead youth numerous temples

Emperor Hadrian. Genius emerges miraculously from the darkness of human history. Hadrian was a wise man such as the world only sees at intervals of several hundred years, a prince of peace, order and integrity who was endowed with an extraordinarily wide range of talents. He reigned from A.D. 117 to 138

Antoninus Pius, one of the most noteworthy occupants of the Roman throne, was an uncommonly handsome man who combined humanity and warmth with generosity and great courtesy. During his reign (A.D. 138–161) the Roman Empire reached the zenith of its power

Annia Galeria Faustina, wife of Emperor Antoninus Pius. On her death in A.D. 140 she was proclaimed 'Diva Faustina' at her husband's request. The worthy Emperor also founded an order for destitute girls, the Puellae Faustinianae, in her honour

Roman historians justify on numerous grounds. Perhaps the Emperor owed the award to his great kindness, friendliness and prudence. Needless to say, the Romans of those days understood by *pius* not Christian 'piety' so much as the moral perfection taught by Stoics. (It is on record, incidentally, that Antoninus did not persecute the Christians.) He was also invested with the title 'Father of the Fatherland', an honour which he at first declined but later accepted, courteously expressing his thanks.

When his wife Faustina died in the third year of his reign, she was officially deified by the Senate. Countless coins were minted in her honour bearing the inscription *Diva Faustina*, or 'divine Faustina'. Faustina had a daughter of the same name. Four years after her mother's death, the younger Faustina, an extremely beautiful girl, was given in marriage by Antoninus to his adoptive son Marcus Aurelius.

The Emperor lived frugally and without ostentation. The fare for his table was furnished by his own slaves, bird-catchers, fishermen and huntsmen. He opened one of his baths to the public free of charge. All his time was spent in the 'House of Tiberius', his palace on the Palatine or on his country estate in Campania. He avoided making any journeys outside the route between his estate and the capital because he considered the expense of travelling with full escort was unjustified.

When in residence at Rome, the Emperor was the true focus of world attention. All nations held him in the highest esteem and treated him with great respect. When the Parthian king was planning an attack on Armenia, a letter from Antoninus sufficed to dissuade him. Antoninus made large cash distributions to the people on nine separate occasions. He gave his soldiers a bonus on the day of his daughter's wedding in the year 145, and founded the *Puellae Faustinianae*, an order for destitute and homeless girls, in honour of his dead wife. He also erected many buildings in Rome and completed Hadrian's imposing tomb, now the Castle of St Angelo, which was then regarded as a miracle of building technique.

In the north of Britain Antoninus authorized the construction of a rampart between the Firth of Forth and the Firth of Clyde as a fresh defence against the barbarian tribes. In the year 148 he advanced the famous *limes*, or defensive rampart designed to keep out the Germans, and replaced all its wooden towers by stone ones. The new *limes* ran in a mathematically straight line from Miltenberg on the Main to Lorch in the Rems valley. Then, abandoning its north–south route parallel with the Rhine and Neckar, it turned and followed the eastward course of the Danube. The military value of this monumental earthwork was open to question, but it was certainly a great feat of organization and a lesson in the use of mass labour. It also demonstrated the Emperor's wish to defend his world empire by peaceful means. Peace, order and security were his dominant ideas. His subjects gratefully declared that Rome needed walls no longer. If Antoninus Pius had not refused the honour, our months September and October would now be known as Antonini and Faustini.

This does not mean that Antoninus' reign was free from disasters and evil omens. The soothsayers were ready with their usual predictions. Famine broke out. The great Circus collapsed. An earthquake occurred, probably in A.D. 140, and destroyed towns in Rhodes, Cos and Caria. Fire broke out in Rome, the Tiber burst its banks, a comet was seen in the sky, a two-headed child was born, an Arabian snake tried to devour itself (it got as far as its midriff) and a woman produced quintuplets — beating Madame Dionne in Canada by 1,800 years.

Antoninus became Emperor at the age of fifty-two and continued to conduct public affairs until his death, twenty-three years later. One of his major preoccupations as an old man was to keep himself fit. He still looked extremely well, but he got the impression that his tall figure was becoming a little bent, so he ordered some corsets made of narrow strips of lime-wood and strapped them to his chest and back to hold himself upright. Anxious not to succumb to the arduousness of his duties, he ate dry black bread every morning before receiving his court officials.

When the Emperor knew he was going to die, he ordered the emblem of his authority, a golden statue of the goddess Fortuna, to be carried from his bedroom into that of his adoptive son and heir, Marcus Aurelius.

For a while he lay there in a delirium, muttering about government affairs and the kings of distant lands. Then he turned over on his side as though he wanted to sleep, and fell asleep for ever.

MARCUS AURELIUS

THE TIME IS AT HAND

The time is at hand when you will have forgotten everything; and the time is at hand when all will have forgotten you. Always reflect that soon you will be no one and nowhere.

Marcus Aurelius, Meditations, vii, 21, and xii, 21.

LIKE Trajan, Marcus Aurelius came of a Spanish family, but he was born on the Caelian Hill in Rome in the year 121. He was seventeen when Hadrian died.

Emperor Hadrian had early recognized the boy's capabilities. If he had not been such a good 'talent scout', Marcus Aurelius would probably have become a run-of-the-mill civil servant or army officer, and we should have known nothing about him.

At Hadrian's bidding, Marcus was given a comprehensive education which he absorbed with notable success. We know the names of his tutors, some of them familiar to us and others quite unfamiliar, some Roman and some Greek. Young Marcus Aurelius was devoted to these distinguished scholars, and his admiration for them, coupled with a passion for learning, prevented him from taking more than the bare minimum of sleep. We know that he was instructed in literature, drama, music, geometry, grammar, rhetoric, jurisprudence and, in particular, philosophy. The boy grew up in the true spirit of the Stoic doctrines, living on a diet of bread and figs, sleeping on the hard ground and devouring one book after another. 'I am so weary that I can scarcely breathe,' he wrote in an extant letter addressed to his old teacher Fronto.

Marcus Aurelius received his *toga virilis*, the garment which a Roman youth wore on coming of age, at fifteen. Emperor Hadrian at once married him to Fabia, the daughter of Lucius Ceionius. But the marriage was not destined to last long. When Hadrian died, Antoninus Pius took over Marcus' education and dissolved his childhood marriage. Marcus then married Antoninus' twenty-three-year-old daughter, a lovely and accomplished girl whose name, like her mother's, was Faustina. Faustina took an active interest in her young husband's studies.

Marcus was now associated with Antoninus Pius in all the more important affairs of State, and Antoninus never undertook any course of action without consulting him. The Emperor and his adoptive son lived harmoniously together in the Palace of Tiberius on the Palatine, where the prince must have learnt a great deal from his conversations with the distinguished old man. He also continued to attend his tutors' lectures.

As an uncompromising Stoic, Marcus Aurelius worked tirelessly to improve himself. All his energies were devoted to the attainment of *ataraxia*, a state of perfect mental equilibrium which involved self-control and a sense of obligation towards oneself and one's fellow beings. He lived unostentatiously, giving daily audiences to the best men in Rome — not in the great public rooms of the imperial palace or attired in his robes of State, but clad simply in a night-shirt. His normal outdoor dress was sombre in colour. He only wore the official toga when accompanying the Emperor, and was never preceded by torch-bearers like other young Roman aristocrats. The thought that he was destined to be master of Rome and the Roman Empire was never far from his mind.

Could he be happy, in view of the immense burden he would have to shoulder one day? No, a mind schooled in Stoic rationalism could always see the negative side of everything. He was not happy. He was even a little apprehensive about the future. His inordinate passion for work, the strain of sleepless nights, the ruthless over-burdening of his memory and a renunciation of the normal amenities of life all conspired to weaken his constitution. And still he continued to study the great philosophers and perfect his Greek and Latin rhetoric.

Marcus Aurelius was forty years old when Emperor Antoninus died. It was in keeping with his shrewdness and deliberation — not to mention his qualms about an emperor's chances — that he summoned Lucius Verus, who had likewise been adopted by Antoninus, and made him co-regent. By investing his adoptive brother with the title Augustus, he placed him on an equal footing with himself. In his ailing condition, Marcus Aurelius felt unable to administer the Empire on his own, and intended Verus to relieve him of some of his military responsibilities. His plan was to divide and share. Thus, for the first time, the Empire was governed by two emperors, one in the west and the other in the east, each with the title Augustus and each with nearly the same measure of authority. It was a prototype of the east–west partition which subsequently came into being. But the plan failed, and Marcus Aurelius was eventually forced to combat single-handed the immense difficulties which arose during his reign.

The first thing Marcus and Verus did was to bury their adoptive father in

Hadrian's mausoleum. It must have been a great moment when the funeral procession, with its long columns of legionaries, marched up to the doors of the gigantic circular tomb, now fully completed. The top of the magnificent building was crowned by a copse of growing trees, and its general appearance was that of an impressive natural feature rather than a man-made edifice.

Marcus Aurelius called a halt to his studies and laid his books aside. The world lay before him, and storm-clouds were gathering above the huge empire. The new Emperor was a philosopher, but he could also be a man of action. That was just what philosophy was designed to equip him for.

In the east the Parthians were getting ready to make war on Rome under their King, Vologaeses III. They had already occupied parts of Armenia and Syria. Marcus Aurelius dispatched his partner and adoptive brother Verus against Vologaeses. Unlike Marcus, Verus liked good food, wine and women. Once he had reached the East and tasted the flesh-pots of Antioch and Daphne he never wanted to see Rome or another Stoic again, and decided to enjoy life while he could. He at once sent the Parthians an offer of peace, which they naturally rejected.

Marcus Aurelius had given his fifteen-year-old daughter Lucilla in marriage to Verus, who was considerably his junior. He was very fond of his adoptive brother-*cum*-son-in-law and wanted to do all he could for him. Although his hopes that Verus would prove a help to him had been dashed, he remained hopeful and confident. He recalled him from the East, and both emperors were invested with the title 'Father of the Fatherland'.

To protect his eastern flank Marcus appointed General Avidius Cassius as governor of Asia. It was a necessary step, for while Cassius was driving the Parthians back across the Euphrates and Tigris fresh danger was looming up, this time in the north. The Germans were on the move, as they had been in the days of the Cimbri and Teutons. The Marcomanni and Quadi had broken through the *limes* north of the Danube and were pushing into Pannonia, or lower Austria. Under the leadership of Ballomar, King of the Marcomanni, they poured into Styria and the districts of Laibach, Ödenburg and Ofen. The Romans were hard put to it to hold the Alpine passes, and in the end the Germans even threatened to burst through this last bulwark at Aquileia in northern Italy. Rome was in very real danger in the year 168. It was, in fact, the beginning of a great migratory trend in the Germanic area.

Taking Verus with him, Marcus marched to the relief of Aquileia and forced the Germans to retreat. Verus wanted to withdraw after this initial success, but Marcus set off in pursuit of the barbarians and crossed the Alps to restore the Danubian frontier. Then Rome suffered a frightful blow. A mysterious epidemic had been introduced into Italy by soldiers from the eastern front, probably from Babylon. Was it the Plague? We don't know, just as we don't know what epidemic struck Athens down during the time of Pericles. Thousands and tens of thousands died year after year. The dead were trundled out of the capital on carts and barrows. It was the longest and most widespread epidemic in ancient history. The two Emperors issued decrees strictly prohibiting the dead to be buried on their own premises. But the epidemic gained ground, ravaged the whole of northern Italy and swooped across the Alps to the Rhine, where it attacked the army, carried off whole legions and put new heart into the Germans.

Some of the German tribes mentioned by the Roman historians Julius Capitolinus and Dio Cassius have names which are totally unfamiliar to us. Mention is also made of eastern tribes which had infiltrated into the Danubian area, like the Osi and Besseri and the Sarmatian Costoboci and Iazyges. Prominent among the German tribes were the Bastarni, the Suebi (whose name survives in the Swabians), the Marcomanni, Quadi and Hermunduri. Then there were the Langobardi with their long beards, and various nomadic tribes who fought on horseback and gave no quarter in battle. Roman legionaries were astonished to find armed women among the bodies of the slain.

The royal brothers agreed that Verus should return to Rome to report to the Senate, but on the way, while still in the company of Marcus, he suffered a stroke and died. The date was A.D. 169.

After a number of sanguinary battles in gloomy forests or on the banks of remote rivers which the Romans had never heard of, the Marcomanni and Iazyges were defeated. Marcus' defeat of the Quadi was attributed to a miracle. It was a scorchingly hot day when the Romans engaged the Quadi, and the legionaries were half dead with thirst. Accordingly, the Emperor prayed to the gods, who obliged by sending a rain-storm. The Christians explained this marvel by alleging that one of the legions in Marcus' army consisted entirely of Christians. On being informed that the Christians could achieve anything by prayer, Marcus asked them to pray to their god, and their prayers were answered. From then on the Christian legion was known as the 'Thunderer'. We are told in moving terms how the Romans caught the precious rain in their shields and helmets, how it mingled with the blood of battle and how many a man shared the heaven-sent liquid with his dying horse.

Meanwhile, further advances by the barbarians were taking place. The Costoboci pushed down as far as Greece and plundered the temple at Eleusis, the Germanic Chatti crossed the Rhine and the Moors invaded Spain from Africa. The Praetorians and other garrison troops were withdrawn from Rome and sent into battle. On the Emperor's orders, training establishments were emptied of gladiators. Slaves were armed and given an assurance that if they proved their mettle they would later be granted their freedom. German tribes entered the service of Rome, too, and Emperor Marcus welcomed them with open arms. A wide strip of territory on the left of the Danube was cleared, and the last of the Quadi roamed away to the east.

By this time, however, the imperial treasury was exhausted. The Emperor decreed public sales, and for two whole months the Forum Traiani was filled with furniture, gold, crystal, ivory and jewels from the royal household. Even the Empress's gold-embroidered robes were put up for sale. The Emperor announced that, as soon as the war against the Marcomanni and the other German tribes had been successfully terminated, everyone would be allowed to sell back the articles which he had bought at their original purchase price.

Marcus Aurelius had taken over the name Antoninus from his adoptive father. His victories are depicted in 116 reliefs on the Antonine Column in Rome. They do not make as powerful an impact as those on Trajan's Column. The places where the Roman legions had repelled the German invaders were too dismal, strange and unfamiliar to provide the same inspiration. The Emperor was absent for quite a time in those barbarian regions, remote and awesome lands of the great beech-tree, dark spruce and lonely fir. He reached Silesia and the borders of Galicia, defying cold and fatigue to lead repeated cavalry charges in person. It was hardly surprising, therefore, that when he had been unable to send news to Rome for some time, a rumour spread round the world that he had died or been killed in action.

Syria was still under the control of Avidius Cassius, the man whom the Emperor regarded as his best governor. Cassius was, in fact, governing his native land, having been born in Cyrrus. He was a successful man, but brutal, violent and utterly ruthless towards his enemies. He crucified prisoners and discouraged deserters by cutting off their legs.

It was unwise to appoint a man viceroy of his own country, especially when it was so far from the seat of government. Scarcely had the false news of Marcus' death reached Cassius when he instigated a revolt with the object of making himself Emperor. It is still uncertain what part Faustina, Marcus' wife, played in this affair. Her husband's weak health and the risks he ran may have convinced her that he would die at any moment. His son Commodus was not only too young but temperamentally quite unsuited to become the Emperor's successor. Not unnaturally, Faustina trembled for her position as Empress, and it is said that she recommended Cassius to take over the throne — and herself — in the event of her husband's death.

Antioch was already swearing allegiance to Cassius when Marcus Aurelius bore down on the renegade general with all sails set. He addressed his troops as follows: 'I would willingly abdicate in favour of Cassius, were it for the good of the State. I have endured immense dangers and hardships. For a long time now, I have lived outside Italy. I am an old and ailing man. I can no longer eat without pain or sleep without care. My one dread is that Cassius may kill himself from shame. I fear this because it would rob me of the finest prize which war against Cassius could bring me: to pardon an offender, to remain friends with someone who has abused my friendship, to keep faith with one who has broken faith.'

Marcus' fears were realized. They cut off Cassius' head — the head which had, for three months and six days, been filled with dreams of imperial sovereignty. A legionary hurried to meet Marcus Aurelius and lay the trophy at his feet, but the Emperor was so saddened by the gift that he ordered it to be buried without taking a look at it. Then, while still on his journey eastwards, he was greeted by a second piece of bad news. Faustina was dead, Faustina, the wife he had loved so dearly, the woman whom the legionaries had called 'Mother of the Camp', the woman of whom Antoninus Pius had said: 'Rather in the desert alone with my daughter than in the imperial palace without her.'

Had Faustina died a natural death?

Had shame or fear at having conspired with Cassius driven her to take her own life?

Emperor Marcus would have nothing to do with such rumours. He ordered some letters which were found in the luggage of a certain Pudens to be burnt unexamined. He did not want to hate anybody, and had no taste for blood. Even the gladiators at Rome were only allowed to fight in his presence if their lives were guaranteed, none of the combatants being permitted to carry sharp weapons. He refused to allow a lion which had been trained to devour human beings in the Circus to enter the arena, in spite of popular demand, and locked up the trainer. On being asked to give him back his freedom, the Emperor pointed out that the man had not done much for freedom himself. 'Heaven forbid,' he once said, 'that anyone be condemned to death by myself or by you senators.'

In the year 176 the Emperor, accompanied by his fifteen-year-old son, returned to Rome in triumph after his difficult and hazardous journey to the East. He was depressed. He had lost a good man in Cassius, perhaps because he had placed too much confidence in him, and he was still mourning for his wife. But the great triumph drowned all other thoughts for a period of days and weeks. Marcus Aurelius laid the foundation-stone of the Antonine Column, an eternal reminder of the repulse, so important historically, of the second great German invasion. An equestrian statue of Marcus Aurelius still stands on the Roman Capitol today. Once gilded, this famous piece is the prototype of all subsequent equestrian statues, but it only owes its survival to an erroneous belief that it portrayed Constantine, the first Christian Emperor.

The Germans' offensive strength was far from exhausted, and the Emperor's spell of leisure in Rome was of short duration. His generals needed him on the Danube, which meant a return to Bohemia and the hardships of camp life. The enemy had been subdued, but danger was still lurking everywhere. Marcus Aurelius decided to clarify the situation by pushing the frontiers of the Roman Empire forward to the Erzgebirge, to the Sudetic and Carpathian Mountains. A new legionary camp, Castra Regina (modern Regensburg), was erected on the Danube as a defence against the Marcomanni, and two new provinces in Bohemia and Hungary (they were to be called Marcomannia and Sarmatia) had just been formed, when the Emperor suddenly died in Vienna of a dangerous infection. It is probable that his constitution was already so severely impaired by continuous stomach-trouble that it broke down under the effect of a strange and unaccustomed diet. He died on March 17th, A.D. 180.

It was there in Moravia and Bohemia, during the long and lonely nights in camp, that the Emperor wrote his world-famous *Meditations*. Composed in Greek, these soliloquies have survived for nearly 2,000 years and brought tranquillity and peace of mind to generation after generation, even though the Emperor himself never intended them for publication. Since the seventeenth century, over 200 different translations of the Emperor's book have appeared in England alone.

The *Meditations* is a devotional work consisting of dialogues between Marcus Aurelius and himself, and himself and God. He talks of 'the gods', it is true, but that is merely his term for the divine object of his prayers, whether a single god or the universe itself. 'Men seek places whither they can retire, abodes on land, on sea, in the mountains ... All such desires are childish, when it is possible, at any given moment, to withdraw into oneself. For nowhere does a man find more peace and tranquillity than in his own soul ... Consider how many men have been at odds with each other, borne each other envy and hatred, fought to the death, and then lain down for the last time and become ashes. ... Consider, too, how quickly all is forgotten, remember the chasm of infinity on either side, the futility of approbation, the fickleness and instability of mankind. ...' Marcus Aurelius had a deep insight into the human soul. 'People of a certain disposition will always act in accordance with their nature.' All great philosophers, both before and after Marcus Aurelius, have recognized that character is an immutable factor and that people must be taken as they are.

Marcus also knew that the only way to make an impression on people was by kindness. 'Does someone hate me?' he asks. His reply is unhesitating: 'That is his own business. For my part, I am kind and well disposed toward everyone and ready to show him his errors, not reproachfully, but ... sincerely and full of kindness.'

The Emperor knew where he stood, too. He knew his place in history, time, and the world. 'Do you grumble at what the course of life brings you? ... What a tiny part of boundless, infinite time is allotted to each of us. Everyone disappears into eternity without more ado. ... And on what tiny portion of the whole earth's surface do you creep about? Reflect on all this and regard nothing as important save to act as your nature impels and endure what Nature brings you. ... The whole world is but a dot. What a small speck of it is occupied by the abode of men, and how few of them there are! And what sort of people are they that shall praise you? ... Do not wait for the perfect State, but esteem it, however small the progress made.'

Such were the sentiments of Marcus Aurelius, and it is not too much to call him the greatest royal philosopher that ever lived. 'The time is at hand when you will have forgotten everything, and the time is at hand when all will have forgotten you. ... Reflect that you will soon be no one and nowhere.'

Could such a man have persecuted Christians? Have we found a flaw in the great emperor-philosopher?

Well, the reign of Marcus Aurelius saw not only the death of Justin and his six companions but the martyrdom of Metrodorus the Marcionite and Pionius the presbyter, the torture and burning of Carpus and Papylus at Pergamum and the voluntary death by fire of Agathonice the Christian. Eusebius gives us the text of a letter written by the churches of Lugdunum (Lyons) and Vienna (Vienne, near Lyons) to the communities of Asia and Phrygia in the year 177. Its frightful tales of mob violence, atrocities and Christians roasted alive, and its descriptions of the torments endured by Blandina the slave-girl and the maltreatment of ninety-year-old Bishop Pothinus are like a shrill cry to the heavens. Our comfortable age can scarcely fathom how those early

Christians triumphed over agony and death, for we have lost the ability to distinguish when heroism is worth while. The Christians, however, were dying for eternal truth.

But none of this took place under the eye of Emperor Marcus Aurelius. He did not personally oppress the Christians. In his edict to the province of Asia, he declined to take any measures against them. Only if they could be proved to have committed political offences against the Roman State was the State permitted to intervene. The governors who persecuted Christians in those days operated at a distance, where the Emperor could not always keep a check on them. Marcus Aurelius was definitely not at the bottom of all this organized suffering. He was the most upright emperor the Roman Empire ever had, a Stoic who was the soul of justice and rooted in the ancient Roman sense of duty, a long-suffering philosopher in a hostile world, one of the luminaries of antiquity.

According to John Stuart Mill, Marcus Aurelius was a better Christian — in the undogmatic sense — than all the avowedly Christian monarchs that have ruled since his day. He was probably more humane than any other ruler in history.

The universe and eternity, the great starry heavens and puny little man, who carries all happiness and unhappiness about inside him and is really without hope, yet should welcome his destiny without complaint: such were the ideas that coursed through the mind of the lonely Emperor as he communed with himself and recorded his meditations during those long nights on the frontiers of the barbarian world, far from Rome. A man of over fifty, he sat there deep in thought, the stillness outside broken only by the muffled calls of sentries changing guard, by the moaning of the wind as it swept across the wild Danubian landscape, or by the distant, infinitely mournful songs of the Marcomanni women as they lulled their wounded sons to sleep. Alone with the huge night sky and man's timid and eternal quest for peace of mind, Marcus Aurelius found an answer: do what your nature demands of you and act as your nature directs. It was a formula which brought him very close to supra-mundane wisdom and supra-mundane peace. For, as he himself wrote: 'It is quite possible to become a godly man, yet remain unrecognized.'

COMMODUS

THE MONSTER

He had slain an ostrich, and brought its head across to where we were sitting. He held the head in his left hand, the bloody sword raised in his right. True, he spoke not a word, but he motioned with his head and smirked as if to show that he had the same thing in mind for us.

Dio Cassius, lxxii, 21.

MARCUS AURELIUS was an amazingly well balanced personality, the soul of kindness and a wise man who almost succeeded in attaining perfect inner contentment and peace of mind 'like the wide sea becalmed'. But in the very kindness and optimism of this philanthropic Emperor lay his one weakness: he deliberately refused to see his fellow-men as they really were. He was boundlessly indulgent toward his wife and made his son Emperor in spite of his patent unsuitability.

Nineteen-year-old Commodus haunted his father's death-bed like a shadow. Dio Cassius insists, allegedly on good authority, that Marcus Aurelius 'did not die of the disease which had attacked him' but because of the ministrations of his doctors, 'who wished to ingratiate themselves with his son'. He even claims that the Emperor realized what was afoot, but, far from betraying that he knew he was being murdered, told his soldiers to serve his successor faithfully.

Rome had had five good rulers. It seems, in history, as though even intelligence and moderation need an occasional break, as though the course of events cannot be without its darker side, as though only despotism and murder can boost the advent of happier days.

Marcus Aurelius left behind the finest code of rules for living which any Roman who was not a Christian could have devised.

What about some rules for his son? Wasn't he in far greater need of them?

We must bear in mind that Marcus Aurelius was the first emperor for some time to depart from the adoptive system of succession, a system which provided an excellent antidote to the degeneracy so prevalent in the second generation of Roman dynasties. Wise and kind though he was, and far beyond time, heaven and earth though his thoughts ranged, Marcus Aurelius was obtuse where his own flesh and blood was concerned. He naturally engaged the finest scholars of his day in an attempt to instruct and educate

Commodus, but it was all wasted effort. As the historian Aelius Lampridius ironically points out, the success of a palace education is determined by the royal pupil's temperament and his tutors' lack of authority.

On the other hand, could it be that Marcus Aurelius really wrote the *Meditations* for his son's benefit? It is possible that Commodus was not his son at all? Was Faustina really as bad as she was painted? Whatever the truth of the matter, the Emperor's educational methods completely failed. History had repeated itself. Seneca was one of the finest educationalists of all time, yet his pupil was Nero. And now another Nero — indeed, a far worse monster — occupied the throne of Rome. Commodus had reigned in partnership with his father for four years, and Marcus Aurelius must have noticed a great deal in that time. But he was a Stoic. He knew how to control himself. Perhaps, too, he was one of those over-rational teachers who give free rein only to their intellect, never their temperament; who never inspire healthy respect because they are incapable of losing their temper; who are like those fathers with criminal offspring who 'always meant well'.

Commodus gave clear evidence of his brutality at the tender age of twelve. Finding his bath too cool on one occasion, he ordered the chief bath attendant to be thrown into the furnace. Fortunately, the slave entrusted with the order did not carry it out, but merely threw a sheepskin on the fire. Commodus sniffed the smell of burning and was satisfied.

Now that Marcus Aurelius was dead, Commodus found himself in sole command of a large army. The young man was faced with the superhuman task of conquering and pacifying the Marcomanni and Quadi and bringing the German wars to a decisive close, but he immediately succumbed to every kind of bad influence.

Before long Commodus had surrounded himself with actors and young degenerates who persuaded him that war in these wild regions was far too dangerous and painted horrific pictures of what lay across the Danube. The upshot was that he gave up the war and concluded a peace treaty with the Germans on very generous terms, abandoning the new provinces which Marcus Aurelius had so laboriously created. This was not at all the policy envisaged by his father, but a retreat undertaken against the advice of the late Emperor's friends. It did not, however, prevent Commodus from staging a triumphal return to Rome. The young Emperor's boon companion Saoterus sat behind him during the procession. Commodus repeatedly turned round and lavished amorous kisses on him in full view of the spectators.

The misbegotten offspring of one of the greatest Roman Emperors then proceeded to squander the resources of his empire as fast as he could. By night he reeled drunkenly through tavern and brothel. By day he sent criminals and their accomplices all over the world to govern Rome's provinces. The Senate hated him, but cringed and fawned as usual. And the more despised the Emperor felt himself, the more blood-thirsty he became.

Before long, plans were made to assassinate him. The conspirators included his sister Lucilla, a man called Quadratus, and Paternus, commander of the imperial body-guard. The murder was to be carried out by a certain Claudius Pompeianus. It was an evening in the year A.D. 183. Commodus was just leaving the amphitheatre by a dark and narrow gateway, bound for home, when Pompeianus sprang out at him with a drawn sword, shouting: 'This weapon comes to you from the Senate!' The foolish man had bungled his opportunity. He was arrested and executed, together with Quadratus and numerous others. Lucilla, the Emperor's sister, was banished to Capri and there murdered.

Rome seethed with the wildest rumours. The Praetorian Guard took it into their heads that the Emperor's unpopularity was due to his friendship with Saoterus, whom they promptly murdered. Paternus, the prefect of the Guard, had hoped that this would change things, but he, too, fell prey to the Emperor's vengeance and was executed in the company of several other alleged saboteurs.

Commodus was scared. He ceased to appear in public and never received letters or messengers unless they had been previously examined by his new favourite, Perennis. Absolutely no one was admitted to the Emperor's quarters without Perennis' prior approval. The court took on an almost oriental atmosphere, the sycophant Perennis administering public affairs and the Emperor devoting himself entirely to his own pastimes. Having safely transferred the burdens of government to the shoulders of Perennis, Commodus rushed from one banquet to the next, staggered round his palace roaring drunk, took an endless succession of hot baths and amused himself with his three hundred concubines, the pick of Rome's prostitutes. He also purchased three hundred young boys specially selected for their physical charms. The Romans had to grin and bear it all, as they had done in the days of Caligula, Nero, Vitellius and Domitian. The Emperor personally performed ritual slaughter at the altar, acting as 'sacrificial acolyte'. He fought in the arena, murdered anyone he disliked, robbed people and broke every conceivable law. He killed his wife Crispina. His concubines were forced to participate in the most riotous orgies. He murdered senators, wealthy women and finally his own son. In the end even his favourite, Perennis, was declared a public enemy and torn to pieces by the soldiery.

The Emperor's new man was called Cleander. Like Saoterus, he was a former slave from Asia Minor. Cleander was obliged to commit even worse crimes on the Emperor's behalf than his predecessor. The Guard commanders were changed constantly. Senior appointments could be obtained only by bribery. There was nothing which the worthy Cleander could not make money out of, and before long nobody at court could see through the maze of intrigue with which he surrounded himself. But no courtier was a good insurance risk under an emperor who was always in need of new scapegoats. Famine broke out, bread became unobtainable and rioters surged through the streets of Rome. Cleander was seized by the mob and stoned to death. It goes without saying that the children which he had fathered on several of Commodus' concubines were also executed. Cleander was succeeded by Julianus and Regillus, each of whom was put to death in his turn. Execution followed execution with monotonous regularity. We can still read the long lists of people, consuls, civil servants and courtiers among them, who perished in the Emperor's blood-bath together with their families.

The Senate introduced a note of crazy irony into the situation by giving Commodus the titles 'Dutiful' (*Pius*) and 'Fortunate'. The dutiful and fortunate Emperor proceeded to stage an attempt on his own life as an excuse for more murders. He became known as 'Roman Hercules', and his statues show him in the guise of that Greek hero, complete with club and lion's skin. Yet another of his names was Britannicus. He cherished a megalomaniac ambition to rechristen Rome 'Colonia Commodiana', encouraged in that idea and others of a like calibre by his mistress, Marcia, who later became a Christian. Since it was their only way of ridiculing him, the Senate at once fell in with these suggestions. They even accorded him divine status.

We read of the most fantastic happenings at court. Commodus got rid of Motelenus, one of his Guard commanders, by giving him a present of poisoned figs. There came a day when one of the palace servants 'accidentally' dropped a writing-tablet out of a bedroom window. It was unfortunate. The tablet bore the names of innumerable people whom the Emperor intended to kill.

Commodus greatly fancied himself in the role of Hercules. Clad in female garb, he would slaughter lions and chained prisoners with his club. Another of his hobbies was to dress cripples up as snakes and shoot them to death with arrows. He appeared in public as a gladiator and recorded for posterity the number of opponents he had killed. It is almost inconceivable how a city like Rome could have tolerated all the Emperor's whims and fancies.

Sometimes Commodus embraced people fondly, sometimes he showered

Emperor Marcus Aurelius and his brother Lucius Verus. The two brothers ruled jointly from A.D. 161 to 169. Marcus Aurelius, who survived Verus by eleven years, was the author of the world-famous *Meditations*, written during lonely nights in camp in Moravia and Bohemia

Detail from the Column of Marcus Aurelius, built by the Roman Senate between A.D. 176 and 193 to commemorate victories over the Marcomanni, Quadi, Sarmati and Jazyges. The column is constructed of Carrara marble and rises to a height of over ninety-seven feet. A missing statue of the Emperor was replaced in 1589 by a bronze statue of St. Paul

Emperor Commodus reigned from A.D. 180 to 192. He ushered in an epoch of bloodshed, ferocity and mass murder. This degenerate son of Marcus Aurelius was eventually strangled by the gladiator Narcissus

Publius Helvetius Pertinax, a general who distinguished himself in Rhaetia under Marcus Aurelius and in Britain under Commodus. After the latter's murder he reigned for two months and twenty-five days

Marcus Didius Julianus was a wealthy senator who bought the Roman throne at an auction organized by his predecessor's assassins. He was murdered in A.D. 193 after a reign of only two months

Emperor Septimius Severus, who reigned from A.D. 193 to 211, was born in Africa and proclaimed emperor at Carnuntum on the Danube. His belief in astrology led him to marry Julia Domna, a girl with a 'royal horoscope'. He died at Eboracum (York)

The triumphal arch of Septimius Severus in the Roman Forum was erected by the people and Senate in honour of the Emperor and his two sons Geta and Bassianus (Caracalla) in A.D. 203. The inscription refers to the tenth anniversary of his reign, and the figures at the base of the pillars represent Parthian prisoners of war

them with obscene nicknames of his own devising. During an inspection he threw Julianus, the Guard prefect, into a swimming-pool and later made him dance naked in public. He was always eating, even in his bath. He would enter the sacred precincts of temples spattered with blood and still lusting for murder. After some artist had painted his mistress, Marcia, as an Amazon, he adopted the title 'Amazonius'. He decided to rename every month in the year after his own grandiose titles. Sometimes he felt immensely strong, sometimes weak and ill. His chest developed swellings which even the finest silken robes failed to disguise. But no sooner had the population begun to wonder whether they had seen the last of Commodus than he surprised everyone by reappearing in the amphitheatre dressed as a woman.

Commodus had become incredibly lazy and almost incapable of serious concentration. He had long ceased to discharge any public business, and his replies to written requests and petitions bore no relation to their subject matter. A large proportion of the Emperor's letters simply consisted of the word 'farewell'. For a fee, men could now get their sentences of death transferred to others. On the Emperor's authority, the famous *acta urbis* or *acta diurna*, a sort of official gazette, was crammed with scurrilous, sensational and vulgar items of news.

The Romans regarded Commodus as the plaything of his own whims. One day he ordered the capital to be burnt down. The credit for dissuading the Emperor at the last moment was laid at the door of Laetus, prefect of the Praetorian Guard. Recognizing that the present state of danger and emergency had to be brought to an end, Laetus enlisted Marcia's co-operation in a carefully planned attempt on the Emperor's life. When poison failed to act quickly enough, they summoned an athlete who was the Emperor's favourite wrestling-partner, and the man throttled him to death.

The Roman populace clamoured for 'the hook'. But, curiously enough, instead of being dragged into the Tiber, Commodus' body was laid in Hadrian's mausoleum.

Dangerous buffoon, monster, gladiator and self-styled hero, Commodus had erected statues and effigies of himself all over the place. Now every reminder of him was torn down. Not having built anything himself, he had been in the habit of putting his name on other people's buildings. Wherever he had done so, it was erased.

It was like the end of some horrible dream. All that remained was a haunting memory of the Emperor's drunken, petulant face and the flowing locks which he made his hairdressers dye blond and sprinkle with gold-dust.

PERTINAX AND JULIAN

AN EMPIRE FOR SALE

It happened in A.D. 193. 'Whoever gave the troops the largest bonus was to become emperor. Julian acquired the hotly contested imperial throne for about 6,000 *denarii* (roughly £210) per man.'

Dio Cassius, lxxiii, 11.

When we received the news, we were seized with fear of Julian and the soldiers. This applied especially to those who had been on close terms with Pertinax, among them myself, who had been honoured by him and nominated quaestor, but had frequently brought Julian before the courts in my fight against injustice.

Dio Cassius, lxxiii, 12.

'PERTINAX was a man of honour. He reigned for only a short time, and was then murdered by his soldiers.' Those are the opening words of the seventy-third book of an eighty-volume history of Rome by Dio Cassius, who was a senator during this period and gives us a graphic description of it. A keen observer of the contemporary scene, he was always there on the spot, watching emperors come and go, sometimes laughing with his fellow-senators, sometimes trembling with them, living dangerously in a Rome where death-sentences and decapitations were a daily occurrence.

'The troops have appointed me Emperor,' declared Pertinax, 'but I am not snatching at this honour. I wish to abdicate immediately. My age, my poor health, and my personal affairs do not make the throne an attractive proposition.' He went to the Senate and asked Glabrio, the foremost patrician there, to assume the imperial throne in his place. Glabrio politely declined, however, and the other senators were equally unforthcoming.

'We therefore applauded the great man with all sincerity,' Dio Cassius relates, 'and confirmed him as Emperor. He was a man of the highest character and soundest constitution. Only his feet troubled him.'

It was December 31st, A.D. 192. Pertinax was sixty-six. The army could not raise much enthusiasm for the mild old man. He appears to have been well-meaning, but scarcely the person to behave like an Imperator or retain the throne for very long. Even though he did nothing wrong, he was not popular, nor was he universally well spoken of. The Romans despised his quiet, stealthy manner, insipid public speeches and greedy acceptance of gifts, and laughed at his apparent ignorance of his wife's continual infidelity to him with her musician lover. Yet Pertinax did have some redeeming features. He was approachable and could always be relied on to make sensible decisions on any matter.

Emperor Commodus had left behind a foul morass of vice, injustice and corruption. His successor did everything within his power to straighten out the muddle, stop the Praetorians bullying the civil population, initiate wise legislation, reduce the high level of taxes and generally put the country on an even keel. He tried to model himself on Marcus Aurelius.

Pertinax organized a grand sale of all the treasures which Commodus had confiscated and hoarded. Among other articles offered for sale were gorgeous silks embroidered with gold, priceless robes and cloaks in the Dalmatian and Greek style, a gladiatorial toga and the gold and jewelled accoutrements that went with it, and vessels of gold, ivory and silver.

Also up for auction were Samnite jars in which Commodus had kept his face-lotions, and chariots of the latest design, with carved wheels and movable seats which the occupant could adjust so that he never had to sit in the sun. Other chariots were equipped with milometers and clocks, and still others were cunningly adapted to suit the late Emperor's highly individual tastes in vice.

Then came the turn of Commodus' slaves. His boys and prostitutes were sold, though many of them were soon brought back to the palace to amuse his elderly successor. With an unusual burst of generosity, Pertinax distributed the proceeds of all these sales to his soldiers.

He found it a hard task to return all the items of property stolen by Commodus (including numbers of confiscated slaves), to their rightful owners, but he did his best. He cut down on court expenditure and made his son live outside the palace in his original home, sending him to an ordinary school. His palace banquets were modest affairs and were not allowed to swallow up vast sums of money. 'He used to invite us to frugal meals,' Dio Cassius records.

The new regime, with its cheese-paring emphasis on economy, not unnaturally aroused widespread displeasure among army officers, civil servants and courtiers. No longer could the soldiers rob and pillage or the Emperor's freedmen behave as they pleased; no longer could the wretchedly paid bodyguards sleep on duty. Laetus, the commander of the Praetorians, soon regretted that he had ever helped Pertinax to become Emperor, for the old man took to calling him a stupid blabbermouth in public and taxed him with giving away secrets. There came a day when 300 soldiers marched on the palace.

The palace guards did not bother to stop them. They hated their close-fisted master. Pertinax was just inspecting the court slaves when he was confronted by the 300 blood-thirsty intruders. Even at that stage he could probably have had them cut down by the sentries and knights on duty in the palace. Instead, odd and easy-going man that he was, he treated them to a long lecture. It utterly failed in its object: a spear pierced the Emperor's chest. Breathing a prayer to Jupiter, Pertinax covered his head with his toga and died under a rain of dagger-blows, a venerable bearded old man who was totally untalented, enjoyed literary discussions and had never tasted roast pheasant in his life.

For a mere two months and twenty-five days Pertinax ruled an empire which had outgrown his kind of innocuous personality. The Senate expressed their deepest regret at the Emperor's death, but then, nobody cared what the Senate thought, least of all the Praetorians who had murdered him.

People who think they are living in dangerous times and bemoan the uncertainty of the future can console themselves with the reflection that things were much less pleasant in Anno Domini 193. A change of emperors was the signal for universal apprehension.

Rome now witnessed what was probably the most shameful and ridiculous farce in her history. The capital and the whole Empire were offered to the highest bidder, with the late Emperor's assassins playing the role of auctioneers, and Sulpicianus and Julianus doing the bidding. The officers made no secret of the fact that they would give the throne to whichever of them offered their men the most money. A wild round of bidding started. 'Sulpicianus is offering such and such an amount,' the brokers shouted. 'How much do you raise him by?' Julian immediately increased his offer. 'What do you say to that?' the brokers asked Sulpicianus. And so it went on. However, Julian continued to bid so unconcernedly, signalling to the soldiery on his fingers, that the imperial throne was finally knocked down to him at 6,200 denarii per head. Having paid — or at least promised to pay — each man this not inconsiderable sum (about £210), Julian marched to the Senate with the Guards at his back and was proclaimed Emperor. His wife Manlia Scantilla and his daughter Didia Clara each received the title 'Augusta', as is shown by the cions of this period. Julian summoned them to join him in the palace. They did so apprehensively, already scenting the imminence of his downfall.

The Roman populace would not have anything to do with a man who had bought his throne. They pelted Julian so violently with stones as he was entering the palace that his escort of guardsmen had to screen him with their shields. Men and women uttered imprecations while the Emperor was doing sacrifice and begged the gods not to accept his offerings. Then they threw more stones. Julian made a feeble attempt to pacify them by suspending the laws, but it did little good. The crowds poured into the Circus, sat down wherever they pleased, and stayed there all night, hooting, yelling and calling down curses on Julian's head. In the end they grew tired and hungry and went home without having achieved anything.

Next, the governors of Syria and Illyria, Pescennius Niger and Septimius Severus, rose in arms against the Emperor. Severus marched on Rome with an army. Julian wanted to send the Praetorians against him, but their enthusiasm was already on the wane because he could not satisfy their renewed demands for money. Severus seized control of the fleet at Ravenna. Julian now proposed to send Vestal Virgins and priests to meet him, thinking to achieve by entreaty what he could not do by force. But the Senate refused him permission, their attitude being that anyone who could not master an opponent by force of arms had no right to rule. Julian did, however, persuade them to declare Severus a public enemy. Meanwhile, Severus marched on inexorably, preceded by large numbers of spies and soldiers in disguise. Panic-stricken, Julian decided to make peace with Severus and share the throne with him, probably intending to murder him later. However, Severus declared that he would rather be the enemy than the colleague of a weakling, which left the desperate Emperor with no choice but to build ramparts and ditches, turn Rome into an armed camp, and prepare to give his rival a bloody reception.

Absolute chaos ensued. There was a stream of conflicting orders. Men, horses and elephants bivouacked all over the place. The citizenry quaked in their shoes. The Emperor's body-guards, corrupt and demoralized, did nothing. Maddened by the battle-turrets on their backs, Julian's elephants stampeded and threw their riders. Julian fitted new locks to the palace doors to protect himself from the enemy. 'Sometimes we had to laugh at it all,' says Dio Cassius, 'especially when the Emperor barricaded the palace and bolted the doors. ...'

Soon poor Julian was abandoned by everyone. The Senate divested him of his imperial authority. His voice echoed dismally through the deserted palace. He was lying on a couch in his huge bedchamber, pale and trembling, when a private soldier flung open the door, rushed in, and plunged a sword into his breast. 'What crime have I committed?' gasped Julian. 'Whom did I ever put to death?'

After a mere two months and five days, Julian's reign was at an end.

SEPTIMIUS SEVERUS

THE GRIM PHOENICIAN

Emperor Septimius Severus was strict, unbending, grim. During the latter years of his life he always had himself carried about in a litter. When they wanted to depose him on that account, he said quietly: 'A man governs with his head, not his legs.'

Aelius Spartianus, *Severus*, xviii, 11.

THE next occupant of the Roman throne was born at Leptis Magna in Africa. This Tripolitanian town had been founded by the Phoenicians in about 1000 B.C., and it is therefore probable that Rome's new Emperor, Septimius Severus, came of seafaring Phoenician or Punian stock. His family, which could be traced back for several generations, still had some Punic blood, even though it had received Roman citizenship much earlier. Emperor Severus spoke fluent Punic, and his Latin betrayed a distinct Punian accent.

His career had been an arduous one: aide to the proconsul in Africa, tribune of the people, praetor in Spain, student at Athens, where he also performed 'certain sacred rites', governor of Gaul at Lyons. His first wife Marcia had died, so, being a keen student of astrology, he proceeded to examine the horoscopes of various marriageable girls. Among them was a beautiful young Syrian whose horoscope indicated that she was going to marry a ruler of men. Her name was Julia Domna, and her father, Julius Bassianus, was priest of the sun-god Baal at Emesa in Syria. Severus was extremely pleased with this gift from the stars — though the stars never told him that Julia would be unfaithful.

As governor, Septimius Severus was supreme commander of the Roman troops in Pannonia, the district between the Danube and the Drave. His legions proclaimed him Emperor on August 13th, A.D. 193, at Carnuntum, a town on the Danube twenty-six miles east of Vienna, between Petronell and Deutsch-Altenburg. He was greeted enthusiastically along the whole route to Rome. The Romans saw their new Emperor as the avenger of the late-lamented Pertinax, but when they realized that he meant to march into Rome at the head of his troops there was general panic. Severus was taking no risks. Ringed by soldiers, although he himself was dressed in civilian clothes, he marched to the Capitol and entered the palace with his bodyguards.

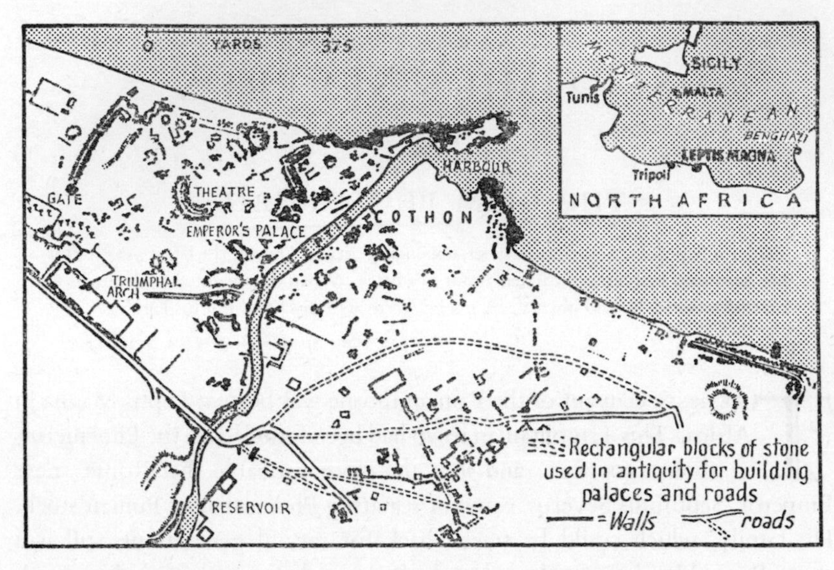

Leptis Magna, founded by the ancient Phoenicians, was the birthplace of Septimius Severus. Here the Romans built a splendid city of marble which now lies in ruins

The troops gathered outside, grumbling. They wanted 10,000 sesterces each, and Severus could not refuse, however little he liked the idea. But no sooner had he established himself firmly on the throne than he began to govern in his own way. First he disbanded the Praetorian Guard and formed a new and stronger force from among his own legionaries. Then he saw to it that the dangerously empty granaries were properly restocked. He dispatched troops to Africa and sent a legion to occupy Greece and Thrace, anxious to forestall any move by his rival, Pescennius Niger, the governor of Syria. Niger had already seized Byzantium, but when he saw that the new Emperor could show his claws he offered to share the throne. Severus refused. Battle was joined near Issus in Cilicia. Niger had the advantage of numbers as well as a vast amount of military equipment, weapons and engines of war, but he was rather a hot-head. He styled himself 'Alexander the Second'. (It was at Issus, about 500 years earlier, that Alexander had defeated Darius.) On being asked what gave him the right to adopt the name, he pointed to his sword and replied: 'This does!' When the battle was over, Niger had lost 20,000 men. He made for Parthia, but only got as far as Antioch. Severus had him followed, arrested and beheaded. He then ordered his opponent's head to be impaled on a stake and planted in the ground in front of Byzantium, hoping that the sight would induce the city's inhabitants to surrender. He punished the citizens of Antioch and Naples because they had supported Niger, and executed every senator who had been well disposed toward his former enemy.

Then Severus besieged Byzantium. Dio Cassius gives some most interesting details about the siege and the city as it was in those days. We read of the fortifications, the massive walls, the towers and the forward lines of defence along the Bosphorus. The entrances to the city's harbours were barred by chains, and lofty towers protected the moles which led out to sea. The Byzantines had huge machines for catapulting rocks and baulks of timber at the enemy, also hooks which descended like lightning and hauled whole ships bodily out of the water. Dio Cassius relates how his fellow-countryman, Priscus, the inventor of these machines, was sentenced to death by Emperor Severus but later pardoned by him because he needed his technical skill — much as we need nuclear scientists today.

The defenders of Byzantium performed miracles of bravery and endurance in the face of hardship and starvation. Slipping into the water under cover of darkness, their divers lopped off the anchors of enemy ships and towed them towards the battlements, where a shower of rocks and timber rained down on them. Completely surrounded, the besieged inhabitants eked out their supplies of ammunition with stones from their theatre, metal statues, even horses. Women cut off their hair to make ropes. In an attempt to combat starvation, people inside the city softened leather and tried to eat it. They finally resorted to cannibalism. The Byzantines made a naval sortie during a storm, only to meet with disaster, and the city eventually abandoned further resistance.

The Romans massacred all soldiers and officials, but spared the ordinary citizens. Severus handed the captured stronghold over to the inhabitants of the neighbouring town of Perinth, who 'treated it like a village and oppressed it in every way'. Dio Cassius says of Byzantium: 'I saw the city in ruins, but I also saw it when it was still intact. And I even heard it speak. There used to be seven towers down by the sea. If you shouted to the first it would echo the sound and pass it on to the second; so sharp of hearing were the walls of Byzantium.'

While the siege of Byzantium was still in progress, the Emperor was conducting operations against the Osrhoeni, Adiabeni and Arabi. He also knocked some sense into the Parthians. Rome offered him a triumph and the Senate conferred on him the titles 'Arabicus', 'Adiabenicus' and 'Parthicus', but Severus refused the triumphal procession and the title Parthicus, not wishing to offend the Parthians.

Then rebellion broke out in Gaul under Albinus. The Emperor had his opponent proclaimed a public enemy and at once marched against him. He encountered Albinus at Tinurtium — probably the modern town of Tournlis, which stands by the Saône some nineteen miles north of Mâcon. There Severus ran into great danger. He was knocked off his horse and wounded by a leaden shot.

Back in Rome, the Senate assumed that the Emperor was already dead and started to look round for a successor. But Severus was tough. He survived. In his hatred of the Rome-bred senators who looked down their noses at him, an African, he became the first emperor to create a provincial majority in the Senate. On the other hand, he liked it to be thought that he belonged to the family of Marcus Aurelius, which was why he officially deified Commodus, the murderous emperor who had been the bane of Rome.

His vanquished opponent Albinus was hauled before him, more dead than alive, and summarily decapitated. Severus sent the head back to Rome and ordered the trunk to be left unburied outside the dead man's house. He then executed countless supporters of Albinus in Gaul, among them noblewomen from France and Spain. Albinus' official residence, Lugdunum (Lyons), which had been the capital of Gaul ever since the time of Augustus, now lost its importance, while Trèves began its climb to fame.

Seething with a tyrant's hatred, Severus returned to Rome, where he executed forty-one noblemen and senators on the spot. Narcissus, the man who had strangled Emperor Commodus, was thrown to the lions.

The Emperor left a trail of blood behind him wherever he went. Anyone who opened his mouth too wide, indulged in witticisms or made equivocal remarks was put to the sword. 'Behold the Emperor, worthy of his name! He is truly steadfast (*pertinax*), truly strict (*severus*).' Among others who forfeited their lives was the punster who coined that ambiguous phrase!

The historian Aelius Spartianus considers that Severus went to war more often out of ambition than absolute necessity. The Emperor now opened an offensive against the Parthians. He took their capital, Ctesiphon, and allowed his troops to loot it, instituted a wholesale massacre and carried off thousands of prisoners. He marched through Mesopotamia and turned it into a Roman province once more. The city of Atra refused to surrender. This fortress had some first-class artillery in the shape of long-range catapults. One of them is said to have been capable of discharging two projectiles at each firing. The inhabitants of Atra also used petroleum, pouring it down on the Romans from their walls and setting it alight. 'Thus God helped his city,' says Dio Cassius. Severus abandoned the siege.

We next see the Emperor in Upper Egypt. Inquisitive by nature and eager to plumb the secrets of this world and the next, he travelled about the country admiring its ancient buildings. He discovered some secret texts and locked them away in the tomb of Alexander the Great, which must still have been intact at that time. No living man was ever to set eyes on them, just as no one was ever to set eyes on Alexander's mummy.

The Emperor travelled onwards to the African provinces. His native city of Leptis was rebuilt on a grand scale, and the ancient Punic capital, Carthage, became a metropolis once again. Septimius Severus placed such emphasis on his Carthaginian descent that he erected a great memorial for Hannibal and for Libyssa, the Bithynian town where he died. Effigies of the ancient patron goddess of Carthage, Tanit Caelestis, appeared on Roman coins. There are reminders of Severus all over North Africa. The spirit of the Punic Roman Emperor still emanates from innumerable ruins, from crumbling temples, triumphal arches, statues, inscriptions, harbour installations, market-places, whole towns. A large and quite well preserved temple to the Septimian family still stands at Ciucul in Numidia. The frontier rampart in the desert which protected caravan traffic into Central Africa was pushed forward. Never in the whole of its history, until today, has North Africa experienced such a golden age as it did under Septimius Severus and his successors.

Emperor Severus was a dangerous man, but Plautianus, the commander of his body-guard, was more dangerous still. His avarice was beyond belief. He left no town, no province unplundered. He accumulated loot from the four corners of the Roman world, even raiding islands in the Red Sea for zebras, which were sacred to the Sun-god.

Plautianus was much more blood-thirsty than the Emperor. He castrated a hundred Roman noblemen in his own house. All his daughter Plautilla's servants and tutors had to be eunuchs. Before long, Plautianus grew more powerful than Severus himself, and statues of him were erected everywhere, in the provinces as well as at Rome.

Severus betrothed Plautianus' daughter to his own son Antoninus. This young man was constantly quarrelling with his brother Geta. Both the Emperor's sons were bad characters, kept bad company and had bad manners. 'I am so fond of Plautianus,' the Emperor declared, 'that I should like him to outlive me.'

Empress Julia had to put up with every sort of hostility from Plautianus. He tried to denigrate her to her husband, conducted investigations into what he termed 'the Julia case' and stretched noblewomen on the rack in his search for incriminating evidence. Poor Julia sought consolation in philosophy and the companionship of sophists.

Meanwhile, Plautianus debauched himself with prostitutes and youthful catamites, caroused, crammed his stomach with food, vomited and generally played the greatest libertine in Rome. Plautianus was firmly in the saddle. No one could dislodge him.

Racius Constans, governor of Sardinia at the time, said: 'The heavens will fall before Plautianus has anything to fear.' One year later Plautianus forfeited his head, but the heavens did not fall.

The Emperor had become wary. Discovering that Plautianus was secretly planning to murder him and his son Antoninus, he summoned him to the palace. Plautianus drove there so furiously that his mules sank to the ground on arrival. The sentries would only allow him to enter if he left his bodyguards behind. Plautianus hesitated, but the guards refused to let him go back. He was admitted to the Emperor's presence. 'What were you thinking of?' Severus asked him. 'What were you thinking of, to plan our murder?' He allowed Plautianus to defend himself, but jumped up in the midst of the man's expostulations and struck him in the face. He was only restrained from killing him by the presence of his old father, and delegated the task to a servant. A few hairs from the dead traitor's beard were handed to Julia and Plautilla. The two women had only just met. Julia beamed. Plautilla wept. In the words of Dio Cassius: 'Thus the most powerful man of my day, who dreamed of climbing ever higher and before whom all quaked and trembled, was put to death and his body thrown out of the palace into the street.'

Plautilla and Plautius, the dead man's children, were exiled to the island of Lipara, where they lived in fear and misery until they were killed by Antoninus. Now that the all-powerful Plautianus was gone for good, Severus' sons, Antoninus and Geta, felt as free as air. They raped women, formed friendships with gladiators and charioteers, and became competitors in crime. They even charged each other during chariot races in a mutual attempt at murder.

One story of this period is rather amusing. Someone was suspected of coveting the imperial throne, and a witness declared that he had seen a bald-headed senator eavesdropping. No names were mentioned. All the senators were panic-stricken, not only the really bald ones but those who were going thin on top, too. Dio Cassius, who was a senator himself, wrote: 'I cannot here refrain from saying what happened to me, ludicrous as it may seem. I was so perturbed that I involuntarily felt around on my head for some hair. It was the same with a number of others.' Then came the further information that the bald-headed man had been wearing a toga trimmed with purple. 'Our eyes now turned to Baebius Marcellius, who hadn't a hair left on his head.'

On his way to the executioner, Marcellius said to his children: 'My only regret is that I have to leave you behind alive.'

Realizing that life in peace-time Rome was spoiling his sons and that his armies were losing their discipline for lack of any large-scale operations, the old Emperor set off for Britain. He guessed that he would never return from the expedition alive. Dio Cassius gives us a rather fanciful portrait of the Britons of those days. 'They lived in tents,' he tells us, 'without clothing or shoes, and shared their wives and children communally.' When Emperor Severus' wife, Julia Domna, who used to accompany her husband on his campaigns and was known among the troops as 'Mother of the Camp', criticized the wife of Argentocorus the Caledonian for her promiscuous sexual habits, the woman replied: 'We conform to Nature far better than you Roman ladies. We openly consort with the best, while you live secretly with the worst and commit adultery with them.' And 'the best' were really tough and intrepid men. Dio Cassius tells us that 'they endured hunger, cold and every kind of hardship with ease'.

Emperor Severus invaded Caledonian territory. He probably led his troops from the sea to the Firth of Forth, but he undoubtedly penetrated quite far into the north of the island, for he noticed 'the sun's long sojourn above the horizon'. Scotland was to be turned into a Roman province. Inscriptions show us that the country had its own cult dedicated to the Carthaginian goddess Tanit, the Emperor's patron deity.

We are told that Severus was carried about in a litter throughout this campaign. He was ill, and afflicted with gout. His sons, too, were a source of worry — especially Antoninus, who seems to have been a complete degenerate. He was quick-tempered and often scarcely in command of himself. On one occasion he nearly killed his father with a sword-thrust in the neck, only to be deterred by the outcry of the Emperor's retinue. Afterwards, in his tent, Severus told him: 'If you want to kill me, do so. You are at your prime, while I am an old man.' Antoninus made no move.

Seeing old Severus lying there racked with pain, the troops had wanted to proclaim Antoninus Emperor in his place. Severus ordered his bearers to carry him to the court-martial, where he punished them all except his son. 'That will teach you,' he said, 'that a man governs with his head, not his feet.'

In the year A.D. 211 the old Emperor decided to return to Rome. But the

Caledonians were still as refractory as ever, and Severus resolved to take the field once more. He died at Eboracum (York) on February 4th, while engaged in preparations for this campaign.

Dio Cassius remarks that the Emperor was always a good friend but a very dangerous enemy. He carried out his plans with dogged resolution. He never lost his Phoenician accent, nor did his daughter, who spoke Latin with such a strong Phoenician intonation that Severus disliked having her in Rome.

Severus was a very early riser. He used to get up even before day-break to listen to reports on every sphere of government activity. He presided in court until midday, when he went riding. After that he took a bath and sat down to a good lunch with his family. The afternoon was spent in completing the rest of the day's affairs and taking Latin lessons. (We have already mentioned his language difficulties.) Late in the afternoon the Emperor took another bath and then sat down to his evening meal. It is surprising, in view of his regular habits, that he only lived to the age of sixty-five.

Shortly before his death he sent for his own burial urn. 'You will soon contain a man who found the globe too small for him,' he said. His last words to his body-guards were: '*Laboremus!* — Let us work!' He wanted to remain active to the last. 'Well, hand it over, whatever there is left to do,' he whispered, and then died.

GETA, BASSIANUS-CARACALLA, JULIA DOMNA

LAUGH, JULIA!

Geta was murdered by his brother Bassianus, later Caracalla, on his mother's knee. And she, Julia Domna, was forbidden to weep on pain of death. 'Geta sustained a fatal wound and, dying, drenched his mother's breast with blood.'

Herodian, Imperial History, iii, 4.

'On thinking the matter over carefully, I am certain that, in general, no genius has ever bequeathed a really distinguished son to posterity. Most of the great men in history have had either no sons at all or offspring which mankind could well have done without.' So writes the Roman historian Aelius Spartianus, who lived circa A.D. 300. He quotes, among other examples, Homer, Demosthenes, Virgil, Caesar and Augustus — we might add Goethe and Napoleon — and considers that the best thing which could have happened to Septimius Severus was never to have begotten Bassianus (Antoninus).

In the Via Giulia at Rome, in the peristyle of the Palazzo Marchese della Rovere-Sacchetti, there is an historical relief known as the 'Sacchetti Relief'. It depicts Emperor Septimius Severus seated on the *sella curulis* or chair of office with Geta on the extreme right, and Bassianus — who later won the nickname Caracalla — behind him on the other side. Between the two princes we can make out the jurist Papinianus and, standing prominently beside the Emperor in the place of honour, Severus' favourite, Plautianus. The figures of Plautianus, Geta and Severus all lack heads. They were purposely mutilated, and we know why.

The relief was commissioned to celebrate the nomination of Bassianus and Geta to the consulship in 205. When Plautianus was beheaded on January 23rd, his head had to disappear from the sculpture as well. Geta's head was obliterated in the year 212, while the Emperor's vanished some time later. Ludwig Budde elucidated the secret of this interesting piece of sculpture in 1955, on behalf of the German Institute of Archaeology.

Shortly before Emperor Septimius Severus died, he urged his sons to get on together and behave as brothers should. Each of them, however, was dominated by an unnatural desire to kill the other. Their father had named them his joint successors in the hope that they would co-operate. Now they stood beside his bier in Eboracum, professing friendship and mutual admiration but secretly planning fratricide. One thing was clear from the first: only one of them could reign, only one of them could rule, only one of them could live. Warily, the two brothers crossed the Channel and travelled through Gaul and Italy, suspiciously watching every sword, drinking with caution and never eating at the same table, for fear of poison.

Geta seems to have been more popular with the troops than Bassianus. His strong physical resemblance to his father Severus encouraged the soldiers to assume that he was like him in character, too. Bassianus was probably the more unscrupulous. He planned to assassinate Geta during the Saturnalia, but made his preparations too obvious.

So the two brothers settled down in Rome, dividing the large imperial palace exactly in half and barring all access to each other's quarters. Every door and passage-way leading from one side of the palace into the other was barricaded and guarded by pickets. On the few occasions when the brothers met, it was either in public or in the presence of their mother Julia Domna — and then only if escorted by their body-guards. All attempts at reconciliation or compromise failed. It was planned to divide the Empire (as the sons of Emperor Theodosius did 185 years later). Bassianus, the elder brother, was to get Europe and the western part of Africa, while Asia and Egypt went to Geta, whose capital was to be either Alexandria or Antioch.

Julia Domna was very unhappy. Although she was still a beautiful woman and numbered lovers as well as philosophers and scholars among her companions, she was mother enough to be pained by the family quarrel. At all costs, she wanted to prevent the Roman Empire from being dismembered because of her sons' intolerance. As the mother and widow of emperors, she felt that she, too, would be torn asunder by the proposed partition.

The Senate tried to reconcile the brothers by offering a solemn sacrifice to the goddess Concordia. The sacrificial beast was already at the altar and the consul on his way to supervise the slaughtering, when someone managed to frustrate the ceremony. The consul could not find the sacrificial acolytes, and the acolytes could not find the consul. It meant bad days ahead for Rome, where nothing was given greater credence than an omen.

Geta was guarded by sentries night and day, and Bassianus saw that he was not going to get at his brother by main force. And so, in February of A.D. 212, he went to his mother Julia Domna and pretended a sensible desire for reconciliation. He asked her to send for Geta. After all, he pointed

Geta, the ill-fated son of Septimius Severus and Julia Domna, who was treacherously murdered by his brother Bassianus (Caracalla) in A.D. 212

Julia Domna, second wife of Septimius Severus, was a beautiful and gifted Syrian woman of intellectual bent. Her son Geta vainly sought refuge in her lap when trying to evade the murderous sword-thrusts of his brother Bassianus

Plautilla, wife of Emperor Caracalla, was murdered by her bloodthirsty and capricious husband

Emperor Caracalla, who murdered his brother Geta, occupied the throne of Rome between A.D. 212 and 217 and was the builder of the famous Baths of Caracalla. His real name was Marcus Aurelius Antoninus Bassianus, Caracalla being a nickname derived from the cloak he always wore

Opellius Macrinus instigated Caracalla's assassination and assumed the throne in his place. This African-born emperor ruled ingloriously from A.D. 217 to 218

out, Geta was his brother, and as the elder of the two he wanted to shake hands with him. He wanted to embrace him alone in their mother's house.

Geta trusted his brother for the first and last time. Unescorted, he went to his mother — and his death. Centurions whom Bassianus had concealed outside rushed into the room with drawn swords. Running to Julia and throwing his arms round her neck, Geta cried, 'Mother, mother, they are killing me!'

Julia Domna was helpless. She embraced her son in an attempt to protect him with her arms, but the centurions stabbed away at him so busily that they wounded her in the hand. Geta died on his mother's knee, soaking her robes with blood. Hence the ghoulish whisper that ran round Rome: 'Did you know? Geta has returned to the lap which bore him!'

Bassianus, the new-fledged fratricide, stood there glowing with the satisfaction of someone who has done a good day's work. His twenty-two-year-old brother was dead. From that moment on, Julia Domna was never allowed to shed a tear or show any emotion. Bassianus kept her under surveillance day and night, forcing her to laugh as though she were the happiest woman alive and noting down her every word and gesture so that she dared not mourn her loss even in secret.

In Bassianus we are confronted by the picture of a haunted and conscience-stricken murderer with absolute power. He became a complete despot, malicious and two-faced, and the Syrian characteristics which he had inherited from his mother degenerated under the influence of terror, superstition and witchcraft.

Bassianus raced through Rome like a hunted man. He was always telling people that he was in deadly peril. 'They want to do away with me. They want to kill me,' he whispered to everyone he met. He promised his soldiers huge bonuses. 'I am only one of you,' he declared. 'I want to live for you alone, to be able to reward you handsomely. My treasures all belong to you.' The new Emperor went on to tell his men that he intended to die with them. Having recalled all exiles, Bassianus launched a campaign of terror unmatched by any emperor before him. He dealt out death-sentences galore and waded in a veritable sea of blood, using Geta as his eternal pretext. Twenty thousand men and women were executed, among them Geta's servants, soldiers who had supported him, and his friends, male and female. It was enough for someone to have been seen in Geta's half of the palace. The very name Geta became an anathema. On all the monuments and inscriptions in honour of Septimius Severus and his family which have ever been found, whether in Italy, Asia Minor, Africa or elsewhere, Geta's name has been erased.

The celebrated jurist Papinianus was another of Bassianus' victims. Emperor Severus had probably confided to him how worried he was about his two sons, and Papinianus may have tried to bring the brothers together. We are told that Bassianus ordered him to justify his murder of Geta to the Senate and the people. Papinianus is said to have replied that it was easier to commit fratricide than to defend it, and that to incriminate an innocent victim of murder was tantamount to murdering him a second time. On his way to execution, the famous lawyer asserted that anyone who took over his post as Praetorian prefect without avenging him was a fool. The gods appear to have heeded his words, for the Emperor was later murdered on the orders of Macrinus, Papinianus' successor.

When Papinianus was dead, the Emperor, who had now adopted the name Antoninus, coolly inquired why the executioner had cut off his head with an axe instead of a sword.

But the Emperor was far from finished with murder. His next victim was his former tutor Cilo. Cilo was sitting in his bath when the soldiers came to kill him. They led him to the palace in wooden clogs and a scanty under-garment, beating him about the face meanwhile, much to the disgust of the onlookers. Hearing the commotion, Antoninus hurried down the street and threw his military cloak round the poor man's shoulders crying, 'Do not maltreat my dear old tutor!' Then he ordered that the military tribune who had been detailed to kill Cilo should be executed for failing to cut off his dear old tutor's head.

Rome became a very sad place. No distinguished or respected man was allowed to survive. Several Romans were executed for having relieved themselves near statues of the Emperor. Antoninus forced a gladiator to fight three opponents in a single day. When he was defeated by the third, the Emperor ordered him to be buried with due ceremony.

CARACALLA

A CLOAK

The cloak became world-famous. *Caracalla* meant a cape, and the emperor who wore it was named after it. He was infatuated with Alexander the Great ... He extended this predilection to Macedonians in general, and once commended a military tribune from Macedonia for his agility in leaping on to his horse. 'Where do you come from?' he asked him. On learning that he was a Macedonian, he questioned him further: 'What is your name?'—'Antigonus.'—'What was your father's name?' When it turned out to be Philip, he said: 'Now I know all I wanted to know.'

Dio Cassius, lxxvii, 7 and 8.

BASSIANUS ANTONINUS yearned to be a celebrated general like Alexander. He was always seeking new excuses for war, kept large armies permanently mobilized and lavished huge sums of money on his soldiers. He had absolutely no sense of proportion and gave his men such extravagant rates of pay that he had to devalue the coinage, just as Severus had decided to do before him. Soon, his father's treasury was exhausted and the public exchequer showed a large deficit. This lack of money was probably responsible for the Emperor's one act of historical importance: his celebrated granting of citizenship to the whole free provincial population of the Roman Empire in the year A.D. 212, which made it a single legal unit for the first time. Since death duties had been carefully increased for all citizens in advance, this extension of civil rights provided an immense source of new revenue.

The Emperor was nearly always on the move. Wherever he made a halt, expensive hotels, amphitheatres and racecourses had to be built. Vast sums were wasted because the Emperor usually failed to turn up at the places which had been prepared for him, and everything had to be torn down again. 'He only does it to provoke us,' whispered the Romans. 'Nobody except me must have money, so that I can give it to my men,' said the Emperor.

Antoninus was hot-tempered, thoughtless and as over-hasty and unsound in his decisions as he was prejudiced in favour of his own judgment. He disliked asking other people's advice, especially people who had put him under an obligation of some sort. He liked no one and hated everyone, most of all those who had distinguished themselves. Such outstanding men as he had not murdered he sent off to regions with unpleasant climates which did not agree with them. These 'marks of high esteem' were a way of removing people whom he disliked from his range of vision. As a result, a number of very able men died of excessive heat or cold in various parts of the world. Others had all their property confiscated and were reduced to penury. In all these measures the Emperor was aided by a certain native cunning, probably a legacy from his Syrian mother.

One year after Geta's murder, in 213, the Emperor left Rome never to return. He did not witness the completion of the huge thermae which were built on his orders and are still among the largest ancient ruins in Rome today, but spent the remaining four years of his reign in various provinces of the Empire. In August 213 he crossed the Rhaetian *limes* and defeated the Germans on the Main, thereafter adopting the title Germanicus Maximus. In the spring of 214 we see him on the Danube.

Bassianus Antoninus marched on through Thrace until he reached Macedonia, where he was totally overcome by his mania to emulate that country's greatest son. Alexander the Great had always been his idol, and he now envisaged himself as the living image of the Macedonian king. He spent hours before a mirror with his head on one side, trying to imitate the posture for which Alexander was famous. (The Alexandrians christened him 'Alexander's monkey'.) He drank from a goblet reputed to have belonged to Alexander, carried weapons which Alexander had used about 550 years earlier, ordered statues of Alexander to be set up in every camp, both at Rome and in the provinces, and recruited a phalanx, 16,000 strong, composed solely of Macedonians. The members of this unit — about the size of a modern division — were armed exactly as Alexander's soldiers had once been. Spartans were also invited to join it. The Emperor negotiated unsuccessfully with the King of Parthia for his daughter's hand in marriage so that, as heir to the Parthian empire, his suzerainty would extend as far as India, as Alexander's had done long ago.

In May 215 the Emperor arrived in Antioch with his mother. He was suffering from nervous hallucinations, persecuted by the spirits of his murdered victims, haunted by the minatory apparitions of his father and brother. Sometimes he fainted dead away. He hardly dared take the field any longer. But Alexandria, the Egyptian city named after the hero he so greatly idolized, temporarily jolted him out of his insanity, weakness and inaction.

The Emperor had heard that the Alexandrians objected to his having murdered his brother Geta and that they reproached and despised him. That was exactly why he had decided to visit their famous city. With his habitual cunning, he invited all the most distinguished citizens to a banquet and then exterminated them. He occupied every street and roof-top, imposed a curfew, executed many thousands of people. Anyone who got in the way of his soldiers' swords was slain out of hand, whether friend or foe. 'The city is very large,' Dio Cassius relates, 'and, since the wholesale slaughter went on day and night, no one could make any distinctions — even if anyone had wanted to.'

Every province had a chance of experiencing the Emperor's rapacity, brutality and lack of scruple. Dio Cassius tells us that no one had a good word to say for him. He became known as 'Tarantas', the nickname for a gladiator who was small and ugly but bumptious and blood-thirsty. However, he went down in history under the name of Caracalla.

Being unequal to great exertion or extremes of heat and cold, Emperor Caracalla ordered himself some special clothes which looked like armour but were not. Clad in these he felt safe from assassination but did not have to endure the weight of real mail. Over his sham armour he wore a red cloak. It is uncertain whether this garment was invented by the Celts, the Syrians or the Mesopotamian Persians. At all events, it was not a one-piece affair like the normal Roman cloak, but tailored from several pieces of cloth and worn heel-length. Its name, *caracallus*, came to be applied to the Emperor himself, Caracalla being an inflection of the original word. His soldiers were obliged to wear these garments, too.

Caracalla had murdered his wife Plautilla long before. His mother, Julia Domna, seems to have managed the affairs of the whole Empire with considerable statecraft, both at Rome and at Antioch in Syria, where she was on home ground. Caracalla paid little attention to Julia's advice, and she had to go very cautiously to avoid arousing his violent temper. She maintained written communication with the Empire at large, answered official correspondence in Latin and Greek and gave audiences to senior civil servants, still finding time to devote herself to philosophical meditation.

It was the Emperor's fondness for murder and depravity, coupled with his habit of leaving the administration of public affairs to others, which finally spelt his undoing. An Egyptian called Serapis, who possessed the gift of clairvoyance, had predicted that Macrinus would soon be master of the Roman Empire and declined to withdraw this prophecy even when he was put in chains and threatened with death.

The Emperor, who was back in Syria again and holding court at Antioch, was notified of this occurrence in writing. Being engrossed in a chariot race at the time, however, he neglected to open his mail — as he often did — and sent the report back to Rome unread. There it was opened by Macrinus, who administered a large proportion of civil affairs on Caracalla's behalf. On reading the fateful document, Macrinus did not waste a moment. Sending for a soldier who was dissatisfied with his lack of promotion, he instructed him to kill the Emperor.

By this time Caracalla was on a pilgrimage from Edessa to Carrhae (modern Haran), the place from which Abraham had once started out for Canaan and where the Romans under Crassus the Triumvir had suffered their first defeat at the hands of the Parthians in the year 53 B.C. There the Emperor indulged his pronounced partiality for oriental magic cults and astrology. He had long ago seen to it that the Semitic or Syrian Sun-cult became the national religion of Rome, and he now decided to pray at the shrine of Luna, the Moon-goddess.

Caracalla hurried along the ancient biblical trails to the Moon-temple, his mind obsessed with magic. In his craving for deliverance and relief from the pangs of remorse, he failed to notice that his soldiers, long used to their high rates of pay, had become sullen and suspicious; that in their secret hearts they despised him, even though his sole wish was to be one of them. A small squadron of cavalry accompanied the hurrying Emperor in the long cloak. Ordering his escort to halt, Caracalla left the main highway and went a short distance into the surrounding scrub. The discontented soldier, whose name was Martialis, approached the Emperor on some pretext and drove a dagger into his heart. He himself was immediately killed by a Scythian archer in the imperial body-guard.

Julia Domna could weep at last. She had lost both her sons now, and with them the rank of Empress. Grief and loss of status proved too much for her, and she took her own life.

ELAGABALUS

THE BEAUTIFUL BOY-PRIEST

> He wanted not only to abolish the Roman forms of worship, but to snuff out the religions of the whole world, dominated by the thought that God Elagabalus alone should be worshipped everywhere.
>
> *Aelius Lampridius, Antoninus Elagabalus*, vi.

IT is extraordinary how quite insignificant people are sometimes raised to the most exalted heights in time of alarm or emergency. They meet with sudden success and attain a prominence which even they would never have believed themselves capable of. Playthings of destiny, they are like kites in the wind which fall in tatters after a short time aloft.

Such a man was Opellius Macrinus. He was no Macbeth. He was not motivated by personal ambition — still less by the ambition of an aspiring wife. No, he arranged his Emperor's murder out of dire necessity, a necessity forced on him by the precariousness of his position. Macrinus, a lawyer by profession, was Emperor Caracalla's Praetorian prefect. It had been prophesied that he, humble though his origins were, would become Emperor of Rome. It was a pleasant prophecy but a dangerous one, so long as another emperor was still alive. And Caracalla was very much alive. He set heads rolling on the slightest provocation, as everyone in the vast Roman Empire was aware. Macrinus knew that Caracalla's myrmidons might come to kill him at any moment.

Caracalla was murdered on April 8th, A.D. 217. Macrinus had beaten him to the punch. Fear had impelled him to become a murderer, just as fear made him seize the throne and adopt the name Antoninus, with all the near-sacred associations which still surrounded it. The earlier Antonines had been good and highly respected rulers. Antoninus Pius, Marcus Aurelius, Lucius Verus — all had become transfigured in retrospect and glowed with a golden aura.

But Macrinus did not belong to the Antonine family, nor did he come of the Severan line. He called himself simply 'Antoninus'. What was more, he made it clear to the Senate that the legions had also conferred imperial status upon his nine-year-old son Diadumenianus, as well as the sacred name Antoninus. It had been Caracalla's honorary title, and Macrinus may have hoped that by keeping the name alive he would disguise the fact that he had murdered its former owner.

Macrinus was an undistinguished character. He was a Mauretanian lawyer, and far from being a soldier's general. But, with the courage of a man who is gambling for his life, he rose to the occasion. It was an unparalleled situation. Never before had a man who was not even a member of the Senate mounted the Roman throne. But the time was ripe. Anyone looked better to the Romans than the frightful Caracalla. With icy calm, Macrinus proposed that the monster whom he had just murdered be declared a god.

It was unheard of for an assassin to honour his victim in such a way. Still more amazing was the fact that the Senate complied with Macrinus' wishes, for his guilt was an open secret. Nevertheless, the new Emperor's proposal did more to cloak his murderous act than any of his other hypocritical declarations.

There is no better way for a despot, dictator or tyrant to obliterate his past than to cover himself with military glory. Still in the summer of A.D. 217 Emperor Macrinus marched against the Parthians. All the army's doubts and uncertainties vanished and street-corner gossip died away. Great military successes were the Midas touch which would turn the Emperor's insecurity into power and glory.

But Macrinus did not win much of a military reputation. After a few minor successes against Parthian camel-riders he put forward peace proposals to Artabanus, which the Parthian King was quite happy to accept. The Emperor then returned to Antioch, where he devoted himself to *recherché* amusements and basked in his exalted rank. He cultivated his beard, strolled slowly and majestically about, and conducted audiences in such an affectedly low voice that no one could understand a word he said.

Herodian reports that back in Rome people could at least enjoy a year's freedom from fear once Caracalla was dead and peace had been signed with the Parthians.

However, the Roman legions soon grew to dislike their new master. They were victors, yet the Emperor's deplorable peace treaty with the Parthians made them look more like a defeated army. Macrinus had even promised to pay Artabanus a large indemnity for war damage, and when he proposed to cap it all by docking the legionaries' pay, the Roman warriors began to grumble. They started to lay plans for the Emperor's murder.

There was still a genuine Severan dynasty in existence, even though it had been by-passed. The surviving members of Severus' line were not going to sit back and let their title, Antoninus, be purloined by someone with

The city of Emesa was famed in ancient times for its Sun-temple. The city's tutelary deity was the Sun-god Elagabalus, who was worshipped in the shape of a meteor. Emperor Varius Avitus, later known as Elagabalus, held priestly office in Emesa at the early age of fourteen

absolutely no right to it. Julia Domna, late wife of the former Emperor Septimius Severus, had a sister called Julia Maesa. Maesa had two daughters, Soaemis and Mamaea, each of whom was the mother of one son: Soaemias of Varius Avitus, and Mamaea of Alexianus. The whole family lived at

Emesa, their native city on the Orontes in central Syria. This place, which lay to the north of Damascus, is now known as Homs. At Emesa, the family provided high priests for the god Elagabalus. In the name Elagabalus (less correctly Heliogabalus) we rediscover the ancient god Baal, whom we have already met in the Old Testament as a heathen deity. Elagabalus, who was a Sun-god and the patron deity of Emesa, was worshipped in the shape of a black conical stone 'which had fallen from heaven' — a piece of the sun, in fact.

Julia Domna herself had been the daughter of a wealthy priest of Elagabalus, and Varius Avitus, the son of Soaemias, occupied the same post in Elagabalus' temple at the age of fourteen. Thus the family was closely connected with the cult of Baal.

Fourteen-year-old Varius Avitus was the legitimate son of Soaemias and the Syrian Varius Marcellus. Now, however, to add to the general confusion, his cunning grandmother Maesa announced that he was a natural son of the late Emperor Caracalla. That made him a Severus: and only a Severus — being entitled to the surname Antoninus — could become Emperor.

To the grandmother, obtaining the throne for her grandson was more important than preserving her daughter's good name. As for the daughter, she did not mind exposing herself to shame, disgrace or scandal as long as her young son became Emperor. The two women actually succeeded in convincing the whole world that the priest's son was Caracalla's bastard. The Antonines were still honoured as gods, and it was not long before the new Antoninus was voted honours by cities all over the Empire.

Grandmother Maesa was as wily as she was wealthy. Daughter Soaemias was ambitious, courageous and hard-headed. Grandson Avitus was an effeminate youth who liked spending money. The handsome young priest was extremely popular with the troops, and his temple was never empty.

Caracalla's alleged offspring was now proclaimed Emperor, and Macrinus once more found himself in deadly peril. A battle was fought between the armies of young Avitus and Emperor Macrinus at the village of Immo, near Antioch. Avitus' army put up a miserable performance, but Julia Maesa and Soaemis jumped down from their chariots and plunged, weeping and wailing, into the fleeing mob of soldiers in an attempt to halt them. Even the worst army can win if there is greater cowardice on the other side. As soon as Macrinus met resistance he fled, taking his son Diadumenianus with him. Both father and son were captured at Chalcedon on the Bosphorus and murdered while on the way back to Antioch. Meanwhile, Julia Maesa had soon won over Macrinus' troops by lavish distributions of largesse. Macrinus was the first emperor in Roman history never to set foot in Rome throughout his reign.

The handsome boy-priest was now undisputed master of the Empire. He was known simply as Elagabalus, after his god—though he did not receive the name until much later on. He became the most Machiavellian monster that ever occupied the Roman throne, diabolical in his vicious eccentricities and far outrivalling Nero himself in perverted ingenuity.

When the Senate heard the news of Elagabalus' accession there were the usual scenes of rejoicing. Tributes were paid to the new 'Antoninus' and curses were heaped on the late Macrinus and his nine-year-old son. To prepare the Romans in some degree for his strange appearance, Elagabalus commissioned a life-sized portrait of himself in the vestments of a Syrian priest and sent it on to Rome in advance, where it was set up beside the statue of Victory in the Senate-house.

In the spring of 219, Elagabalus made his ceremonial entry into Rome. Swathed in gorgeous robes, rouged like a young girl, his eyes artificially luminous with essences, a pearl necklace about his throat and diadems in his hair, the new Emperor entered the city on the Tiber, bringing a breath of the Orient with him. At his side sat his mother and grandmother, misty-eyed with rapture and devotion but confronted by the onerous task of controlling the unruly instrument of their ambitions.

The Romans witnessed scenes such as they had never known before. They saw the sacred meteorite pass by in solemn state, borne on a lofty carriage. The Syrian youth had removed his Sun-god's image from the temple at Emesa and brought it all the way to Rome. He walked backwards in front of the carriage so that he should never lose sight of it. Two temples were at once erected for this Baal, one on the Palatine Hill and the other near what is now Porta Maggiore. All Rome's other gods now had to withdraw, leaving the stage free for the great god Elagabalus. Emperor Elagabalus wanted to merge the numerous Roman cults and make Elagabalus the supreme deity. He even wanted to bring Judaism and Christianity into his temples and enlist them in the service of his god. Elagabalus very soon divorced his first wife Julia Paula. The surviving sculptures of this young woman reveal a beautiful but sad and rather sullen face.

To publicize the amalgamation of Rome's gods with those of the East and set the seal on his strange religious merger, Elagabalus married Aquilia Severa, who, being a Vestal priestess, was sworn to everlasting chastity. He announced that, in his opinion, a marriage between a high priest and a priestess was most appropriate, and expressed his confident belief that any children of such a union would be godlike.

That was the first shock which the Emperor gave his Roman subjects. Seeing that he had aroused the indignation of the whole Empire, he hastily divorced his Vestal priestess and brought the image of Tanit ('the Heavenly'), principal goddess of Carthage, together with all her sacred treasures, into his own temple, the 'Eliogabalium'. This goddess seems to have been worshipped in association with Magna Mater, the Great Mother, whose cult involved the performance of peculiar magical and orgiastic rites and was bound up with the horrible custom of child-sacrifice. Elagabalus wanted not only to abolish the religions of Rome but to coerce the whole world into worshipping his own god. The Emperor of Rome danced round the altars at public festivals to the sound of cymbals, drums and weird anthems sung by Syrian women.

All Rome marvelled at the sacred sky-born stone, the new priest-emperor and the oriental display of exotic colours, incense and music.

But who really was Elagabalus' god — this god to whom he sacrificed beautiful children from aristocratic families all over Italy? His god was a combination of self-indulgence, debauchery and vice. Elagabalus liked to surround himself with every form of witchcraft. The sorcerers and magicians performed their daily sacrifices and the people got their hand-outs. Instead of throwing them gold and silver, Elagabalus distributed fattened cattle, camels, donkeys and slaves. When asked why, he replied: 'That's what real emperors do.'

DROWNED IN BLOSSOMS

Emperor Elagabalus installed a reversible ceiling in his dining-room and released so many violets and other flowers on to his guests that some of them lost their lives because they could not dig their way out of the avalanche of blossoms and into the open air.

Aelius Lampridius, Antoninus Elagabalus, xxi.

ELAGABALUS was fourteen when he came to the throne, and eighteen when he died.

There were riotous scenes in the imperial palace, where he opened a large bath-house to the public — not, it may be added, in the service of Roman hygiene, but in order to find victims for his idiotic amusements.

The Emperor was constantly accompanied by a huge athlete from Smyrna called Aurelius Soticus. Soticus, the son of a cook, had been brought with great ceremony to Rome, where Elagabalus welcomed him into his palace, specially illuminated for the occasion, and appointed him his Chamberlain. At sight of his stalwart new henchman the Emperor jumped up, all of a twitter, and coyly averted his head. Soticus took the most outrageous advantage of his friendship with Elagabalus and amassed a large fortune by selling promises and concessions to all and sundry. 'I told the Emperor this about you,' he would whisper to everyone he met, or 'The Emperor said that about you.' Elagabalus solemnly went through a form of marriage with Soticus and insisted that someone should act as 'mother of the bride'.

Elagabalus nominated a ballet dancer as prefect of the Guard, a charioteer as commander of the watch and a barber called Claudius as supervisor of the grain supplies. None of these men had any qualifications for their jobs except debauchery. Aurelius Victor reports that, generally speaking Elagabalus 'gathered about him the most obscene people from all over the globe'. He gave the three senior posts in the department of death-duties to a muleteer, a messenger and a smith. Whenever he visited the Senate or a military camp he took his grandmother with him. No one showed him any respect, otherwise. It was, incidentally, the first time that a woman had ever set foot in the Senate-house.

Mamaea, the sister of Elagabalus' mother Soaemias, had meanwhile ensured that her son Alexianus was also promoted to imperial rank. It was quite obvious that Elagabalus could not go on 'reigning' by himself for much longer. His cousin Alexianus was a very able young man. He was popular with the army and greatly respected by the Senate. Elagabalus turned morose at the very mention of Alexianus' name, realizing only too well that the people much preferred his cousin to himself. He became suspicious of everyone. Seeing Alexianus' continued existence as a threat to his own position, he hired some soldiers to assassinate him. However, the soldiers occupied the palace to protect Alexianus, not to kill him.

Elagabalus concealed himself and waited, with a pounding heart, for news of the murder. Hearing the tramp of soldiers' feet, he was suddenly seized by a nameless fear and hid behind a curtain in his bedroom. He only escaped with his life on this occasion thanks to the commander of his body-guard. But he did not abandon the idea of murdering his cousin. Because he knew that the Senate was on Alexianus' side, he decreed that all its members must leave Rome immediately. Despite this, one courageous senator called Sabinus stayed on in the dangerous city. The Emperor ordered a centurion to kill him but, luckily for Sabinus, the centurion was deaf. Another man who risked his life on this occasion was Ulpian, the famous Syrian jurist.

Elagabalus was a great devotee of banquets, wine, flowers and perfume. He inaugurated various summer carnivals, each with a different colour as its theme. There was a green festival, a pink festival, a violet festival, a blue festival — a special colour for each warm summer's day. He blended wine with the most exotic additives, enhancing the bouquet of rose-wine, for instance, by mixing it with fragrant fir-cone essence. He showered his banqueting-halls with roses, lilies, violets, hyacinths and narcissi, and waded happily through oceans of blossom. Having installed a reversible ceiling in his dining-room, he tipped such quantities of violets and other flowers on to his guests that some of them lost their lives because they were unable to struggle out of the suffocating avalanche of blossoms and into the open air.

Elagabalus would swim in his pool only if the water had been perfumed. He presented his favourites with whole swimming-pools and rose-scented water in which he himself had bathed. The rarest and most precious oils were provided whenever he went bathing with his court. He had swimming-pools built a considerable distance from the coast, where it was difficult to fill them with sea-water, and then gave them to his friends. Once, wanting to see a mountain of snow, he had one transported from far away in huge buckets. His pillows and couches had to be stuffed with hare's fur and the finest turkey's feathers, and he always reclined on them surrounded by rare flowers and perfumes. He once had himself and his favourites served with a dish of 600 storks' heads, of which he ate only the brains. On another occasion he offered his guests twenty-two unusual meat dishes and compelled them to bathe with him in mixed company between each course, swearing all the time how much they were enjoying themselves.

The Emperor collected snakes and was fond of letting them loose among the spectators at evening entertainments so that people were injured in the ensuing panic. Sometimes he harnessed lions to his chariot, sometimes tigers or elephants, always donning the costume of the deity to which these animals were sacred. His pets included small Egyptian snakes, hippopotami, crocodiles and even a rhinoceros. When he got bored, he drove around naked with lovely young girls harnessed in pairs, threes or fours to his chariot. At night he would disguise himself in a wig and visit disreputable taverns, where he enjoyed himself riotously. Sometimes he would sit on the threshold of one of his palace chambers, pulling aside the curtain on its golden rings and soliciting any of his courtiers who happened to be passing in a reedy, languishing voice. He always behaved with extreme effeminacy and used, among other things, to spin wool, wear a hair-net, paint his eyes with white lead and carmine and pluck his beard. Wherever Elagabalus went and whatever he was doing, whether sacrificing, receiving visitors or addressing the people, he used to dance. He also played charioteer, dressed in a green robe, with his body-guards, grandmother, mother and numerous concubines acting as umpires. Bowing low, the Emperor begged gold pieces from his officers and the other 'umpires' like a common racing-driver.

Elagabalus had a very good singing-voice and could play the flute, horn, organ and a three-stringed instrument. He is said to have been the first Roman to dress entirely in silk, a material which he prized above all others. He owned a *tunica* of pure gold, another of purple, and another, from Persia, encrusted with precious stones, which he often complained was too heavy for him. He even wore jewels on his shoes and a bejewelled diadem calculated to enhance his girlish beauty.

At the theatre he sometimes laughed so loudly that the audience could not hear the performers. He assembled all the prostitutes in the capital in a large public building and made obscene speeches to them.

When his friends had got drunk at one of his wild parties, Elagabalus used to dowse the lights, lock them in and let lions, leopards and bears into the room without warning. The animals were docile and harmless, their teeth having been removed. The Emperor only wanted to give his friends a shock, not kill them — but in fact many of them died.

Elagabalus appears to have been the inventor of the air-cushion. He used to get his slaves to let the air out under his friends so that they rolled beneath the table. Again, he lashed several of his boon companions to a water-wheel, set it in motion, and enjoyed himself hugely at their expense.

He ordered imitation food to be made out of wax, wood, ivory, clay, marble or stone, and served these cunning replicas to his unsuspecting guests while at table with them. He once told his slaves to gather half a ton of spider's web, offering prizes as an encouragement, and, when they collected five tons, remarked that it showed how large Rome was. He used to present his friends with jars containing frogs, scorpions, snakes and even captured flies. He bought himself a very beautiful concubine for 100,000 sesterces and then kept her untouched, 'as a virgin'. He sank fully-laden ships in harbour on the grounds that such an act demonstrated the greatness of his soul. He executed all the day's business at night and luxuriated in bed for most of the morning. He seldom dismissed his courtiers after an audience without giving them a present — unless they were the thrifty type, of course. The Emperor detested thrifty people.

On being told by Syrian priests that he would die an unnatural death, Elagabalus provided himself with red silk cords with which to hang himself, golden swords on which to impale himself and every conceivable type of poison. He even went to the lengths of building himself a tall tower from which to plunge to his death when the critical moment arrived. But his soldiers and body-guards, especially the latter, did not let it come to suicide.

Once again Elagabalus was contemplating the murder of his cousin. Once again all he had succeeded in doing was to direct the murderous inclinations of his body-guards against his own person. In a last-minute attempt to pacify them and save his life, he visited their camp accompanied by his cousin Alexianus and their respective mothers.

The soldiers never shifted their gaze from him, but watched him like a rat in a trap. The atmosphere took on a note of sinister farce when the two mothers started to squabble, heaping the fuel of their hatred on to an already explosive situation. Elagabalus tried to escape and hid in a latrine with Soaemias, who sat there trembling with her arms clasped tightly about her beloved son. But mother and son were discovered and killed. Their heads were cut off and their bodies dragged through the gutters to the Tiber, where they were thrown off the Aemilian Bridge with weights attached, to prevent their floating to the surface.

The actor, practical joker, charioteer and dancer, the insane voluptuary, the painted woman in masculine attire who had occupied the throne of a world empire, was dead at last. He was only eighteen.

Emperor Elagabalus reigned between A.D. 218 and 222. During his reign Rome witnessed scenes of debauchery unequalled by anything in her previous history

Julia Mamaea, mother of Alexianus, the thirteen-year-old boy who was proclaimed co-regent with Elagabalus. As Emperor, Alexianus took the name Alexander Severus. Mamaea controlled her son and through him the whole Empire

Julia Paula, beautiful first wife of the priest-king Elagabalus. Here we see her as a young woman of about twenty-six 'wrapped in a strange melancholy. She is immersed in her own thoughts, her gaze directed inwards rather than at her surroundings or at the beholder'. (Hans Weber)

Alexander Severus (reigned A.D. 222–235) had such fine and brilliant eyes that it was said to be hard to meet his gaze. He was a favourite of the Romans and ruled with integrity and moderation. He was too dependent on his mother, however, and was eventually murdered with her

The nerve-centre of ancient Rome. The Roman Forum was the focal point of the greatest empire in the ancient world and the hub of Roman life, which reached a peak of activity at about 11 a.m. each day. All traffic was banned here between sunrise and 4 p.m. To identify the various buildings, see sketch

1 Monument to Victor-Emmanuel II, 2 Roman State Archives, 3 Temple of Saturn, 4 Triumphal arch of Emperor Septimius Severus, 5 Forum of Caesar, 6 Curia (Roman Senate-house), 7 Monument of Emperor Phocas, 8 Basilica Julia, 9 Temple of Castor and Pollux, 10 Monuments, 11 Basilica Aemilia, 12 Temple of Emperor Antoninus Pius and his wife Faustina, 13 Temple of Divus Julius (Julius Caesar deified), 14 Temple of Vesta, 15 House of the Vestals, 16 Temple of Romulus (son of Emperor Maxentius), 17 Basilica of Maxentius or Constantine, 18 Triumphal arch of Titus, 19 Trajan's Forum, 20 Capitol, 21 Roman State prison (Carcer Mamertinus), 22 Ancient shopping-street

And his god?

His god followed him, banished from Rome. The sacred meteorite, the temples and altars, all disappeared.

That was the end of a man whose life, as the contemporary Roman historian Aelius Lampridius declared, was as perverse as his name.

ALEXANDER SEVERUS

THE DARLING OF THE ROMANS

Alexander Severus was a seventeen-year-old Syrian boy with beautiful, brilliant eyes. He obeyed his mother, and she ruled. 'He intended to build Christ a temple and include him among the gods—a project which Hadrian is said to have contemplated earlier.'

Aelius Lampridius, Severus Alexander, xliii.

AFTER his half-demented cousin Elagabalus, Alexianus looked to Roman eyes like a gift from the gods. It was A.D. 222, or 975 years 'after the founding of the city' — *ab urbe condita*, as the Romans termed it. It was an age when people believed in miracles and heavenly manifestations and saw divine portents whenever there was a change of government. A story at once became current that a great star had appeared in the sky above the house at Arca Caesarea in Syria where Alexianus had been born. People had doubtless heard something about a 'king of mankind' and his birth-star, and the idea of an omen of salvation above the new Emperor's place of birth was the logical outcome.

A mere boy of fourteen, Alexianus owed his throne to the Praetorian Guard. It was hoped that he would model himself on Alexander the Great, which was why, as Emperor, he bore the names Marcus Aurelius Severus Alexander. The Senate loaded him with imperial honours and titles. However, power really lay in the hands of two Syrian women, his mother Mamaea and his grandmother Maesa. Maesa died shortly after Alexianus' accession, leaving her astute but avaricious daughter Mamaea to rule her grandson and, through him, the whole Empire. Mamaea formed a permanent Privy Council composed of sixteen wise and respected senators. Its president was the well-known Syrian jurist Ulpian, who, in his additional capacity as commander of the body-guard, was invested with supreme imperial jurisdiction.

Mamaea never wanted to be an empress: she merely wanted to hold the reins of power from behind her son's back. She wanted to restore order. She alone was to be allowed to shape her son's ideas, and she would not tolerate another woman near him. Alexander married the daughter of a patrician, chosen for him by Mamaea, but his happiness was shortlived. His father-in-law, who had received the title Caesar, was executed for high treason when he started taking his new status too seriously. The unhappy bride, whose name may have been Memmia or Herennia Orbiana, was chased out of the palace by her mother-in-law and banished to Africa. It so happened that Alexander was deeply in love with her.

Mamaea moulded her young son's character with the utmost care, enlisting the aid of the greatest living teachers. What was more, she was successful, for his nature, not in itself a strong one, was illumined by integrity, orderliness, inner cleanliness and an unquestioning devotion to his mother. Admittedly, this young Emperor whom the Romans honoured and revered like a god never willingly made a decision of his own. Mild as the gentle wind from Lebanon which blew across his native land, he merely bowed to his responsibilities. But he never shirked a decision — as long as Mamaea was within reach. He was dominated by his mother and never dared to contradict her. The Romans conferred on her the extravagant titles 'Mother of the Fatherland' and 'Mother of All Mankind'.

Alexander had beautiful, brilliant eyes, and people used to say that it was difficult to meet his gaze. He had a remarkably good memory and was even credited with telepathic powers. Being a distinguished astrologer himself, he permitted the 'Chaldeans', who had been banished from Rome since 139 B.C., to install themselves there once more and pursue their profession freely. It was believed that anyone who could predict the future was a great asset to the State.

The Emperor studied geometry, painting and singing. In contrast to Nero and Elagabalus, however, he sang only in privacy, i.e. in front of his slaves. Roman historians attributed a large number of other talents to this greatly respected Emperor, some of which were no doubt invented out of admiration, regard or a sense of relief that he had survived his villainous cousin and that Elagabalus was a thing of the past. A Syrian by birth, Alexander was far less Asiatic in manner than Elagabalus. In his anxiety to be a Roman, he always tried to gloss over or disguise his alien origins, and was furious when the citizens of Antioch and Alexandria jokingly referred to him as a Syrian priest.

The Emperor used to visit the temple at dawn each day. If we are to believe the Roman historian Aelius Lampridius, Alexander addressed his prayers not only to the Roman gods and the emperors who had been raised to divine rank, but to the spirits of Orpheus, Christ, Abraham and, when in his private chapel, to Apollonius of Tyana. This remarkable itinerant preacher and worker of miracles from the first century A.D. was represented by legend sometimes as a magician, sometimes as a god-like man. At the instigation of Maesa's sister Julia Domna, who was also a devotee of Apollonius, the Greek author Philostratus wrote a romantic biography of the man. It has survived, but appears in many respects to have been modelled on the New Testament.

We are told that Alexander Severus intended to build Christ a temple, a project which Hadrian may secretly have contemplated earlier — Hadrian, the strange emperor who erected several temples and left them bare of gods. It appears, however, that Alexander's advisers successfully opposed this plan. They warned him against building a temple to the god of the Christians, arguing that everyone would turn Christian and the other temples would be deserted. For all that, the Jews were now granted freedom of worship, and it was forbidden to persecute the Christians. That great Father of the Church, Origen of Alexandria, was even invited to levees by Julia Mamaea, the Emperor's mother, and the Christian historian Julius Africanus was on such good terms with Alexander that he dedicated his work to him.

The Emperor spent the early part of the morning hunting, fishing or walking. Then he devoted himself to affairs of State, which never seemed to tire or irritate him. After that he would do some reading. He often dipped into a biography of Alexander the Great, but also studied Plato (whose work on the ideal State was his favourite book) and read Cicero and Horace. Then came athletics, after which Alexander had himself oiled and swam for an hour. He followed his bathe with a snack of milk, bread and eggs which often enabled him to do without a midday meal. In the afternoon he answered official correspondence and worked with his secretaries. After that he was at home to friends and visitors. Ulpian was always at his side during the more important interviews.

Alexander was very abstemious and often drank nothing but cold, clear water. In summer he used to mix his wine with a little rose-water, his fondness for the bouquet this produced being all he really had in common with his cousin Elagabalus.

Alexander made a clean sweep of the parasites whom Elagabalus had provided with cosy sinecures in the civil service. The Senate, palace and army were all purged of ballet dancers, catamites and uneducated upstarts. The Emperor discharged all the palace eunuchs and made them the slaves of women commoners or gave them to his friends, declaring that this 'third sex' should not be tolerated either by men or by upper-class women. His predecessor Elagabalus had been the slave of his eunuchs. Now the boot was on the other foot. 'If these loafers do not settle down to an honest job of work, you may kill them without a hearing,' the Emperor announced.

Dwarfs, jesters, male singers with female voices, clowns and buffoons were all proclaimed State property, as were women of easy virtue. There were hard times ahead for corrupt magistrates. The young Emperor, so mild in other respects, could be brutal when it came to legal graft. On going to the Senate one day and encountering Septimius Arabianus, a notoriously crooked lawyer, Alexander flew into a rage and cried: 'Ye gods! So Arabianus is still alive and actually comes to the Senate!'

The Emperor made it a principle not to grant appointments to the first to crowd round the trough. Far more often he promoted modest men of genuine ability who stayed quietly in the background. Doctors, technicians and scholars of all kinds received commissions and well-paid posts, while orphans and children from poor homes got interest-free loans from the State. The whole Senate was given a hearing before any new senator was nominated. The Senate was also consulted in the matter of elections to the consulship, as it had been in the old days. When Mamaea advised her son to be rather more strict and severe, Alexander answered that his kind of rule was at least safe and enduring.

The young Emperor seems to have been extraordinarily hard-working. He sat for nights on end poring over the lists of officers and other ranks in his army, checking their strength, ranks and rates of pay, noting the names of men who had earned promotion, and drawing up extensive plans for supply depots and ration dumps which would spare his soldiers the necessity of carrying heavy packs.

On military expeditions through enemy territory, Alexander always provided an ample number of sturdy draught-animals. He personally visited the sick and wounded in their leather-tented hospitals and had them transported in carts during long marches. Severely wounded men were left behind in towns in the gentle and efficient care of leading citizens.

Alexander planned all his military enterprises with great forethought. He let his soldiers know the date and time of departure long in advance and informed them how far they had to go. The one thing he never told them was his objective and his plan of operations, fearing that he might alert the enemy and play into their hands. The soldiers liked their young Emperor. They felt that he had their interests at heart. They were well clothed, well quartered and excellently armed. They had swift thoroughbred horses and regulation saddles. Their splendid appearance was living proof of the power and glory of Rome.

However, the fact that it was composed of so many different nationalities made this Roman army a brittle affair. Moreover, the men who had served under Alexander's predecessors were spoilt, enervated and fundamentally demoralized. Alexander's well-intentioned plan to settle largish bodies of troops as yeomen farmers in the neighbourhood of their frontier garrisons had the unfortunate effect, from a military point of view, of diminishing both their state of readiness and their value as a fighting force.

Alexander attracted business men to Rome from all over the world by smoothing over trade difficulties and regulating financial relations. He imposed reasonable taxes on tailors, linen-weavers, glass-manufacturers, blacksmiths, silversmiths and goldsmiths, and founded guilds for greengrocers, wine-merchants and shoe-makers. When the populace asked him to lower prices, he asked them which items of food were too expensive. 'Beef and pork,' came the reply. Instead of lowering prices, Alexander imposed a ban on slaughtering. When he lifted it two years later, there was a glut of meat on the market — and it was dirt-cheap!

The Emperor preferred the normal linen toga to robes interwoven with purple or gold. In his opinion, gold thread made any material stiff and unpleasant to wear. He also wore puttees and close-fitting white trousers. On Trajan's Column, trousers were the distinguishing mark of a barbarian, yet by the second century A.D. they were already being worn by some of the Roman troops on the Rhine and the Danube, who were encouraged by the colder climate and the example of the betrousered Celts, Germans and Dacians. Now, in the third century, the Emperor himself took to wearing trousers.

Alexander entertained the idea of putting all his courtiers into uniforms denoting their rank. They were not to be military uniforms but merely a means of showing the Emperor at a glance whom he was dealing with. He also decreed special clothes for slaves which would make it harder for them to mingle undetected with freemen. However, the legal experts Ulpian and Paulus seem to have put a damper on Alexander's sartorial plans. Apart from anything else, slaves were becoming fewer because many of them had been given their freedom on humanitarian grounds. 'According to the law of Nature, all human beings are equal,' was the enlightened verdict of Ulpian.

The Emperor decreed that mixed bathing should be strictly prohibited — as it had always been except under Elagabalus, who had wrought such havoc with Roman traditions. To prevent the public baths (there were 800 of them in Rome) from getting into financial difficulties, Alexander gave them the usufruct of the State forests. Baths could be taken in the evening and at night, too, since the Emperor provided abundant supplies of oil for artificial lighting. In the year A.D. 222 Alexander built what was the last Roman aqueduct on the ancient pattern. Coins dating from the year 226 and bearing pictures of thermae show us how important to the Roman his bath was.

Life in Rome was good and the citizens were contented. The soldiers, too, were fond of their young Emperor. But, because he was just and reasonable and did not load them with money like Elagabalus, they found his integrity almost more trying than the vices of his imperial forerunner. Ulpian, who, as prefect of the Guard, was responsible for justice and discipline, soon came to be regarded by them as an enemy. The Guards spread a story that he had done away with his predecessors Flavianus and Chrestus, and mutiny broke out. Pursued by the Guards, Ulpian sought refuge in the imperial palace. The dramatic scene which followed clearly shows how dangerous life was for the young Emperor and what a tense atmosphere prevailed in the capital. The guardsmen threw themselves on Ulpian. Alexander tried to protect his best friend and adviser with his purple cloak, but the soldiers murdered their brilliant and erudite general before the Emperor's very eyes.

Alexander's reaction was sluggish. He could not summon up the courage to take proceedings against the ringleader of the mutiny, a man called Epagathus, so he first appointed him prefect of Egypt and then sent him on to Crete. Only when the Guards' memory of Epagathus had faded slightly did the Emperor have him tried before a court on the island and executed.

ARDASHIR'S GREAT ACHIEVEMENT

There is no power without an army, no army without money, no money without agriculture, no agriculture without justice.

Ardashir, King of Persia.

On the throne of the Roman Empire sat a well-meaning youth, governed for and guided by his mother. Mamaea and her son both hoped that his reign would be unmarred by bloodshed. Like a fine ray of light out of an overcast sky, a new and quite un-Roman sentiment came to the notice of young Alexander Severus during this period (A.D. 222–235): 'Do not unto others that which you would not have them do unto you.' The non-Christian Emperor had this golden rule, which originated in the Proverbs of Solomon in the Old Testament, inscribed on the wall of his palace. He must have heard it from Jews or Christians.

Once, when a soldier had maltreated a poor old woman, the young Emperor drummed him out of the army and made him the old woman's slave. We are told that, being a skilled wheelwright, the soldier was well able to support her, but we are also told that the army grumbled at his punishment. This dissatisfaction and internal unrest became a threat to the Emperor and the Empire in general, and Alexander was forced to disband a whole legion, first giving its members a lengthy and severe lecture in which he addressed them as 'citizens', not 'soldiers'.

The Emperor often sat down in his legionaries' dining-tent and ate the same food as his men. He gave silver shields to the élite of his body-guard, but showed that he personally could live like a common soldier. Apparently he never felt afraid of his legionaries. 'A soldier is harmless,' he used to say, 'as long as he is well clothed, well armed and well quartered: as long as he has a full belly and some coins in his money-belt.'

But were the soldiers really so harmless? The great English historian Gibbon asserts, in his famous work on the decline of the Roman Empire, that from the reign of Augustus to the time of Alexander Severus Rome carried two sorts of enemy within her: tyrants and soldiers.

Almost at the same time as Alexander Severus became Emperor of Rome, the distant highlands of Iran witnessed what was probably one of the most momentous events in their fascinating history. The Romans never really grasped what was going on in Asia between Mesopotamia and India, the

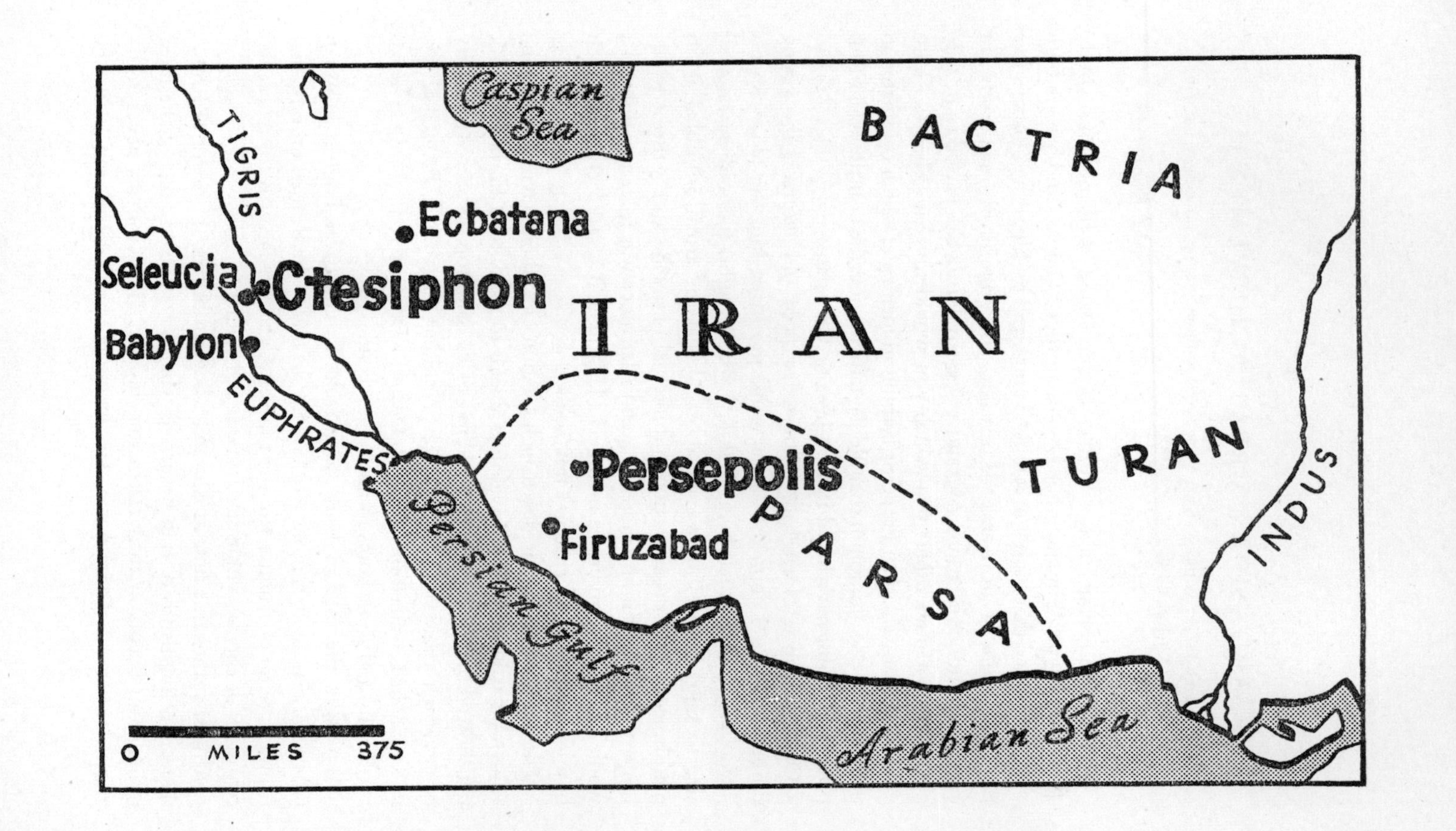
Caspian Sea
BACTRIA
TIGRIS
Ecbatana
Seleucia
Ctesiphon
Babylon
IRAN
EUPHRATES
Persepolis
Firuzabad
PARSA
TURAN
INDUS
Persian Gulf
Arabian Sea
0 MILES 375

Caspian Sea and the Persian Gulf. Even though, at this date, China carried on a trade in silk with Iran and Roman diplomats and business men occasionally visited China, the Romans still regarded the Parthians' highland plateau as 'the edge of the world'.

But Rome was not to remain the sole mistress of the world for ever. She was soon to be joined by another empire. A second eye was to open in the face of the world: the Sassanian empire of Persia. Parsa (the original form of the modern name Persia) was once a small province in the huge kingdom of Media. In the year 550 B.C. an intrepid son of this small province overthrew the Median King, captured Ecbatana, the Iranian capital, and made himself 'King of Kings'. The glory of Cyrus' royal dynasty, the Achaemenids, lasted for about 220 years, until that day in 330 B.C. when Alexander the Great vanquished the Persian empire with his decisive victory at Gaugamela in the plain of the Tigris.

When Alexander's successors, the Macedonian Seleucids, had been ousted in their turn, yet another non-Persian dynasty mounted the throne of Iran. These were the Parthian Arsacids, members of a race of steppe-dwellers and horsemen who came from the region of the Aral Sea in Central Asia and were called the Parni. The Arsacids ruled for 500 years.

Then, in A.D. 226, there was an exact repetition of what had happened in 550 B.C. Once again the small province of Parsa produced a daring young world-conqueror. Once again a youth from Parsa overthrew the Great King. Once again a Persian conquered the empire and founded a new royal line.

Thus, Iran was conquered by the little province of Parsa on two separate occasions: by Cyrus in 550 B.C. and by Ardashir in A.D. 226. Both princes came from the heart of Iran, the ancient region of Parsa which is now known as Fars and represents the earliest and most genuine part of Iran. There in the native land of such conquerors as Cyrus, Darius and Xerxes, ancient tradition lived on. Even though they had been dead for more than 700 years, people

---

In 550 B.C. Cyrus emerged from *Parsa*, the ancient heart of Iran, overthrew the Median King of Kings, captured the Iranian capital, *Ecbatana*, and founded the Achaemenian dynasty. The imposing ruins of the Achaemenids' palaces and tombs stand at *Persepolis*. Their dynasty survived until Alexander's conquest of the Persian Empire in 330 B.C., after which the (non-Persian) Parthian Arsacid dynasty held sway for 500 years. Then, in A.D. 226, Iran was again conquered by Parsa and Ardashir founded the Sassanian dynasty. The Sassanids' native city was *Istakhr* or *Stakhr* and their new capital was *Ctesiphon*, royal seat of the powerful kings Ardashir and Shapur

still remembered the great days of the Achaemenids and the way they had tried, setting whole nations in motion as they did so, to conquer Greece and, through Greece, Europe. People still dreamed of world conquest and an empire such as the world had never seen before.

Like so many conquerors, Ardashir came of the humblest origins. Later on, as so often happens in history, it was carefully proved that he belonged to a princely house. Our most important source of information is the Arab historian Abu Jafar Mahommed Tabari, who wrote a history of mankind from the Creation to his own day (circa 950).

Ardashir was the outcome of an affair between a private soldier called Sassan and the wife of a dyer called Babec. Many people insist that Sassan was a high dignitary in the temple of Anahita at Istakhr, the capital of Parsa. In any case, it was from Sassan — whether private soldier or priest — that the name of the Sassanian dynasty was derived. Of course, Persian poets and historians soon refurbished Ardashir's lineage. They established that he belonged to an ancient branch of the Persian royal family and was a descendant of the world-renowned kings Cyrus, Darius and Xerxes. The workings of time and destiny, they said, had reduced the members of that ancient royal line to the status of commoners.

Invoking his family tree, Ardashir proclaimed himself the only rightful heir to the ancient monarchy. He rebelled against his elder brother Shapur and autocratically made himself King of Parsa. His aim was to liberate his Persian countrymen from the Parthian yoke and set the ancient Persian line, which Alexander the Great had swept aside, on the throne of Iran once more. It took three battles to defeat the Parthians. During the last great struggle in A.D. 227, the Parthian King Artabanus V was killed. His descendants were ousted from every foothold save Armenia. Ardashir now called himself 'King of Kings', as his forefathers and predecessors had done.

Power had once more passed to the district of Parsa, the real heart of Iran, as it had once done long ago after Cyrus' victory over the Median Empire. There was a revival of interest in the ancient doctrines of Zoroaster. For centuries now the Iranians had believed in Ahura-Mazda the god, Ahriman the devil and Zoroaster the prophet. But many fire-altars lay in ruins with their sacred flames extinguished, and the priesthood of the Magi had lost its power. Ardashir made 'Mazdaism' a State religion and reinstalled the Magi in their official positions. At his bidding the sacred texts of the Avesta were compiled and translated afresh. All rival faiths were banned, their temples and images demolished. Jews and Christians were persecuted, and the Persian ranks were ruthlessly purged of all heretics.

The Empire was rigidly welded into a single, well-organized unit. Feudal overlords were still allowed to govern the individual parts of the Empire, but the old multiplicity of kings was abolished. 'There is no power without an army, no army without money, no money without agriculture, no agriculture without justice,' said Ardashir. He also realized that throne and altar are inseparable and that a ruler without a religion automatically becomes a tyrant. He thus created not only a new empire but a world Power.

The emergence of this neo-Persian Empire was, historically, the most important event in the third century A.D. Rome was no longer the only world Power: she had a mighty rival in the Sassanian-Persian Empire. Spiritually, this new Empire soon found itself fighting on two fronts. In the West it tried to repel the onslaughts of victorious Christianity, and in the East it resisted the impetus of Buddhism. King Asdashir reigned from A.D. 223 to 241, and his equally distinguished successor Shapur (Sapor) I from 241 to 271. Both these kings strengthened their Empire, reached acquisitively eastwards and westwards, and competed with Rome at every opportunity.

The great cultural influence of the Sassanian Empire was still making itself felt in the Middle Ages. It was from the Sassanids that we inherited knighthood and nobility, tournaments and mounted duels with the lance, court dress and ceremonial, feudalism and the idea of an established church. The Sassanian era lasted until the victory of Islam in the year 651, when Iran became part of the Caliphate.

To return to Ardashir. It was obvious that the King's lust for power and prestige would soon encounter Roman opposition. Proclaiming himself heir to the Old Persian Empire, he demanded the return by the Romans of all territory in Asia. Simultaneously, he invaded Roman Mesopotamia and Syria. His cavalry pushed on into Asia Minor, showing an audacity and determination which Rome had never met before.

Alexander Severus sent the Persian King a letter warning him not to invade foreign territory or try to stir up insurrection in Asia. War, wrote the mild and peaceable Roman youth, would be a dangerous undertaking. He pointed out that war with Rome was something quite different from war against barbarian hordes, and reminded Ardashir of the victories won by Augustus, Trajan and Septimius Severus.

Ardashir retorted by sending a delegation to Antioch in Syria. Here the Emperor was one day confronted by 400 enormous Persians, splendid, handsome fellows armed with golden weapons and a reply from their master, the 'King of Kings': the Romans must give up Syria and all their

Asian possessions, leaving the Persians in control of their ancient Empire, the vast empire which once attacked Greece.

The Emperor answered this arrogant request by immediately arresting the 400 envoys and treating them as prisoners of war.

Still dependent on his mother but with characteristic thoroughness, young Alexander Severus instituted counter-measures. While wintering in Antioch with Mamaea in 231–2, he made a last attempt through diplomatic channels to avert hostilities. But Rome's greatest source of danger loomed up once more. The Emperor's troops spent an enjoyable winter visiting women's bath-houses, drinking and amusing themselves generally. They made it clear what they thought of the 'petticoat regime' which Mamaea directed from behind her son's back. Alexander had the most unruly of his men arrested and put in chains, but mutiny threatened to develop. From the tribunal the young Emperor delivered one of the long homilies for which he was renowned. He addressed himself both to the accused men and to those soldiers who had not been arrested. 'If our discipline fails, we shall lose our good Roman name and our Roman empire. Some Roman soldiers, comrades of yours and men of mine, are leading a depraved life. They drink, they loiter about in baths, they behave like Greeks.' The listening soldiers gave a murmur which turned into a shout. 'You should shout in battle,' cried Alexander, 'not in front of your Emperor! You should display your strength to the Germans and Persians, not to me. If you despise Roman laws you are not fit to be called Roman citizens!'

There were outbreaks of mutiny among Roman troops in various other parts of the world. It was not a good omen for the trial of strength in which Rome was soon to be engaged.

In the year 232 three Roman armies took the field against Ardashir. The first army marched through Armenia, the second through northern Mesopotamia, and the third, commanded by Alexander himself, moved on the Persians to the south of the Euphrates. The first army met with initial success and advanced as far as Media, looting as it went, but suffered heavy losses on its return journey along the ice-bound and inadequate mountain roads. The army which took the route through Mesopotamia had scarcely reached the marshy plains of Babylonia when it was scattered by the numerically superior Persians and their armoured cavalry. Roman casualties were severe. Alexander's column, moving too slowly and lacking resolute leadership, suffered from disease and exhaustion.

The whole plan of campaign had been destined to failure from the start. Apart from the fact that it was most unwise to split up such a large army, the three columns marched much too far apart and were never able to give each other mutual support. The outcome of this great clash between Rome and Persia was obvious: Persia had won. For the time being, however, the Persians were unable to hold Mesopotamia. They, too, had suffered losses, and Ardashir decided to postpone any further aggression. The Romans were allowed to reoccupy their abandoned frontier forts. No peace treaty was signed, but Alexander went back to Rome pluming himself on having won a great victory, even though his losses had been far too heavy to warrant any such claim.

It was then that the Emperor and Rome were faced by a new danger, this time from the Germans in the north.

THE WALL OF DESTINY

> If there had never been a *limes*, the indigenous culture of Central Europe would today be entirely different. A fully united Europe would probably have been in existence for many hundreds of years, and almost the whole of the Continent would be speaking Romance languages.
>
> *The Author.*

In the year A.D. 83 Emperor Domitian made a decision which has retained its vital influence on European history until the present day. In order to secure the approaches to the frontier fortress of Moguntiacum (Mainz), call a permanent halt to German encroachments and protect Roman possessions in Gaul and south-west Germany, Domitian erected a frontier rampart, the *limes*.

This *limes* made world history by largely insulating the Germanic way of life from Roman civilization. Whereas France, as a part of Gaul, remained a Roman province for more than 500 years — from 50 B.C. to A.D. 476 — adopted Rome's culture and, above all, her language; whereas the French lost their ancient Celtic tongue and became a unified nation, the *limes* ensured that the German language remained virtually unaffected, German tribal distinctions were preserved, and the Germanic world was divorced from the Roman. For better or worse, the *limes* shaped German destiny and, with it, the destiny of Europe.

The word *limes* originally suggested an impassable boundary such as a cliff, a river or a mound of stones. Later it came to be applied to the path running between two pieces of land. Thus a *limes* was primarily a narrow balk marking the border between two fields or settlements. In its simple meaning of 'boundary-path' it was also applied to the strip of unpopulated waste-land on the German frontier. Domitian's contribution was to turn the *limes* from a no-man's-land into a fortified line. The first move was to cut a path through the forests which could provide the frontier guards with a patrol-line.

The idea of a fortified *limes* suited the mood prevailing at the end of the first century A.D. The Roman Empire longed for security. Many fields of creative endeavour in the ancient world were showing clear signs of decline and retrogression. Social apathy was setting in. During the second century A.D. the process of spiritual debilitation became even more marked, and in the third century we witness the breakdown of ancient civilization.

Emperor Maximinus, an uneducated Thracian peasant, was proclaimed emperor in Mainz and ruled from A.D. 235 to 238. He was a first-class army officer

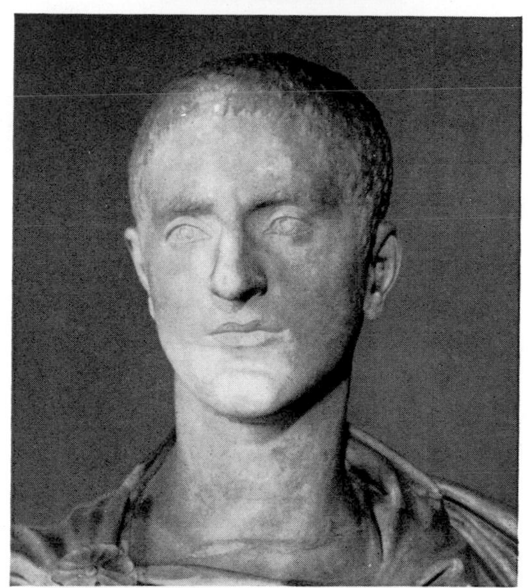

Maximinus' strikingly handsome son shared the throne with his father and was murdered with him on May 10th A.D. 238

Emperor Gordian II reigned in partnership with his aged father for a few weeks in A.D. 238 and was then killed

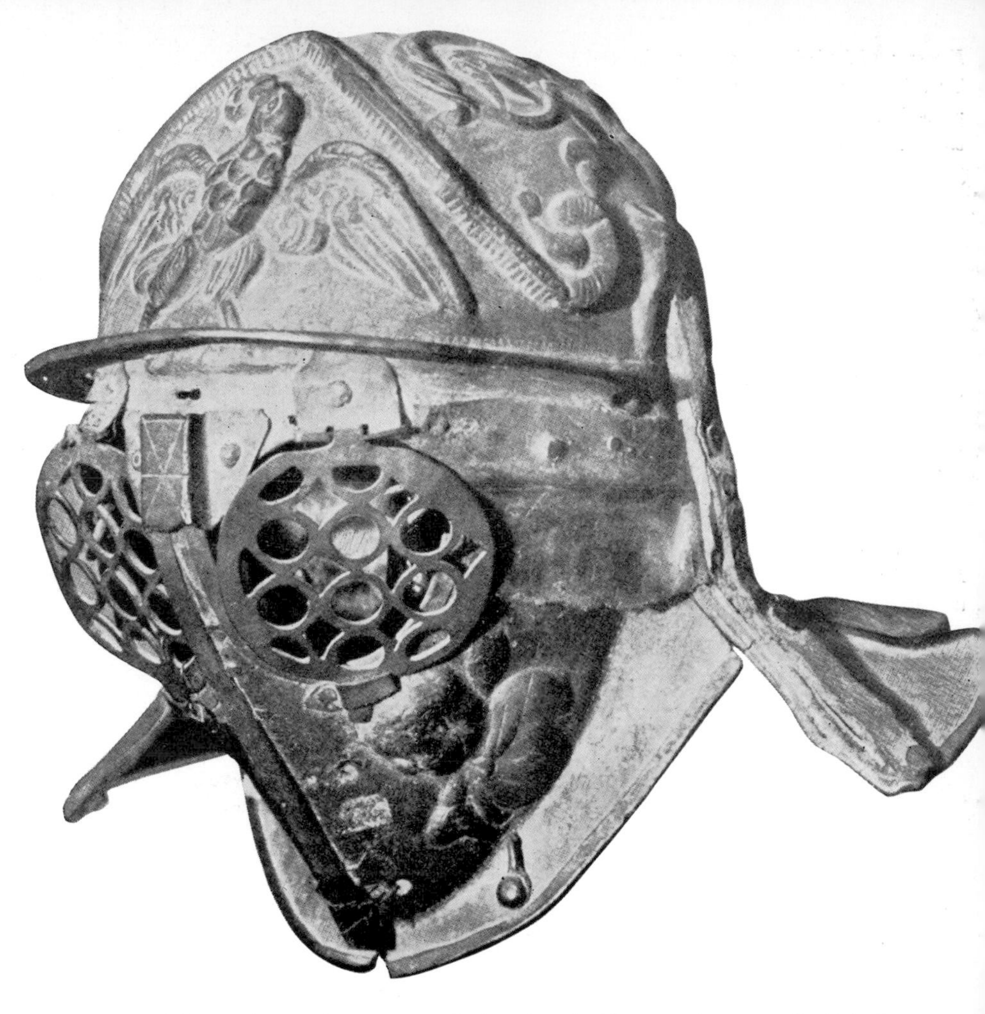

This bronze helmet with vizor is a mute reminder of the lavish entertainments of which the empero
and people of Rome never tired

A Roman shoe, once worn by a legionary in about A.D. 200. Note the excellent workmanship and th
up-to-date style designed to keep the foot cool. It was found in an old well-shaft, where it ha
remained in amazingly good condition

Ever since Edward Gibbon's classic work was published, a stream of books have been written about the cause of the Roman Empire's decline and fall. It is, as the well-known ancient historian Ernst Kornemann has said, 'the problem of problems'. It is for ever being formulated and solved anew. We probably come closest to the truth by attributing the downfall of the ancient world to a large number of heterogeneous causes. Its deterioration took place in the political, social, economic and, last but by no means least, the spiritual sphere. Among political enemies it was the Germans who, by their struggle with Rome, gave the map of Europe a completely new look.

But there was once a time when Rome made an attempt, of great historical significance, to push farther and farther northwards and draw the whole of German territory into the Roman Empire, as Caesar had probably once planned. It must be remembered, even though German history books like to forget the fact, that in A.D. 6 the region between the Rhine and the Elbe was a Roman province under the administration of P. Quinctilius Varus, a relative of Augustus.

Arminius' act of liberation in the year A.D. 9 put an early end to the Romans' struggle for possession of the whole of Germany. The Roman historian Tacitus concedes with amazing objectivity that Arminius was 'without doubt the liberator of Germania'. Varus' three legions were annihilated in the battle of the Teutoburger Wald, and Varus himself was killed. But the battle certainly did not take place at the spot where the Hermann Memorial stands today, near Detmold. Emperor Augustus' legionaries did not fall beneath the swords of the Cherusci and their allies (other Germanic tribes also took part) anywhere near the Osning. The Roman general Varus was ambushed and his forces annihilated *in a region of forests and marshes*, not in a mountain range like the Teutoburger Wald, and modern researchers adduce a great deal of complex evidence to support the theory that the site of the battle should be sought much farther to the west, on the upper or middle Lippe or somewhere in the neighbourhood of Hamm.

What is more, the Germanic version of Arminius' name was not Hermann. Arminius is known to have been the son of the Cheruscan prince Segimer. Together with his brother Flavus, he entered the service of Rome and was proclaimed '*amicus populi Romani*' (friend of the Roman people). On his return the young German prince married Thusnelda, daughter of the Cheruscan Segestes, against the latter's wishes.

The assumption that Arminius is the Latinized form of Hermann is untenable, and no plausible explanation of the word has yet been found — though it was certainly the name by which the German prince was known

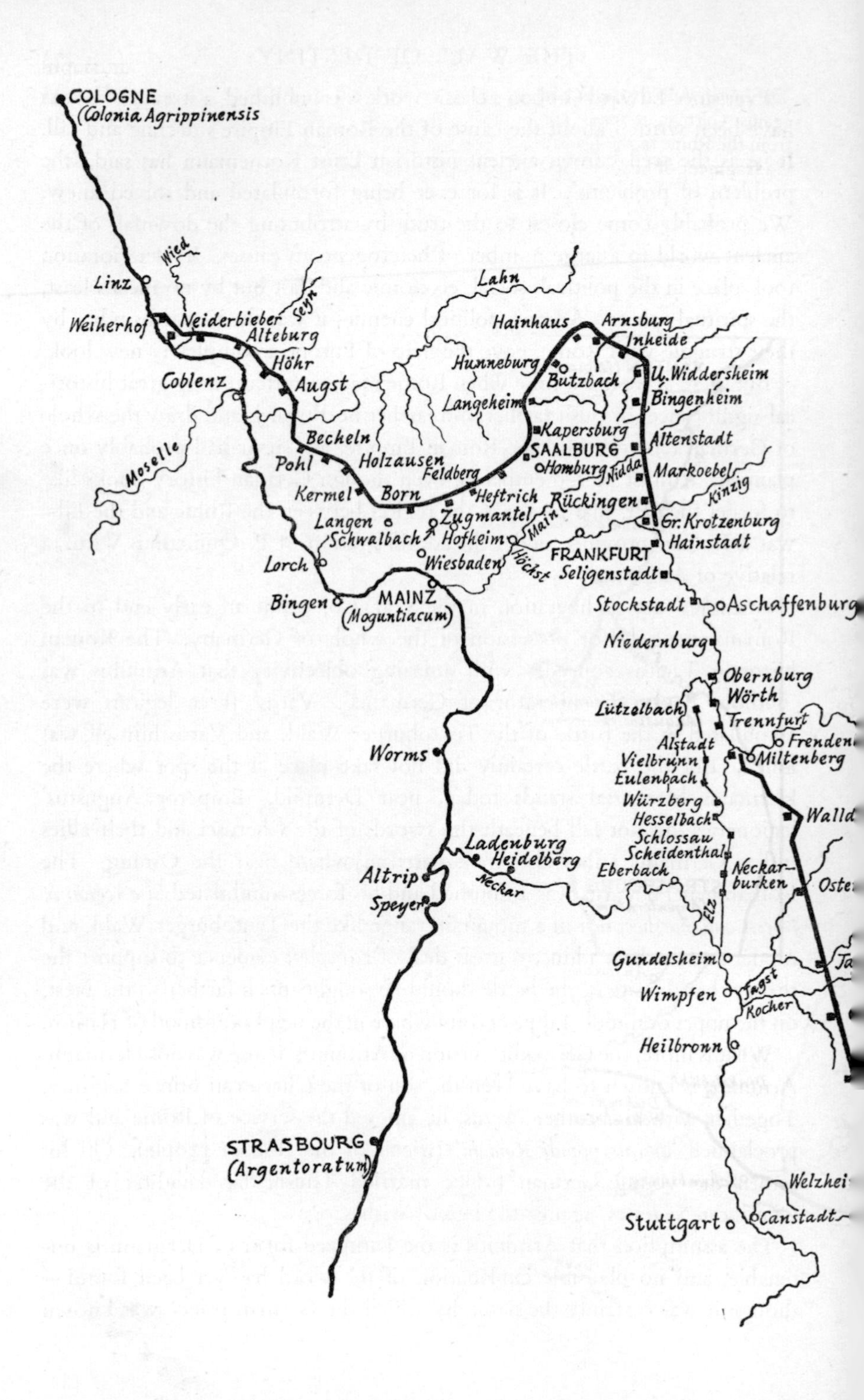
COLOGNE
(Colonia Agrippinensis
Wied
Linz
Weiherhof
Neiderbieber
Seyn
Alteburg
Höhr
Coblenz
Augst
Moselle
Becheln
Pohl
Holzausen
Kermel
Born
Langen
Schwalbach
Lorch
Bingen
Lahn
Hainhaus
Arnsburg
Inheide
Hunneburg
Butzbach
U. Widdersheim
Bingenheim
Langeheim
Kapersburg
Altenstadt
SAALBURG
Homburg
Nidda
Markoebel
Feldberg
Heftrich
Rückingen
Kinzig
Zugmantel
Gr. Krotzenburg
Main
Hofheim
Hainstadt
Wiesbaden
Höchst
FRANKFURT
Seligenstadt
MAINZ
(Moguntiacum)
Stockstadt
Aschaffenburg
Niedernburg
Obernburg
Wörth
Lützelbach
Trennfurt
Alstadt
Vielbrunn
Miltenberg
Eulenbach
Würzberg
Hesselbach
Schlossau
Scheidenthal
Worms
Ladenburg
Heidelberg
Eberbach
Neckar-
burken
Altrip
Neckar
Speyer
Elz
Gundelsheim
Jagst
Wimpfen
Kocher
Heilbronn
STRASBOURG
(Argentoratum)
Stuttgart
Canstadt

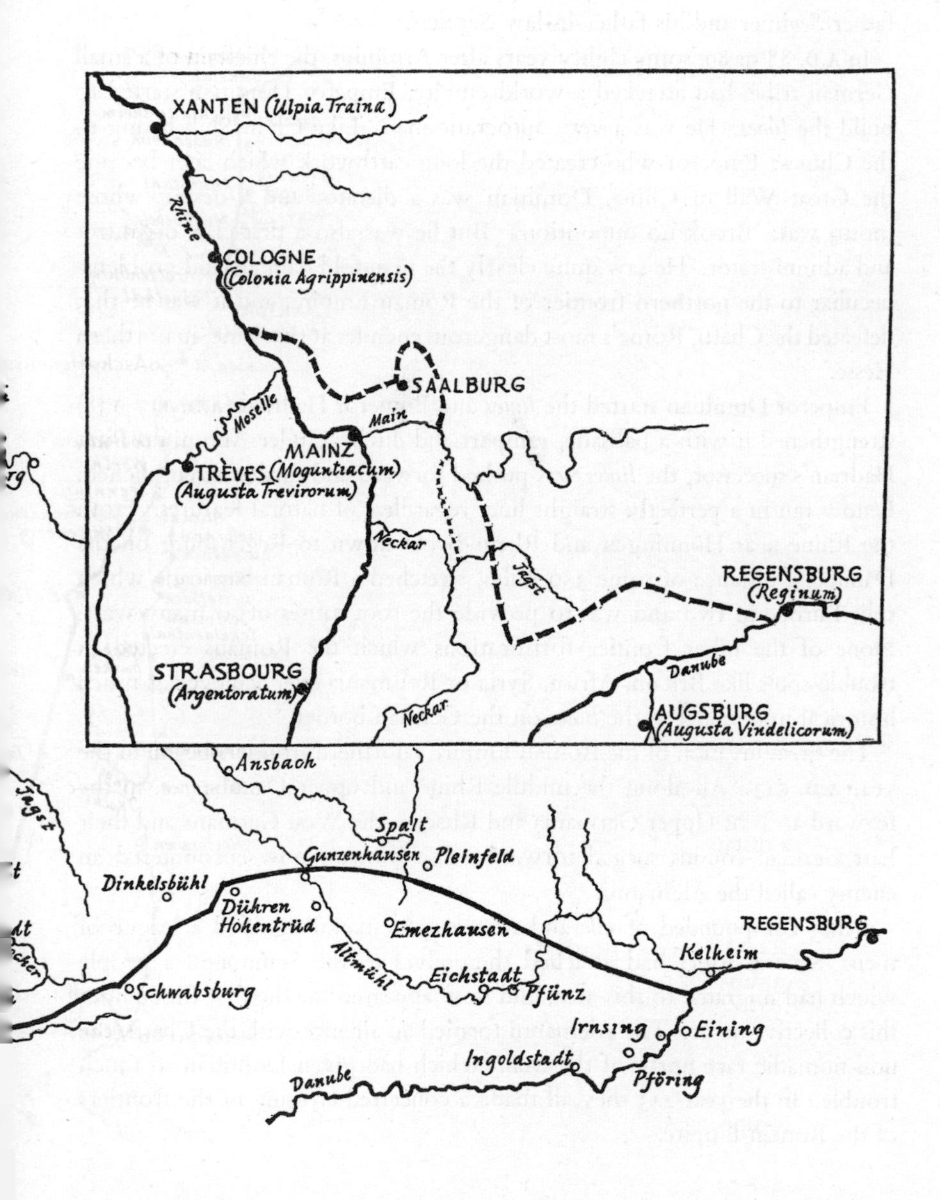

The Limes, built by the Roman emperors between A.D. 83 and 138 as a powerful bulwark against German attacks. This wall of palisades and stone extended for about 350 miles from the Rhine to the Danube and was supported by towers, forts and military roads. It is a fragment of history which is gradually sinking into oblivion beneath ploughed field and woodland

during his time as a Roman officer, just as his brother was known as Flavus ('blond'). One doubtful theory is that Arminius won his appellation by distinguishing himself in battle on the Romans' behalf in Armenia. In Strabo the word appears as *Armenios*. Other scholars, who believe that Arminius was the Siegfried of the Nibelung saga, place their reliance in the fact that his German name was probably compounded with 'Segi', as was that of his father *Seg*imer and his father-in-law *Seg*estes.

In A.D. 88 or 89, some eighty years after Arminius, the chieftain of a small German tribe, had attacked a world empire, Emperor Domitian started to build the *limes*. He was a very autocratic man. Like Ch'in Shih-huang-ti, the Chinese Emperor who created the long earthwork which later became the Great Wall of China, Domitian was a dictator and a despot whose motto was: 'Brook no opposition'. But he was also a first-class organizer and administrator. He saw quite clearly the manifold dangers and problems peculiar to the northern frontier of the Roman Empire, and it was he that defeated the Chatti, Rome's most dangerous enemies at that time, in northern Hesse.

Emperor Domitian started the *limes* and Emperor Hadrian (A.D. 117–138) strengthened it with a palisade, rampart and ditch. Under Antoninus Pius, Hadrian's successor, the *limes* was pushed forward and further strengthened. It now ran in a perfectly straight line, regardless of natural features. From the Rhine near Hönningen and Rhein-Brohl down to Regensburg on the Danube, a distance of some 350 miles, stretched a Roman barricade which split Europe in two and was to provide the root causes of so many wars. None of the other frontier fortifications which the Romans erected in trouble-spots like Britain, Africa, Syria or Roumania ever achieved as much historical importance as the *limes* on the German border.

The great invasion of the Roman Empire's northern frontiers began in the year A.D. 213. All along the middle Rhine and upper Danube, i.e. in the forward areas of Upper Germania and Rhaetia, the West Germans and their East German cousins surged forward. The Romans now encountered an enemy called the Alemanni.

Being compounded of *alle* and *Mannen*, Alemanni signified a league of men. Several tribes had attached themselves to the Semnones, a people which had migrated to this area, and now appeared for the first time under this collective name. The Alemanni formed an alliance with the Chatti, the non-nomadic race north of the Main which had given Domitian so much trouble. In the year 213 they all made a concerted crossing of the frontiers of the Roman Empire.

The Romans improved the roads in their northern territories, Rhaetia and Noricum, and made extensive preparations. Then, still in 213, Emperor Caracalla defeated the Alemanni in the vicinity of Miltenberg-am-Rhein. In place of the now decaying palisade, there arose along the Rhaetian *limes* north of the Danube a stone wall between six and nine feet high and some four feet thick — the so-called *Teufelsmauer* (Devil's Wall), an imposing rampart over 100 miles long. Elsewhere the *limes* was an earthwork with a large ditch on the German side. In front of this ditch was another, smaller, ditch, and into this smaller ditch were driven the stakes which formed the pallisade The stakes were between ten and fourteen feet high and about a foot thick, and the whole network of defences was never less than sixty-five feet in depth.

We know all this now. A 130-foot section of this palisade has been reconstructed at Sayn and can be admired from the Pulver-Berg. But for a long time the palisade bothered students of the *limes* a great deal. Tracing the smaller ditch was easy enough, but it was so narrow that it could never have presented any serious obstacle to an attacking enemy, and it was hard to see what the purpose of this outlying hollow could have been. In it were found stones, charcoal, iron nails and fragments of slate. Eventually some wooden stakes were discovered in a marsh in the Odenwald where, thanks to the boggy ground (always a splendid preservative), they had remained in excellent condition. The riddle was solved at last. The narrow outlying ditch served as the foundation of a stockade which ran for mile after mile through forests, over hills and across obstacles. The materials found in the ditch had been used to wedge the stakes securely.

However, the *limes* did not consist only of a rampart, ditch and stockade. It also comprised wooden block-houses which gave a good view of the surrounding country. Traces of more than a thousand such watch-towers have been found all along its length. The guards could pass information from one tower to the next. During the day, smoke-signals were used. A shutter in the roof of each tower enabled puffs of smoke to be sent up at varying intervals. At night, communication was maintained by fire-signals. A flaming torch held motionless indicated the approach of friends: hostile activity was indicated by waving the torch to and fro. So much for 'telegraphy' in the first centuries A.D. In cases of emergency, trumpet-calls could also be exchanged between the towers, thus alerting mile after mile of the defence system.

At regular intervals immediately to the rear of the *limes* stood the quadrangular forts of wood and earth in which the outposts were quartered, while still farther to the rear stood large fortresses like Heddesdorf, Bendorf and

Niederberg. The corner-stone of the defence network was represented by the famous legionary camp at Mainz.

The *limes* fortifications also included stone towers. We can get an exact idea of what they looked like from portrayals of them on the Columns of Trajan and Marcus Aurelius at Rome. A reconstruction of one of these small stone towers has been erected on the Pulver-Berg at Sayn, close to the ruins of a genuine Roman tower. Visitors can climb up to the little gallery and enjoy the magnificent view across Sayn and the Brexbachtal to Andernach in the far distance.

Few people know that West Germany boasts a complete reconstruction of a Roman fort. It is well worth a visit, as is the *limes* itself, large stretches of which can still be identified today. This fort, known as the Saalburg, stands near Bad Homburg. The name Saalburg is a modern one, and can only be traced back as far as 1604. The fort's Roman name is unknown, but we do know that during the reign of Emperor Hadrian (A.D. 117–138) the second cavalry cohort was sent there on detachment from its depot at Wiesbaden. The fort was reconstructed between 1898 and 1907. All the buildings and perimeter walls were erected on the old Roman ground-plan, but reconstructions were made only of those buildings assumed to have consisted of stone. The only reason why the project was carried out at all was that Professor Louis Jacobi managed to interest Kaiser Wilhelm II in the idea.

In the year 232 the Alemanni invaded the Roman Empire once again, pouring across the *limes* not only on the Rhine frontier but also in the northern part of the province of Rhaetia. Large numbers of provincials hid their money and valuables in pots and buried them beneath the ground, and since many of them never got a chance to dig their treasures up again it is not uncommon for people to come across caches of coins today. Rome hastily sent forces from all over the world to the trouble-spot. Even Spain had to supply troops. Alexander Severus personally led his legions on a forced march to the *limes*, archers and Parthian deserters were brought over from the East to help deal with the mounted hordes of Alemanni, and the Romans hurriedly threw a pontoon bridge across the Rhine near Mainz. The first engagements went well.

Then something appalling happened. Before the opening of any decisive operations, mutiny broke out in various parts of the Roman army. The young Emperor disbanded several units. His mother, who, needless to say, was also at headquarters, suddenly hit on the idiotic idea of cutting down the soldiers' pay — at this time of all times. She was either being mean, or danger had robbed her of her common sense. Wanting to avoid a pitched battle, Alexander opened negotiations with the enemy on his mother's advice. His soldiers (probably the Pannonian units) disagreed with this. If the Emperor was negotiating with the Alemanni it might well mean that he was offering them money, and the soldiers preferred to have the money themselves. They wanted to fight, not negotiate.

The air was fraught with danger. Had not a Druidess called to the Emperor, at the very moment of his departure for the war: 'Go, but do not hope for victory or rely on your soldiers!'?

As usual, the Emperor did not take these threats and omens too seriously. As usual, he ate his evening meal in an unguarded tent. Afterwards, at about the seventh hour, he lay down for a short rest. His tent must have stood by Mainz, near the village of Bretzenheim. It was a cool evening in March, A.D. 235. 'What is it?' called the Emperor, starting up. 'Have you news of the enemy?'

A Roman soldier stood there, pale and trembling. The man had simply lost his way, and now he found himself standing by Alexander's bed. Suddenly struck by the thought that the Emperor's continued existence could spell his own undoing, he rushed out, calling to his comrades to come and kill the Emperor without more ado. Grabbing their swords, the men raced into the tent and stabbed their defenceless master to death.

The young Emperor had always obeyed his mother, and now she had to die with him. She had given birth to a man of integrity, not a hero.

The tragedy of it all was symbolized by what the murderers saw, once the Emperor was lying dead in his own blood. The supper-dishes had not been cleared away, and on them were the remains of ordinary rations like those which they themselves had just eaten.

MAXIMINUS THRAX, THE THREE GORDIANS, PUPIENUS AND BALBINUS

THE BAITED BEAR

He dashed himself against the wall, threw himself on the ground, shouted loudly and incoherently, and gripped his sword as though he wanted to kill the whole Senate there and then. He rent his royal robes, beat the palace servants, and nearly tore out his young son's eyes.

Julius Capitolinus, The Two Maximini, xvii.

MAXIMINUS was the son of a Goth and an Alana. He was born in a Thracian village at a time when his native land was still a cultural desert. In him we are confronted by a self-made man from the outermost edge of the Roman Empire who suddenly emerged at the hub of world activity, although he never came to Rome as Emperor. History knows this Caesar as Maximinus Thrax.

A big fellow, violent, uncouth, arrogant, but not unhandsome, he is said to have drunk no less than a Capitoline amphora of wine every day. A Capitoline amphora was a jug whose original was kept on the Capitoline Hill, rather as the standard metre is in the vaults of the Bank of Paris today. It held about forty-six pints! In addition, Maximinus ate forty pounds of meat daily — but no vegetables. He didn't like them. He could knock a horse's teeth out with a single blow of his fist. His enormous size and physical strength encouraged him to believe that he was immortal, but in the theatre people used to laugh at him behind his back. 'A man who cannot be killed by one is killed by many,' they quipped.

In the year A.D. 232 Maximinus was commander of the second legion ('Trajan's Own') in Egypt, and during the war with Persia he was governor of Mesopotamia. Having won a reputation as a gallant and distinguished officer, he was then given command of all the recruits in the Roman army on the Rhine by Emperor Alexander Severus. Maximinus became, in effect, the Roman Director of Military Training. Although a disciplinarian, he gave his men the feeling that they were doing a worth-while job. He refused to allow his legionaries to ply a trade as a side-line, and considered that hunting was the only leisure occupation worthy of a fighting soldier.

Maximinus Thrax was a general after the legionaries' own hearts, and it was not surprising that the mutineers made him Imperator in place of Alexander Severus. When news of his accession reached Rome, the Senate resigned itself to the *fait accompli*, although a sizeable body of senatorial opinion was opposed to having an upstart on the throne.

Right at the very outset Maximinus had to cope with an attempt on his life organized by some centurions. He only just managed to foil their plan, which was to lure him across the Rhine into hostile German territory, then cut off his retreat and kill him. The ringleader of this murderous plot is said to have been a man of consular rank called Magnus, who naturally wanted to become Emperor himself.

But Maximinus was on the alert. He at once condemned the conspirators to death without the benefit of a trial. Four thousand people died and their property was confiscated. The Thracian peasant had shown his hand.

Crossing the Rhine, Maximinus advanced deep into German territory. Along the Main and in what is now Württemberg he burnt villages, drove off cattle, took thousands of prisoners, plundered and devastated everything made by German hands. The Emperor's oriental bowmen and African spearmen, Syrians and Mauretanians respectively, seemed in German eyes to be diabolical supermen.

And the Germans? This was how the Roman historian Tacitus described them 100 years earlier: 'Their shields are black, their bodies painted. They choose dark nights for battle. They spread alarm by the very appearance, gruesome and dismal, of their ghostly ranks. No enemy can withstand the startling, almost hellish sight. For, in every battle, eyes are the first things to fall.'

The first pitched battle took place in fen country, probably on the borders of northern Württemberg and Baden, and was fought by the Romans and their foreign mercenaries against the Alemanni, the same Alemanni who had broken through the *limes* shortly before. Even as Emperor, Maximinus still fought in the front line. It never occurred to him to do otherwise.

The year 236 saw the German threat banished once more. The remains of new *limes* fortifications erected during this period show that peace had been restored on the Rhine and upper Danube. Henceforth the Emperor called himself 'Germanicus Maximus', and he now proclaimed his son, a remarkably handsome man, Caesar and joint Emperor. Great victory celebrations were held at Sirmium, their winter quarters on the Save near Belgrade. We are told that Maximinus gained successes against the Sarmatae and Dacians during 236 and 237, and in the spring of 238 we see him back in Sirmium, holding court and receiving envoys from Rome and the provinces. Rome itself did not attract him. He felt far more at home in the broad valley of the Save among his soldiers and horses. He was now planning to subjugate the Germans between the Danube and the North Sea.

Emperor Maximinus never ceased to victimize those who had supported his predecessor's dynasty, now extinct. He is said to have been extremely brutal in his methods of revenge, crucifying people, crushing their skulls and throwing them to starving beasts. Perhaps he thought that, as a man of humble origins, his only way of keeping the throne was by cruelty.

'Essentially, his rule was more frightful than that of any other emperor,' was Jacob Burckhardt's verdict on him. His sense of personal inferiority, erroneous as it may well have been, made Maximinus hate the Senate and the whole of the aristocracy. His wife Caecilia Paulina did her best to mitigate this dangerous characteristic, but she soon died. Maximinus detested everything that had any connection with his predecessor. So deep was his loathing of Alexander's memory that he decreed a new spate of anti-Christian persecution, merely because Alexander had tolerated the Christians.

Hippolytus and Origen, who had probably been on friendly terms with Mamaea, the mother of Alexander Severus, now found themselves in great danger. The Christians Pontianus and Hippolytus were exiled to Sardinia. In Cappadocia and Pontus, too, Christians were persecuted by Governor Serenianus. But, in spite of all this, Emperor Maximinus is not to be numbered among the classical persecutors of Christianity. He himself ensured the continued existence of the priesthood in Christian communities for reasons of public policy. Nor were the persecutions in Cappadocia and Pontus carried out at his instigation, but because the Christians there had been held responsible for an earthquake.

Maximinus was always in need of money. The Empire was large, the enemy active on every frontier and defence costly. That meant that taxes had to be high and harsh methods employed in collecting them. Wealthy families never had a moment's peace, wondering when their property would be confiscated. The Emperor cast an especially predatory eye at the temples, with their valuable dedicatory offerings of gold and silver. Using any old pretext, he melted down sacred images, memorial statues and consecrated objects of every description, and turned them into money. But this caused resentment, and it was hardly surprising that some young Roman aristocrats in Africa murdered the imperial procurator at Thysdrus, a coastal town 100 miles south-east of Carthage, near modern El Djem, when he prepared to expropriate their estates at the Emperor's bidding.

The rebels repudiated Maximinus and swore allegiance to a venerable old proconsul called Gordianus. It was the last thing the old man wanted. He screamed, threw himself on the ground and begged his 'benefactors' to leave him alone, but they threatened him with their swords and wrapped him in the purple willy-nilly. The date was 238, and Gordian was eighty years old.

Gordian walked stiffly, was extremely rich, took an interest in literature and usually fell asleep during meals. Eventually he reconciled himself to the idea of spending the rest of his days on the throne, and moved to Carthage with his son, who was proclaimed joint Emperor. The Roman Senate ratified the two Gordians' accession and deposed Emperor Maximinus, and the inhabitants of the capital celebrated the 'tyrant's downfall' amid scenes of tumultuous rejoicing. Many supporters of the Thracian peasant-emperor were killed during these disturbances.

Among Maximinus' adherents in Africa was the governor of Numidia, a man called Capelianus, who now began to incite his province to rebel against the Gordians. Young Gordian was sent by his father to restore order, but was killed after a fierce and desperate engagement. Gordian senior thereupon took his own life.

When the terrible news of the Gordians' death reached Rome, with its threat of retribution on the part of Maximinus, the Senate hurriedly elected two emperors from its own ranks: Clodius Pupienus Maximus and Caelius Calvinus Balbinus. They were to have exactly equal status and were, with the help of a committee of twenty senators, to organize the defence of Italy against Maximinus. The people and the army quickly supplied yet a third emperor in the shape of Gordian's grandson, who later became Gordian III. With three emperors, Rome felt itself a match for the fourth, who was lurking in the north on the German border.

The fourth emperor behaved like a huge, tormented bear. He could not grasp what had happened. Convulsed with rage, he dashed himself against walls, threw himself on the ground, bellowed, lashed out at his servants, tried to claw his son's eyes out and finally drank himself into a stupor. Then, sober once more, he mustered his army — which included many German deserters — and marched over the Alps into Italy, taking cavalry and a large baggage-train with him. When the German horsemen in his advanced guard reached Emona (modern Laibach), they found it a scene of sinister desolation. They were hungry, but nothing edible was to be found. Five hundred wolves, dread harbingers of famine, had visited the town shortly before. The same thing greeted Maximinus' troops in every town they came to. Rome was opposing them with that most terrible of all foes:

silent, gnawing hunger. The first place to offer resistance was Aquileia, and all attempts by Maximinus to take that fortress failed. Knowing that their town would be razed to the ground if it were captured, the citizens of Aquileia defended themselves with every means at their disposal. In the end, the Emperor's second Parthian legion took a hand — though not by capturing Aquileia. Tired, hungry and desperate, they murdered their own master, Emperor Maximinus, and his handsome son.

One month after the death of this ferocious monarch the Praetorian Guard murdered Pupienus and Balbinus, the two senatorial emperors, who had by that time fallen foul of each other. A thirteen-year-old boy was now nominated as ruler of the Empire.

Army, Senate and people all welcomed the choice, for this third Gordian was a grandson of the worthy old man whom fate had treated so badly. Fundamentally, however, young Gordian's accession represented a triumph for the soldiery, who had once more assumed the arbitrary right of choosing an emperor. When it nominated Pupienus and Balbinus, the Senate was participating in an imperial appointment for the very last time. From now on it became a dead letter. For 800 years it had helped to shape the course of world history. Now it was leaving the stage. It had mismanaged things, and lived on as a mere shadow of its former self.

The following passage by Ernst Kornemann neatly sums up the importance of this vital moment in Rome's history: 'With the Senate went the aristocratic basis of the Roman State. A blatantly militaristic regime had no room for a high economic and intellectual standard of living. It was as though a tempest had swept across the Empire or as though it had been inundated by a deluge comparable with the Great Flood of popular legend. All that was beautiful and good in Nature and the living world was set aside. All that remained was the barren land.'

But the famous 'year of the six emperors', A.D. 238, saw yet another event of great historical significance. It was the year when the Goths crossed the frontiers of the Roman Empire at the estuary of the Danube.

PHILIPPUS ARABS AND DECIUS

THE COMING OF THE GOTHS

In a list including tigers, hyenas, giraffes, leopards and hippopotami, one Roman historian mentions the item: 'a thousand brace of imperial gladiators'.

'He (Gordian III) was a gay youth, handsome, endearing, universally popular, merry in his life, serious in his letters. There was nothing which could have made him unfitted to rule save, perhaps, his youth.'

Julius Capitolinus, The Three Gordiani, xxxi.

SINCE October 1st, A.D. 226, a new world Power had been in existence: the Sassanian dynasty's Persian empire. The first two Sassanid kings, Ardashir and his son Shapur, had created a power in the East to be reckoned with. Between them, father and son reigned for half a century, and under their leadership Asia knocked brusquely at the door of Europe once again. Both remarkably able men, they ushered in an era in world history which lasted until A.D. 642.

In A.D. 238, the year when Maximinus Thrax died, Rome was once more sandwiched between two terrible dangers, the German tribes in the north and the Persians in the east. Ardashir died in 239. His son Shapur proceeded to show the world that, unless it is checked by force, Asia will always creep irresistibly westwards. Ardashir had already captured Nisibis and Carrhae. Shapur now reached out an eager hand for Roman Mesopotamia and Rome's Syrian provinces, even threatening Antioch and the Orontes.

There is something almost pathetic about the way in which Rome sent her boy-emperor to meet the menacing avalanche from the east. Emperor Gordian III was only thirteen years old, but he had extricated himself with great courage and skill from a web of court intrigue, the apron-strings of his vacillating and weak-minded mother and the machinations of the palace eunuchs. In him we see the rare picture of a pupil who remained unwaveringly loyal to his teacher. And in the teacher we recognize a man who, like Seneca, stood head and shoulders above his contemporaries. His name was Timesitheus.

While still a prince, young Gordian had married his tutor's daughter, a lovely girl with an even lovelier name: Furia Sabinia Tranquillina. Now, as Emperor, he appointed Timesitheus to the highest government posts, and the Senate conferred on him the honorary titles 'Father of the Prince' and

'Protector of the State'. For all his new-found authority, Timesitheus remained staunch in his loyalty to the Emperor. The two of them, tutor and pupil, set off on a forced march to the East. Timesitheus showed himself a thoroughly competent commander, and Gordian was an intelligent boy. Here is a passage from a letter which he wrote to Timesitheus: 'Woe to the ruler to whom no one dares speak the truth. Since such a king cannot mingle with the people, he must accept what he is told or overhear what the majority are saying.'

On the way to Asia, the Romans picked up more troops from the army on the Danube. Bands of Germans, prominent among which were the Carpi, at once tried to penetrate the gaps in the frontier defences. But Timesitheus fought back. He pacified the frontier, hurried on eastwards with the Emperor and liberated Syria from the Persians. A decisive battle at Resaena won back the whole of Mesopotamia for Rome.

Another interesting personality who was with the Roman army at this time was the Egyptian-born philosopher Plotinus. He was probably the last intellectual in the ancient world to embody in himself and his philosophy the ancient world's whole range of thought. He was not merely an intellectual, however, but a near saint whose main concern was with the soul. His life was, in fact, dedicated to the eternal quest for an invisible god. Plotinus joined the eastern expedition as a scientist in search of information. He wanted to see India and, in particular, he wanted to understand the philosophies of Persia, India and the Far East. That was why he had entrusted himself to his Emperor and to Timesitheus, who had organized the whole expedition so brilliantly. Timesitheus was everywhere at once, paying incognito visits to the sentries at night and asking after their welfare, or strolling through the sleeping legionaries' tents. His superb organizing ability made this army, far from home as it was, a fighting force of unparalleled efficiency. 'And, because he loved the Emperor and the State so greatly, he was respected by all,' says the chronicler.

Eastwards: that was the dream of this man who emerges so dimly from the distant past. Timesitheus wanted to push on, following in the footsteps of Alexander the Great, to the Indus and perhaps even to China. But it was not to be. He died of a sudden attack of influenza. Such, at least, was the official cause of death, but the suspicion of poison could not be discounted. It was rumoured that he had been given a laxative just before his death by some doctors in the pay of a man who coveted his position: to wit, one Julius Philippus, the forty-five-year-old son of an Arab or Syrian sheikh from the desolate region of Trachonitis in Transjordania. Philippus at once began to

Balbinus and Pupienus were elected joint emperors by the Senate after the death of Gordian I in A.D. 238. Balbinus took over the civil administration, and Pupienus the supreme command of the Army. This division of power lasted only a few days. The emperors became jealous of one another. After a rule of three months they were assassinated

The famous philosopher Plotinus from Lycopolis in Egypt, 'the last man of antiquity', followed Gordian's campaign against Persia (A.D. 242–243). In Rome the philosopher had had numerous discussions with the emperor and his wife. The plan whereby a 'city of philosophy' was to be created for Plotinus – 'Plato's Republic' – was given up after the assassination of the emperor. Plotinus believed in *one* creator of all things

Emperor Decius, the first Roman emperor to be killed in action on barbarian soil. He lost his life while fighting the Goths – very probably because he had been betrayed by General Trebonianus Gallus

Trebonianus Gallus was proclaimed emperor by the army after the battle of Abrittus. His two years of rule were dogged by misfortune: the Persians overran Mesopotamia, the Goths invaded Moesia, and the Plague raged. Trebonianus and his son were murdered in A.D. 253

Gordian III and his murderer Philippus Arabs. Emperor Philippus (reigned A.D. 244–249) succeeded in inciting the army against young Gordian, who was eventually murdered

undermine Gordian's popularity with the troops by sabotaging their supplies, and young Gordian proved no match for him. As a man, Philippus was uncouth, ill-bred, arrogant and ruthless. Jacob Burckhardt says, probably with justification: 'It is doing Philippus too great an honour to regard him as an Arab sheikh. He came from the disreputable tribe of southern Syrians east of the Jordan.' Gordian tried first to oppose Philippus, then to co-operate with him, finally to suffer under him, all to no avail. He was killed.

We know the spot where Gordian III was murdered. There, between Circesium and Dura-Europos, quite near the confluence of the Euphrates and the little Chaboras, a memorial was erected to the young Emperor which still stands today. Philippus had the mortal remains of his nineteen-year-old victim taken back to Rome, informing the Senate that he had died of an illness.

As for Plotinus, after the campaign was over he managed to reach Antioch, whence he travelled back to Rome.

An African and a Syrian had occupied the Roman throne: now it was an Arab's turn to rule the Roman Empire. Philip the Arab made peace with the Persians in return for territorial concessions and entrusted the further defence of the eastern frontier to his brother Priscus. This step was an urgent necessity, for Philip himself had to hurry back to the northern frontier. He conducted successful operations against the Carpi in the autumn of A.D. 246, and celebrated them by adopting the triumphal title 'Carpicus Maximus'. Dacia had been held once more. Near what is now Sheba, south of Damascus, Philip founded the city of Philippopolis and conferred on it the rights of a colony. The impressive ruins of its splendid buildings, which were modelled on the palaces, theatres, temples and baths of Rome, still survive. The Thracian city of Philippopolis, which had been founded by Philip of Macedon, father of Alexander the Great, was also raised to colonial status.

It was in this year, A.D. 248, with decay gnawing at the heart and extremities of the great Roman Empire, with the soldiers electing new emperors all along the frontiers, with Roman sovereignty on the wane, that Philip the Arab held a magnificent festival at Rome. It was the thousandth anniversary of Rome's foundation. Ten centuries had passed since Romulus and his small band of shepherds fortified their humble encampment on the banks of the Tiber.

The date of the great festival should really have been April 21st, A.D. 247, but Philip had postponed it for a year. It was celebrated with great pomp. Foreigners were not allowed to attend and slaves were forbidden to show their faces. Choirs composed of twenty-seven boys and twenty-seven girls of the noblest birth invoked the benediction of the gods. There were sports in the

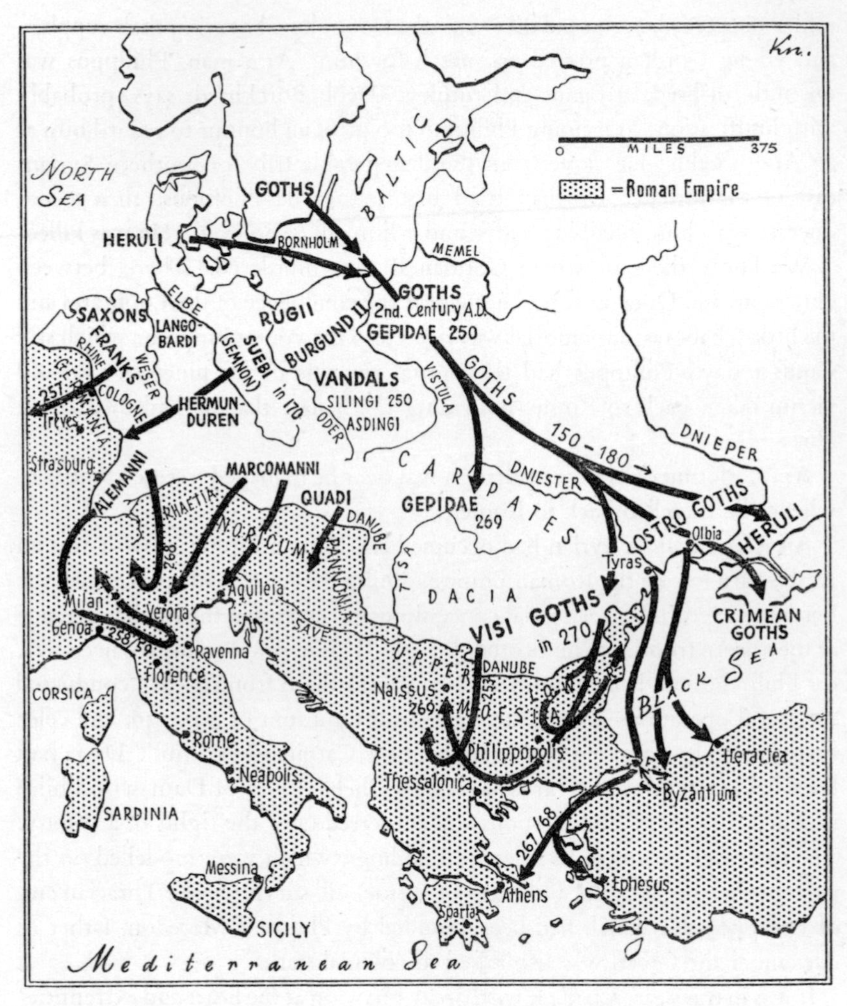

The Goths came partly from the island of Gotland and partly from Öster—and Väster-götland in southern Sweden, where their name has survived. Their vast hordes swept like a tidal wave down to the Black Sea, Asia Minor and Greece

Circus Maximus, coloured lanterns, torches, and dancing and music on the Field of Mars. Sacrifices were offered to the gods on the banks of the Tiber for three nights running. The Roman historian Julius Capitolinus describes what Rome could offer its inhabitants in the way of entertainment during these festivities. Young Gordian had made advance preparations for the triumphal procession which he intended to hold in Rome in celebration of his own and his tutor's victories over the Persians. Now Gordian was dead.

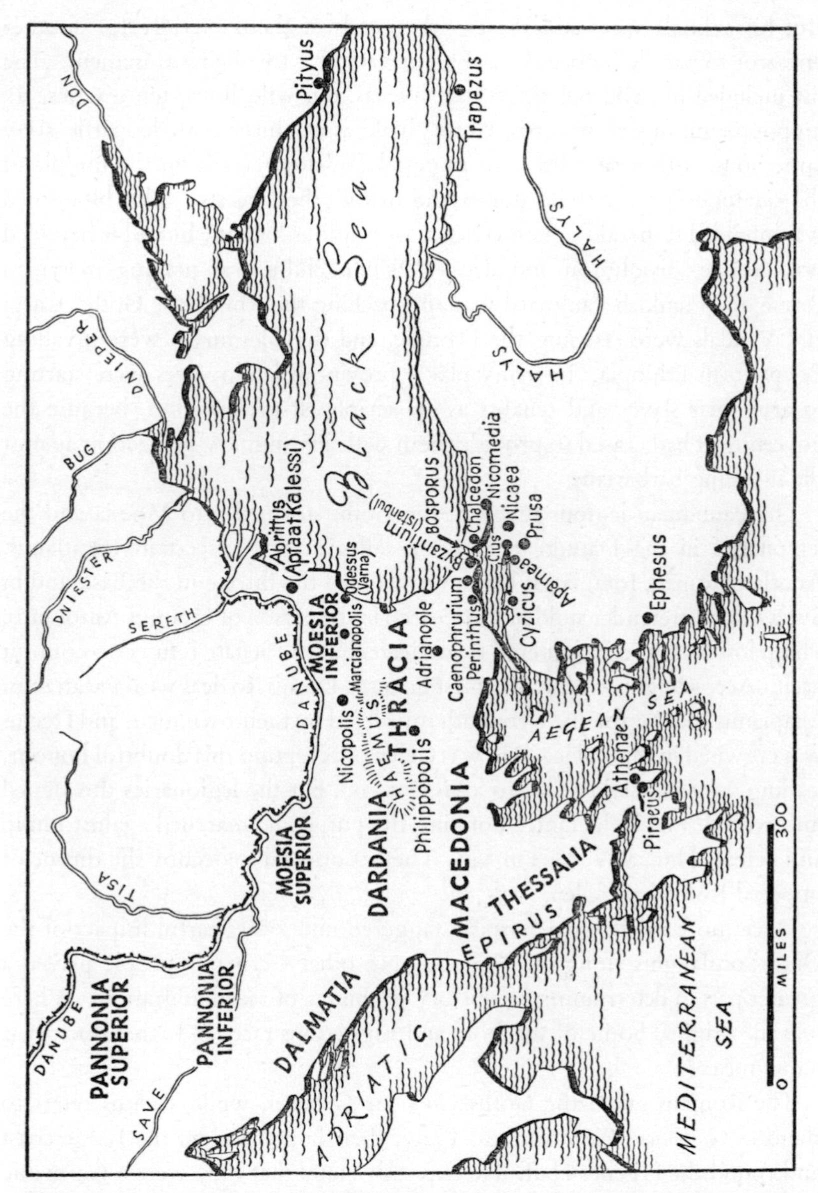

During the reign of Emperor Philippus Arabs (244–9) the Goths threatened *Dacia* and besieged *Marcianopolis*, the capital of *Moesia*. Emperor Decius (reigned 249–51) suffered a crushing defeat at the hands of the Gothic king, Kniva. The Goths then captured *Philippopolis*, and in 251 Decius lost his life in battle. All the places indicated on this map were besieged, captured, looted and destroyed by the Goths

But his animals were still there — thousands of them — ready for another emperor to parade before the public or slaughter for their amusement. The list included ten elk, ten tigers, ten hyenas, ten wild lions, ten giraffes, six hippopotami, one rhinoceros, twenty wild asses, thirty tame leopards, sixty tame lions, 'a thousand brace of imperial gladiators' (right in the middle of the catalogue!), forty wild horses and many other 'beasts'. This bloodshed was intended to herald a new century of glorious history, but all it heralded was decline, dissolution and decay. While Philip was making merry in Rome, the Frankish vanguard was approaching the Rhine, the Goths, Carpi and Vandals were crossing the Danube, and the Blemmyes were invading Egypt from Ethiopia. In many places provincial landowners were starting to arm their slaves and tenants as an act of self-preservation, because the government had ceased to provide them with any military protection against the invading barbarians.

The Pannonian legions rebelled, the Goths stormed into Moesia and the legionaries in the Danube area swore allegiance to a certain Pacatianus. Another Roman, Iotapianus by name, claimed the throne in the East, and in Syria a third pretender suddenly appeared in the person of Uranius Antoninus. Philip lost his nerve and offered to abdicate, but the Senate refused to commit itself. Accordingly, he sent his ablest general, Decius, to deal with Pacatianus. Iotapianus and Pacatianus were both murdered by their own men, and Decius was crowned in their place. He was chary of accepting this doubtful honour, leading, as it inevitably did, to a violent end, but the legionaries threatened him with death. Reluctantly donning the purple, he marched against Philip and defeated him at Verona in 249. The last oriental to occupy the throne of imperial Rome had fallen.

Once more the Roman Empire staggered under the fearful impact of the Goths' onslaughts along the Danube. No other Germanic people played a greater part in determining the history of this era of racial migration. Where was the original home of this bold and mysterious race, and what does their name mean?

The Romans called the Goths *Gothi* or *Guttones*, while Tacitus refers to them as *Gothones*. According to Pliny, their home was on the Baltic coast and round the Frisches Haff. He expressly states that they were a Germanic people. The Goths called themselves *Gutans* or *Gutos*. In their own country they described themselves as *Gutthiuda*, *gut* and *thiuda* meaning 'people-together'. In all probability some of them came from the island of Gotland and others from Öster- and Västergötland in southern Sweden, where their name has survived. They then settled in the estuary of the Vistula and started to force their way into eastern Europe. Their emergence at the beginning of the third century A.D. as a powerful nation on the coasts of the Black Sea coincided with the appearance of the Alemanni in the West. During the reign of Philip the Arab (244–9) they threatened Dacia and besieged Marcianopolis, the capital of Moesia. Decius forced them to give ground at Nicopolis in the year 250, but they later annihilated a Roman army and sacked the city of Philippopolis in the Haemus range, led by King Kniva. Without any thought of retreat, the Goths stormed across Macedonia, pushed southwards as far as Thermopylae, then veered to the north and, in June, A.D. 251, wiped out the greater part of the Roman army at Abrittus in Moesia (now Aptaat-Kalessi in the Dobrudja).

Right at the start of this battle Decius' son, Herennius Etruscus, was killed by an arrow. Emperor Decius himself was lured into a marsh and cut down by the Goths.

These attacks by the Goths, who loom up so suddenly out of the mists of history, seem almost like irresistible natural phenomena. Fanning out along the Black Sea coasts, the Goths laid the foundations of their maritime power by capturing the Bosphorus. In 253 they set off in a large number of flat-bottomed boats and captured the city of Pityus. They took Trebizond and acquired a fleet there. Then, in 258, they withdrew to their settlements on the Sea of Azov.

But the Goths could not sit still. In 259 they marched on the Thracian Bosphorus. They captured Chalcedon, Nicomedia, Nicaea, Prusa, Apamia and Cius. In a third great wave, 500 ships destroyed Cyzicus. Crossing the Aegean Sea, the Goths landed at the Piraeus near Athens. From there they advanced as far as Epirus. Nothing escaped looting and devastation, from the southern tip of the Peloponnese to Thessaly in the north. Then, weary at last, the vast hordes made their way back over-land to the Danube, although some of them sailed down the coasts of Asia Minor in search of further loot and destroyed the world-famous Temple of Diana at Ephesus before starting out on their homeward journey.

GALLUS AND AEMILIANUS

THE HOUR OF CRISIS

One emperor succeeded another, and each was murdered. We can only marvel at the great demand for the imperial purple during the third century A.D. When applied to the Caesars, death by natural causes now meant death by dagger or poison.

The Author.

It was ominous that the Roman head of State should have lost his life in battle.

Decius was the first Roman Emperor to die a hero's death on the battle-field. He fell far from Rome, where his men could not even recover his body. But his sacrifice was futile. He could not prevent a Gothic victory. There in the east, on the Danube, a terrible wound had been torn open. Paradoxically, only more Roman blood could stanch the bleeding.

As far as Rome was concerned, anyone who restored the desperate position, closed the breach in the Empire's defences and once again saved Rome and the Roman Empire from extinction, would be only too welcome to the throne and all the honours that went with it.

Vibius Trebonianus Gallus was governor of Lower Moesia (Moesia Inferior), the region south of the lower Danube. He was well placed, therefore, to redeem Rome's honour and avenge the death of Emperor Decius. The Danubian country-side had been devastated. The Goths had carried off the surviving inhabitants of Thrace as prisoners, looting, murdering and taking anything of apparent value with them.

Gallus came of an old Etruscan clan. He may have been cunning, but he was certainly no match for the present situation. The remnants of the Roman army of the Danube proclaimed him Emperor, and Rome applauded. Gallus abandoned immense quantities of booty to the Goths. He was obliged to guarantee them freedom of withdrawal and to watch senior Roman officers and dignitaries being led off into barbarian captivity. Worst of all, he promised them a huge annual tribute in gold.

In the course of the centuries the Romans had grown accustomed to *receive* tributes, but to be forced to shower their barbarian enemies with such a fortune in gold each year was something quite new to them. They grumbled, and fashionable society in the capital mocked and despised Gallus for having made such undignified concessions.

In an attempt to improve his own invidious position, Emperor Gallus appointed Hostilianus, the still-surviving second son of his late predecessor Decius, as joint regent. But Hostilianus died. Last of the Decians, he succumbed to the plague which was raging through eastern Europe at that time and attacked Asia Minor shortly afterwards.

Like a forest fire, the rumour at once swept through Rome that Gallus had murdered the son of Decius, the late lamented hero. People began to ask ugly questions. Hadn't Gallus been in reserve while Emperor Decius was doing battle with the Goths? And, if he had been stationed behind Emperor Decius' ranks, why hadn't he gone to his commander's aid? If it weren't for Gallus, it was whispered in the streets of Rome, Decius might still be alive.

There was a widespread conviction that Gallus had betrayed his Emperor.

Gallus immediately travelled to Rome. He treated the Senate with great deference and then proceeded to snap his fingers at all the sinister rumours. He laughed, drank and made merry in the capital of his menaced empire.

Meanwhile, on the Danube in Lower Moesia, Aemilius Aemilianus had assumed command. Reassembling the weary Roman troops, he attacked the barbarian Goths and drove them back across the Danube. His soldiers naturally hailed him as a friend in need and at once proclaimed him Emperor. Aemilianus raced to Italy by forced marches, intending to take Emperor Gallus by surprise and dispose of him.

We can be certain that Gallus was reluctant to give up his carousals by the Tiber for a bloody encounter with the advancing Aemilianus, but he did so, and met his rival in the plain of Spoleto. There the armies of the two imperial adversaries faced one another, well within visual range. Gallus could not prevent his soldiers from making unfavourable comparisons. Their own commander had bought peace on the Danube with Roman gold and had been forced to abandon their best officers to a terrible fate as prisoners of the Goths. Aemilianus, on the other hand, had victoriously stemmed the barbarian invasion. When they learnt that he was willing to reward every deserter that came over to his side, that settled it. The legionaries murdered Emperor Gallus and — as was now the invariable custom — his son Volusianus as well.

So ended the civil war. The Senate confirmed Aemilianus as Emperor and conferred on him the resounding titles 'Hercules the Victor' and 'Mars the Avenger', titles in whose glamour the dazzled Aemilianus basked for four short months. They are to be found on coins of the period, of which many are in our possession. People only buried their money in time of danger, which is why our most comprehensive collections of coinage always date from mankind's darkest hours.

Shortly before his death the unfortunate Gallus had hastily dispatched a general called Valerianus to Gaul and Germany to fetch reinforcements. A gentleman to the marrow, Valerianus was obedient and loyal at a time when loyalty was at a premium among the Romans. Having arrived too late to save his Emperor, he decided to avenge him.

Aemilianus' troops now behaved exactly as those of Gallus had done. They, too, made comparisons. They, too, peered inquisitively out into the world from their camp on the plain of Spoleto. They, too, recognized the advancing enemy as the better man. They, too, saw at once that the army sweeping down on them was stronger than their own. They murdered their Emperor on a hot, sunny day in August, A.D. 253. He had reigned for only four months. In Rhaetia the troops from Germany and Gaul proclaimed Consul P. Licinius Valerianus as Emperor. It was unusual for a Roman of this period to become Emperor without steeping his hands in blood, but Valerian was such a one. This time the new Augustus commanded the support not only of the Senate but of the whole Roman world as well.

Emperor Valerian, the self-styled 'enemy of tyrants', is one of the most tragic figures in Roman history, for he suffered a fate which no other ruler of Rome ever had to undergo. He was sixty years old when he donned the purple. A very erudite man, a wise and experienced monarch and a good judge of character, he furthered the careers of efficient officers like Claudius, Aurelian and Probus who were destined to preserve the Empire in years to come. But, like other good men before and since, he had his Achilles' heel: he adored his son and was blind to his unique and remarkable lack of principle. He was only too happy, therefore, when the Senate invested the apple of his eye with the title Augustus. The name of this joint regent, who was one of the most original personalities in the history of Rome, was P. Licinius Egnatius Gallienus.

Father and son had been left a sad legacy. The Roman Empire was threatened on every frontier. Of all potential enemies in the contemporary world the Germans were the most dangerous and aggressive and the Persians the most powerful and cunning. Rome now had to defend herself against both these enemies. Persia was already a world Power like Rome herself, and the Germans were trying, for the first time in their history, to build an empire north of the Black Sea. They were the vanguard of the great interracial migration which was ultimately to sweep across the whole of Italy. Frankish hordes were already looting their way through Gaul and into Spain. Very soon, in 257, they were to reach North Africa via Gibraltar.

The desperate situation prevailing in the year 254 prompted Valerian to divide the Empire. He himself went to the East and installed his court at Antioch in Syria, while his son took over the defence of the West.

It was a crucial decision — crucial because it publicized the greater importance of the East for the first time. The father, as senior emperor, went to the Greek Orient, while the son and subordinate emperor remained in the Latin West. It meant that the Empire had been divided and that the curtain had risen between the 'stage' in the East and the 'audience' in the West. It meant that the scales had now tipped in favour of the eastern half of the Empire, and that Rome's importance had waned so much that she was gradually ceasing to be the focal point in world history.

It was while Valerian and his son Gallienus were taking their leave of one another, never to meet again, and while the barbarian Goths and Borani were swooping down from the Black Sea to ravage sea-coast and country-side, that Persia's strong-man recognized his moment. Shapur was without doubt the most important king to rule Iran since Darius I. He now began to make history.

VALERIAN

A LIVING DEATH

In A.D. 260, the world was shaken to hear the news of Valerian's dreadful fate. Money-changers stared aghast at coins bearing the old Emperor's portrait. Persia's King Shapur treated Valerian like a slave until his life's end.

The Author.

THE city of Baghdad in Iraq is partly built of stones found on the banks of the Tigris, some twenty-four miles away. The ruins of an imposing palace with a huge curved reception-hall had always stood there, among the rubble of a vanished settlement, providing a convenient and inexpensive supply of good building material.

This ancient ruined city has a much more illustrious history than modern Baghdad. Ctesiphon, as it was called, was the winter residence of the Parthian rulers, and it was there that the powerful King Shapur I had his royal seat. He was the second major statesman of the Sassanian dynasty, and was responsible for building the palace. It was his ambition to realize his father Ardashir's dream of dominating 'the whole world'. Shapur was an energetic, resolute man with great organizing ability. Could it only remain a dream, this idea of a universal empire, of a kingdom holding sway over the whole of Asia and Europe, of a world inured to Persian supremacy? Was it only a dream, with the splendid goal so nearly attained?

Like his father, Shapur I was a devotee of fire-worship. His priests, the Magi, with the powerful backing of State religious sponsorship, were the sole arbiters of ritual orthodoxy, sin and atonement, oracular decrees and the magic arts. The smoke of burnt offerings rose into the sky from towers on the hill-tops. A vast, visible empire lay at the feet of Ahura-Mazda, the invisible god, and the spirit of his prophet Zarathustra celebrated a great revival in the neo-Persian Empire. King Shapur was strict and unyielding, but he could also be tolerant. It was during his reign that Mani the Babylonian, one of the most unique figures in the history of religion, propagated his mysterious 'doctrine of light and darkness'. The first Manichean sermon was delivered on March 20th, A.D. 242. On that day young Mani first proclaimed his religion at Ctesiphon, capital of the Empire, under the aegis of King Shapur.

Thirty years later Mani followed the example of so many religious founders and was executed. But his doctrines spread throughout the world, became known to the Romans and even penetrated to the British Isles. They became one of the greatest threats to Christianity, but were eclipsed in the ensuing struggle.

In Manicheism light and darkness appear as two eternal beings. At one time they were distinct from one another, but darkness insinuated itself into light like the Serpent into Paradise, since when evil has existed in the world. Mani's doctrine is really an aberrant off-shoot of Christianity, a strange compost of ancient Persian, Hellenistic and Christian ideas. Indeed, Mani called himself an apostle of Jesus Christ. The Manichean faith recognized certain prophets who had spread 'the light', among them Adam, Noah, Abraham, Buddha, Zarathustra, Mani himself and, most important of all, Jesus, who according to Mani's own words 'appeared in Judaea'. Christ was 'the last prophet before Mani', and Mani regarded himself as 'the greatest prophet and apostle of Jesus Christ'. All this information is to be found in the writings of St Augustine, but the very close relationship between Manicheism and Christianity has been illustrated by ancient Manichean inscriptions discovered quite recently at Turfan (in the Chinese province of Sinkiang) and in Egypt. It is interesting to note that Mani wrote in Aramaic, Christ's native tongue.

Shapur treated the young religious fanatic with a great deal of understanding and allowed him to propagate his doctrines throughout the Empire by missionary activity. Having at first tried to stamp out the Christian faith, which was gaining ground all over the contemporary world, Shapur one day forbade the Magi to persecute the Christians further. He decided to let everyone in the huge Persian dominions seek salvation in his own way. The Magi were allowed to uphold their ancient Iranian god Ahura-Mazda and his prophet Zarathustra, the Manicheans 'the Light' and its various prophets, the Jews their Yahweh, the Christians their Christ, the shamans their animistic phenomena and magic spirits, and the Brahmans their huge collection of gods. And all the adherents of every religion were to be permitted to pursue their own ideas and forms of worship in peace and freedom.

At the same time King Shapur tried to extend and perfect his father Ardashir's religious life-work. Ardashir had commissioned a senior religious official (Tansar) to collect the various texts of the sacred Avesta, and had published them as an authorized version. His son Shapur added scientific texts to this canon, including medical, astronomical and metaphysical works from India, Greece and other parts of the world. The new Persian King was an extremely open-minded man of liberal interests.

It is quite remarkable what a wealth of religious ideas pervaded the world in about A.D. 250. Five great world-conquering ideologies were competing for support among the inhabitants of Europe and Asia: the Jewish–Christian faith in the West, the religion of Ahura-Mazda and Mani's doctrines in Persia, Buddhism in India — with its finest cultural achievements in the Afghan province of Gandhara — and, influencing all four, Greek philosophy or Hellenism, as its dilution with oriental ideas is called. Hard pressed by Christianity and Buddhism, Mazdaism gained new reserves of strength and a fresh lease of life under the Sassanian regime in Persia, probably just because Zarathustra's ancient god was under such heavy fire from every other religion.

Whereas Ardashir had contented himself with being lord of Iran, his son described himself as 'Great King of Iran and all other countries'. His Persian title ran: *Shahansha i Eran u Aneran* or 'Great King of Iran and non-Iran'. Shapur was enterprising, cunning and cruel, but he possessed a harem, and there — as with most Persian kings — lay his one weakness and only vulnerable spot.

Anyone who wanted to rule the world would have to deal with the Romans. More precisely, he would have to defeat the Romans and drive them out of Asia. As a good strategist, Shapur knew that before he could do so he would have to secure his right flank. And there on his right flank lay Armenia. In the year A.D. 252 the Persian King occupied the rugged and mountainous country which King Chosroes had defended so successfully for thirty years against every external and internal threat. An exciting book could be written about this able ruler's life. Shapur eventually succeeded in bringing about his assassination. Chosroes' son Tiridates was only a child when the throne passed to him. His kingdom, too, like so many others in history, was destined to be overthrown from within. Opposed by other members of the Armenian royal family, Tiridates had to seek asylum with the Romans, and the opposition party, with Artavasdes at its head, was only too happy to accept Persian suzerainty. The contemporary world was not only under the spell of King Shapur: it was also dazzled by the Iranians' revived faith in the prophet Zarathustra and his god Ahura-Mazda. The Sassanians' neo-Persian Empire was not dependent solely on the two great statesmen, Ardashir and his son Shapur, who had created and sustained it: it was borne aloft on the mighty wings of Mazdaism and Manicheism. The collapse of Armenia tore a dangerous breach in Rome's eastern defences. Shapur invaded Mesopotamia, marched through Syria leaving a trail of devastation in his wake, besieged Antioch for a time and overran Cappadocia. The city of Tyana fell, and Caesarea was hard pressed.

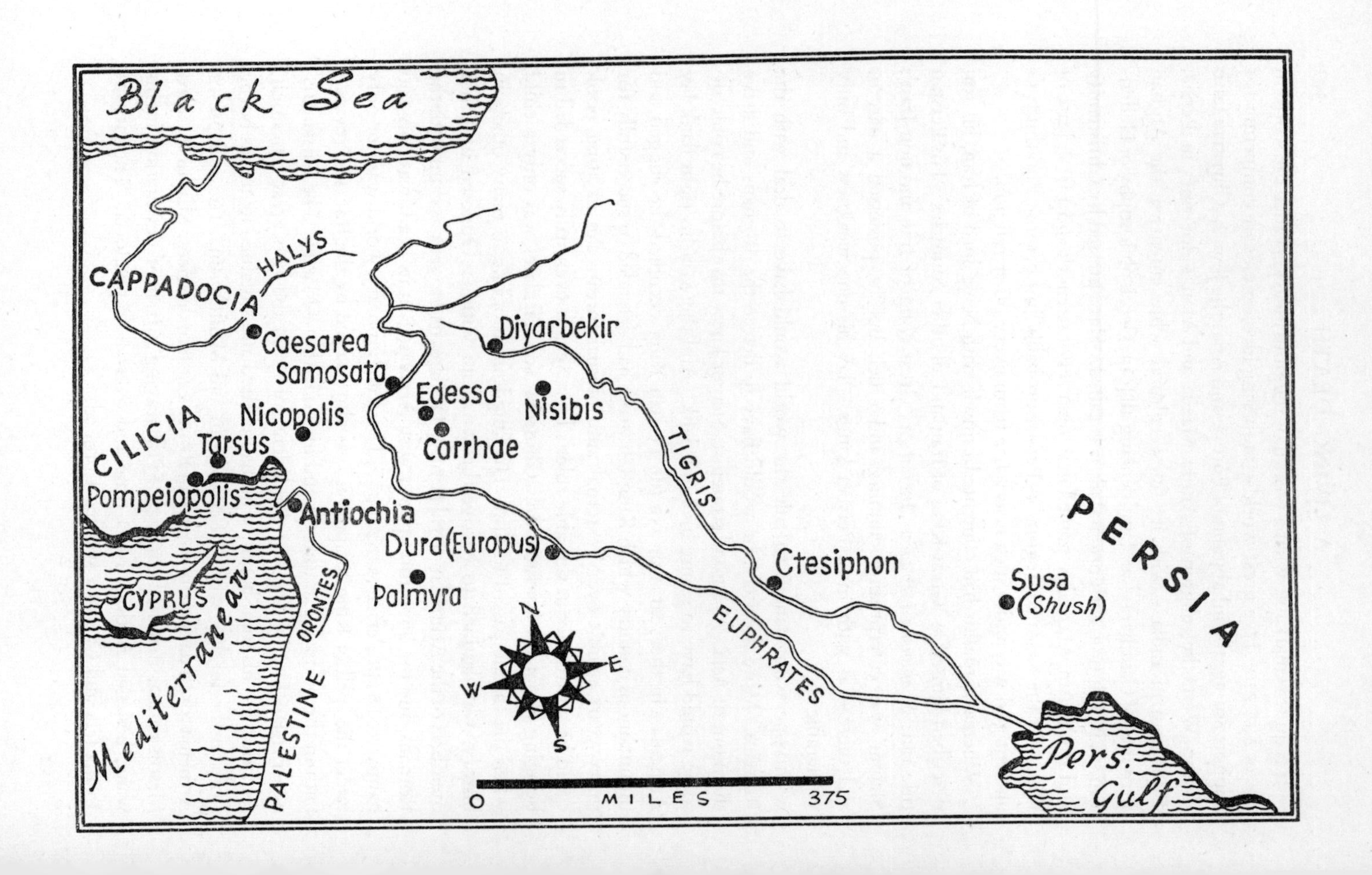

Black Sea
CAPPADOCIA
HALYS
Caesarea
Samosata
Nicopolis
CILICIA
Tarsus
Pompeiopolis
Antiochia
CYPRUS
Mediterranean
ORONTES
PALESTINE
Edessa
Carrhae
Diyarbekir
Nisibis
Dura (Europus)
Palmyra
TIGRIS
EUPHRATES
Ctesiphon
Susa
(Shush)
PERSIA
Pers.
Gulf
N
E
S
W
0
MILES
375

Emperor Valerian was scarcely equal to this situation. He was getting on in years, being a man of over sixty, and the Persian coup came just as the Goths and Borani were emerging from their Black Sea bases once more and renewing their land attacks and piratical raids. The elderly Roman monarch must have won several victories over the Persians, for coins dating from the year 259 bear inscriptions such as *Victoria Parthica* and *Restitutor Orientis*, and were evidently struck to commemorate victory over the Persians (Parthians) and the pacification of the East. Be that as it may, Valerian was finally reduced to a mood of terrible fear and uncertainty.

This was a period when any Roman general who had gained military successes reached out an eager hand for the imperial purple. Dictatorial power was, then as now, a drug which induced dreams of domination, brief dreams which inevitably resulted in the addict's death. Emperor Valerian was most reluctant to entrust large expeditionary forces to any one of his generals. It was dangerous to bestow far-reaching powers on a deputy. True, he sent Successianus to deal with the Borani and appointed him Praetorian prefect or commander-in-chief. True, he dispatched a certain Felix to Byzantium with orders to prepare the city for a siege. But none of these measures presented any real obstacle to the determined Goths. It seems, in general, as though every measure undertaken by this interesting old man was contaminated by hesitancy and weakness.

Leaving his official residence at Antioch, Valerian travelled to Cappadocia, but turned back abruptly on receipt of bad news and finally made his headquarters at Samosata, a stronghold on the upper Euphrates. There, supported by the stout fortress of Edessa, he proposed to meet the Persian advance.

King Shapur sent his son Hormizd to the Euphrates, and the Persians effected a break-through at Dura-Europos. This caravan-city on the central Euphrates, one of the largest archaeological sites in the world, has been gradually excavated by the French Academy and Yale University since 1928. At the foot of a steep cliff in the north-east corner of the city flowed the Euphrates. High above the river stood an acropolis or citadel, and identifiable

---

Valerian left *Antioch*, his royal residence, and marched into *Cappadocia*, but turned back abruptly on receipt of bad news and eventually made his headquarters at *Samosata*, a stronghold on the upper Euphrates. There, supported by the stout fortress of *Edessa*, he intended to stem the Persian advance. However, the Persians effected a breakthrough at *Dura-Europos*. (Excavations have been carried out there since 1928.) At *Naksh-i-Rustam* a scene was hewn into the rock for all time depicting Emperor Valerian kneeling in chains before the Persian king Shapur, who is seated on a horse. The Roman emperor was destined to die in captivity

among the ruins are stone bastions and towers, a rectangular street system, a Roman court-house and palaces for officials. Part of the city was probably undermined by the Euphrates and fell into the depths below. On its walls were found pictures of horsemen in Persian dress. Excavations have proved how stubbornly the Persians besieged the city and how desperately they were resisted. Battles raged beneath the ground as the defenders met tunnel with counter-tunnel. Archaeologists have found the remains of soldiers with coins in their purses dating from the year 255.

Then, just when things were at their blackest, the Romans were hit by a disaster which increased the hazards of their unfortunate position a thousand-fold. Valerian's ranks were ravaged by the plague. The old Emperor brooded day and night as to how Rome had offended the heavens, while his soldiers, as though struck down by an invisible hand, perished in their thousands. The only idea which occurred to the old man in this state of dire emergency was to vent his wrath on the Christians. The tragic situation demanded a scapegoat and, since Valerian's main concern was to propitiate the heavens and regain the favour of the ancient gods of Italy, he diverted the Romans' gaze from the conflagration in the East to the evils of Christianity.

The Christians prayed for the life and welfare of the Emperor, but they prayed to their own god. As Bishop Cyprian said, when subjected to a rigorous cross-examination by the Roman governor of the province of Africa: 'I am a Christian. I know no other god than the true god. That is the god whom we Christians serve. We pray to him night and day for ourselves, for all men, and for the preservation of the Emperor.' But sincerity did not save the Christians' heads, and many of them were executed. The Christian Bishop of Rome was slain in the catacomb of the Praetextatus just as he was celebrating Mass. The deacon Laurentius was tortured to death, and in Carthage Cyprian was sentenced to die by the sword. In Spain, Bishop Fructuosus died a martyr's death. 'That is what comes of neglecting to worship the gods and refusing the Emperor's countenance a pious salute!' the Roman judge shouted at him. Yes, thought Valerian in despair, if one ceased to worship the gods of Rome they sent plagues, Persians and plagues. The vacillating old man managed to wreak havoc among Christians everywhere, but he failed to stop the Persians.

In the year 260 Shapur appeared before Edessa. True to its reputation, the city defended itself with great gallantry. Valerian decided to fight it out. His army took the field depleted by the Black Death, demoralized, enervated and half-starved. It soon became known in the ranks that the Emperor himself had abandoned all hope.

Emperor Gallienus was the son of Valerian, who died in Persian captivity. Gallienus wanted to counter Christianity with Plotinus' doctrines and his sincere quest for God. This interesting emperor, who was little understood by his contemporaries, reigned from A.D. 253 to 268

Marcus Aurelius Probus would be numbered among the great figures in world history if our information about him were not so scanty. He introduced viticulture into Germany and Hungary and was an extremely successful general. He was killed at Sirmium in A.D. 282

Valerian took a last desperate step. He tried to negotiate with the Persians, offering them a fantastic sum in gold in an attempt to pacify them. The cunning Shapur had a first-class intelligence service, however. He knew exactly how hopeless things were in Valerian's camp.

Shapur at first refused point-blank to negotiate, but he later allowed himself to be 'talked into' a conference. His only proviso was that Emperor Valerian should attend it in person. The unwitting Valerian came, and was taken prisoner. It was a sly and infamous breach of international law, but that did not worry Shapur.

A Roman Emperor in barbarian hands, captured, enslaved and — worst of all — still alive. It was a terrible tragedy, not only for the Emperor but for the Roman Empire as a whole.

The world had sharp ears in those days. News raced fast from country to country despite the lack of telegraph, telephone or aeroplane. The report of the Emperor's capture smote Rome's armies and provinces like a crippling hammer-blow. At Rome the incessant cries of the bargemen on the Tiber were hushed, the rumble of wagon-wheels died away, the carts stopped rattling through the winding lanes, curses froze on the muleteers' lips. Money-changers stared in horrified amazement at coins bearing the old Emperor's portrait. Copper-smiths, snake-charmers, even beggars held their breath as the shocking rumour ran through fifty miles of Roman streets.

The Persians poured westwards like a tidal wave. Antioch fell, betrayed to the Persian King's soldiers by Mariades, one of its leading citizens. Having been expelled from the city council for embezzling public funds, he decided to turn Quisling. He probably arranged the escape of several prominent Antiochians, and the city's mint and treasury were hurriedly removed to a place of safety. But the masses had no inkling that Mariades had betrayed them. They were sitting in the amphitheatre, applauding, when the murderous Shapur broke in. The Persians at once put everything to the torch, not even sparing the surrounding country-side. Mariades was burnt alive on Shapur's orders, probably because he had not been wholehearted enough in his treachery and had allowed the city's store of gold and treasure to disappear in advance.

Numerous small townships and the capitals of Cilicia and Cappadocia, Tarsus and Caesarea, all fell prey to the Persians' savage fury. In Paphlagonia, in northern Asia Minor, Persian cavalry reached the shores of the Black Sea. Endless columns of prisoners trudged over the desert tracks of the East, driven to water once a day like cattle. The great Band-i-Kaisar (Mole of the

U

Caesar) at Sostra (Shushtar) in Susiana is said to have been constructed by these prisoners.

We are told that Shapur treated Valerian like a slave until the day he died. From time to time he would parade him in imperial purple and chains. Whenever Shapur mounted his horse, the Roman Emperor had to lie down on his belly so that the Persian king could step on his back. 'That is what I call a real triumph,' laughed Shapur, 'not just painting triumphs on walls, as the Romans do.' Valerian had to endure this treatment for the rest of his life, and it appears that he survived for many years. When he at last died, Shapur had him stuffed, painted red and exhibited in a temple 'to the everlasting shame of Rome'.

It is always possible that the Christians exaggerated the horrors of Valerian's captivity because he had persecuted them so relentlessly. Indeed, a number of historians consider the Emperor's hardships to have been very much overdrawn.

One thing seems certain: Shapur was so harassed by the Romans and their allies in the ensuing years that he must have vented some of his spleen on his distinguished prisoner, and it is also well known that Persians of this period were exceedingly brutal. At Naksh-i-Rustam, near the ruins of Persepolis, a scene depicting the Roman Emperor kneeling in chains before the Persian king Shapur, mounted on a horse, was carved into the rock for the benefit of future generations. This well-preserved relief can still be seen there today.

At first, nothing could stem the Persian tide, and Shapur's armies murdered and looted at will. But the retreating Romans regrouped themselves under a general called Callistus. Callistus, nicknamed 'Ballista', attached himself to Macrianus, the Roman Quartermaster-General. Collecting some ships in Cilician ports, he set off for beleaguered Soloi (Pompeiopolis), killed several thousand Persians and gained what was probably the most important victory of this period: he succeeded in capturing the Persian king's harem!

Shapur's attitude changed at once. The unexpected loss of his concubines, not to mention the personal baggage that went with them, apparently cut him to the quick. He set off in the direction of Ctesiphon, his capital, travelling by forced marches. When asked what urgent business he had to attend to at home, he alleged that he 'had to celebrate a festival'.

Throughout this turmoil the city of Edessa had held fast against time, plague and Persian attack. King Shapur's line of withdrawal took him through terrain commanded by that fortress. He knew Edessa too well to risk a fight with his army in its present weakened and depleted condition. So the citizens of Edessa lived to see the triumphal day when Shapur, aspirant to world domination, was forced to purchase free passage through their territory with all the money which he had captured from the Romans.

After that the wild, restless and titanic energy of the power-hungry Persian king seems to have waned. Shapur eventually found, in the rulers of the oasis of Palmyra, opponents who were either a match for him or at least curbed his ambition. Towards the end of his reign he was so occupied with internal affairs that he had no time to contemplate a new trial of strength with the Romans. The war-weary king spent the rest of his days carrying out grandiose building projects.

Who knows? Mani's dualistic philosophy may also have played a part in toning down and moderating the Persian king's restless nature. Perhaps Mani wanted to take the Christian, Persian and Buddhist faiths, popular religions which were dividing the world, and fuse them into a higher unity. Who can tell what heavenly power the great Persian ruler acknowledged as the true divinity at the end of his life, after thirty years of rule?

Shapur's coins would indicate that he remained faithful to the ancient Persian deity Ahura-Mazda or Ormuzd, God of Light. Seventeen hundred years old, these coins portray a remarkably shrewd and alert face and bear the legend: 'Worshipper of Ormuzd, excellent Shapur, King of the Kings of Iran, heavenly scion of the gods.'

GALLIENUS

THE GRECOPHILE

Rome never understood this emperor. He hated his father and loved his wife. It was he who passed on to us the spirit of Greece.

The Author.

GALLIENUS was a brilliant man but a bad son. He stayed in Rome and made no move to free Valerian from Persian captivity. He did not even send envoys to the Persian king to beg for his father's release or improve his conditions. On the contrary, he was glad to be rid of his stern and severe parent. In the triumphal march which he staged to commemorate the tenth anniversary of his accession he included some men dressed in Persian costumes to simulate prisoners of war. Several comedians threaded their way through the ranks as though searching for someone. When asked what they were doing, they replied that they were looking for the Emperor's father.

Gallienus was quite a unique figure in the history of Rome. He at once abandoned his father's anti-Christian policy and issued an edict of toleration whereby Christian communities had their confiscated property, churches and cemeteries restored to them. The Emperor became almost a patron of Christianity, which is why adherents of the ancient Roman faith credited his memory with so few good traits, while the Christians made the most of the merits, probably considerable, which he did possess.

During his reign the Graeco-Roman world experienced a last brief Hellenistic renaissance. Like Hadrian, Emperor Gallienus was an admirer of Athens and an enthusiastic champion of Greek culture. He, too, travelled to Greece and had himself initiated into the mystery-cult of Eleusis. Eleusis in Attica was the chief centre of worship of the goddess Demeter. All who participated in the mysterious rites were sworn to secrecy, and no author in antiquity ever broke silence on the subject—hence our almost complete ignorance of the rituals involved. We do know, however, that they included certain dramatic performances designed to stimulate religious emotion. Gallienus struck coins depicting himself as Demeter and adopted the name 'Galliena' in his capacity as a female deity. Ludicrous though this may seem to us, we must remember that people of the time were much closer to the goddess's secret.

Gallienus' wife was a remarkably sensitive and cultured person called Cornelia Salonina, a Greek from Bithynia. Unfortunately, students of history have neglected this interesting woman far too much. When she died a coin was minted in her honour bearing the words *Augusta in pace*, the first Christian inscription to appear on Roman imperial coinage. Was Salonina a Christian?

The Emperor and his consort were both devotees of the greatest contemporary Greek philosopher, Plotinus of Nicopolis (Egypt). The creator of 'neo-Platonism', Plotinus was in a certain inward sense a Christian, without actually having adopted the faith. Neo-Platonism was a rebirth of the old Platonic ideas, a time when Greek philosophy revived once more, once more proclaimed its great mission and, in an era of chaos, disclosed its deep yearning for God. Plotinus described man's goal as 'to become godlike'. There is little doubt that he was acquainted with Christianity; his pupil Porphyrius wrote a work which attempted to compromise with the Christians. Neo-Platonism was born at a period when those who believed in the ancient gods of Rome and the mysteries and cults of the East were, in many respects, not so far removed from the Christians and their novel beliefs, for the ancient faith and the new were both Europeanized by Hellenistic philosophy. Gallienus did not end the persecution of the Christians because he regarded them as harmless. He decided that the only way to refute them was with the spirit, not the sword.

The Emperor wanted to counter Christianity with the ideas of Plotinus and his sincere, moving quest for God, influenced, perhaps, by his wife Salonina, who accompanied him wherever he went and was actually in camp with him when he was assassinated. All over the Roman world, in Athens, Syria and Egypt, men of intellect — Christians among them — were enjoined by the Emperor to promote the most valuable concepts of ancient classical culture. Europe is indebted to Gallienus for passing on a large measure of the Greek genius and way of life.

Ironically enough, the sorely tried Roman Empire was subjected during his reign to a series of disasters. In A.D. 262, numerous towns in Asia Minor were destroyed by earthquakes, and year after year outbreaks of plague took their frightful toll.

Gallienus patterned himself on Augustus. He tried to deal with every threat, every infringement of the Roman frontiers, with a vigour, alacrity and vigilance worthy of his illustrious model. Yet at other times, so Eutropius tells us, he could be strangely immobile and apathetic.

Gallienus repelled German attacks on the Rhine for seven long years and succeeded in halting the wild hordes of Alemanni, Heruli and Goths. He fortified threatened cities. (One can still clearly distinguish, at Verona for example, the speed and urgency with which walls were built on his orders.) At the same time, he was constantly harassed by would-be usurpers. So many ambitious men cast covetous eyes at the throne during this period that Roman history lumps them together under the heading of 'the Thirty Tyrants'.

A man called Postumus set himself up as an independent emperor at Trèves (Augusta Treverorum). He erected magnificent buildings there, ruled Gaul, Britain and Spain, and issued coinage which gave an impression that the whole world belonged to him. Despite the numerous successes which he won over Postumus, Gallienus eventually had to concede that the traitor was master of the Gallic provinces. When, anxious to spare the lives of many thousands of soldiers, Gallienus nobly challenged him to a duel, Postumus replied that he was not a 'gladiator'. The pretender was finally murdered by his own men at Mainz. The *limes*, Hadrian's ambitious system of defence, had been meant as a guarantee of lasting peace. Now a constant state of war prevailed, and the frontier fortifications had completely given way.

Gallienus was a great army reformer. He created a mobile reserve ready for instant use, recruiting his cavalry, now the most important arm, from among the Dalmatians, Moors and Germans. This 'flying squad', designed for speedy dispatch to threatened frontier regions, was stationed at Milan. It was as mobile as the new conditions of war demanded. The Persian campaign had shown that infantrymen were not manœuvrable enough to cope with the swift Iranian cavalry. For all that, the infantry remained what it was 2,000 years earlier and still is, nearly as long afterwards: the hard core and essential backbone of any powerful army.

Gallienus is the only emperor in this violent and sanguinary epoch who was able to celebrate the tenth anniversary of his accession. This he did in the autumn of 263. Five years later, the Emperor could be seen hurrying back to Italy from the Danube, fresh from his victories over the Goths and Heruli, whose plundering raids had brought them as far as Athens and Corinth. Gallienus now besieged the insurgent cavalry general Aureolus in Milan.

The Emperor was a vigorous and wide-awake man who always acted quickly. It was this alertness and capacity for lightning-like decision which spelt his doom. He was told that Aureolus, beleaguered in Milan, had made a sortie. It was a ruse. Conspirators were lurking outside the Emperor's tent. He rushed out without helmet or armour and fell, mortally wounded.

Gallienus stood at the cross-roads between Christianity and the ancient religions. He was a man who hated his father and loved his wife, a personality of the first order, an utter individualist with a mind of his own who was little understood by his contemporaries. Even death did not win him immunity from the misfortune which had dogged him throughout his life, for his family was massacred with him. But, hard-pressed defender of a world in dissolution that he was, he passed on to us the spirit of Greece. He was one of the great figures in Roman history, despite our comparative lack of information about him.

The most amazing thing of all is that, in a period made tragic for the Empire by attack, defeat and betrayal, the ruler of Rome found time to forge plans for a unique project. He proposed to instal the great Plotinus in a settlement in Campania, modelled on Plato's political doctrines, where all devotees of the spirit of Plato could forgather and engage in exalted creative activity. Even though Platonopolis, as the ideal city was to be called, never became a reality, the project remains a silent memorial to the singular mind that conceived it.

ZENOBIA AND AURELIAN

SHE RODE LIKE A SOLDIER

The Queen of Palmyra, who reigned from A.D. 267 to A.D. 272, was perhaps the greatest female ruler in ancient history. She was defeated by Emperor Aurelian and led through Rome on a golden chain.

The Author.

IN the Syrian desert stand the lonely ruins of Palmyra. This once-flourishing caravan-city in the sands of northern Arabia is now a rubble-strewn plain. No one who wanders among the silent colonnades, through the shattered temples and palaces, and over the debris of a myriad tumbled stones, can fail to recognize that hundreds if not thousands of years went into the building of the place, and that a great past lies buried there.

Standing half way between the Mediterranean and Euphrates, Palmyra was once the main junction between the civilization of the Persian Gulf and the metropolitan cities of the Mediterranean. It was a rendezvous for caravans from the whole of the ancient world and the Far East. Wares from Emesa on the Orontes and valuable merchandise from Dura-Europos and the Euphrates area arrived on camel-back and were unloaded there. Dealers in precious stones and rare pearls plied their trade there. The city's market-place was piled high with goods from China, India, Persia and southern Arabia: bales of silk, incense-candles, ivory — the treasures of a world as yet unknown to mankind at large.

The oasis was famed for its abundant water supply, which was stored in huge subterranean tanks. Beside the broad, mile-long main avenue, bounded at one end by a triumphal arch, stood the great Sun-temple. Seven hundred-and-fifty rose-white pillars (of which 150 are still standing) gleamed in the sun, and massive buildings soared into the deep blue Syrian sky. It was a true feast of Greek, Roman and oriental architecture. A number of archaeologists have worked on the oasis during the last twenty years, and new ruins are constantly being unearthed. A careful examination of the temple of Baal-Shamin the Sun-god has yielded the discovery of an altar and a ritual banqueting-hall, while Palmyra's splendid theatre has only recently been excavated.

Palmyra is a Greek word meaning 'place of the date-palms'. Before its

Greek period the oasis-city was known as Tadmor, *tamar* being the Hebrew for date. Oddly enough, date-palms never grew in Palmyra, but the city was surrounded by magnificent gardens renowned the world over for their gorgeous flowers.

Anyone who spends a little time strolling through these ruins will find it hard to understand how so large a commercial centre could ever have met its end with such finality. Palmyra made world history. More than that, Palmyra once aspired to world domination, and the hands which reached for that prize were the slender hands of a woman.

The inhabitants of Palmyra were Arabs who spoke and wrote Aramaic, the language of Christ. Greek was used as a secondary language, but the noblemen and millionaires of Palmyra undoubtedly belonged to the Arab race. Merchant-clans with hundreds of years of tradition behind them, traders who rivalled Marco Polo in their expeditions to China and back, and the best archers and armoured cavalry in the contemporary world: those were the pillars of Palmyra's strength. How wealthy her people were can be deduced from the 'high houses' or towers of eternity which they erected as tombs during their lifetime. These turrets and their burial-precincts are still visible on the hills near the city.

With Valerian captured by the Persians, and the Empire, under his son Gallienus, menaced on every side, it was left to an Arab to save the Roman world. The name of this man, an Arab prince of Palmyra, was Septimius Odaenathus. Far away in the desert, in the eastern world, he and his city kept faith with Rome. He even disposed of a pretender to the Roman throne and drove the Persians out of Mesopotamia and Armenia. Gallienus gratefully entrusted him with the defence of the East, and before long he had become Governor-General of the whole Orient. Odaenathus and his splendid city attained a unique status. To all intents and purposes, the lord of the oasis was an emperor. Odaenathus was murdered in the year 267 at the height of his career. Perhaps he had become too powerful for the Emperor's liking. Perhaps Rome had instigated his murder. The sheikh was succeeded by his son, Prince Vaballathus. Since the boy was much too young to rule, the administration of Palmyra's affairs was taken over by his mother, the widow of Odaenathus. For the first time in world history, a woman of Arab blood stood at the helm of a huge empire. That woman was the celebrated Zenobia.

Zenobia was a Greek name, the Queen's oriental name being Bat-Zabbai or 'daughter of Zabbai'. Queen Zenobia traced her ancestry back to the rulers of Egypt, to the dynasty which had produced the great Cleopatra, who was of Macedonian stock. However, she is said to have been more beautiful than

Cleopatra and considerably more chaste — exaggeratedly so, in fact. History relates that she only permitted her royal husband Odaenathus to embrace her once a month for the purpose of procreation.

Zenobia had dark hair, very white teeth and fiery black eyes. She had worked hard to school her almost masculine intellect under the famous philosopher and rhetorician Cassius Longinus, who instructed his beautiful pupil in Greek language and literature. He had a cosmopolitan background, having taught in Athens and being himself the pupil of a very well-known Egyptian. In his own and his pupil's eyes, Egypt was the absolute and universal criterion of greatness. Longinus was one day to become the most trusted adviser of the queen of the world.

A woman of wide interests and unusual intelligence, Zenobia spoke fluent Syrian, Aramaic, Greek and Latin. The amazing military successes of her husband Odaenathus were in no small part due to his consort's advice, courage, determination and presence of mind. Imagine what it must have meant when the Arab Prince attacked the mighty Persian Empire and knocked at the very gates of Ctesiphon, the Persian capital! The contemporary oriental world admired and respected the gallant couple, and the Romans at first looked upon Odaenathus and Zenobia as the avengers of their captured Emperor, Valerian.

Whenever King Odaenathus was not occupied with affairs of State at Palmyra or actually engaged in a military campaign, he used to go hunting. We learn that he killed lions and panthers. There must have been large forests in Syria at this time, for bears are also mentioned. Zenobia used to accompany Odaenathus on these hunting expeditions, and showed no less dash and bravery than her husband. Having successfully inured herself to heat and cold, she never travelled in a closed carriage but rode like a cavalryman and often marched for many miles at the head of her troops. When Odaenathus died, Palmyra was a flourishing caravan-city which controlled the whole of Syria and a large part of the East. Neighbouring countries such as Arabia, Armenia and Persia feared Zenobia's enmity and sought her favour.

But Zenobia was still dissatisfied. Wasn't Longinus always rhapsodizing about Egypt? Wasn't Egypt the crowning glory of civilization, the 5,000-year-old pearl of the contemporary world? Wasn't Egypt the granary of the whole Roman Empire? And hadn't Zabdas, Zenobia's chief of staff, spent many nights expounding to her the best plan of attack? Zenobia wanted to rule Egypt, the land of the Pharaohs and, so she claimed, of her forefathers. She would not rest until she had plucked this tempting fruit for herself and her infant son. Accordingly she sent a large army to the Nile under the supreme command of Zabdas, and simultaneously launched an attack on Arabia. It was an ideal moment. Probus, the Roman prefect, was absent from Egypt. He hurried back at top speed, but it was too late. The Palmyrenes had conquered Egypt, and Probus committed suicide.

At Rome, Emperor Gallienus had been succeeded by Claudius II, an extremely efficient army officer from Illyria (modern Yugoslavia). He fought Rome's battles with notable success for one-and-a-half-years, defeating the Alemanni at Lake Garda and decisively worsting the Goths at Nisch. His victories laid the foundations of the Empire's reconstruction, but he died of the plague in the year 270.

Claudius II was followed by Aurelian, a man who combined great physical strength with a coolly calculating mind and well-disciplined military ability. He was outstandingly courageous and carried each of his military operations through with copy-book precision and extreme tenacity. Once he had decided on a plan he would never deviate from it. By far the most distinguished of all the Roman officers in Illyria, Aurelian had made his mark in the war against the Goths and was the obvious successor to the throne.

The new Emperor lacked three things: charm, tact and a subtle appreciation of the intellectual. For all that, his reign was a time of unparalleled achievement. First, he signed a treaty with Zenobia to protect his rear, intending to rule the West himself and leave the eastern half of the Empire under the control of Zenobia and her son. Then he began to tidy up. The Roman Empire was being eaten away on every side. Aurelian repelled a Vandal invasion of Pannonia. The Juthungi and Alemanni heavily defeated him at Piacenza and Rome itself was threatened, but he saved the situation and was finally victorious at the battle of the Ticino. It was his invariable policy to recruit defeated enemies into the Roman army. He fortified Rome with walls twenty feet high, thirteen feet thick and twelve miles long. This mighty bastion of defence, which is still one of the sights of the city, was interspersed with towers and eighteen gates. It was built by non-combatants and prisoners of war, Rome's legionaries having better things to do in the outside world. The Emperor abandoned the province of Dacia and left it to the Goths. At long last he had his hands free for the great game in the East.

The world waited expectantly for the clash between the tough and brilliant soldier and the worldly-wise, ambitious Queen. Flushed with success, the Palmyrenes remained in Egypt and minted coins at Alexandria with the head of their own King Vaballathus on one side and that of Emperor Aurelian on the other. Before long (from March 11th, 271, onwards) they were striking coins on which only the Palmyrene King's head appeared. In the summer of 271 Zenobia raised her own status to that of 'Augusta' or Empress, and entitled her son 'Augustus'. Palmyra had seceded from the Roman Empire and thrown down the gauntlet.

Aurelian was not a man to tolerate this sort of behaviour. Breaking off relations with Palmyra, he assembled a large army and wrested Egypt from Zenobia's control. At the close of 271 the Emperor's massive columns rolled eastwards. The city of Tyana, on the borders of Cappadocia, offered resistance, but was taken. The Emperor treated the citizens with great leniency, and the news of his behaviour encouraged a large number of other cities to open their gates to him. Zenobia now relied on getting some support from the King of Persia, but King Shapur was very old and quite unwilling to come to her aid.

At Antioch, battle was joined anew. Zenobia was present in person, but her run of military success was at an end. Although outnumbered, Aurelian defeated the Palmyrene cavalry and Antioch fell into his hands. Once more the Emperor shrewdly spared the lives of the civil population.

Zenobia's defeated soldiers trudged back along the endless caravan trails, their morale at a low ebb. Aurelian offered the Queen peace terms. He called on her to surrender, pointing to the large number of men who had lost their lives in the battles on the Orontes. 'Yes, but they were only Romans,' retorted Zenobia, and engaged the Emperor yet again at Emesa. After a bloody battle, the Roman legionaries won the day.

'The Sun-god of Emesa has deserted his home and given victory to Rome,' declared Aurelian. He adopted this God of Light, an oriental deity which had been subjected to the refining influence of Greek culture, as the Romans' national god. The Sun-temple was dedicated on the Field of Mars at Rome on December 25th, 274. It was an attempt at heathen monotheism, for only a universal and omnipresent god like the Sun-god could hope to make a fight of it with the new god of Christendom.

But Rome's soldiers were exhausted. They advanced on Palmyra by forced marches, broiled by the pitiless sun. The city had ample supplies, and a siege presented almost insuperable difficulties, for the Romans were perpetually short of water. Aurelian was wounded by an arrow, but the greatest officer on the throne since Trajan refused to abandon his cause. Zenobia, who was opposed in this bitter struggle by a tough adversary and a shrewder brain, gave up too soon, convinced that time was taking no toll of Aurelian's army and that the Roman legionaries were insusceptible to hunger or demoralization. She made off in the direction of Dura-Europos on the

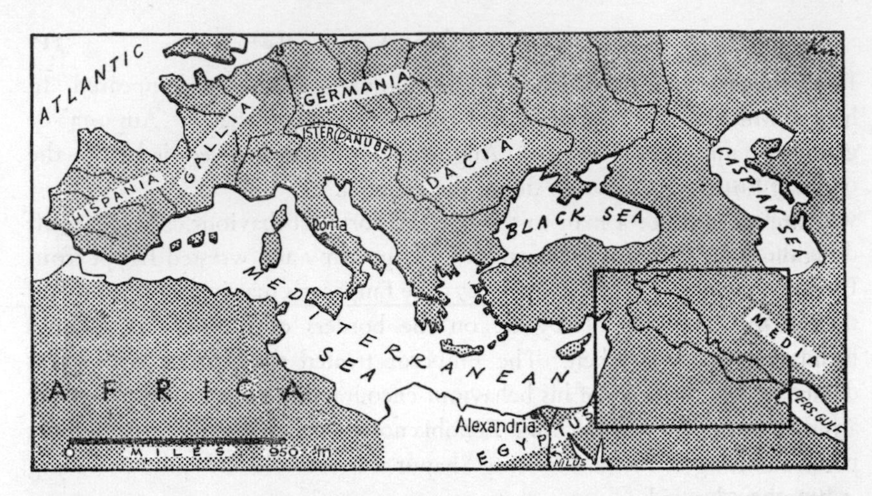

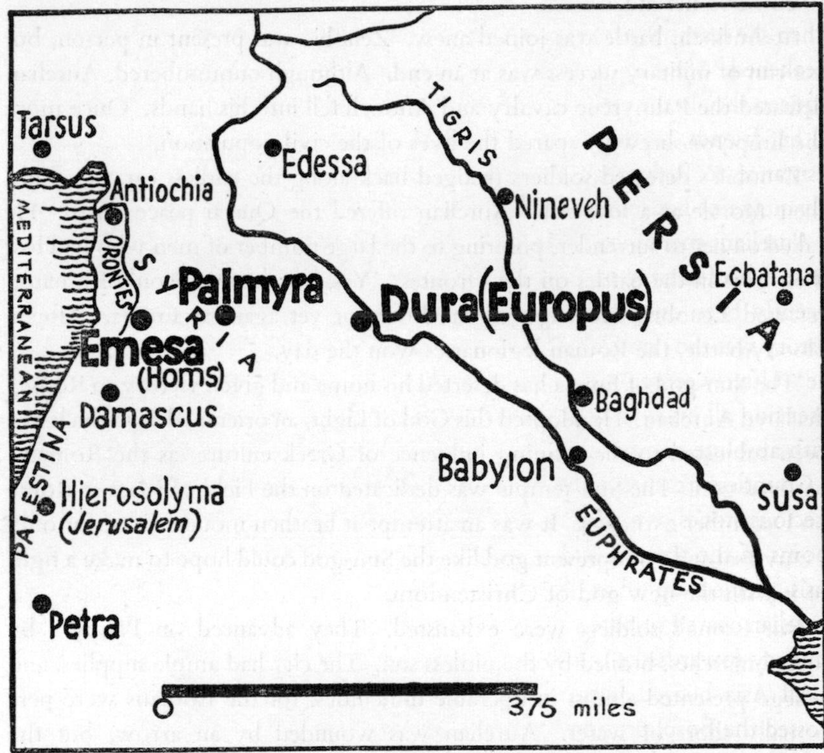

Palmyra used to be the commercial rendezvous between the metropolitan cities of the Mediterranean and the cultural area of the Persian Gulf. This caravan-city reached its zenith under the Arab Queen Zenobia. Her army was defeated by Emperor Aurelian at *Emesa*, and she was finally captured at *Dura-Europos* just as she was about to escape across the Euphrates

Euphrates, swaying along on dromedary-back. Her intention was to seek help from the Persians once more, relying on her personal charm and glamorous appearance to secure it without delay. But Roman cavalry set off in pursuit. Zenobia had already reached the Euphrates and was just stepping into the boat which was to take her to the other bank and the freedom she longed for, when she and her son were seized by the Romans. Palmyra, unnerved by Zenobia's flight, abandoned further resistance. When the Syrian Queen was led before Emperor Aurelian, he asked her how she had dared to rebel against the masters of Rome. Zenobia answered with great dexterity that she had never been able to regard his predecessors or, indeed, any men who had forcibly taken possession of the throne, as Roman Emperors, and added: 'You alone are my conqueror and lord.'

But the captured Queen soon lost her initial sang-froid. She trembled when she learnt that the legionaries were clamouring for her execution. She weakened. She forgot that Cleopatra, her model, had taught the world that a queen should die rather than live in dishonourable captivity. She betrayed all her friends, teachers and confidants, claiming that her obstinacy and her resistance to Rome had been engendered by bad advisers who had taken advantage of her feminine weakness.

Aurelian thereupon beheaded Zenobia's leading counsellors. Among those who fell prey to the fear and desperation of this woman who had so recently been one of the most courageous feminine personalities in world history was the famous teacher Longinus. He died as a philosopher ought to die. Utterly serene, never complaining, comforting his fellow-victims and reserving all his sympathy for his unfortunate mistress, he went to his death with absolute composure.

Countless treasures fell into the Roman Emperor's hands: gold, silver, silk, precious stones, weapons, horses, camels. The treasure-chambers and storerooms in the temples and public buildings of the world's most prosperous oasis yielded up their contents to the victorious Romans. Apparently, Aurelian spared private property, and he again exercised his now proverbial leniency towards the inhabitants of the city.

All Asia buzzed with the news of Aurelian's victory. He had already crossed the Bosphorus on his way home when he heard that the Palmyrenes had risen against him once more. This time, with truly Asiatic brutality, he vented his rage on men, women and children alike. Not even the peasants who lived in the neighbourhood of the city were exempted. The Emperor ordered everything to be destroyed. Nevertheless, when he saw Palmyra lying in ruins, he regretted his decision and gave the few surviving inhabitants permission to rebuild the city. His act of clemency came to nothing. Palmyra was never to rise again, and its ruins have lain untouched for 1,700 years.

The Emperor had almost reconquered the Roman world when a new and singularly interesting figure appeared on the scene. Firmus was a ship-owner and paper-maker of Greek origin who had left Seleucia in Syria and settled down in Alexandria, where he made a vast fortune out of papyrus manufacture. He also did a thriving trade in Chinese silk, using the town of Coptos as his base. During the years circa 270 'Firmus silk' was being transported by ship and camel-train from one end of the world to the other, and Firmus' ships were making regular trips across the Indian Ocean. Clothes-conscious ladies in Rome and Palmyra dressed themselves in his silks. No sooner had Firmus heard that Aurelian had left for home after his first conquest of Palmyra than he joined forces with some Nubian desert tribes, instigated a revolt, and decided, at the beginning of 273, to promote himself from paper-king to Roman Emperor. However, Aurelian's legions restored order here, too, and we learn with some regret that the enterprising paper and silk magnate took his own life.

The Emperor's triumphal procession through Rome outshone anything which the Eternal City had seen before. Twenty elephants, four royal tigers, 200 of the rarest animals in the contemporary world and 1,600 gladiators all paraded by, bound for the sadistic entertainments in the amphitheatre. There were banners captured from many defeated nations, treasures from all over Asia, ambassadors from Ethiopia, Arabia, Persia, India and even China, and endless columns of prisoners, among them Goths, Vandals, Sarmatae, Alemanni, Franks, Gauls, Syrians and Egyptians. Then came the gorgeous wardrobe of the captive Zenobia and, finally the Queen of the East herself, choicest prize of all. A slave led her along on the end of a golden chain welded about her neck. The lovely woman looked ready to collapse under the weight of her own jewellery. She had been forced to walk along on foot in front of her magnificent battle-chariot — the very same chariot in which she had hoped to enter Rome in triumph.

Aurelian's triumphal chariot was drawn by a team of four stags captured from the Goths. Hour after hour the amazing procession wound through the streets of Rome. At first the crowds were lost in silent admiration, then they cheered. Then they fell silent again and stared with bated breath. For in the parade of prisoners was Tetricus, senator and would-be emperor who had arbitrarily seized control of Gaul. Aurelian had made sure of his presence on this day of days. By defeating him, he had won Gaul back for the Empire. Never before had a Roman senator marched through Rome as a prisoner in a triumphal procession. The Emperor was lenient with him, however, and gave him a government post in southern Italy.

We are told that Emperor Aurelian treated Zenobia with the greatest consideration and gave her a villa at Tivoli. The Syrian Queen, once so proud and courageous, proceeded to lead a blameless existence as the wife of a Roman senator. Her daughters married into leading Roman families, and her descendants are said to have been living in Rome as late as the fifth century.

DIOCLETIAN

THE ADMINISTRATIVE GENIUS

Diocletian was a shrewd character, gifted with sharp-sightedness and a penetrating intelligence. He tried to divert on to others the bitterness caused by his severe measures. He spent his old age as a private citizen on his country estate at Salonae. His rare magnanimity was demonstrated by the way in which he voluntarily relinquished his lofty status for the rank and condition of a private citizen — the only man to do so since the foundation of the imperial regime.

Eutropius, History of Rome, ix.

As a great soldier-emperor, Aurelian had fought with success against the Goths and Vandals. He had brought the Alemanni to a standstill and made Rome the strongest fortress in the world. He had reunited Gaul with Rome. He had destroyed Palmyra and captured Queen Zenobia, first exhibiting her to the Romans as an item of booty in his triumphal parade and then settling her in a villa at Tibur (modern Tivoli) and marrying her to a senator. Or was the slim little woman's end really as uncomplicated? Only if a kind fairy had been making history in those days, and not an unsentimental man like Emperor Aurelian! I cannot personally believe in the Tivoli story and regard it as far more likely and more in keeping with the times that she died in chains.

Zenobia's conqueror was now master of the world and God's deputy on earth. His lonely supremacy brought him gradually closer to the Christian emperors who were later to rule 'by the grace of God'. But Aurelian's god was not the god of Christianity. It was the Sun-god which had given him victory over Zenobia and, with it, mastery of the world. Jupiter Capitolinus, hitherto the senior member of the Roman pantheon, was now superseded by the oriental Sun-god, the invincible national deity who was greater than all other gods. By promoting a single god, Aurelian's Sun-cult illustrated the astonishing development of the ancient mind and, being virtually monotheistic, foreshadowed the possibility of future State recognition for the god of Christianity.

Aurelian was the first in the line of great rulers from Illyria who governed in the oriental manner, godlike and by divine right. His grasp extended to every quarter of the world, to north, east and west, to the skies and the sun.

But, incomparable soldier-emperor that he was, he died through a stupid mischance, either through blind fate or human folly.

At the end of 274 he had set off for the East once more, intending to wrest Mesopotamia from the Persians and reconquer it for Rome. The final act unfolded at Caenophrurium, between Perinth and Byzantium, in the autumn of 275. The man who had set a nearly impotent empire on its feet again, the only man of his day with any creative ideas, owed his death to the machinations of an insignificant private secretary.

This secretary, Eros by name, had for some trivial reason aroused the Emperor's disfavour. Over-apprehensive of Aurelian's anger, Eros forged a letter purporting to show that the Emperor meant to execute all his bravest warriors. He then showed it to the men involved, and they, imagining that they were in mortal danger, resolved to murder their inflexible master. They only discovered their mistake after the great monarch was dead. Eros was executed.

The army was so dismayed that it did not select a new emperor from its own ranks for once, but left the choice to the Senate. The long-departed era of senatorial supremacy seemed to have returned. In September, 275, Senator Tacitus was elected Emperor. Such an honour was tantamount to a death-sentence, considering how few emperors died from natural causes. Tacitus, who was quite unconnected with the historian of that name, was seventy-five years old. He conscientiously marched against the Goths in Asia Minor, but was murdered at Tyana in April 276.

The army of the East now chose another Illyrian, M. Aurelius Probus, the ablest officer in the Roman service. Had history been kinder to him, this Emperor would be ranked among the greatest. He succeeded, by a series of bold strokes, in restoring Roman possessions to full strength. He liberated Gaul from the Germans in a single year, repelled hostile attacks on every frontier of the Empire, on the Rhine, the Danube and in Upper Egypt, dealt with insurgent mountain tribes and usurpers in the provinces, settled large numbers of German prisoners in the Roman Empire, did a great deal for his native Pannonia, launched soil-improvement schemes and introduced viticulture into Germany and Hungary. He was killed at Sirmium in 282, just as he was preparing for a Persian campaign. He reigned one year longer than Aurelian, achieved as much or even more than he did, and was known, like Aurelian, as 'God and Lord'. Yet historical records give him such poor coverage that we know relatively little about him.

Probus' successor, Carus, and his sons Carinus and Numerianus, rulers of West and East respectively, made only fleeting appearances on the imperial stage. All three died a violent death, as was only to be expected. Numerian took part in a successful Persian expedition commanded by his father Carus, and led a victorious army back from Ctesiphon. In autumn, 284, the Roman forces reached Nicomedia, where a gruesome discovery was made. For some time an unbearable stench had been issuing from the Emperor's litter. It was found to contain a putrefying body. Numerian was dead, and his litter-bearers had been toting a corpse round Asia. The murderer was his father-in-law, Arrius Aper. It was not long before he paid for his deed.

Men are complex creatures. No one can be summed up in a few catch-phrases, which is what makes good historical writing such an art. It crams a lot of truth into a little space. C. Aurelius Valerianus Diocletianus was one of the most complex figures in world history, a character with a multitude of lights and shadows, neither an ordinary man nor a universal genius, no soldier but one of the greatest administrators of all time, a human being with human failings, a ruler who made several big and serious mistakes. The last great heathen Emperor, Diocletian marked the end of an epoch, not the beginning.

Before his accession he was known as Diocles. He came of very humble origins. His native land was Dalmatia and his home town is assumed to have been Salonae, since he later built a large palace there. The precise year of his birth is unknown, but coin portraits dating from 305, the year of his abdication, show him as a man of about seventy, so he may have been born in 235.

The troops proclaimed him Augustus, or Emperor, at Nicomedia in Bithynia, on November 17th, 284. Addressing the army, he gazed up at the sun with drawn sword and swore a sacred oath that he was innocent of Numerian's death. Then, quick as lightning, he drove his blade through the man who was standing next to him. It was the Praetorian prefect Arrius Aper, his predecessor's father-in-law.

The story has a point. It had once been prophesied to Diocles that he would become Emperor if he killed a wild boar — in Latin *aper*. Now the boar lay dead at his feet. The prophecy had been fulfilled — no trivial matter in those days of dark superstitions, magic incantations and mysterious formulae. The soldiers were dumbfounded. They liked that sort of thing. The new Emperor was obviously a quick thinker, and the gods were on his side.

But Diocletian did not possess the conventional daring and magnanimity of the heroic figure who seeks danger and glory, abhors intrigue and challenges bold men of his own stamp. His gifts were practical rather than brilliant. Edward Gibbon, who drew a very subtle portrait of him, thought that his already strong character gained further schooling from experience and a study of human nature, that he was a blend of generosity and meanness, lenience and severity, stubbornness and flexibility, and that he often cloaked extreme hypocrisy under a bluff soldierly exterior. But above all, Gibbon said, Diocletian had acquired the ability to subordinate his own and other people's emotions to the dictates of his ambition. He could always find the most elaborate and cogent reasons for any action he undertook. H. Mattingly describes the effect of such a man on his contemporaries. Apparently he was an object of the deepest admiration — not unmixed with a certain uneasiness and distrust.

Diocletian surrounded himself with imperial pomp and soon made it clear that he regarded himself as God's agent on earth. There was a religious aura about Diocletian's monarchy which stemmed from an emphasis on his divine right to rule, the supernaturally sacred character of the imperial office, oriental-style court ceremonial and emperor-worship as a means of paying direct homage to the highest earthly ruler, God's deputy in the world. This restatement of the Emperor's central authority probably suited the mood of the time. People were tired of the frightful national crises of the third century. 'If any means of saving the Roman Empire still existed — and this was the nation's general belief — it had to come from above,' writes Rostovzev.

While he sometimes held court at Nicomedia (modern Ismid, not far from Istanbul), arrayed in his State robes of silk and gold, a pearl-encrusted diadem on his head and pearls and precious stones on his shoes, Diocletian spent most of his time travelling through Asia and Europe, receiving the homage due to a god. The Emperor of Rome had become unapproachable. The supernatural radiance which people ascribed to the Emperor now began to appear as a *nimbus* or aureole in portraits of him. The master of the world sat in his 'Sacrum Palatium' in solemn isolation. Anyone who wanted to see him was passed on from one steward and eunuch to the next until he reached the Holy of Holies, where he had to fall before the monarch and address him as a god. This custom of *proscynesis*, which entailed falling on one's knees and kissing the hem of the imperial purple, hailed from the court of ancient Persia. Even the Emperor's own family were required to comply with it. The Emperor's title and normal mode of address was now 'Lord' (*dominus*), not 'First Citizen' (*princeps*), as Augustus had once styled himself. The 'Principate' had become the 'Dominate'.

Diocletian had one daughter, Valeria, but no son. He realized that the

Empire was much too large for one man to govern alone, and so, in midsummer 285, he promoted his comrade-in-arms Maximian to the rank of Caesar and sent him to Gaul. Shortly afterwards, in recognition of his achievements there, he proclaimed him 'Augustus' or joint Emperor.

There were now two Emperors, Maximian in the West and Diocletian in the East. The Augusti were looked on as brothers, an honorary relationship which put Diocletian's co-Emperor on a par with himself. Diocletian still retained the premier position in the Empire, however. He had chosen the East because it presented the knottiest diplomatic and military problems. It was there that the frontiers had to be held against the Persian Sassanids and there that the greatest economic strength lay. The scales of power had tipped in favour of the East.

Diocletian had mounted the throne at Nicomedia, the city which would one day see him take his leave of the purple. He made it his royal residence and ornamented it with splendid buildings. A generation later, the orator Libanius called the city 'the most beautiful metropolis in the world'. The eastern half of the Empire had stepped into the spotlight, while Rome, profligate, spoilt, sadistic city of arenas, magnificent thermae and amphitheatres, was forced to retire to the wings.

Emperor Maximian spent very little of his time in Rome. In order to be nearer the threatened northern frontiers he lived in Milan, which at this period began to exceed Rome in importance. The dual sovereignty of Diocletian and Maximian functioned excellently and lasted for seven years. Diocletian was wise and careful enough to invoke the gods in sanctifying and perpetuating his new system of government. From now on, he reigned under the aegis of Jupiter Optimus Maximus, the supreme god, and adopted the religious title 'Jovius', while his partner Maximian received the title 'Herculius'. Since Hercules was also a god and acted as Jupiter's 'right-hand man' in heaven, the titles symbolized the two holy Emperors' collaboration on earth.

Between them, Diocletian and Maximian defeated a whole host of enemies — Burgundians, Alemanni, Franks, Sarmatae, Goths, Arabs — none of whom had been giving the Romans a moment's peace since the victories of Claudius, Aurelian and Probus.

The two rulers met in Milan. Despite the vast distances and the absence of telephone or telegraph, they kept in the closest touch. The inhabitants of Milan gave them an enthusiastic reception after their journey across the snow-covered Alpine roads. The worthy citizens' only worry was how to deal with two emperors: their ceremonial was only adapted to one.

When, in 293, Diocletian realized that even two emperors were no match for the unremitting threats from outside the Empire and the vast administrative problems within, he founded his famous tetrarchy, or 'rule of four'. Each of the Emperors, the eastern and the western, took on an assistant. The title of the premier Emperor remained Augustus, while the assistant Emperor assumed the title of Caesar. Both the new Caesars had previously commanded their respective Emperors' body-guards and were reliable men whom Diocletian had selected with characteristic skill.

Maximian's assistant, Constantius, was to govern Gaul from Trèves, which made Trèves an imperial residence and turned it into one of the loveliest and most important cities in the West. Galerius became Diocletian's Caesar, and administered the whole region south of the Danube from the Inn to the Black Sea. His residence was at Sirmium (Mitrovitza) on the lower Save. In order to draw the bonds between the four Emperors even tighter, the Caesars were adopted by their Augusti. They were to succeed their seniors after twenty years, thus giving the latter a chance to abdicate and leave the throne alive, rather than be assassinated. But it did not stop there. The junior Emperors had to divorce and marry the daughters of their exalted patrons. The imperial quartet is immortalized in the Piazza San Marco at Venice by a harmonious group of four porphyry statues which can still be seen today.

Diocletian still occupied the dominant position. At his own bidding he was honoured as 'the founder of everlasting peace' and accorded the title *Invictus*, or 'invincible'.

Only rarely in human history has so artificial a device been such a practical success. Always working hand in hand, the four Emperors governed, guarded and gained victories in their respective corners of the world. When Carausius, governor and commander-in-chief in Britain, seized control of the whole island and had himself proclaimed Emperor, he was blockaded in Boulogne and defeated. Britain was reconquered for the Roman Empire.

The history of Roman achievements between the years 295 and 305 includes a great victory over the Alemanni, victories on the Danube, successful operations in Africa, the quelling of an Egyptian revolt, the expansion of Roman sovereignty in the East across the Tigris and the building of more *limes* fortifications.

This period also saw the erection of a contemporary wonder of the world: the magnificent Baths of Diocletian at Rome. This building surpassed in size and splendour all the other 800 baths in the capital — not excluding the Baths of Caracalla. Out of the central hall of these baths, with their high cross-shaped vaults and pillared façades, Michelangelo made his Church of Santa Maria degli Angeli. The rest of the site is now occupied by Italy's national museum.

Planning, co-ordination, organization and construction were all second nature to Diocletian. He built arsenals at Antioch, Edessa and Damascus, and probably at Irenopolis (Cilicia) and Caesarea (Cappadocia) as well. Dye-works and wool and linen mills sprang up, new roads were constructed throughout the Empire, frontier defences erected. Imposing buildings and palaces took shape in the four royal residences, Nicomedia, Sirmium, Milan and Trèves. The gloomy, crag-like Roman ruins at Trèves are still there to remind us of this period. Carthage, Antioch and countless other places all showed visible signs of the inaccessible Emperor's urge to build. At Daphne in Syria there arose two palaces, five baths, a stadium and a shrine to Hecate. The temple of Apollo at Miletus was extended and a new bathing establishment at Alexandria brought welcome relief from the heat.

But that was not all. Emperor Diocletian's passion for organization prompted him to create the greatest totalitarian regime in the ancient world. An increasing number of civil servants were appointed. The city councils and individual government officials lost all their autonomous powers. Everyone was responsible to a superior. The official hierarchy grew with startling rapidity until it reached unheard-of dimensions. Every aspect of administration in the huge political system had to be dealt with by an all-powerful bureaucracy. Self-government vanished, and supervisory organs were controlled by other supervisory organs. The system was brutal in its simplicity. Even the central government officials were no more than servants and slaves of the State. The Emperor's provinces were redistributed and organized into large administrative regions or *dioeceses*.

Were all these measures merely the product of megalomania, of a demoniac thirst for power and craze for uniformity? Were they merely the obsession of a monomaniac who wanted to probe every last government department with a myriad fingers, just to find himself confirmed in each facet of a vast empire's existence? Did Diocletian want to turn the Imperium into a huge looking-glass which would reflect nothing but his own divine omnipotence?

Well, something radical had to be done after the disasters of the third century. Reforms were urgently necessary and the Roman Empire had to be safeguarded, once and for all, against internal and external dangers. The ancient Roman virtues had vanished long ago, and where the old-fashioned disposition was lacking, only a system could take its place. In this case it was Diocletian's government machine. Nothing else could have saved the Empire.

National moods come in waves. A warlike mood, soon exhausted, is followed by a peaceable mood of longer duration. That is why, when normally volatile nations develop a much-vaunted love of peace, it is usually no more than a symptom of fatigue and not a sign of 'reformed national character'. After Caesar's victory over Pompey and a century of bloody civil war, the Romans were affected by a sort of fatigue, a peaceable inertia which never really deserted them again.

Once the battle of Actium had been won in 31 B.C. and Egypt had been conquered in 30 B.C., Augustus demobilized. He cut down the army almost to half strength, leaving only twenty-eight legions in service. These were stationed on the frontiers, and no reserve army was provided in the interior. The danger of such disarmament was demonstrated in A.D. 9 at the battle of the Teutoburger Wald, in which Varus lost three legions. Augustus, the great statesman and founder of the Principate, was really the heathen author of the ideal of universal peace, as is testified by the famous Ara Pacis Augustae or Altar of Augustan Peace at Rome. And this romantic mood permeating the Augustan age, this exalted yearning for eternal peace, this light which preceded the Christian Gospel, passed from one Emperor to the next. Even though Trajan, Rome's last great soldier-emperor, took the offensive against the Dacians and Parthians, a plan which Caesar entertained and was only prevented from carrying out by the fatal coup on the Ides of March, 44 B.C., Rome's new world policy remained essentially defensive.

After Augustus there was a second renunciation of Caesarism or retreat from militarism. This was the policy of Emperor Hadrian, the highly sensitive admirer of Greece who wore a philosopher's beard and was nicknamed *Graeculus*, 'the little Greek'. On his accession in 117, he renounced the aggressive policy of his predecessor Trajan. Overflowing with the idea of Pax Augusta, he wanted to be the 'illustrious servant' of State and people, an emperor of peace ruling with the wisdom of Hellenism.

That was how the Empire came to be weakened by demilitarization yet again, at a time when Rome was hemmed in by nations whose appreciation of culture and standard of civilization were rudimentary, nations in the first flush of their strength who were only waiting for a chance to fall on the wealth of the Roman Empire. What made the third century A.D. so exceedingly dangerous for Rome was that cultural dissolution had set in. People had developed a penchant for mystery-religions, and the romantic concept of Augustan peace had been transformed into pacifism proper. Quite uninfluenced by such peaceable ideals, the Germans in the north were building their gloomy strongholds or surging to the attack with fearsome war-cries and primitive momentum, while the East, dormant since Alexander's day, had awoken to new vigour, since the year 226, under a Persian Empire resurrected by the Sassanids.

The Roman legions stationed on the frontiers were now quite un-Roman in appearance, having long been recruited not from Italy but from the frontier territories. As the blessings of Roman civilization had penetrated to the outskirts of the Empire, so camp life had become soft and the frontier army had degenerated into a sort of border militia. The sands were fast running out when Diocletian reinforced these frontier troops by creating a highly mobile reserve or army of the interior.

It was only to be expected that the sweeping efforts to revitalize national defence, the expansion of the army, the powerful and omnipresent bureaucratic system, the enlarged and much more costly royal household and the extensive building programme all combined to produce a need for fiscal reform. The Emperor fixed the level of taxation at the beginning of each year, and no one knew in advance what he would have to pay in the coming twelve months. Rates of payment were assessed by *iugum* and *caput*, iugum being a yoke of land (about 0·6 of an acre), and caput being the 'head' (c.f. 'poll'-tax) of the man who worked the iugum. Female labour was rated at half a head.

Iugatio or taxation took into account not only the number of yokes and heads, but also the number of cattle. Everything had to be declared. The peasant-farmer, being responsible for his land and his 'heads', was in duty bound to pay the taxes imposed. To make the whole business easier for the State, his freedom of movement was restricted and he was tied to his plot of land for better or worse. The towns had to levy the money and manufactured articles needed by the Government. A group of rich town councillors or *curiales* were held responsible for the prompt payment of their fellow-citizens' dues and had to underwrite them with their own resources. Understandably, the councillors would often have preferred to evade this duty, but a ban was imposed on their movements, too, and their responsibilities devolved on their children when they died. Manual labourers and shop-keepers had to join obligatory guilds or corporations and were taxed accordingly. An army of civil servants worked night and day to prevent tax-collectors from bilking the exchequer and the tax-payers to any serious degree.

In this way, farmers, labourers and tradesmen were kept in total subjection, the economy was paralysed and the whole of every-day life was fettered to a ruthless government machine. The officials, while growing ever more powerful, had their own fears and worries. Dishonesty was rife. By his sweeping controls and the thorough system of taxation which produced the constant flow of money needed to finance his immense building programmes, the administration and the armed forces, Diocletian had induced general apathy. The three maxims of existence were: keep mum, obey and pay. Only the city of Rome was granted exemption from taxes, the ancient capital's last remaining privilege.

The influence of early Christian writing has evoked much harsh and negative criticism of the non-Christian Emperor and his measures. But there was no accurate market research or advanced theory of economics in those days, and the science of sociology had not yet been invented. Recent history had shown that the Empire's decay could not be halted unless its economic and financial resources were properly organized, and that military security could not be achieved without great public sacrifices. Diocletian's solution of the problem was a totalitarian or war-economy, as we would term it today. His prime object was the maintenance of an army.

We know now that Diocletian's planned economy had many failings. What is remarkable is that our own century, despite its exact knowledge of history, has experimented with these methods all over again, only to stand aghast when they break down. Price-ceilings were tried out at this period. In the year 301 the Emperor froze all prices, wages and salaries at a uniform level throughout the Empire. This was supposed to prevent the imperial court and the imperial army from being over-charged. Anyone who exceeded the maximum prices was executed. The system met with no lasting success, even though it was preceded by an attempt at currency stabilization on the basis of a gold standard. The goods disappeared from the shops, a flourishing black market sprang up and blood flowed. 'People were now too frightened to bring anything saleable to market, and the cost of living increased to a much worse degree,' wrote the Christian author Lactantius in his *De Mortibus Persecutorum*.

Diocletian's tariff of maximum prices appeared as an edict in 301, and was published throughout the Empire on stone tablets. Several of these tablets have survived. Their lists of goods for which maximum prices were fixed give us a glimpse of every-day existence in a long-vanished age and bring the Roman Empire to life once more.

The Romans of this period kept a good table, and the profusion of items bought and sold make amazing reading. In the poultry line, geese, partridge, wild and domestic pigeon, grouse, duck and peacock were all normal fare for the well-to-do. Sparrow, thrush, goldfinch, dormouse and quail were regarded as delicacies. Starlings, it appears, were not popular. In addition, 'individually fed' or fattened turtle-doves could be purchased.

For vegetables there were carrots, artichokes, asparagus and most of the other species of vegetable known to us today. A lot of fruit was eaten, too, of course. We read of rose-apples, figs from Syria, dates, peaches, cherries, apricots and sweet melons. There were also almonds, walnuts, 'rock-fish' and Egyptian wine.

The maximum-price tablets, fragments of which are continually being unearthed in former Roman provinces, their text engraved sometimes in Latin, sometimes in Greek and sometimes in both languages together, provide us with a complete guide to contemporary modes of travel. There were sleeping-cars, freight-cars and saloon-cars. Axles, wheel-hubs, carriage-seats and horse-shoes (though not of the modern nail-on type) were manufactured. We read of dust covers for litters, hooded cloaks, garments with simple fasteners, short capes and close-fitting underclothes of hare's fur. There was a trade in sheepskin for hats and caps, linen cloths, bedclothes, mattress-covers and pillow-cases, reed pens, ink, and parchment processed with saffron.

One or two of the handicrafts and professions mentioned are also very interesting. There were craftsmen who specialized in marble overlays for floors and walls, mosaic artists, polishers, veterinary surgeons, sheep-shearers, barbers, seamsters, tailors, bath-attendants, schoolmasters and solicitors. As far as the study of economic history is concerned, Diocletian's maximum-price law is the most important and comprehensive piece of evidence to have survived from antiquity.

We do not know how long this law remained in force, but it was probably repealed by 305 at latest, the year of Diocletian's abdication. The stone tablets give us a thousand indications about the life of the time. But they reveal it as a life regimented down to the last detail. Co-ordination was the watchword of the period, and co-ordination involved a general simplification of life within the totalitarian confines of the State, in spite of the distinction still drawn between a slave (*servus*) on the one hand, and a bondsman peasant (*colonus*) or member of a compulsory trade union on the other.

Emperor Diocletian was a staunch believer in the ancient Roman god Jupiter and his proved omnipotence. However, he also recognized the Iranian god Mithras, not merely because Mithras hailed from the East, but because the legionaries were fonder of worshipping him than any other god. The Emperor demanded unconditional obedience or *adoratio*, as it was called in Latin, from all his subjects.

In the year 303, when Diocletian saw that the Roman world was disintegrating under the impact of Christianity, he launched an oppressive campaign against the Christians, probably at the instigation of Galerius. Diocletian's persecution of the Christians had a prologue. One of the Emperor's sacrifices miscarried, and Galerius, who was present, managed to attribute its unfavourable outcome to the clandestine activities of the Christians. All the serving-men and women in the palace were at once ordered to sacrifice to the gods of Rome, and anyone who refused was flogged.

Since it had come to light that the palace itself was cankered by the doctrines of Christianity, the Emperor decided on a 'purification' of the army, and extended the purge to the civil service as well. Compulsory sacrifice throughout the armed forces and the Government resulted in the dismissal of countless nonconformists.

Lactantius, who was born in the Roman province of Africa in A.D. 250 and went over to Christianity in 301, described the horrors of persecution and God's judgment on the persecutors in his above-mentioned work, *How the persecutors died*.

Diocletian was much too clever to decree a Christian 'pogrom' in the grand manner. But in religious conflicts one evil leads to another, and the early morning of February 23rd, 303, saw the ominous beginning of a brutal campaign against the Christians.

Within sight of the imperial palace at Nicomedia stood a Christian basilica. From the palace, the Christians could be seen going to daily service, a peaceful community, but one which was growing at an astonishing rate.

All at once the doors of the church were flung wide. There was a feverish search for 'the effigy of God', sacred texts were burnt and the Emperor's troops, officers and men alike, milled about in disorder, looting and robbing. Shoulder to shoulder, Diocletian's guardsmen marched up with axes and demolition tools, and before many hours were past the tall church had been razed to the ground. The edict of purgation was now extended to the whole Empire. Such Christians as had clung to their civil or military appointments in defiance of the first purge were threatened with imprisonment, but there was no bloodshed as yet.

One courageous Christian in Nicomedia pulled down the proclamation and tore it into little pieces with the scornful words: 'Only victories over Goths and Sarmatae are posted here!' Diocletian and Maximian sentenced him to be burnt at the stake for *lèse-majesté*. There is a report on this in the

Roman martyrology. The Emperors apparently gave orders that 'no form of torture should be left untried, but the man endured them all with such serenity of mind and expression that no one could detect in him the slightest sign of anguish'. He was, Lactantius tells us, 'duly roasted, exhibiting marvellous endurance throughout, and finally burnt to ashes'.

Shortly afterwards Diocletian's palace at Nicomedia was set on fire and the two old Emperors were nearly burnt to death. Diocletian ordered his whole staff to be put to the rack.

After another fortnight had elapsed the palace went up in flames once more. Galerius immediately cast suspicion on the Christians, although, according to Lactantius, 'he had again ordered the fire to be kindled himself'. Lactantius' description is detailed, dramatic and full of fierce vitality, but we have no reason to distrust him, by and large, for he was an eye-witness of these events. Moreover, the Christian historian Eusebius confirms that Galerius was the real instigator of the persecutions.

Diocletian was in a difficult position. Even his wife Prisca and his daughter Valeria had been convinced by the new Christian ideas, and both were secret converts to Christianity. Now they, too, were compelled to do sacrifice. Members of the palace staff who refused to follow their example were tortured to death in the most ingenious manner. Bishop Anthimus of Nicomedia died a martyr's death, and any Christian in that city who fell into the hands of the Emperor's executioners was treated as a convicted incendiary. There was no time for legal proceedings: the slaughter went on without trial or verdict. Diocletian's chamberlain, Petrus, died from the effects of the rack. Donatus, who refused to betray his faith, lay in a dark dungeon for six years, was stretched on the rack no less than nine times, and emerged alive. Dorotheus and Gorgonius, two senior court officials who opposed the persecution of the Christians, were put to death in the most cruel fashion. They were followed by thousands of martyrs, of whom the most famous were St Sebastian and St Agnes who died at Rome, St Lucia at Syracuse, St Catherine at Alexandria and St Barbara at Nicomedia. More Christians died in Egypt, and at Tyre, Saragossa and Trèves, and were 'crowned with the crown of martyrdom'. If the Christians buried those who had died for their faith, the bodies were dug up again and flung into the sea, in case the homage paid to the dead should attract new converts to the Christian religion.

In many parts of the Empire the Christians encountered overt or secret indulgence from officials who were unwilling to participate in the bloodshed. In Gaul and Britain, which were governed by Constantius, churches were pulled down but Christians suffered no bodily harm. There were farcical scenes in several provinces when the governors dragged Christians in front of pagan altars and, having once got them there, released them on the grounds that they had done sacrifice. The Christians repudiated this by loudly reaffirming their faith. On the other hand, there were sadistic governors who invented brand-new methods of torture and execution. When a small town in Phrygia — it may have been Eumenia — resolutely declared for Christianity, it was cordoned off by legionaries and its inhabitants burnt alive. Then there were governors who did their utmost never to put Christians to death, not out of leniency, but cruelty. They bragged that they had never killed a Christian: their ambition was to break the believers' morale. Lactantius reports that when a Christian prisoner 'cracked' after two solid years of resistance, the governor of Bithynia was as proud as if he had defeated a whole tribe of barbarians. Among the most humane governors were those who executed the Christians as quickly and painlessly as possible. But elsewhere, particularly under Galerius' jurisdiction in the East, the witch-hunt raged on a scale hitherto unknown in the Roman Empire. No atrocity was too horrible for the ancient gods of Rome and heathendom as, in their death-throes, they decided to sell their sovereignty as dearly as they could. It was an eye for an eye and a tooth for a tooth. Christianity's triumph was won with pain and anguish, not to the jubilant sound of Sunday hymns.

There was another side to it, of course. We must not forget the Christians' readiness, their willingness to sacrifice themselves — even, in some cases, the way they jostled one another in their eagerness to die a martyr's death. Some believers, especially women, actually clamoured to be executed because they were Christians. Others threw themselves in front of wild beasts in the arenas, and still others were so outspoken that they simply compelled governors to take notice of them and their beliefs.

The Christians never made any concerted attempts to thwart their persecutors by rebellion. They yielded to the heathen authorities and rendered to the Emperor what was the Emperor's. Nevertheless, they showed great courage and endurance. In sublime emulation of Christ, they triumphed by fortitude, not force. Their sheer ability to endure pain was beyond all belief and cannot adequately be described here. These intermediaries between Christ and ourselves, who, by giving their lives for a Christian victory and refusing to let the Gospel be silenced, were directly responsible for passing on to us all the concepts of Christianity — which embraces the bulk of our ideas and of Western culture in general — belonged to a different age from the cynical, sceptical and often faint-hearted age in which we live today. They clung tenaciously to their point of view, and died for it because they

Emperor Diocletian (reigned A.D. 284–305) had an amazing gift for organization. He ruled the world for twenty years and then retired to his palace at Salonae in modern Yugoslavia. Only very few sculptures of this unique historical figure exist

Constantius Chlorus, born in Illyria, was nominated by Diocletian as Caesar of the West. His wife Helena, who built numerous Christian churches and was later canonized, bore him a son who was to become Constantine the Great. Constantius was a victorious general of great ability and a magnanimous ruler. He died in Britain, at York

The Porta Nigra at Trèves was the most massive gatehouse ever built by the Romans and formed part of the imposing city fortifications constructed in the 4th century A.D. It is possible that the gate was built by Constantine

firmly believed that eternal bliss awaited them when they had drawn their last breath. But this belief in a reward hereafter cannot diminish the merits of their self-sacrifice. The very existence of such a faith is marvellous enough. It demonstrates Christ's enormous influence, the stupendous power of his initial impact on the world, his amazing spiritual strength. It explains how Christianity was able to set out on its everlasting journey through time and eternity.

Emperor Diocletian at first restrained the outbursts of hatred against the Christians in Nicomedia. He wanted to keep the situation under control. His second edict did no more than order the arrest of Christian clergy. One repeatedly gets the impression that Diocletian himself was in favour of moderation. It must be admitted, in all fairness, that to call him 'heathen' is something of a prejudgment. Far from being 'superstitious', he was a man who had an implicit faith in the gods of Rome, the gods who had made Rome great, the elder deities invoked by Romans and those who wanted to be Romans. The African author Arnobius gave an intelligent, forceful and courageous exposé of their failings in a seven-volume work written at the height of the persecutions in 305: 'Your cause, too, was new when it began. But the value of a religion must not be judged by its god, nor by its duration, and it matters not on what day one begins to worship, but whom one worships. Is anyone older than He? To whom does eternity owe that which makes it eternity? Is it not His uninterrupted existence which ensures that the everlasting ages continue to unfold? But your gods were men. For where there are weddings, marriages, births, wet-nurses, handicrafts and infirmities, where conditions of liberty and slavery prevail, where wounds, blows, blood, amours, desires and sensuality are, where all emotions are borne of changeability, there nothing divine can exist.'

Diocletian thought otherwise. The tall, lean man with the pale face and the powerful nose was firmly rooted in the ancient beliefs. He respected the ancient religion, watched anxiously for divine omens, and gazed with half-tremulous curiosity at the entrails of slaughtered animals for manifestations of the will of Heaven. His real hatred was reserved for the Manicheans, members of the Persian sect which followed the religious founder Mani. Diocletian burnt these men alive with their scriptures, executed them or sentenced them to penal servitude in the mines, seeing in them not only religious fanatics but political enemies who were supporters and agents of the Persian King. To his way of thinking, there was inherent in any propagation of the Manichean religion a danger that the gods of Persia and his Persian enemy would gain ground. Jupiter, and only Jupiter, was Diocletian's god and the tutelary god of the Empire. Firmly believing that Jupiter had made him great, he wanted to safeguard the ancient forms of worship.

Diocletian was not prone to religious ecstasy, not a fanatic, anything but a visionary. As a hard-headed organizer, he was quite unimpressed by Christianity. The idea of adopting new gods, let alone *one* incomprehensible foreign god, seemed far too chancy. It might mean courting the vengeance of the ancient Roman pantheon. Diocletian's faith in the perpetuity of Roman civilization, the Latin tongue and Rome's world mission was unshakeable. He is the only emperor in late antiquity who was still anxious to carry out a Roman political concept. The Graeco-Byzantine State in the East was a counter-blow to the ideals of this last genuine prophet of Romanism.

In the year of the Christian persecutions, Diocletian met Maximian at Rome to celebrate the twentieth anniversary of his reign. His mental condition was disturbed and growing worse all the time. A year later, while travelling to Nicomedia, he suffered a nervous breakdown and nearly died.

It is uncertain what actually happened, but the Emperor may have had a seizure or perhaps a stroke. On December 13th, 304, prayers were said for him in the expectation that his end was near. But it was as if the Emperor's mental powers had rallied in sympathy, for, though a shadow of his former self and greatly weakened in health, he appeared in public again on March 1st, 305. Two months later, on May 1st, he and his co-Emperor abdicated with due ceremony. Maximian resigned at Milan. Diocletian's formal abdication took place at the foot of a hill not far from Nicomedia, in front of the army which he had led to so many victories. With tears in his eyes he declared that he was old, ailing and in need of rest.

The two 'Caesars', Constantius and Galerius, now stepped into the shoes of their seniors and a second tetrarchy or rule of four was born.

For twenty years Diocletian had ruled the world. For twenty years he had defended the Empire and built up his vast and formidable administrative machine. Now, after twenty years, the great planner was retiring to Salonae in his native Dalmatia, just as he had envisaged long ago when he formed the tetrarchy.

All the old man wanted was complete peace and quiet. He was determined to enjoy his retirement, too, which was why he had taken the precaution of building the vast palace at Salonae. It was designed, in keeping with his thorough and orderly nature, on the austere lines of a Roman camp. Diocletian's palace was, in fact, castle, country house and town all rolled into one. The soldier-emperor wanted to live in a fortress because he was concerned for his personal safety. There were many secret Christians at court, and Diocletian still did not trust Christians.

The east and west sides of the palace were over 700 feet long, and the whole structure formed a trapezoid or irregular-sided quadrangle. The massive walls enclosing it on the north, east and west were nearly seven feet thick. The south face of the palace, which looked out over the sea, was eighty feet high and just under 600 feet long.

Thirty feet above the ground and built into the side facing the sea was a pillared gallery with twenty-four arches. There the old Emperor strolled up and down, day after day, a prey to depressing thoughts and disquieting memories, gazing out to sea and listening to the muffled roar of the waves pounding away at the foundations of his giant's castle.

Advancing age had made the Emperor increasingly cautious and mistrustful. An underground passage leading to the sea provided him with instant means of escape in case of emergency.

The fortified palace of Salonae was so enormous that during the Middle Ages a whole town grew up around and inside it. This was the town of Spalato, or what is now Split in Yugoslavia. As late as 1926, the old palace still contained 278 houses and 3,200 inhabitants. No modern visitor to Diocletian's massive sea-side retreat can fail to be amazed by the Emperor's will to build.

Diocletian's living-quarters in the south face contained all that an emeritus ruler of the world could want: a *triclinium* (dining-room), *cubicula* (bedchambers), *nymphaea* (halls with pools, fountains and statues), *bibliothecae* (libraries), *balnea* (baths) — every possible comfort and amenity known to Roman and Hellenistic architecture.

Along the inside of the walls at ground level ran store-rooms, granaries, slaves' quarters, stables and bake-houses, while the upper storey provided accommodation for officers and courtiers. (The Emperor had brought his whole court with him.)

Three large gates led into the palace. The main gate, which faced Salonae, was the famed Porta Aurea, some fifteen feet high and thirteen feet wide. Diggings undertaken between 1904 and 1910 have established that this gate went down for another nine feet below the surface.

Diocletian installed a temple to Jupiter in the palace so that he could always be close to the ancient Roman god whom he worshipped.

An aqueduct five miles long, running partly beneath the ground and partly high above it, brought fresh water to the palace from the river Jadar. For 730 yards of its journey this conduit was supported on arches whose pillars soared, in places, to a height of fifty-five feet. What is more, when the aqueduct was restored in 1878–9, one-third of its original length needed virtually no repairs before use. Water was important to the old Emperor because the ruling passion and greatest solace of his latter years was his vegetable garden.

Freemen and slaves, Greek master-craftsmen and Greek artisans, local masons and stone-porters all worked on Diocletian's palace. The masonry for the walls was obtained from neighbouring quarries, but the material for all the pillars — rose-granite, porphyry, grey, red and white marble — came from marble quarries in Egypt. Colossal statues were also ferried across from Egypt to beautify the place.

The Emperor's retirement was destined to be disturbed only once. In response to an urgent request, he hurried to a conference at Carnuntum on the Danube to help Galerius restore internal order. He declined an invitation to reassume the office of Emperor, only to see his great system decay, and his wife and daughter victimized and brutally murdered while on their way to visit him.

Diocletian's mind was clouded now. He tottered through the halls of his immense palace shouting unintelligible names. He could not grasp how the gigantic political edifice which he had built to last for all time could be crumbling away so quickly. He died — the almost incredible exception in a long series of emperors who were murdered to a man — quite alone.

Inside the palace at Salonae Diocletian had built himself an octagonal mausoleum enclosed by twenty-four pillars. In the middle, beneath the central dome, may have stood the dark-red porphyry sarcophagus of the mighty champion of the spirit of ancient Rome. The imperial coffin was screened by purple hangings. When the rays of the setting sun fell on it through the one small half-oval window, the gloomy twilight inside became a ruddy gold. The Emperor meant to lie there in everlasting peace, but his repose was brusquely disturbed just over a century later, when his sarcophagus was stolen.

Even in death, Christianity wreaked its revenge on him. The Emperor who had wanted to save the Roman world and the gods of Rome from extinction and had yearned to sleep in his mausoleum under the protection of those gods lost the final battle. His last resting-place was transformed into a Christian church, the Cathedral of Spalato.

CONSTANTINE

THE WORLD'S FIRST CHRISTIAN EMPEROR

About the hour of noon, when the day was already declining, the Emperor had seen with his own eyes, so he said, the victorious emblem of the Cross formed out of light, up in the sky above the sun, and near it the words: 'Through this sign you will conquer'.

Eusebius, Life of Constantine, I, xxviii.

OLD Emperor Diocletian whiled away the time in his palace at Salonae, the largest in the contemporary world, planting magnificent vegetable gardens and keeping a remote eye on the turbulent world which had given him so much to do in the past. Did he really think that his four-emperor system was going to last? Did he foresee the collapse of his new order? Or did he regard the framework of his vast administration as indestructible?

His great colleague Maximian had followed his example and laid aside the purple, just as the two supreme masters of the Empire had agreed long ago. But at the time of the double abdication Maximian was still interested in government. His health was probably stronger than Diocletian's, and he had not lost his taste for forging plans and playing the great game of imperial chess in which the pawns were countries, armies and enemies. He craved a life of action. Inactivity, leisure and 'honourable retirement' were abhorrent to him, and we shall soon see how long such a man could tolerate voluntary exile.

Once more there were four rulers, two Augusti or senior emperors, and two Caesars or assistant emperors. It was another tetrarchy on the Diocletian pattern, though the two Augusti, Constantius in the West and Galerius in the East were quite dissimilar in character.

Constantius, the elder, was a man of education, poise and good taste, for all that his Illyrian parents bore an undistinguished name. He was big-hearted and loved good wine, good living and pretty girls. He had distinguished himself as a young general in Illyricum, where he had occupied a senior appointment. It is uncertain whether the general brought his young mistress, Flavia Helena, with him when he moved to Naissus (modern Nisch) or whether he first met her there in the Roman fortress on the banks of the Nissava. At all events, she was the daughter of an innkeeper, and her

Illyrian lover, being of humble origins himself, was very happy with her. Constantius never married Helena, but there was no stigma attached to concubinage, governors and army officers being at that time debarred under Roman law from contracting *iustum matrimonium* with local women. Constantius and Helena were heathens, but the child that lay in its cradle at Naissus was destined to become the world's first Christian Emperor.

Helena was the truly inspired woman who later found Christianity through her son, built numerous churches (among them the Church of the Nativity at Bethlehem), rediscovered Christ's cross and was eventually canonized. When Constantius was admitted into the tetrarchy by Emperor Diocletian he had to repudiate his beloved Helena and marry Theodora, the daughter of his senior emperor, Maximian. His legal wife bore him two sons and three daughters. Constantine, Constantius' first child, having been born outside the sacred bounds of Diocletian's political system, was separated from his parents and his step-brothers and sisters and brought up by strangers. The boy could not, therefore, have been exposed to any early pro-Christian influence on his father's part. However, his father had an instinctive feeling for the religious climate of his day. He had shown the Christians that heathens, too, could be tolerant. Like other Romans in authority, he had been obliged to pull down many churches in the course of Diocletian's anti-Christian campaign, but he never sentenced any believers to death. As a worshipper of the Sun-god he was a heathen with monotheistic leanings, like Seneca, Epictetus, Marcus Aurelius, Apollonius of Tyana and Plotinus. His son later liked to paint him as the first Christian emperor. 'My father alone practised works of gentleness and invoked the Saviour with admirable piety in all his actions.' It is worth noting that Constantius called one of his daughters Anastasia, a name which was only favoured by Jews and Christians at that time. He is also said to have summoned Christian priests to his court.

In very recent times a new bust of the Emperor has been discovered in England. Constantius Chlorus (his surname meant 'pale') reconquered Britain for Rome. He sailed up the Thames and stood on the site of London. What is more, he died in England, at Eboracum (York), the very same town where Emperor Septimius Severus had breathed his last.

Emperor Galerius was quite another character. He was hard and merciless. Lack of forethought frequently led him to commit blunders, but he was incredibly ambitious and persecuted the Christians ruthlessly in the years 303–4. He was the Caesar who convinced Diocletian of the need for a reign of terror. The self-assurance with which he had persecuted the Christians was matched by his cock-sure attitude towards his new mission as Augustus and one of the senior members of the tetrarchy. Regarding himself as Diocletian's successor and leader of the imperial team, he acted as such without bothering to consult Constantius, his partner in the West, who being the elder, was really entitled to the senior position.

The two Augusti, pale Constantius in Gaul and robust Galerius on the Danube, watched one another suspiciously. A factor which heightened the tension was that the new assistant emperors or Caesars, Severus and Daia, were cat's-paws of Galerius and blindly devoted to him. As a consequence, Galerius was virtually sole master of a world ruled by four emperors. Constantius could not do anything which did not suit Galerius, and every move he made was carefully noted by Galerius' two henchmen.

Constantius was in a strait-jacket. His son Constantine was at Galerius' court, in the power of his undeclared enemy. The boy had grown up in the East, away from his father and his mother Helena. He had gone through a hard school and received his military training under Diocletian. There at Nicomedia, in the palace of the great man who was shaping and reorganizing the world, he saw world policy in the making and felt the hot, exciting breath of history on his cheek. As an outsider and the son of a woman unrecognized by the tetrarchy, he was kept under strict and unremitting supervision. There came a day when he was promoted to '*tribunus primi ordinis*', and there is little doubt that Diocletian's keen eye sometimes lighted on the tall, handsome, fair-haired youth as a potential successor. But it could not be. The tetrarchy was not a hereditary system and senior emperors could not select a Caesar from their family circle, so the young man had the disappointment of seeing himself passed over time and time again. He was present when Diocletian abdicated and appointed Daia 'Caesar' instead of him. From then on he was obliged to stay with Galerius, still under the same careful observation. Invisible chains bound him to Galerius' court like a hostage, for his presence there guaranteed the suspicious Emperor immunity from any hostile move on the part of Constantius. True, the brave and ambitious young man was given a senior post at Galerius' court and distinguished himself in battle against the Sarmatae on the Danube frontier, but he was never allowed to evade the watchful attentions of the Emperor or his spies.

Meanwhile, Constantius was preparing for an expedition against the Picts and Scots in Britain. We now come to a most interesting moment in world history. Constantius sent messengers to Galerius requesting his imperial colleague point-blank to send his son over to assist him in his campaign. Galerius was in an awkward position. He could not refuse to release

Constantine: that would have been construed as open hostility. But to grant Constantius' request was to give father and son freedom of action. Always an ugly customer in a tight spot, Galerius chose a third course. To reach his father, Constantine would have to pass through territory under the control of Severus. Galerius sent him off on his long journey, but apparently instructed Severus to have him intercepted and arrested on the way. Only this would explain why Constantine hurried furtively from one post-station to the next like a criminal on the run, always killing off his exhausted horses so that his pursuers could not use them.

The long-awaited meeting between father and son took place on the coast at Boulogne, just before the crossing was made. Constantine fought the British tribes at his father's side. The young man was very popular with the troops, who were mainly Germans, and Crocus or Erocus, a friendly Alemannic prince, looked on him as the future Augustus, as did his own father. When, after a long illness, Constantius finally died at Eboracum, the Romans' barbarian army at once proclaimed Constantine Emperor. It was July 25th, 306. Once more a delegation set off on the long journey to Galerius with orders to inform him of what had happened and request his confirmation. Galerius reacted with great cunning. He appointed his faithful henchman Severus 'Augustus' or senior emperor, and recognized Constantine as a Caesar. Constantine declared himself satisfied with his subordinate status. He possessed, as his best modern biographer, Josef Vogt, emphasizes, 'the happy knack of being able to wait'. His father's death had put new heart into the Alemanni and the Franks, but he attacked without delay. Capturing their kings, Ascarius and Ragaisus, he threw them into the dark dungeons of the amphitheatre at Trèves and had them torn to pieces by wild animals in the arena there. He reorganized the Rhine fleet and built a bridge across the river near Cologne.

While all this was going on, ex-Emperor Maximian, who had withdrawn from public affairs at the same time as Diocletian, was at home on his country estate in Lucania in southern Italy. He was restive. He, too, had a son, Maxentius. He found it hard to understand why Constantius' illegitimate offspring should have been proclaimed Emperor and had his Caesarship confirmed by Galerius when his own son had been denied such an honour. Maxentius bided his time in the vicinity of Rome, while his father forged plans and brooded angrily in southern Italy.

Severus, who governed Italy, was exceedingly unpopular at Rome. Rome's importance as a world centre had already been short-circuited by Maximian's choice of Milan as his official residence. Diocletian had always ruled far from Rome, and the city and its inhabitants had made a poor impression on him when he paid them a visit. Severus now proposed to disband the Roman guards and subject Italy to a penal level of taxation. The Romans' embitterment knew no bounds. Rome was an imperial city, the city which had made the Empire great. Rome was due to celebrate another century of existence in the coming year, and her inhabitants wanted to be able to hold up their heads proudly, citizens of an imperial city once more. The guardsmen refused to let themselves be disbanded. They defiantly stayed put, and Maxentius, who was conveniently to hand, was proclaimed Emperor. Rome had regained her imperial status for the last time.

This time, Galerius was unco-operative. He had reluctantly sanctioned Constantine's promotion, but now he decided to show his claws. Although Maxentius was his son-in-law, being the husband of his daughter by his first marriage, he had an irresolute, unsoldierly nature — well compensated by arrogance — which Galerius particularly detested. He ordered Severus to march against him. Maxentius and his father made an efficient combination, however. They managed to capture Severus by a ruse and put him to death just as Emperor Galerius himself was taking the field against them.

Odd things happened in those days, and no holds were barred in an imperial wrestling-match. Ex-Emperor Maximian won Constantine over to his own and his son's side by giving him his daughter's hand in marriage. Fausta, as she was called, was not yet of marriageable age, but Constantine was obviously very much in love with her and had been engaged to her since his boyhood days. Maximian, old age and impatience getting the better of him, proclaimed Constantine 'Augustus' on condition that his new son-in-law accorded him the same status. The bond between the two men was duly sealed by public professions of mutual esteem. But old Maximian's cup of contentment could never be full while his son was still lording it at Rome. Arriving there after a hurried journey, he tore the imperial purple from Maxentius' shoulders in the presence of his assembled troops. However, Rome's legionaries were on the son's side, not the father's. Maxentius was their own Emperor, whereas Maximian had always ruled from Milan. The old man had miscalculated and, being in the weaker position, was forced to flee. He sought refuge with his son-in-law Constantine.

The tetrarchy was in ruins. Diocletian's grand design had collapsed. It had never been anticipated that an ex-emperor would re-emerge from oblivion with an unabated thirst for power. Only a *deus ex machina* could save the day, and Emperor Galerius decided to produce one. He invoked the aid of Jupiter himself, or rather 'Jovius', the old pensioner of Salonae. Almost a forgotten man after his three years of retirement, Emperor Diocletian was invited to attend a conference at Carnuntum in the year 308. Carnuntum was the most important Roman fortress on the Danube front. It stood on the present site of Petronell and Bad Deutsch-Altenburg, twenty-six miles east of Vienna. Diocletian left his majestic palace by the sea and travelled to the Danube as a private citizen to preside over the celebrated conference, at which Maximian and Galerius were present. It was the last time anyone managed to coax him away from his vegetable-gardens and into the world of imperial administration.

To stroll through the ruins of Carnuntum, to see the foundation-stones of the fine palaces and houses there, to trace the outlines of the army camp, to stand in the silent arenas of the once-pulsing civil or military amphitheatres and absorb their atmosphere, to read the intensely human messages of filial and parental affection on the numerous tombstones, or visit the *Museum Carnuntinum*, Austria's newest museum devoted to Roman history, and stand in front of the altar to Mithras, is to be brought strangely close to the vanished age of Rome. There on the altar-stone, consecrated in the year 308, are engraved the names of Diocletian, Maximian, Galerius and Licinius. It was there that old Diocletian himself once stood. It was there in Carnuntum that he said, when the discussions were at their height, 'If only you would grow cabbages far away in Salonae, as I do, you would be the better for it.' Mommsen once said of Carnuntum: 'The Viennese have a Pompeii on their doorstep, but they do not know how to make the most of it.' Well, today they do. A whole world lies there, unearthed before our eyes: religious sculptures and consecrated altars, statues and statuettes, dancing maenads and stark torsos, coins, bowls, jugs, urns, glass beakers, glass bottles, spoons, tweezers, surgical instruments. The visitor to Carnuntum will carry away with him a vivid impression of the decisive influence exerted on the world by Roman emperors far from home, of the efforts they made to defend the Danube frontier, and of the immeasurable strength with which the long arm of Rome's civilization and creative energy thrust its way into what was once barbarian territory. He will also realize that, even for an old and weary emperor like Diocletian, distances simply did not exist.

The results of the conference were threefold: Maximian had to promise to retire from politics for good; Licinius (one of Galerius' comrades-in-arms) was promoted to Augustus in place of the murdered Severus; and Maxentius, the Roman rebel, was declared a public enemy.

The old fox had once more brought his matchless genius for administration to bear on a disintegrating world. He had restored order. But several men

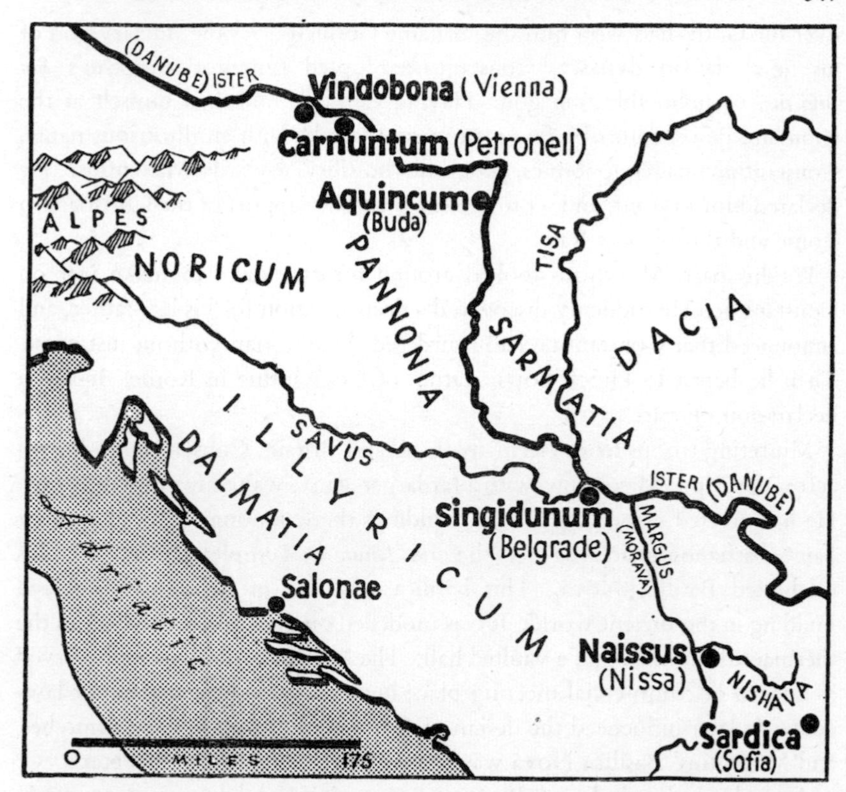

Salonae (modern Split in Yugoslavia) is the site of an impressive palace which Emperor Diocletian built *circa* A.D. 300 and to which he retired after his abdication in the year 305. *Carnuntum*, the most important Roman fortress on the Danube front (near what are now Petronell and Deutsch-Altenburg), witnessed the famous Conference of the Three Emperors in A.D. 308. Those present included Diocletian, Maximian and Galerius. Constantine the Great was born at *Naissus* (modern Nisch)

were missing from the conference couches at Canuntum, ambitious rulers who still wanted to transform the world or make it tremble.

Jealousy raised its head once more. Naturally enough, Constantine and Daia did not take kindly to Licinius' sudden promotion to 'Augustus'. Constantine felt slighted. Both he and Daia wanted full imperial rank. As for Maximian, the turbulent old man found retirement as distasteful as ever. He tried to turn his daughter Fausta against her husband and stirred up insurrection among his son-in-law's troops, but was captured and ultimately executed.

Constantine now broke away from the whole chaotic system. He announced that he was descended from Emperor Claudius II, whose victories over the Goths had won him the surname Gothicus. As the tutelary god of his new Flavian dynasty, Constantine adopted Emperor Aurelian's *Sol Invictus*, or invincible Sun-god. Having calmly established himself as the scion and descendant of a famous imperial family with an illustrious name, Constantine made no bones about his hostility towards Maxentius. He declared him a tyrant, and set to work to win the support of the Christians in Rome and throughout Italy.

For his part, Maxentius looked around for an excuse to make war on Constantine. He suddenly discovered a deep affection for his late father, and announced that Constantine had murdered the old man without just cause. Then he began to knock down statues of Constantine in Rome. It was a declaration of war.

Mustering troops from Germany, Gaul and Britain, Constantine led them across the Alps. Maxentius, with a far larger army, waited for him in Rome. He had erected some magnificent buildings there, among them a Circus at San Sebastiano outside the city, the *urbis fanum* or Temple of Rome, and his celebrated Basilica Nova. This basilica was the most massive covered building in the ancient world. It was modelled on the great bathrooms in the thermae and consisted of a vaulted hall. The Roman basilica not only served as a social or commercial meeting-place but also housed the *tribunal* or law-court. It later influenced the design of Christian basilicas, or early churches, and Maxentius' Basilica Nova was Michelangelo's model for St Peter's.

As we have already heard, Rome was preparing to celebrate a centenary in the year 313. She was anxious to regain her status as queen and focal point of the world, but to do so she needed a victorious emperor with an illustrious name. Her citizens at first thought that Maxentius was the answer to their prayers, but they soon found out that their idol was nothing but a ruthless, vicious and self-seeking despot.

Constantine arrived outside Rome with 90,000 infantry and 8,000 cavalry. Maxentius, whose forces numbered 170,000 and 18,000 respectively, decided to shut himself up in the city, and accordingly demolished the bridge across the Tiber. His plan was to repel all Constantine's attacks from within the impregnable confines of the metropolis. There he stayed, sacrificing to the gods and poring over the Sibylline Books. Sibylla is a very ancient name which originated among the eastern Greeks in Asia Minor, and the Sibyls were prophetesses and priestesses of Apollo whose inspired predictions are described by Virgil in the Aeneid. Maxentius read in their pagan prophecies that he was bound to repel Rome's attackers. He had built a pontoon-bridge across the Tiber, chained together in two sections so that it could be cut apart in case of necessity. Now he led his army across it and engaged the enemy on the other side of the Tiber by the Pons Mulvius.

Constantine's first move was to launch a cavalry attack. His infantry followed it up in good order.

His legionaries were inspired by something hitherto unknown, something new and irresistible which gave them an overwhelming superiority in courage and morale. Maxentius' troops fought badly, eager to be rid of their tyrannical master. Their ranks wavered, then broke, and the whole army streamed back across the bridge into the city. The bridge parted and Maxentius plunged to a watery death in the Tiber. Nobody dared to evince any joy when the news of his death filtered into the streets of Rome. The citizens were obviously terrified of Maxentius and doubted the truth of the report. Writing in about 450, the Greek historian Zosimus painted a graphic picture of the atmosphere in the city. Not until Maxentius' head was exhibited on the end of a spear did the paeans of rejoicing burst forth.

Constantine executed a number of his late adversary's supporters. The Senate rededicated Maxentius' buildings to him and proclaimed him supreme Augustus. On October 29th, 312, the Emperor made a triumphal entry into Rome, where he was hailed as a liberator and harbinger of peace. He led his army along the Via Flaminia and into the city through the Porta Triumphalis. 'Constantine's Arch' was, in fact, started by Maxentius on his own behalf. It was not completed until 315, three years after the triumph itself.

A Roman triumph was invariably accompanied by a visit to the Capitol, where the victorious Emperor was expected to sacrifice to the supreme god. Constantine, however, waived the visit to the Capitol and did not offer sacrifice. This was unusual, for the whole of the heathen world expected him to do so as a matter of course, especially since it was his first visit to Rome. The Senate, in particular, deep-rooted in the Roman faith, viewed any recognition of the ancient gods with satisfaction. But Constantine avoided the Capitoline temple. Something extraordinary must have taken place inside him before the battle of the Mulvian Bridge. So it appeared, at least, and so legend would have us believe. Scholars have written numerous works on the subject of this inner transformation and modern authorities believe that we are very near the heart of the mystery. It is easy to understand why so many theologians and historians have been preoccupied with Constantine's religious experience. We are products of an age which is poor in faith, barren of great religious experience, hungry for revelation, lacking in inner perception. Vision is something almost totally denied to our age of speed, logic and scepticism. But, apart from Christ's influence and the conversion of St Paul,

Constantine's spiritual transformation was the most momentous religio-psychological event in world history. In the year 312, before the battle of the Mulvian Bridge, the Roman Emperor from Illyria became the first ruler in the world to recognize the omnipotence of the Christian god. Eusebius, the ablest and most prolific author in the Christianized Roman Empire and a contemporary and favourite of Constantine, describes the Emperor's experience as a vision. Lactantius, who was also alive at this time, differs from Eusebius in calling the medium of Constantine's revelation a dream.

Apparently, Constantine saw a phenomenon of light — a sign made up of sun and cross united in the sky — and was told in his sleep to put the heavenly symbol on his soldiers' shields. Constantine complied with this suggestion and ordered his men to carve the Greek letter χ on their shields — representing the *ch* in Christ's name. At the top of the rising stroke he added a hook to express the letter *r* in 'Christ', thus transforming the emblem into a sort of monogram: ☧.

Further evidence of Constantine's vision is supplied by his military helmet, which also bore a replica of the two initial letters in Christ's name, the Greek letters *chi* and *rho*. Portrayals of the Emperor's monogrammed helmet can still be seen on coins minted only a few years after the battle at the Pons Mulvius. The battle was fought in 312. Three years later, in 315, the silver medallion of Ticinum was struck. It displayed, at the tip of the crest on the Emperor's helmet, the monogram ☧. In this case the *rho* was vertically superimposed on the *chi*, but they still represented the first two letters in Christ's name. An example of this early Christian emblem is to be found in the State Numismatic Collection at Munich.

Is Constantine's vision authentic or apocryphal? Did he really see it? Was it fact or fiction?

Our most important source, Eusebius' *Vita Constantini*, is still an object of controversy today. Eusebius, who was one of the leading scholars of his day, pursued his biblical studies in Palestine, at the theological school in Caesarea. The school had been founded by a man called Pamphilus (hence Eusebius' surname 'Pamphili') and possessed one of the most famous libraries in the contemporary world, the library of Origen, the father of the Church. Origen was tortured during the Christian persecutions under Emperor Decius, and died in 254 as a result of his maltreatment.

Eusebius (circa 260–340) wrote a number of important works. His *Life of Constantine* is a true hymn to the triumph of Christianity — with the emphasis on 'true', for modern scholars are becoming increasingly convinced that all Eusebius' main assertions are correct.

However, a number of authorities seek to prove that Eusebius did not write the *Vita Constantini* at all. Had such a work existed in the fourth century, they say, it would have been mentioned or quoted by authors of that period. Because fourth-century authors make no reference to a biography of Constantine by Eusebius, their silence is taken to imply that the work was a Christian forgery of later date. The Belgian scholar Henri Grégoire makes out an erudite and ingenious case for this point of view.

But Eusebius was a pious man, and, to him, love of truth and Christianity went hand in hand. He was writing about an age in which he himself lived and a man whom he knew extremely well. Constantine told him all about his vision of the cross in the sky with his own lips. According to Eusebius, before his battle against Maxentius at the Mulvian Bridge, the Emperor called upon God to reveal to him who HE was. While Constantine was praying, a divine symbol appeared to him. High in the sky above the sun he saw, formed by light, the victorious emblem of the cross, and near it the words 'Through this sign you will conquer' or, in Latin, '*in hoc signo vinces*'.

Constantine certainly told people about his vision. On that point there is general agreement. Whether the vision was genuine, on the other hand, is a matter of interpretation. No vision can be anything but *subjectively* genuine, i.e. genuine only so far as the recipient is concerned, and every vision presupposes a *readiness* to receive it. What will always remain a mystery, of course, is the connection between visual image and subjective idea, the way in which one arises from the other, and the part played by the extrasensory factor which we call divine power. The important question is whether Constantine was expecting such a vision, whether he was ready for it, whether he wanted to see the sign of the only true god, whether he talked about it, whether he believed in it. Remarkably enough, modern authorities are coming to the conclusion that the vision was genuine and not fabricated, simply because the former assumption is more probable. Heinz Kraft argues very convincingly that the invention of visions does not fit in with Constantine's personality. 'The vision is spendidly attested, and Constantine's Christianity after 312 cannot seriously be disputed.' Kornemann, the well-known classical historian, says: 'It is a vital and no longer deniable fact that the god of Christianity was made manifest to the soul of the greatest and most powerful man of his time, and became a personal experience.'

The views of Burckhardt, who regarded the Emperor as a clever practical politician and a brilliant, if irreligious and self-seeking man, have now been completely superseded. Jakob Burckhardt, Swiss historian, art expert and philosopher, unfortunately saw in Constantine a man whose religion was either second-hand or superstitious and who made the most of Christianity purely for political ends. Henri Grégoire's verdict on the vision of the cross is that it was a piece of apocryphal, tendentious and utterly worthless legend.

The fact that the vision has acquired a legendary flavour over the years and that the Emperor's conversion strikes one as abrupt and almost miraculous is due to the lack of attention bestowed upon Constantine's spiritual development. His gravitation towards Christianity was not an abrupt step but the logical outcome of his sense of mission, his 'growing Christianization and belief in his own calling' (Heinz Kraft), not a feat of spiritual gymnastics, but a slow and gradual process. Finally, Constantine was deeply aware of his vocation and must have had an abundant source of inner strength. That alone could explain his decision to do battle with Maxentius in the year 312, when his prospects looked so bleak. Rome was thought to be impregnable, the opposing forces were numerically superior, and experience gained in numerous German campaigns could not be put to advantage in besieging the most modern fortress in the world. And, apart from anything else, the heathen prophets or *haruspices* had advised the Emperor not to open hostilities.

So it was his sense of mission alone which spurred him on. That was why he embarked upon the most vital struggle in his life under the emblem of the invisible god, and why he turned increasingly towards Christ, God's mediator, whose doctrines and adherents no emperor before him had ever managed to eradicate.

Constantine knew all that. He had seen the futility of Christian persecution while at the courts of Diocletian and Galerius. As a young man who probably, even at that stage, sympathized with the Christians, he had detested both men. And who knows what he saw and never gave away? An extremely interesting discovery was made in Diocletian's palace at Split. On one of the bricks was scratched the outline of a fish rather like a dolphin. Everything indicated that the sign had been left there in great haste, possibly in fear, and whoever was responsible had turned the brick round so that the fish faced inwards and was hidden from sight. The fish, usually represented as a dolphin, was the emblem of Christ, because the Greek word for fish — *ichthus* — contained the initial letters of the expression *Iesos Christos Theou Uios Soter*, 'Jesus Christ, God's son, Redeemer'. We shall never know who felt impelled to bear witness to his secret love for Christ while the palace was being built, but Constantine probably saw many such evidences of hidden faith during his young days at court there, and they must have given him food for thought. Two additional factors were the influence of his tolerant father and the tragic death of Galerius, the anti-Christian Emperor. Galerius died in

Constantine the Great, the world's first Christian emperor. By linking Christianity and throne together for the first time in history he became the pioneer of a new era. Recent research has greatly enhanced our understanding of this emperor

The Praetorians formed the bodyguard of the Roman emperors. They served for sixteen years, received treble pay, were permitted to wear sumptuous armour, golden accoutrements and tall plumes, and frequently influenced accession to the throne by selling their allegiance to the highest bidder. Their normal strength was ten cohorts each of five hundred men (or, from the time of Septimius Severus onwards, about a thousand). Constantine disbanded the Praetorian Guard in the year A.D. 312

frightful agony, a victim of cancer. In his terror, he imagined that the dread disease had been sent by the god of the Christians. And so, on April 30th, 311, shortly before his death, the brutal persecutor of the Christians issued an edict granting religious freedom to all believers.

All this must have left its mark on Constantine, quite apart from the fact that the world had reached a critical point in its spiritual development. Constantine had himself passed some well-defined landmarks in his intellectual career. He had groped his way forward slowly and cautiously. He had believed in Jupiter, Hercules and Apollo. Then he had reached something much nearer Christianity, a monotheistic belief in the invisible, invincible Sun-god. He ended by identifying the invisible Sun-god with the god of Christianity. That was why his sacred emblem may also have been a cross without a tip: $\hat{\mathrm{T}}$ — a T surmounted by the sun. As yet, Constantine made no explicit mention of Christ's name. That would have been forcing the pace. The Senate was still unconverted, as were most of the Empire's inhabitants. Hence the inscription on Constantine's triumphal arch: 'By inspiration of the deity'. The sculptural ornamentation on it was still appropriate to the Sun-god. But the expression 'deity' in the dedicatory text distinctly shows that the point of transition between Sun-worship and Christianity had been reached.

Constantine probably believed with all sincerity that he owed his victory to the Christian god, for he handed over the Lateran, Empress Fausta's palace, to the Pope as an episcopal residence. According to Roman Catholic tradition, there has been a papacy ever since the time of St Peter, over whose grave stands the great church which was named after him and begun by Constantine in 324. Constantine also authorized the building of the Lateran Basilica, 'mother and chief of all Christian churches'. Finally, he returned all property confiscated from the Christian communities in Africa and exempted ecclesiastical dignitaries from taxation.

The man who linked Christianity and the crown for the first time in history became the pioneer of a new world era.

SUBLIME HAPPINESS

He alone among Roman emperors worshipped God the supreme lord with extraordinary piety, he alone proclaimed with candour the teaching of Christ, he alone glorified his Church like none other within the memory of man, he alone eradicated every error of polytheism and all kinds of idolatry.

Eusebius, Vita Constantini, lv, 75.

CONSTANTINE'S vision was a watershed in world history. It marked the moment when the sign of the Cross was handed over to Western civilization. If the transformation of gods and symbols was a gradual and carefully controlled process, it was only due to Constantine's remarkably keen instinct for what the Roman Empire would tolerate and what it was ready to accept. We now accept the Cross as a matter of course. But we can scarcely assess what it meant for the emperor of a heathen world first to find his way inwardly to this symbol of an alien religion and then to give his spiritual discovery practical expression.

All attacks on our chief witness, Eusebius, have foundered to a greater or lesser extent for lack of evidence. In the opinion of Vogt, the great expert on Constantine who has spent many years in intensive research, no convincing textual refutation of Eusebius' authorship has ever been produced. His touching, almost naïve sincerity, his directness and his jubilant tone are all unmistakable pointers. Eusebius was a friend and contemporary of the Emperor — an eye-witness, one might say: that was why he wrote with such realism.

Modern textual research has again veered towards Eusebius and acknowledged Emperor Constantine as a Christian monarch. Constantine's conversion to Christianity is regarded as sincere and authentic by most of today's authorities, among them Alföldi, de Cavalieri, Baynes, Palanque and Vogt. But, modern authorities apart, the sincerity of the Emperor's Christian faith is vouched for by someone whose probity cannot be disputed, Constantine's own nephew Julian 'the Apostate'. This highly individual personality, who occupied the imperial throne from 361 to 363, was brought up on a strict brand of ascetic Christianity but later renounced the Christian faith and tried to further the Empire's reconquest by heathendom. Julian can hardly be described, like Eusebius, as one of the Emperor's panegyrists, since he deeply detested him, but his hostile tirades against Constantine contain repeated allusions to his uncle's abandonment of the Sun-god and conversion to Christianity.

Emperor Constantine was greatly affected by his miraculous vision. Summoning Christian priests, he questioned them about their god and the meaning of the sign which he had seen. They told him that Christ was the only-begotten son of God and that the sign was a symbol of immortality and of the victory which he had won over death during his sojourn upon earth. They also described the nature of his influence on mankind.

How old was the monarch who posed such fundamental questions and received the momentous answers which were to decide the course of European civilization? Constantine's date of birth is hotly disputed. Joseph Vogt puts it at 285. If this is correct, Constantine would have been only twenty-seven when he saw the sign and became a young man with a great spiritual mission, a mission in which he believed with ever-increasing certainty until the hour of his death.

After his victory over Maxentius, Eusebius tells us, Emperor Constantine publicly conveyed tidings of the Son of God to the Romans. And all nations 'who dwelt as far as the western ocean joyfully celebrated their sense of redemption at festive gatherings. They never tired of singing hymns of praise to the victorious hero, pious servant of God, and benefactor.' By the grace of God, salvation had come to the whole human race in the person of Constantine.

There were still three emperors in the Roman Empire: Constantine, Licinius and Maximin Daia. Constantine sought to strengthen the ties between himself and Licinius by putting their relationship on a firm basis. In February of the year 313, an impressive wedding took place at Milan. Constantine gave Licinius his step-sister Constantia in marriage. Important man though Licinius was, being ruler of the Balkan and Danubian territories, Constantia cannot have regarded her forthcoming marriage with any great joy. Being past the age when he could reasonably expect to have children, Licinius forced her to adopt a son whom he had had by a slave. It was a political marriage. Constantine had wanted it so, and Constantia, as a dutiful Roman, complied with her step-brother's command.

At Milan the two Emperors agreed to grant universal freedom of worship. (Christianity also came within the scope of this decree.) They publicly professed their allegiance to the *summa divinitas* or 'supreme deity'. It was still a little too early to make any explicit reference to the god of Christianity. The Milan agreement also restored Christian property and places of assembly and granted recognition to individual Christian communities. In future, everyone was to be allowed to live according to the religion of his choice, a right which naturally benefited the Christians most of all. In order to win Licinius' support for this ideal, render Christianity even more attractive to him, and enable the new religious policy to be carried out on the widest possible scale, Constantine promised his colleague territorial expansion at the expense of Maximin Daia, then ruling in the East.

Daia must have seen the threat inherent in the Milan agreement, for he decided to anticipate Licinius by launching an attack on the Balkan provinces, choosing a moment when Constantine was engaged in operations against the Rhenish Franks and could not come to his partner's aid. Daia was not a congenial character. He was a brutal and superstitious Illyrian of very lowly origins whose rise to power had brought on megalomania, a sensualist with a predilection for wine and women, and an utter political and military failure. The severity with which he persecuted the Christians, on the other hand, far outrivalled that of Emperor Diocletian, even though the latter's brilliant organizing ability had lent his punitive and exterminatory measures an especial horror. Maximin Daia prided himself on being the most autocratic of all autocrats, appropriated whatever he took a fancy to, and declined to recognize the rights of private individuals. In the winter of 312–13, he decided to alienate the troops in Thrace and Illyria from Licinius, their thrifty, almost miserly master, by indulging in reckless bribery. Daia did not know the meaning of caution. He whipped his pack-animals savagely across the snow-covered mountains of Asia Minor, sustaining heavy losses from exhaustion and exposure on the way. He captured Byzantium after a siege lasting eleven days, took Perinth and Heraclea, and marched on Adrianople. Battle was joined on May 1st, 313, not far from Heraclea in Thrace.

As at the Pons Mulvius, each side invoked different gods. It is worth noting that Licinius' soldiers prayed to the 'invisible Sun-god' before the battle, not to the god of the Christians. Christian tradition, however, records the appearance of an angel.

The soldiers of Maximin Daia had to rely on the ancient Roman gods, on soothsayers and heathen oracles. Although outnumbered, Licinius won the day. It was yet another triumph for the invisible god, if not explicitly for the god of Christianity.

Maximin executed as frauds and swindlers the soothsayers who had forecast that he would be victorious. Eusebius describes how harshly he was punished by fate. He evidently became a victim of leprosy or syphilis. 'His innermost entrails were ceaselessly gnawed away. ... For the whole of his body had been transformed as a result of his gluttony into a vast mass of fat, which was now decomposing.' In his pain and distress, Maximin acknowledged his guilt before God, suspended persecution of the Christians, ordered their churches to be rebuilt by imperial decree and begged them to pray for him. Eusebius tells us that Maximin richly deserved his punishment; that he not only burnt, beheaded and crucified Christians, threw them to wild beasts or hurled them into the sea, but also maimed large numbers of men, women and children in one eye and one foot and sent them to the mines, where they wasted away pitiably and died. He ended by becoming blind himself. Despite great pain, he lived long enough to escape to Asia Minor. He died at Tarsus in the autumn of 313. 'Personal experience has taught me to acknowledge the god of the Christians as the only god,' he said. Licinius ordered Maximin's wife to be thrown into the Orontes and executed his son and daughter, aged eight and seven respectively.

That left only two rulers, Emperor Constantine in the West and Emperor Licinius in the East. Diocletian's four-emperor system had collapsed for good and all. The imperial brothers-in-law were now free, if they wanted, to construct a new Roman Empire based on peace and religious toleration.

Still under the influence of his Milan meeting with Constantine, Licinius began by ordering the governors of the eastern provinces to sanction freedom of worship. Gradually, however, his tolerance towards the Christians gave way to hatred, and he started to persecute them.

Emperor Constantine recognized the danger. In order to create a buffer State between his own world and that of Licinius, he married his step-sister Anastasia to a certain Bassianus, whom he appointed Caesar and put in charge of Italy and Illyricum.

Licinius, in his heart of hearts pugnacious and quarrelsome, was an unreliable individual who never kept his word, a rebel by nature and an intriguer of the worst sort. He arranged for Bassianus' brother Senecio to incite the new Caesar to murder Constantine. Constantine unmasked the plot, executed Bassianus, and demanded that Licinius hand over Senecio. Licinius refused, and in 314 war broke out between the two Emperors for the first time. On October 8th of that year, Constantine won a battle at Cibalae on the river Save. After a second but indecisive battle in Thrace, an uneasy peace was concluded. Each ruler was to confine himself to his own half of the Empire. This left Constantine with by far the larger share, and marked the first actual division of the Roman world. Henceforth, two large and distinct States confronted one another with mutual distrust, their rulers forbidden to set foot in each other's domains.

In summer 315 Constantine visited Rome to celebrate the tenth anniversary of his accession. Once again he omitted to sacrifice to the heathen gods. On the other hand, a meeting took place between him and Pope Silvester at which it must be assumed that the building of the first churches in Rome was discussed. Christians were now entrusted with high offices, the image of Sol Invictus vanished from Roman coinage, and Sunday became a national holiday.

This latter measure symbolizes the whole period of flux and development in which the momentous transition from Sun-worship to Christianity took place. *Sun*day or *dies solis* formed a bridge between the two religions. It had always been the first day in the heathens' planetary week, while to the Christians it was a day of reunion for all believers. Now *dies solis* became the national day of rest, which suited both Christians and worshippers of the Sun-god. Until the introduction of this arrangement, the first day of the week had never been a holiday. It was at about this time, too, that the Christians began to celebrate the birth of Christ on December 25th, the birthday of Sol Invictus. That was how Constantine, as a servant of the great religious enlightenment of his day, built a Christian world out of heathendom and its feast-days.

His rival went in the other direction. In the year 321 Licinius opened an all-out campaign against the Christians. Churches were torn down, ecclesiastical dignitaries condemned to death, believers thrown into gaol. Eusebius tells us that 'Licinius was convinced that we were doing everything and seeking to attain God's grace only for Constantine's sake'. Many Christians 'even had to undergo an entirely novel form of death. Their bodies were cut up into many pieces with the sword and, after this cruel and atrocious punishment, thrown into the depths of the sea as food for the fishes.' When the Goths crossed the Danube and invaded Roman territory in 324, Licinius should have driven them back, but he refused to budge. In order to defend the Roman world, Constantine was forced to violate the frontiers of the eastern empire and march through Licinius' territory on his way to meet the Goths.

There followed a last bitter struggle for undivided sway over the Roman world. Licinius once more resorted to the gods of heathendom. Surrounding himself with soothsayers, Egyptian prophets, poisoners, sorcerers, priests and augurs, he sacrificed to the heathen gods and questioned them as to the outcome of the war. With long-winded dictum and sonorous verse, hymn and oracular pronouncement, the motley crew of visionaries declared that he, Licinius, would win. The augurs, too, saw victory for Licinius in the flight of birds, and the priests read the same thing in the quivering entrails of slaughtered animals.

'This moment will show which of us is mistaken in his beliefs' said Licinius. 'If our gods are victorious we shall take the field against all the ungodly' — in other words, the Christians.

Constantine once again fought beneath the 'redeeming emblem of victory'. On July 3rd, 324, he won a great battle against Licinius at Adrianople. He was now master of Europe, but Byzantium was still occupied by his rival, so he gave orders for a siege. Licinius fled to Asia and was finally defeated by Constantine at Chrysopolis. Byzantium and Chalcedon surrendered shortly afterwards.

Licinius was, as we have already heard, married to one of Constantine's step-sisters. Constantia implored her brother to pardon him. The Emperor acceded to her request and allowed Licinius to settle down peacefully in Thessalonica.

But life without power and intrigue was not for Licinius, and he treacherously opened negotiations with the barbarians on the Danube. This breach of good faith resulted in his being condemned to death by the Roman Senate and executed at Constantine's instigation. We are left to wonder how the Emperor's step-sister felt about it all.

Sole ruler and first Christian emperor of the world, Constantine now proclaimed the triumphal power of his miraculous emblem. He felt that he was the elect of God. Sweeping aside all remaining obstacles to Christian faith and religious observance, he professed himself the executor of divine will.

Christians now occupied senior government posts, and in Rome a Christian became *praefectus urbi* or governor of the city. The Christian communities received imperial grants for the building or restoration of their churches. Senior Christian bishops formed a sort of Privy Council about the Emperor, who began to regulate and direct ecclesiastical affairs.

The Christian communities were far from being a united and harmonious whole. There were too many theological schools, too many dogmas, too many conflicting views. The Christian doctrines were veiled and obscured by problems, doubts, contradictory opinions, sectarianism and heresy — that ominous hall-mark of the period. A Greek word, *hairesis* originally meant 'choice' and was used to express doctrinal unorthodoxy. It was a time when the Christians, 'at odds with the ancient philosophy, were fashioning their belief into a doctrinal system'. (Vogt.)

Constantine longed above all else for the unity of the Christian Church, a unity which was, for him, summed up by the word 'catholic', *katholikos* being the Greek for 'universal'. But the outlook was unpromising, especially in the East. The most diverse views were being passionately upheld. At Alexandria in the year 318, a priest called Arius proclaimed a new Christian dogma. He held that Christ and God the Father were two distinct entities, similar but not consubstantial. Arius was excommunicated by his own bishop, Bishop Alexander, but received support and encouragement from other bishops in the East. He began to propagate his views, thus reducing Christians to a state of turmoil and agitation.

In an effort to settle the dispute, Emperor Constantine summoned bishops from all over the Empire to a conference in the imperial palace at Nicaea in Bithynia between May and July, 325. He decreed the inauguration of a public 'mail service' to enable all the bishops to attend and ordered the necessary draught-animals to be put at their disposal.

So the servants of God assembled at Nicaea, no less than 320 of them, predominantly bishops fron the eastern part of the Empire. There were men noted for their wisdom and deliberation, others who had distinguished themselves by their austere way of life, and still others who had won fame by their very humility. There were venerable old grey-beards and young Christian fire-brands only recently recruited into the service of God. The Emperor spoke in Latin, and it is indicative of the polyglot nature of the assembly that his words had to be translated. He was more widely understood when he used Greek. Persuading some and shaming others, he finally succeeded in achieving unanimous agreement on all the points at issue. It was resolved, at the Emperor's request, to celebrate Easter on the same day throughout Christendom, 'for our Saviour bequeathed to us but one day of redemption, the day of His most holy Passion; and His Catholic Church was to be one Church, in accordance with His will'.

The synod's most important single act was to settle the controversy which Arius had aroused. The orthodox Christian faith was laid down for all time in the so-called Nicene Creed.

At a second Nicene council held in the year 327, Constantine attempted to convert Arius to this creed, only to encounter the opposition of Bishop Athanasius. After a dispute lasting many years, Athanasius was removed from office and banished to Trèves.

Between the two councils, in the year 326, Emperor Constantine did something which was to lie heavy on his conscience as a Christian. His wife Fausta fell in love with his eldest son Crispus, who was the outcome of a liaison with a concubine called Mamertina.

Desperately disappointed when she found herself rebuffed by her step-son, who was only twenty years old, and realizing that her blandishments were falling on deaf ears, Fausta reached a frightful decision. She slandered Crispus to Constantine by pretending that the young man had tried to rape her. The details of the affair are obscure, but that seems to be the main outline. One cannot help thinking of Philip II of Spain and Don Carlos, or Peter the Great and the execution of his son Alexis. Burckhardt reminds us of Soliman the Splendid and his worthy son Mustapha, who met his doom through the machinations of Roxolane.

Constantine was on the point of celebrating the twentieth anniversary of his reign. Had Crispus reminded his father of the proximity of this jubilee, which would, under Diocletian's system, have marked the time when he ought to relinquish the throne? Was Fausta playing Phaedra to her step-son's Hippolytus? She had three sons of her own by Constantine, and it could well be that she was maligning her step-son in order to guarantee their right of succession. The Emperor, normally so circumspect, lost his head on this occasion. He had his son Crispus executed at Pola in Dalmatia without giving him a chance to explain the true facts of the case. Young Crispus, who had himself been married at the age of fourteen, was entirely innocent. The hoax was discovered by Helena, the Emperor's pious mother. Now it was Fausta's turn to die. They induced her to take a steam-bath in the palace thermae and then boosted the temperature until she was asphyxiated. After these tragic events, Constantine published an edict prohibiting cohabitation with concubines throughout the Roman Empire. He clearly regretted his own part in the affair and felt that it was his own infidelity which had driven his wife to attempt adultery.

Another event falls into this period: the epoch-making foundation of Constantinople as the capital of the world. The place was still known as Byzantium, but from now on it was to bear the name of the first Christian emperor. Constantine had considered other cities as potential world capitals, among them Serdica (Sofia), Solonici, Sirmium, even Troy. But he finally settled on Byzantium, which stood not far from the administrative metropolis of his predecessor Diocletian. Byzantium was to become a Christian Rome, a Rome of the East, and the new city was, in fact, laid out very much on the Roman pattern. Building began on November 26th, 326. On May 11th 330, Constantinople was officially inaugurated.

Constantine solved the problem of succession by allotting one portion of the Empire to each of his three sons and a fourth to his brother's son. During Easter Week, 337, the ruler of the world fell ill. He hurriedly set off for the medicinal springs at Drepanum, which he had renamed Helenopolis in his mother's honour. But his health failed to improve, and so, filled with forebodings of death, he had himself taken to Ancyrena, a suburb of Nicomedia in Bithynia.

He was not baptized by Bishop Eusebius of Nicomedia until he was on the point of death. The moment was deliberately chosen. Having committed all his life's sins as a non-Christian, he could now enter the world to come entirely free from sin.

Constantine had really wanted to be baptized in the Jordan, 'in the waters of which our Redeemer Himself received baptism as an example to us,' as he put it. 'This is the moment for which I have hoped so long, craving for it and yearning to find salvation in God.' On the last day of Whitsuntide, 337, the Roman Emperor who had seen God's sign and passed it on to the West as a sacred legacy closed his eyes for ever.

The great man's body was brought to Constantinople in a golden coffin and set on a lofty bier in the largest and most splendid room of the imperial palace. Candles sparkled round him in golden candlesticks as he lay there motionless in his baptismal gown, his only adornment a diadem, for he refused to touch the imperial purple once he had been baptized. Sentinels stood guard over him night and day. Senior officials, dignitaries and military commanders tip-toed in silently at the normal hour of audience, fell on their knees and paid homage to the monarch. Court ceremonial continued to be observed with unwavering, clock-work regularity 'for him who, alone among mortals, was still an emperor after his death'.

Not until Constantius, the only one of the Emperor's sons to put in an appearance, had arrived in the grief-stricken city, was the coffin transferred to the Church of the Apostles. This was the church which Constantine himself had erected 'to an incredible height', as we are informed, near the walls on the outskirts of his new metropolis. Eusebius tells us that its roof gleamed so brightly in the sun's rays that it could be seen from a great distance. Constantine had built his mausoleum in conjunction with this church. It contained twelve memorial stelae, one for each of the Apostles, and the Emperor's sarcophagus was hauled into the centre so that it was guarded by six Apostles on either side. The master of the world had aspired to become the thirteenth herald of the true faith. He had hoped, with joyous and invincible confidence, that after his death he would be regarded as an apostle.

His body did not lie there forlorn or neglected. He had decreed that services should be held in the mausoleum so that he could hear the prayers spoken in honour of the Apostles who stood close by his coffin.

Constantine died a sublimely happy man. Not only had he won his way through to the only true faith, but he was to lead countless millions of other men to the same religion after his death. He was sublimely happy because he knew that immortal life awaited him, life everlasting and divine light.

LIST OF ROMAN RULERS FROM MARIUS TO CONSTANTINE

THE REPUBLIC
(*Circa* 510 B.C.–30 B.C.)

Period covering the dictatorships of Marius	107–86
Sulla's dictatorship	82–79
Pompey's exercise of abnormally wide dictatorial powers	67–61
Julius Caesar's dictatorship	46–44

THE PRINCIPATE
(30 B.C.–A.D. 284)

The Julian–Claudian Dynasty (30 B.C.–A.D. 68)

Augustus (Octavian)	30 B.C.–A.D. 14
Tiberius	14–37
Gaius (Caligula)	37–41
Claudius	41–54
Nero	54–68
Galba, Otho, Vitellius	68–69

The Flavian Dynasty (69–96)

Vespasian	69–79
Titus	79–81
Domitian	81–96

The adoptive emperors (96–138)

Nerva	96–98
Trajan	98–117
Hadrian	117–138

The Antonine Dynasty (138–192)

Antoninus Pius	138–161
Marcus Aurelius, Verus	161–180
Commodus	180–192
Pertinax, Didius Julianus	193

The Severan Dynasty (193–235)

Septimius Severus	193–211
Caracalla (Bassianus)	212–217
Opellius Macrinus	217–218
Elagabalus	218–222
Severus Alexander	222–235

The soldier-emperors (235–284)

Maximinus Thrax	235–238
Gordian I, Gordian II, Balbinus, Pupienus	238
Gordian III	238–244
Philippus Arabs	244–249
Decius	249–251
Trebonianus Gallus	251–253
Valerian	253–260
Gallienus	260–268
Claudius II Gothicus	268–270
Aurelian	270–275
Tacitus	275–276
Probus	276–282
Carus, Carinus, Numerian	282–284

THE DOMINATE
(284–337)

Diocletian	284–305
Galerius, Constantius Chlorus, Severus, Licinius, Maximian, Maximin Daia, Constantine	305–324
Constantine the Great	325–337

BIBLIOGRAPHY

I. Ancient Sources

AMMIAN *c.* A.D. 332–400. Ammianus Marcellinus, with English translation by J. C. Rolfe, 3 vols. 1935 and 1937 in Loeb's Classical Library. — APPIAN, *c.* A.D. 160. Appiani Historia Romana, ed. by L. Mendelssohn and P. Viereck, Leipzig 1905 and 1939. — ARNOBIUS *c.* A.D. 305. Adversus nationes, ed. by C. Marchesi, 2nd edition Turin 1953. — ARRIAN *c.* A.D. 95–175. Arrian of Nicomedeia, ed. by A. G. Roos, 2 vols, 1907 and 1928. — AUGUSTUS 63 B.C.–A.D. 14. Imperatoris Caesaris Augusti operum fragmenta, publ. by Henrica Malcovati, 3rd edition Turin 1948. — MARCUS AURELIUS, A.D. 121–80. Marcus Aurelius with English translation by C. R. Haines in Loeb's Classical Library, London 1924. Transl. by W. Capelle, Stuttgart 1953. — AURELIUS VICTOR, *c.* A.D. 360. Sexti Aurelii Victoris Historia Romana cum notis integris Dominici Machanei, Eliae Vineti, Andreae Schotti, Jani Gruteri, Amsterdam 1733; or, publ. by F. Pichlmayr, 1911. — CAESAR, 100–44 B.C. C. Juli Caesaris Commentarii, De bello Gallico and De bello civili, publ. by A. Klotz, Leipzig 1950 and 1952. Alexandrian, African and Spanish War, with English transl. by A. S. Wag, London 1955 in Loeb's Classical Library. Guerre d'Afrique, Texte établi et traduit par A. Bouvet, Paris 1949; also A. Klotz, Gnomon 23, 1951, 40 et seq. — CICERO, 106–43 B.C. M. Tulli Ciceronis scripta quae manserunt omnia, Leipzig 1923. The Correspondence of M. Tullius Cicero, arranged according to its chronological order, with a revision of the text, comment., and introduct. Essays by R. Y. Tyrrell and I. C. Purser, Dublin and London, Vol. I 1904, Vol. II 1906, Vol. III 1914, Vol. IV 1918, Vol. V 1915, Vol. VI 1899, Vol. VII 1901. — INSCRIPTIONS. Inscriptiones Graecae, Vols. I–XIV 1890 onw., and Corpus Inscriptionum Latinarum, Vols. I–XVI, Berlin 1893 onw., publ. by the Prussian Academy of Sciences. Cagnat, R.: Inscriptiones Graecae ad res Romanas pertinentes, 4 vols. Paris 1901–1927. — CASSIUS DIO, *c.* A.D. 155–235. Cassius Dio Cocceianus, ed. by Ph. U. Boissevain, 4 vols., 2nd edition Berlin 1955. — CASSIODORUS, *c.* A.D. 487–583. Flavius Magnus Aurelius Cassiodorus: Orationes, fragments ed. by L. Traube; Variae, ed. by Th. Mommsen in Monumenta Germaniae Historica, Auct. Antiquiss. XII, Berlin 1904; Chronica, ed. by Th. Mommsen, MGH A.A. XI, Berlin 1904; Historia ecclesiastica, ed. by W. Jacob–R. Hanslik, Vienna 1952. — EUSEBIUS, *c.* A.D. 260–340. Eusebius von Caesarea, Ausg. der Historia ecclesiastica by E. Schwartz, 5th edition Berlin 1955. — EUTROPIUS, *c.* A.D. 364–378. Breviarum ab urbe condita, ed. by F. Rühl, Leipzig 1909. — HERODIAN in the 3rd century A.D. Herodianus, ed. by K. Stavenhagen, Leipzig 1922. — HISTORIA AUGUSTA, possibly *c.* A.D. 400. Scriptores Historiae Augustae, ed. by E. Hohl, 2 vols., Leipzig 1927. — JOSEPHUS, *c.* A.D. 37–100. Flavius Josephus, collected edition by B. Niese, 7 vols., 2nd edition Berlin 1955. — JULIAN, A.D. 332–363. The Works of the Emperor Julian, with English transl. by Wilmer Cave Wright, 3 vols. in Loeb's Classical Library, London–New York 1953. — LACTANTIUS, *c.* A.D. 250–318. Ed. by S. Brandt in Corp. Script. Ecclesiast. Latin. XXVII, 2, Vienna 1897. Also ed. by I. Pesenti, Turin 1921. De mortibus persecutorum, ed. by I. Moreau, Paris 1954. — MALALAS, 6th century A.D., publ. by L. Dindorf, Corp. Script. Byzant., Vol. XV, Bonn 1831. A. Schenk Graf von Stauffenberg, Die Röm. Kaisergeschichte bei Malalas, Stuttgart 1931 (part edition of Malalas with commentary). — NEPOS, *c.* 99–24 B.C. Cornelius Nepos, De viris illustribus, Halm edition, Leipzig 1871. Also ed. with commentary by K. Nipperdey–K. Witte, 11th edition, Berlin 1913. Text and transl. by W. Gerlach, 2nd edition, Munich 1952. — Orosius, 5th century A.D. Paulus Orosius, Historiae adversus paganos, ed. by C. Zangemeister, Leipzig 1889. — Petronius, 1st century A.D. Cena Trimalchionis, ed. by H. Schmeck, 4th edition, Heidelberg 1954. Also ed. by W. B. Sedgwick, 2nd edition, Oxford 1950. — Plutarch, *c.* A.D. 45–125. Plutarchi vitae parallelae, ed. by C. Lindskog and K. Ziegler, Leipzig 1914–39. — Pliny the Elder, A.D. 23–79. Gaius Plinius Secundus, Naturalis Historia, ed. by L. Jan, Leipzig 1854–65. 3rd edition C. Mayhoff 1892–1909. — Pliny the Younger, *c.* A.D. 62–113. Gaius Plinius Caecilius Secundus, Epistulae and Panegyricus, ed. by M. Schuster, Leipzig 1933. — Plotinus, *c.* A.D. 204–270. Writings, transl. by R. Harder, Leipzig–Hamburg, 1930–56. Procopius, *d.* A.D. 565. Prokop von Caesarea, ed. by Haury, 3 vols., Leipzig 1905–1913. — Res Gestae Divi Augusti, Monumentum Ancyranum, publ. by Th. Mommsen, 2nd edition, Berlin 1883. — Sallust, 86–*c.* 35 B.C. Sallusti Catilina, Iugurtha, Fragmenta ampliora, ed. by A. W. Ahlberg–A. Kurfeys, 2nd edition, Leipzig 1955. Appendix Sallustiana (epistulae, investivae), ed. by A. Kurfeys, 2 vols., Leipzig 1950–55. — Seneca, *c.* A.D. 4–65. Divi Claudii Apokolokyntosis, ed. by C. F. Russo, 2nd edition Florence 1955. — Suetonius, *c.* A.D. 69–140. Gaius Suetonius Tranquillus, De vita caesarum, lge. edition by M. Ihm, Leipzig 1922. Also ed. by J. C. Rolfe in Loeb's Classical Library, 1914. Transl. by A. Lambert, Zürich 1955. New edition by I. Lana, Turin 1952. — Tacitus, A.D. 55–120. Cornelii Taciti Annales, ed. by C. D. Fisher. Historiarum libri, ed. by C. D. Fisher. Opera minora, ed. by H. Furneaux in Scriptorum classicorum bibliotheca Oxoniensis, London 1952. Or: Historien und Annalen, ed. by C. Halm–G. Andresen–E. Koestermann, Leipzig 1950–1952. Germania, Agricola, Dialogus, ed. by the same, Leipzig 1949. De origine et situ Germanorum, Turin 1949 (Corp. Script. Lat. Paravianum). Historical essays, transl. by K. Büchner, Stuttgart 1955. — Tertullian, *c.* A.D. 160–230. Tertullian, Apology, De Spectaculis, Minucius Felix, Octavius, with English transl. by T. R. Glover in Loeb's Classical Library, London 1953. Or: Quintus Septimius Florens Tertullianus, compl. edition in Corpus Scriptorum Ecclesiasticorum Latinorum, Vol. XX, Vienna 1890. Apologeticum, ed. and transl. by C. Becker, Munich 1952. — Xiphilinos, 11th century text in above-mentioned edition of Cassius Dio. Also: Histoire Romaine écrite par Xiphilin, Zonare, Zosime, transl. from the Greek by Cousin, Paris 1778. — Zonaras, 12th century text ed. by L. Dindorf, Leipzig 1868–75, and Th. Büttner-Wobst, in Corp. Hist. Byzant., Vol. III, Bonn 1897. — Zosimos, *c.* A.D. 500. textual edition by L. Mendelssohn, Leipzig 1887.

II. General Reading

Albertini, E.: L'empire romain, 3rd edition, Paris 1938. — Altheim, F.: Niedergang der Alten Welt, Vols. I and II, Frankfurt a.M. 1952. Also: Literatur und Gesellschaft im ausgehenden Altertum, Halle 1948–50. — Thompson, E. A.: Journ. Rom. Stud. XLI, 1951, 204 et seq.: also Gesicht vom Abend und Morgen (Fischer Bücherei), Frankf. a.M.–Hamburg 1955: also, Die Soldatenkaiser, Frankf. a.M. 1939: also Rom und der Hellenismus, Amsterdam–Leipzig. — Bengtson, H.: Einführung in die alte Geschichte, 2nd edition, Munich 1953: also Griechische Geschichte von den Anfängen bis in die Römische Kaiserzeit, Munich 1950. — Bernhart, M.: Handbuch zur Münzkunde der römischen Kaiserzeit, 2 vols., Halle 1926. — Bickel, E.: Geschichte der römischen Literatur, Heidelberg 1937. — Cambridge Ancient History, ed. by S. A. Cook, F. E. Adcock, M. P. Charlesworth, Vol. IV (The

Persian Empire and the West), Cambridge 1939; Vol. IX (133–44 B.C.), Cambridge 1951; Vol. X (44 B.C.–A.D. 70), Cambridge 1952; Vol. XI (A.D. 70–192), Cambridge 1936; Vol. XII (A.D. 193–324), Cambridge 1939. — CARCOPINO, J.: Das Alltagsleben im alten Rom zur Blütezeit des Kaisertums, transl. fr. the French by L. Schaukel, Innsbruck–Vienna 1949. — CUMONT, F.: Lux Perpetua, Paris 1949. — DAREMBERG, C. and SAGLIO, E.: Dictionnaire des antiquités grecques et romaines, 10 vols., Paris 1877–1918. — DELBRÜCK, H.: Weltgeschichte, Part I, Altertum, Berlin 1925. — DESSAU, H.: Geschichte der römischen Kaiserzeit, 2 vols. in 3 pts., Berlin 1924–30. —v. DOMASZEWSKI, A.: Geschichte der römischen Kaiser, 2 vols., 3rd edition, Leipzig 1922. — DUNBAR, F. L.: Rom. Sechshundert Bauwerke der Ewigen Stadt, Berlin 1943. — FRANK, T.: Economic history of Rome, 2nd ed., Baltimore 1927: also An economic survey of ancient Rome. I. Rome and Italy of the Republic, II. Egypt, III. Western Provinces, IV. Eastern Provinces, V. Rome and Italy of the Empire. Baltimore 1933–1940. — FRIEDLÄNDER, L.: Darstellungen aus der Sittengeschichte Roms, publ. by G. Wissowa, 4 vols, 9th and 10th ed., Leipzig 1920–22. — GELZER, M.: Das Römertum als Kulturmacht, Histor. Zeitschr. 126, 1922. — GIBBON, E.: Decline and Fall of the Roman Empire, Everyman's Library 434, 6 vols., London 1954. — GLOTZ, G.: Histoire générale, Histoire romaine II–IV, Paris 1933–47. — GROEIG, E.–STEIN, A.: Prosopographia Imperii Romani, 4 vols., Berlin 1933–52. — v. HARNACK, A.: Mission und Ausbreitung des Christentums in den ersten drei Jahrhunderten, 2 vols., Leipzig 1924. — HOMO, L.: Les institutions politiques romaines, L'évolution de l'umanité, Vol. XVIII, Paris 1933; also L'empire Romain, Paris 1925; also La civilisation romaine, Paris 1930; also Les empereurs romains et le christianisme, Paris 1931; also Le haut empire (collection histoire générale, Glotz), Paris 1933; also Nouvelle histoire romaine, Paris 1941; also Le siècle d'or de l'empire romain, Paris 1947. — JEFFERSON LOANE, H.: Industry and commerce of the city of Rome (50 B.C. to A.D. 200), Baltimore 1938. — KAHRSTEDT, U.: Geschichte des griechisch-römischen Altertums (Weltgeschichte in Einzeldarstellungen, Vol. II), Munich 1952; also Kulturgeschichte der römischen Kaiserzeit, Munich 1944. — KORNEMANN, E.: Römische Geschichte, 2 vols., 3rd ed. by H. Bengtson, Stuttgart 1954; also Weltgeschichte des Mittelmeer-Raumes, ed. by H. Bengtson, 2 vols., Munich 1949. — MATTINGLY, H.–SYDENHAM, E. A.: The Roman imperial coinage, 5 vols., London 1923–33. — MOMMSEN, TH.: Römische Geschichte, I–III, Leipzig 1854–56, V, 1885. — NIEBUHR, B. G.: Römische Geschichte I and II, Berlin 1811 and 1812; III, 1832. — NIESE, B. and HOHL, E.: Grundriss der römischen Geschichte nebst Quellenkunde, 5th ed., in »Handbuch der Altertumswissenschaft«, edited by W. Otto, Munich 1923. — NORDEN, E.: Die römische Literatur, Leipzig 1954. — THE OXFORD CLASSICAL DICTIONARY, ed. by M. Cary, J. D. Denniston, J. Wight Duff, A. D. Nock, W. D. Ross, H. H. Scullard, Oxford 1953. — PARIBENI, R.: L'Italia imperiale, Storia d'Italia illustrata, 1938. — PARKER, H. M. D.: The Roman Legions, Oxford 1928. — PAULY, A.–WISSOWA, G.: Real-Encyclopädie der classischen Altertumswissenschaft, neue Bearbeitung, Stuttgart 1894 onwards. — PIGANIOL, A.: Histoire de Rome, 3rd edition Paris 1949. — REALLEXIKON FÜR ANTIKE UND CHRISTENTUM, ed. by T. Klausner, Vol. I, 1950; Vol. II, 1954, also supplements 17–19, 1955–56, Stuttgart. — RODENWALDT, G.: Die Kunst der Antike, Hellas und Rom [Propyläen-Verlag], Berlin 1927. — ROSTOVTZEFF, M.: Gesellschaft und Wirtschaft im Römischen Kaiserreich, 2 vols., Leipzig 1929. Original Engl. ed., Oxford 1926. Ital. transl. (new ed.), Florence 1946. — also A History of the Ancient World, 2 vols., Oxford 1926 and 1927. German: Geschichte der Alten Welt, 2 vols., Leipzig 1941–42 [New impression Wiesbaden]. — DE RUGGIERO, E. — CARDINALI, G.: Dizionario epigrafico di antichità romane,

Roma 1886 onwards. — SALMON, E. T.: A history of the Roman world from 30 B.C. to A.D. 138, London 1944. — SCHANZ, M. — HOSIUS, C.: Geschichte der römischen Literatur, I–IV, Munich 1914–35. — SEECK, O.: Geschichte des Untergangs der antiken Welt, 6 vols., Berlin 1920–21. — STEIN, A.: Der römische Ritterstand, Munich 1927. — TAEGER, F.: Das Altertum, 5th ed. Stuttgart 1953. — DE TILLEMONT, M. L.: Histoire des Empereurs, 3 vols., Paris 1911 [orig. ed. in 6 vols., Paris 1690–1738]. — VOGT, J.: Römische Geschichte, I, Die Römische Republik [as Vol. VI of »Geschichte der führenden Völker«], Freiburg i, Br. 1932, 2nd ed. 1951. — WAGENVOORT, H.: Roman Dynamism, Studies in ancient Roman Thought, Language and Custom, Oxford 1947.

III. Special Publications

Descriptions contained in encyclopaedias, handbooks and general histories (under II.) are not individually noted here.

Marius and Sulla

BERVE, H.: Sulla, Neue Jahrb. f. Wiss. u. Jugendbild. VII, 1931, 673 et seq. — CARCOPINO, J.: Sylla ou la monarchie manquée, Paris 1931. — v. DOMASZEWSKI: Bellum Marsicum, Sitzungsber. d. Wiener Akad. 201, 1, 1924. — HILL, H.: Sulla's military Oligarchy, Proceedings of the Classical Association, XXVIII, 1931. — LANZANI, C.: Mario e Silla, Catania 1915. — also L. Cornelio Sulla dittatore, Milano 1936. — LEVI, M. A.: Silla, Milano 1924. — PASSERINI, A.: Caio Mario come uomo politico, Athenaeum 1934. — REINACH, TH.: Mithradates Eupator, König von Pontos, Leipzig 1895. — ROBINSON, F. W.: Marius, Saturninus and Glaucia, Bonn 1912. — SCHUR, W.: Das Zeitalter des Marius und Sulla [Klio-Supplement 46], Leipzig 1942.

Cicero

BOISSIER, G.: Cicéron et ses Amis, Paris 1865. — also La Conjuration de Catilina Paris 1905. — CARCOPINO, J.: Les secrets de la correspondance de Cicéron, 2 vols., Paris 1947; also J. P. V. D. Balsdon, Journ. of Rom. Stud. XL, 1950, 134 et seq. — CARY, M.: Pompey's Compromise. Classical Review XXXIII, 1919, 109. — CIACERI, E.: Cicerone e i suoi tempi, 2 vols., Milano, Roma, Napoli 1926, 1930, 2nd ed. of Vol. 1 1939. — COWELL, F. R.: Cicero and the Roman Republic, London 1948. — FRISCH, H.: Cicero's Fight for the Republic, Copenhagen 1946. — HARDY, E. G.: The Catilinarian Conspiracy, Oxford 1924. — KLINGER, F.: Ciceros Rede für den Schauspieler Roscius, Munich 1953. Also Schmid, W., Gnomon, 26, 1954, 317. — KROLL, W.: Die Kultur der Cic. Zeit, 2 vols., Leipzig 1933. — VOGT, J.: Ciceros Glaube an Rom, Stuttgart 1935. — SEEL, O.: Cicero, Stuttgart 1953. Also John H. Collins, Gnomon 27, 1955, 279 et seq. — ZIELINSKI, TH.: Cicero im Wandel der Jahrhunderte, Leipzig 1929.

Pompey

BOAK, A. E. R.: The extraordinary Commands from 80 to 48 B.C., Amer. Hist. Rev. XXIV, 1918–19, 14 et seq. — GELZER, M.: Gn. Pompeius Strabo und der Aufstieg seines Sohnes Magnus, Abh. Preuß. Akad., phil.-hist. Kl. 1941, No. 14. — also Das erste Konsulat des Pompeius und die Übertragung der großen Imperien, Abh. Preuß. Akad., phil.-hist. Kl. 1943, Nr. 1. — also Pompeius, Munich 1949. Also F. E. Adcock, Journ. of Rom. Stud., XL, 1950, 135 et seq. — GROEBE, P.: Zum Seeräuberkrieg des Pompeius Magnus, Klio X, 1910, 374 et seq. — GUSE, F.: Die Feldzüge des dritten Mithridatischen Krieges in Pontus und Armenien, XX, Klio 1926,

332 et seq. — MEYER, E.: Caesars Monarchie und das Principat des Pompeius, Stuttgart and Berlin 1922. — VAN OOTEGHEN, S. J.: Pompée le Grand, bâtisseur d'empire, Brussels 1954. — SCHULTEN, A.: SERTORIUS, Leipzig 1926.

Caesar

COLLINS, J. H.: Caesar and the Corruption of Power, Historia IV, 1955, 445 et seq. — COLOMB, G.: La bataille d'Alesia, Lons-le-Saunier 1950; also F. Miltner, Gnomon 23, 1951, 210. — GELZER, M.: Caesar der Politiker und Staatsmann, 1943. — GUNDOLF, F.: Caesar, Geschichte seines Ruhmes, Berlin 1925. — HOLMES, T. R.: Caesar's Conquest of Gaul, Oxford 1911. — KLOTZ, A.: Caesarstudien, Leipzig 1910. — MOMMSEN, TH.: Die Rechtsfrage zwischen Cäsar und dem Senat, Ges. Schr. IV, Berlin 1906. — RAMBAUD, M.: L'art de la déformation historique dans le Commentaires de César, Paris 1953 [Annales de l'Université de Lyon]; also Collins, J. H., Gnomon 26, 1954, 527ff. — STRASBURGER, H.: Caesars Eintritt in die Geschichte, Munich 1938. — SYME, R.: The Roman Revolution, Oxford 1951. — TAYLOR, L. R.: Party Politics in the Age of Caesar, Berkeley 1949. — WALSER G.: Caesar und die Germanen, Historia, Einzelschriften, Part 1, Wiesbaden 1956.

Mark Antony, Cleopatra, Augustus

ANDERSEN, H. A.: Cassius Dio und die Begründung des Principates, Berlin 1938. — BÉRANGER, J.: Recherches sur l'aspect idéologique du principat, Bâle 1953; also Wickert, L., Gnomon 26, 1954, 534 et seq. — CARCOPINO, J.: Le mariage d'Octave et de Livie et la naissance de Drusus, Revue Historique CLXI, 1929, 225 et seq. — McCARTHY, J. H.: Octavianus puer. Classical Philology XXVI, 1931, 362 et seq. — GARDTHAUSEN, V.: Augustus und seine Zeit, 2 Pts. in 6 vols., Leipzig 1891 to 1904 with supplement in 1916. — GRANT, M.: From Imperium to Auctoritas, 1946. — HAMMOND, M.: Hellenistic influences in the structure of the Augustan principate, Mem. Americ. Acad. Rome XVII, 1940. — HEINZE, R.: Die augusteische Kultur, Leipzig–Berlin 1933. — HOLMES, T. R.: The Architect of the Roman Empire, Oxford, I, 1928; II, 1931. — HÖNN, K.: Augustus und seine Zeit, Vienna 1953. — HOMO, L.: Auguste, Paris 1935. — KLINGER, F.: Tacitus über Augustus und Tiberius, Munich 1954; also Béranger, J., Gnomon 27, 1955, 436 et seq. — KRENCKER, D., und SCHEDE, M.: Der Tempel in Ankara [Archäol. Institut d. Deutschen Reiches], Berlin and Leipzig 1936. — LEVI, M. A.: Ottaviano Capoparte, 2 vols., Florence 1933. — MAGDELAIN, A.: Auctoritas principis, Paris 1947. — OTTO, W., and BENGTSON, H.: Zur Geschichte des Niederganges des Ptolemäerreiches, Munich 1938. — v. PREMERSTEIN, A.: Vom Werden und Wesen des Prinzipats, Munich 1937. — REINHOLD, M.: Marcus Agrippa, New York 1933. — RODENWALDT, G.: Kunst um Augustus, Berlin 1942. — SCHMITTHENNER, W.: Oktavian und das Testament Caesars, Munich 1952. — SCHÖNBAUER, E.: Die Res gestae Divi Augusti in rechtsgeschichtlicher Beleuchtung, Vienna 1946 [Sitz.-Ber. Akad. Wien, Phil.-hist. Kl. 224, 2]. — SEECK, O.: Kaiser Augustus, Bielefeld–Leipzig 1902. — STUDI in occasione del bimillenario Augusteo, Rom 1938. — VOLKMANN, H.: Kleopatra, Munich 1953. — WEBER, W.: Princeps I, Stuttgart 1936. — WEIGALL, A.: Cléopâtre, sa vie et son temps, Paris. — also Marc-Antoine, sa vie et son temps.

Tiberius

BAKER, G. P.: Tiberius Caesar, London 1929. — CIACERI, E.: L'imperatore Tiberio e i processi di lesa majestà. Processi politici e relazioni internazionali, Roma 1918, 249 et seq. — also Tiberio successore di Augusto, Milan 1934. — DREXLER, H.: Die

Germania des Tacitus, Gymnasium 59, 1952, 52 et seq. — DÜRR, F.: Die Majestätsprozesse unter dem Kaiser Tiberius, Heilbronn 1880. — EHRENBERG, V., and JONES, A. H. M.: Documents illustrating the Reigns of Augustus and Tiberius, Oxford 1949. — KOESTERMANN, E.: Die Majestätsprozesse unter Tiberius, Historia, IV, 1955, 72 et seq. — MARAÑÓN, G.: Tiberius [transl. fr. the Spanish], Munich 1952; also M. Gelzer, Gnomon 26, 1954, 345. — MARSH, F. B.: The Reign of Tiberius, Oxford 1931. — MOMMSEN, TH.: Römisches Strafrecht, Das Staatsverbrechen, S. 537–594, Leipzig 1899. — ROGERS, R. S.: Criminal trials and criminal Legislation under Tiberius, Middletown 1955. — SCHOTT, W.: Die Kriminaljustiz unter dem Kaiser Tiberius, Erlangen 1893. — also Studien zur Geschichte des Kaisers Tiberius, 2 vols., Bamberg 1904–1905. — SCOTT, K.: Tiberius Refusal of the Title of Augustus, Classical Philology, XXVII, 1932, 43 et seq. — VITTINGHOFF, F.: Der Staatsfeind in der römischen Kaiserzeit [Neue Deutsche Forschungen, Vol. 84], Berlin 1936. — WALKER, B.: The Annals of Tacitus, Manchester 1953, 82–110.

Caligula

BALSDON, J. P. V. D.: The Emperor Gaius [Caligula], Oxford 1934. — MAURER, J. A.: A commentary on C. Suetonii Tranquilli vita C. Caligulae Caesaris, Chapters 1–21, Philadelphia 1949. — UCELLI, G.: Le navi di Nemi, Rome 1952.

Claudius

BELL, H. J.: Jews and Christians in Egypt, London 1924. — The Acts of the PAGAN MARTYRS. Acta Alexandrinorum, ed. by H. A. Musurillo, London 1954; also W. Schubart, Gnomon 27, 1955, 212 et seq. — MOMIGLIANO, A.: L'opera dell'imperatore Claudio, Florence 1932. — SCRAMUZZA, V. M.: The emperor Claudius, Cambridge Mass. 1940. — STÄHELIN, F.: Kaiser Claudius, Bâle 1933. — SUHR, E. G.: A Portrait of Claudius, American Journ. of Archaeology 59, 1955, 319 et seq.

Nero

CHARLESWORTH, M. P.: Nero, some Aspects, in Journ. of Rom. Stud. XL, 1950, 69 et seq. — HENDERSON, B. W.: The life and principate of the emperor Nero, London 1903. — LEVI, M. A.: Nerone e i suoi tempi, Milan 1949; also Ernst Hohl in Gnomon 23, 1951, 108 et seq. — LIETZMANN, H.: Petrus und Paulus in Rom, Berlin 1927. — SCHUR, W.: Die Orientpolitik des Kaisers Nero, Klio-supplement 15, Leipzig 1923. — WEEGE, F.: Das goldene Haus des Nero, Jahrb. d. Archäol. Inst. XXVII, 1913, 127 et seq.

Petronius

BAGNANI, G.: Arbiter of Elegance, Toronto 1954. — HERAEUS, W.: amplified and edited for his 75th birthday by J. B. Hofmann, Die Sprache des Petronius und die Glossen, Heidelberg 1937.

Seneca

BENOÎT, P.: Sénèque et St-Paul, Rev. Bibl. 53, 1946, 7–35. — DEISSNER, K.: Paulus und Seneca, 1917. — GIANCOTTI, F.: Saggio sulle tragedie di Seneca, Rome–Naples 1953; also Händel, P., Gnomon 27, 1955, 183 et seq. — PAUL, A.: Untersuchungen zur Eigenart von Senecas Phoenissen, Bonn 1953. — WALTZ, R.: La vie politique de Sénèque, Paris 1909.

Galba, Otho, Vitellius

HENDERSON, B. W.: Civil War and Rebellion in the Roman Empire, 1908. — HOHL, E.: Der Prätorianeraufstand unter Otho, Klio XXXII, 1939, 307 et seq. — KLINGER, F.: Die Geschichte des Kaisers Otho bei Tacitus, Leipzig 1940. — ZANCAN, P.: La crisi del principato nell'anno 69 d.C., 1939. — PASSERINI, A.: Le due battaglie presso Betriacum, Studi di antichità classica offerti a E. Ciaceri, 1940, 178 et seq.

Vespasian

BERSANETTI, G. M.: Vespasiano, Rome 1941. — GRAF, H.: Kaiser Vespasian, Untersuchungen zu Suetons Vita Divi Vespasiani, Stuttgart 1937. — HENDERSON, B. W.: Five Roman Emperors [Vespasian–Trajan], Cambridge 1927. — HOMO, L.: Vespasien, l'empereur du bons sens, Paris 1949; also E. Hohl in Historia, II, 1954, 474 et seq. — WEBER, W.: Josephus und Vespasian, Stuttgart 1921.

Titus

COMPANION to the study of Pompeii and Herculaneum, Rome 1938. — CONTE CORTI, E. C.: Untergang und Auferstehung von Pompeji und Herculaneum, 7th ed., Munich 1951. — MAJURI, A.: Pompeji, Novara 1953. — FURCHHEIM, F.: Bibliografia di Pompei, Ercolano e Stabia, Naples 1891. — SCHEFOLD, K.: Pompejanische Malerei, Bâle 1952.

Domitian

CASE, S. J.: Josephus' anticipation of a Domitianic persecution, Journ. Bibl. Lit. XLIV, 1925, 10. — GSELL, S.: Essai sur le règne de l'empereur Domitien, Paris 1894. — HERZOG, R.: Urkunden zur Hochschulpolitik der röm. Kaiser, Vespasian und Domitian, Sitz.-Ber. Preuß. Akad., 1935, No. 32, 967 et seq. — KÖSTLIN, E.: Die Donaukriege Domitians, Tübingen 1910. — PATSCH, C.: Der Kampf um den Donauraum unter Domitian und Trajan, Sitz.-Ber. Wiener Ak. 217, 1937, 1. Abh. — PICHLMAYR, F.: T. Flavius Domitianus, ein Beitrag zur röm. Kaisergeschichte, Amberg 1889. — SYME, R.: The imperial finances under Domitian, Nerva and Trajan, Journ. of Rom. Stud., XX, 1930, 55 et seq., also Sutherland, C. H. V., ibid. XXV, 1935, 150 et seq.

Trajan

ALFÖLDI, A.: Zu den Schicksalen Siebenbürgens im Altertum, Budapest 1944 [Ostmitteleurop. Bibl., publ. by E. Lukanich, 54]. — CICHORIUS, C.: Die Reliefs der Trajanssäule, 2 vols., Berlin 1896–1900. — v. DOMASZEWSKI, A.: Die Dakerkriege Traians auf den Reliefs der Säule. Philologus, LXV, 1906, 321 et seq. — GARZETTI, A.: Nerva, Rome 1950; also H. Volkmann in Gnomon 24, 1952, 115 et seq. — LEPPER, F. A.: Trajan's Parthian War, Oxford 1948. — PARIBENI, R.: Optimus Princeps, 2 vols., Messina 1926–27. — PARVAN, V.: Dacia, Cambridge 1928. — PETERSEN, E.: Trajans dakische Kriege, 2 vols., Leipzig 1899–1903. — WEBER, W.: Traian und Hadrian in »Meister der Politik«, I, 2, Stuttgart 1923. — also Rom, Herrschertum und Reich im 2. Jahrh. n.Chr., Stuttgart 1937.

Hadrian

VON BUREN, A. W.: Recent Finds at Hadrian's Tiburtine Villa, Am. Journ. Arch. 59, 1955, 215 et seq. — DÜRR, J.: Die Reisen des Kaisers Hadrian, Vienna 1881. — FRASER, P. M.: Hadrian and Cyrene, Journ. of Rom. Stud. 1950. — GRAINDOR, P.:

Athènes sous Hadrien, Cairo 1934. — HENDERSON, B. W.: The Life and Principate of the Emperor Hadrian, London 1923. — KÄHLER, H.: Hadrian und seine Villa bei Tivoli, Berlin 1950; also R. Naumann in Gnomon 23, 1951, 216 et seq. — OLIVER, J. H.: Documents concerning the emperor Hadrian, Hesperia X, 1941, 361 et seq. — D'ORGEVAL, B.: L'Empereur Hadrian, Paris 1950. — PERRET, L.: La titulature impériale d'Hadrien, Paris 1929. — PRINGSHEIM, F.: The Legal Policy and Reforms of Hadrian, Journ. Rom. Stud. XXIV, 1934, 141. — STRACK, P. L.: Untersuchungen zur röm. Reichsprägung des 2. Jahrh., 3 vols., Stuttgart 1931–37. — WEBER, W.: Untersuch. z. Gesch. des Kaisers Hadrian, Leipzig 1907. — also Römisches Herrschertum und Reich im 2. Jahrh. n.Chr., Stuttgart 1937.

Antoninus Pius

BRYANT, E. C.: The Reign of Antoninus Pius, Cambridge 1895. — DODD, C. H.: The cognomen of the Emperor Antoninus Pius, Numismatic Chronicle XI, 1911 6 et seq. — HÜTTL, W.: Antoninus Pius, I. Prague 1936; II. 1933. — LACOUR-GAYET, G.: Antonin le Pieux et son Temps, Paris 1888. — SCHELL, F.: Untersuchungen zur Geschichte des Kaisers Pius, Hermes LXV, 1930, 177 et seq. — TOYNBEE, J.: Some »programme« coin-types of Antoninus Pius, Classical Review XXXIX, 1925, 170 et seq.

Marcus Aurelius

CARRATA THOMES, F.: Il regno di Marco Aurelio, Turin 1953. — DODD, C. H.: Chronology of the Eastern Campaigns of the Emperor Lucius Verus, Numismatic Chronicle, XI, 1911, 209 et seq. — FARQUHARSON, A. S. L.: The Meditations of the Emperor Marcus, 2 vols., 1945. — LAMBRECHTS, P.: L'Empereur Lucius Verus. Essai de réhabilitation. L'Antiquité classique, III, 1934, 173 et seq. — MARTINAZZOLI, F.: La »Successio« di Marco Aurelio, Bari 1951; also D. A. Rees in Gnomon 24, 1952, 274 et seq. — MOMMSEN, TH.: Der Markomannenkrieg unter Kaiser Marcus, Collected Works IV, 487 et seq. — NEUENSCHWANDER, H. R.: Marc Aurels Beziehungen zu Seneca und Poseidonios, Bern und Stuttgart 1951; also Leeman, A. D., in Gnomon 24, 1952, 277 et seq. — VON PREMERSTEIN, A.: Untersuchungen zur Geschichte des Kaisers Marcus, Klio XI, 1911, 355; XII, 1912, 167; XIII, 1913, 70. — SEDGWICK, H. D.: Marcus Aurelius, a Biography, Yale Univ. Press 1921. — v. WILAMOWITZ-MOELLENDORFF, U.: Kaiser Marcus, Berlin 1931.

Commodus

CUMONT, F.: Jupiter summus exuperantissimus, Arch. f. Relig.-Wiss. IX, 1906, 323 et seq. — HOHL, ERNST: Kaiser Commodus und Herodian, Berlin 1954. — MOMMSEN, TH.: Perennis, Collected Works IV, 514 et seq. — VON PREMERSTEIN, A.: Protest des Gymnasiarchen Appianos gegen seine Verurteilung durch Commodus, Philologus, Suppl. XVI, 1923, 2, 28. — ROSTOVTZEFF, M.: Commodus-Hercules in Britain, Journ. Rom. Stud. XIII, 1923, 91 et seq. — WEBER, W.: Probleme der Spätantike, Stuttgart 1930, 67 et seq. and 87.

Pertinax and Julian

WERNER, R.: Der historische Wert der Pertinaxvita in den Scriptores Historiae Augustae, Klio, XXVI, 1933, 283 et seq. cf. Barbieri, G., in Stud. ital. fil. class. XIII, 1936, 183.

Septimius Severus

HASEBROEK, J.: Untersuchungen zur Geschichte des Kaisers Septimius Severus, Heidelberg 1921. — NEUGEBAUER, K. A.: Die Familie des Septimius Severus, Antike 12, 1936, 155 et seq. — PLATNAUER, M.: The Life and Reign of the Emperor Lucius Septimius Severus, Oxford 1918. — RÉVILLE, J.: La Religion à Rome sous les Sévères, Paris 1886. — SCHULZ, O. TH.: Vom Prinzipat zum Dominat, Paderborn 1919.

Geta, Julia Domna, Caracalla

BICKERMANN, E.: Das Edikt des Kaisers Caracalla in P. Gießen 40, Berlin 1926. — KORNEMANN, E.: Große Frauen des Altertums [Julia Domna], 252 et seq., Wiesbaden 1952. — REUSCH, W.: Der historische Wert der Caracallavita in den Scriptores Historiae Augustae, Klio, Supplement XXIV, 1931. — SCHULZ, O. TH.: Der römische Kaiser Caracalla: Genie, Wahnsinn oder Verbrechen, Leipzig 1909. — WILLIAMS, M. G.: Studies in the lives of Roman empresses: 1. Julia Domna, Amer. Journ. Archaeol., VI, 1902, 259 et seq.

Elagabalus

BASSET, H. J.: Macrinus and Diadumenianus, Diss., Michigan 1920. — BESNIER, M.: in Glotz, Histoire Romaine, IV, 76–80. — BUTLER, O. F.: Studies in the Life of Elagabalus, Univ. of Michigan Studies, New York 1908. — HAY, J. S.: The amazing emperor Heliogabalus, London 1911. — HÖNN, K.: Quellenuntersuchungen zu den Viten des Heliogabalus und des Severus Alexander in Corpus der S.H.A., Berlin 1911. — KORNEMANN, E.: Große Frauen des Altertums [Julia Maeṣa und Julia Mamaea, 273 et seq. and 280 et seq.], Wiesbaden, 1952. — ROOS, A. G.: Herodian's Method of Composition, Journ. Rom. Stud. V, 1915, 191 et seq. — SMITS, J. S. P.: De fontibus e quibus res a Heliogabalo et Alexandro Severo gestae colliguntur, Diss. Amsterdam, 1908.

Alexander Severus

GORLICH, E.: Alexander Severus und der Ausgang des Principates, Aevum XI, 1937, 197 et seq. — HOPKINS, R. V. N.: The Life of Alexander Severus, Cambridge Historical Essays, XIV, 1907. — JARDÉ, A.: Etudes critiques sur la vie et le règne de Sevère Alexandre, Paris 1925. Cf. Göttinger Gelehrte Anzeigen, 1929, 504. — MACCHIORO, V.: L'Impero romano nell'età dei Severi, Riv. stor. ant. X, 1905–6, 201; XI, 1906–7, 285 and 341. — VON SICKLE, C. E.: The terminal dates of the reign of Alexander Severus, Class. Philol. XXII, 1927, 315 et seq. — THIELE, W.: De Severo Alexandro Imperatore, Berlin 1909. — WILLIAMS, M. G.: Studies in the Lives of Roman Empresses, Julia Mamaea, University of Michigan Studies, Human. Ser. I, 1904, 67.

The Sassanids

CHRISTENSEN, A.: Les gestes des rois dans les traditions de l'Iran antique, Paris 1936. — also L'Iran sous les Sassanides, Copenhagen–Paris, 2nd ed. 1944. — ENSSLIN, W.: Die weltgeschichtliche Bedeutung der Kämpfe zwischen Rom und Persien, Neue Jahrb. f. Wissensch. und Jugendbild. IV, 1928, 399. — HERZFELD, E.: Archaeological History of Iran, London 1935. — NÖLDEKE, TH.: Tabari. Geschichte der Perser und Araber zur Zeit der Sassaniden. Transl. from the Arabian Chronicle by Tabari, Leyden 1879. — PAGLIARO, A.: Notes on the History of the Sacred Fires of Zaroastrianism. Orient. Studies in Honour of C. E. Pavry, London 1933, 373 et seq. — ROSTOVTZEFF, M.: Res gestae divi Saporis and Dura, Berytus VIII, 1943, 17 et seq. — SARRE, FR., and HERZFELD, E.: Iranische Felsreliefs, Berlin 1920. — SCHAEDER, H. H.: Iranica, Abh. Gött. Gel. Ges. 1934, 10.

Battle of the Teutoburger Wold and Limes

DRAGENDORFF, H.: Westdeutschland zur Römerzeit, 2nd ed. Leipzig 1919. — FABRICIUS, E.: Die Entstehung der römischen Limesanlagen, Trèves 1902. — HALLER, I.: Der Eintritt der Germanen in die Geschichte, Berlin 1944. — HETTNER, F., v. SARWEY, O., FABRICIUS, E.: Der obergermanisch-rätische Limes des Römerreiches, 14 vols. 1894–1938. — JACOBI, H.: Das Kastell Saalburg, Berlin 1937 [Limeswerk, 56th Supplement] — JOHN, W.: Die Örtlichkeit der Varusschlacht bei Tacitus, Göttingen 1950; also E. Hohl in Gnomon 23, 1951, 211 — JUDEICH, W.: Die Überlieferung der Varusschlacht, Rhein. Mus. 80, 1931, 301 et seq. — KOEPP, F.: Die Römer in Deutschland, 3rd Ed., Leipzig 1926. — also Lichter und Irrlichter auf dem Wege zum Schlachtfeld des Varus, »Westfalen« 13, 1937. — also Varusschlacht und Aliso, Münster 1940. — KOLBE, W.: Forschungen über die Varusschlacht, Klio XXV, 1932, 141 et seq. — KORNEMANN, E.: Die neuesten Limesforschungen im Lichte der römischen Grenzpolitik, Klio VII, 1907, 73 et seq. — also Die Varusschlacht, in »Gestalten und Reiche«, Wiesbaden 1943. — MOMMSEN, TH.: Der Begriff des Limes, Collected Works V [1885], 456 et seq. — NORDEN, E.: Altgermanien, Leipzig–Berlin 1934.

Maximinus Thrax

BERSANETTI, G. M.: Massimino il Trace e la rete stradale dell'impero romano. Atti III congr. nazionale di studi romani I, 1934, 590 et seq. — also Studi su Massimino il Trace, Rivista Indo-Greco-Italica XVIII, 1934, 215 et seq. — also Studi sull'imperatore Massimino, Epigraphica III, 1941, 5 et seq. — HOHL, E.: Maximini duo Juli Capitolini. Aus dem Corpus der sog. Historia Augusta herausgegeben und erläutert, Berlin 1949; also R. Nierhaus, Gnomon 23, 1951, 464 et seq. — HOMO, L.: La grande crise de 238 ap. J.-C. et le problème de l'Histoire Auguste, Rev. Hist. CXXXI 1919, 201 et seq., and CXXXII, 1919, et seq. — VAN SICKLE, C. E.: A Hypothetical Chronology for the year of the Gordians, Class. Philol. XXII, 1927, 416 et seq., also XXIV, 1929, 285 et seq. — UHLHORN, G.: Maximinus Thrax, in Realencyklop. für protest. Theol. XII, 456.

Philippus Arabs and Decius

FOUCART, P.: Les certificats de sacrifice pendant la persécution de Decius [250], Journ. des Savants, 1908, 169. — JENSEN, P. J.: Plotin, Copenhagen 1948. — KNIPFING, J. R.: The Libelli of the Decian Persecution, Harv. Theol. Rev. XVI, 1923, 345 [Greek text with English transl.]. — MANLEY, I. J.: Effects of the Germanic invasions on Gaul 234–284 A.D., Univ. of Calif. Publ. in History, XVII, no. 2, 1934, 25. — LIESERING, E.: Untersuchungen zur Christenverfolgung des Kaisers Decius, Würzburg 1933. — RAPPOPORT, B.: Die Einfälle der Goten in das römische Reich, Leipzig 1899. — SALISBURY, F. S.: The reign of Trajan Decius, Journ. Rom. Stud. XIV, 1924, et seq. — SCHMIDT, L.: Geschichte der deutschen Stämme bis zum Ausg. der Völkerw. I. Die Ostgermanen, 2nd ed., Munich 1934; II. Die Westgermanen, 2nd ed. Munich 1938. — UHLHORN, G., and GÖRRES, F.: Philippus Arabs, in Realencyclop. für protest. Theologie, XV, 331.

Gallus and Aemilianus

ALFÖLDI, A.: Die Hauptereignisse im römischen Osten zwischen 253 und 260 im Spiegel der Münzprägungen, Berytus IV, 1937 [1938]. — MATTINGLY, H.: The Reign of Aemilian, in Journ. of Rom. Stud. XXV, 1935, p. 55. — MOMMSEN, TH.:

»Weltreich der Caesaren« [Phaidon Publ. Co.'s title], Amsterdam 1955, pp. 216–219 [Gallus to Aemilianus]. — PROSOPOGRAPHIA Imperii Romani, Art. über Aemilianus, Vol. I, no. 430.

Valerian

ALFÖLDI, A.: The reckoning of the regnal years and victories of Valerian and Gallienus, Journ. Rom. Stud. XXX, 1940. — ROSTOVTZEFF, M. I., BELLINGER, A. R., BROWN, F. E., WELLES, C. B.: The excavations at Dura-Europos conducted by Yale Univ. and the French Acad. of Inscr. and Letters, Prelim. Report, 1935–36, Part III, New Haven 1952.

Gallienus

ALFÖLDI, A.: Der Usurpator Aureolus und die Kavallerie-Reform des Kaisers Gallienus, Zeitschr. f. Numismatik XXXVII, 1927, 198 und XXXVIII 1928, 200. — also Die Vorherrschaft der Pannonier im Römerreich und die Reaktion des Hellenentums unter Gallienus in 25 Jahren röm.-germ. Kommission, Frankfurt 1920. — HOMO, L.: L'empereur Gallien et la crise de l'empire romain au 3e siècle, Revue Hist. CXIII, 1913, 1 et seq., 225 et seq. — MANNI, E.: L'impero di Gallieno, Rome 1949; dazu Hohl, E., in Gnomon 24, 1952, 116 et seq. — SCHLEIERMACHER, W.: Römische Archäologie am Rhein 1940–50, Historia, II, 1953, 94 et seq.

Zenobia and Aurelian

CLERMONT-GANNEAU, CH.: Odeinat et Vaballat, Rev. biblique XVII, 1920, 382 et seq. — CREES, J. H. E.: The papyri and the chronology of the reign of the emperor Probus, Aegyptus I, 1920, 297 et seq. — DAMERAU, P.: Kaiser Claudius II, Gothicus [Klio-Beiheft XX, 1934]. — DANNHÄUSER, E.: Untersuchungen zur Geschichte des Kaisers Probus, Jena 1909. — FÉVRIER, J. G.: Essai sur l'histoire politique et économique de Palmyre, Paris 1931. — FISHER, W. H.: The Augustan »Vita Aureliani«, Journ. Rom. Stud. XIX, 1929, 125 et seq. — HOMO, L.: Essai sur le règne de l'empereur Aurélien [270–275], Paris 1904. — also De Claudio Gothico Romanorum imperatore, Paris 1903. — JORGA, N.: Le problème de l'abandon de la Dacie. Rev. hist. du Sud-Est. Européen, I, 1924, 37. — KORNEMANN, E.: Große Frauen des Altertums, Zenobia, 288 et seq., Wiesbaden 1952. — SCHLUMBERGER, D.: La Palmyrène du Nord-Ouest, Paris 1951; also Kahrstedt, U., Gnomon 24, 1952, 446 et seq. — SEYRIG, H.: Palmyra and the East, Journ. Rom. Stud., 1950, Parts I and II. — STARCKY, J.: Palmyre, Paris 1952; also Kahrstedt, U., Gnomon 24, 1952, 446 et seq. — RICHMOND, I. A.: The City-Wall of Imperial Rome, Oxford 1930.

Diocletian

BULIĆ, F.: Kaiser Diokletians Palast in Split, Zagreb 1929. — BOTT, H.: Die Grundzüge der diokletianischen Steuerverfassung, Frankfurt 1928. — DÖRNER, K.: Ein neuer Porträtkopf des Kaisers Diokletian, Die Antike, Vol. XVII, Berlin 1941. — ENSSLIN, W.: Zur Ostpolitik des Kaisers Diokletian, Sitz.-Ber. Bayer. Akad. d. Wiss., Phil.-Hist. Kl., Munich 1942. — HERAEUS, W., amplified and published in honour of his seventy-fifth birthday by J. B. Hofmann, Zum Edictum Diocletiani und Neue Studien zum Maximaltarif Diocletians, Heidelberg 1937. — HUNZINGER, A. W.: Die diocletianische Staatsreform, Rostock 1899. — MELONI, P.: Il regno di Caro, Numeriano e Carino, Cagliari 1948. — MOMMSEN, TH., and BLÜMNER, H.: Der Maximaltarif des Diocletian, Berlin 1893. — NIEMANN, G.: Der Palast Diokletians in Spalato, Vienna 1910. — SESTON, W.: Dioclétien et la tétrarchie, I. Paris

1946. — STADE, K.: Der Politiker Diokletian und die letzte große Christenverfolgung, Frankfurt 1926. — TAUBENSCHLAG, R.: Das römische Recht zur Zeit Diokletians, Cracow 1925. — WEILBACH, F.: Zur Rekonstruktion des Diocletians-Palastes in Bulićev Zbornik, Naućni prilozi posvećeni Franu Buliću, Zagreb-Split, 1924.

Constantine

ALFÖLDI, A.: The Conversion of Constantine and Pagan Rome, Oxford 1948; also Straub, J., Gnomon 24, 1952, 117 et seq. — also On the foundation of Constantinople, Journ. Rom. Stud. XXXVII, 1947, 10 et seq. — CARNUNTUM-Jahrbuch 1955 [Roman researches in Lower Austria, edited by E. Swoboda], Vienna 1956. — DE' CAVALIERI, P. F.: Constantiniana, Città del Vaticano 1953; also Vogt, J., Gnomon 27, 1955, 44 et seq. — BURCKHARDT, J.: Die Zeit Constantins des Großen, Leipzig 1880, 5th ed. Stuttgart 1929. — DELARUELLE, E.: La conversion de Constantin, Etat de la question, Bull. Lit. ecclés. 54, 1953, 80 et seq. — DÖRRIES, H.: Das Selbstzeugnis Kaiser Konstantins, Abh. der Gött. Akad. d. Wiss. 3. F. No. 34, 1954. — EICHHOLZ, D. E.: Constantius Chlorus' invasion of Britain, Journ. Rom. Stud. XLIII, 1953, 41 et seq. — FESTGABE zum Konstantins-Jubiläum 1913 für Antonio De Waal, Freiburg i. Br. 1913. Comprising: Dölger, F. J., Die Taufe Konstantins und ihre Probleme. von Landmann, K., Konstantin der Große als Feldherr. Leufkens, J., der Triumphbogen des Konstantin. Müller, A., Lactantius' De mortibus persecutorum. Pfättisch, J. M.: Die Rede Konstantins an die Versammlung der Heiligen. Wittig, J., Das Toleranzreskript von Mailand 313. — FREND, W. H. C.: The Donatist church, a movement of protest in Roman North Africa, Oxford 1952; also v. Campenhausen, H., Gnomon 25, 1953, 194 et seq. — GRÉGOIRE, H.: Les persécutions dans l'empire romain, Brussels 1951; also v. Campenhausen, H., Gnomon 25, 1953, 464 et seq. — JANIN, R.: Constantinople-Byzantine, Paris 1950. — KÄHLER, H.: Konstantin 313, Jahrb. d. Deutsch. Arch. Inst., 67, Berlin 1953. — KRAFT, H.: Kaiser Konstantins religiöse Entwicklung, Tübingen 1955. — L'ORANGE, H. P.: Studien zur Geschichte des spätantiken Porträts [Instituttet for sammenlignende Kulturforskning], Oslo 1933. — MONCEAUX, P.: Histoire littéraire de l'Afrique chrétienne 5, 1920, 147 et seq. — MOREAU, J.: Zum Problem der Vita Constantini, Historia IV, 1955, 234 et seq. — NESSELHAUF, H.: Das Toleranzgesetz des Licinius, Hist. Jahrb., ed. by J. Spörl, 74, Munich-Freiburg 1955. — PIGANIOL, A.: Histoire Romaine IV, 2e partie: L'empire chrétien, Paris 1947. — v. SCHOENEBECK, H.: Beiträge zur Religionspolitik des Maxentius und Constantin [Klio-Beiheft 43], Leipzig 1939. — SCHWARTZ, E.: Kaiser Constantin und die christliche Kirche, 2nd ed. Leipzig-Berlin 1936. — STEIN, E.: Geschichte des spätrömischen Reiches I, Vienna 1928. — STRAUB, J.: Konstantins Verzicht auf den Gan zum Kapitol, Historia IV, 1955, 297 et seq. — SWOBODA, E.: Carnuntum [Rom. Researches in Lower Austria], 2nd ed. Vienna 1953. — VOGT, J.: Die Bedeutung des Jahres 312 für die Religionspolitik Konstantins des Großen, Zeitschr, f. Kirchengesch. 61, 1942, 187 et seq. — also Constantin der Große und sein Jahrhundert, München 1949; also Ensslin, W., Gnomon 21, 1949, 328 et seq., also N. H. Baynes, Journ. Rom. Stud. XLI, 1951, 155 et seq. — also Streitfragen um Konstantin den Großen, Mitteil. d. Deutsch. Arch. Inst., Röm. Abt., 58, 1943 Munich — also Die Vita Constantini des Eusebius über den Konflikt zwischen Constantin und Licinius, Historia II, 1954, 463 et seq. — VITTINGHOFF, F.: Eusebius als Verfasser der Vita Constantini, Rhein. Museum 96, 1953, 330 et seq.

INDEX